SELECTED
THEATRE
CRITICISM

Volume 3: 1931-1950

Edited by
Anthony Slide

The Scarecrow Press, Inc.
Metuchen, N.J., & London 1986

In the Same Series

Selected Theatre Criticism, Volume 1: 1900–1010
Selected Threatre Criticism, Volume 2: 1920–1930

Also Edited by Anthony Slide

Selected Film Criticism: 1896–1911
Selected Film Criticism: 1912–1920
Selected Film Criticism: 1921–1930
Selected Film Criticism: 1931–1940
Selected Film Criticism: 1941–1950
Selected Film Criticism: 1951–1960
Selected Film Criticism: Foreign Films 1930–1950

Library of Congress Cataloging-in Publication Data

(Revised for vol. 3)
Main entry under title:

Selected theatre criticism.

  Includes index.
  Contents: v. 1. 1900–1919 -- [etc.] -- v. 3. 1931–
1950.
  1. Theater--New York (N.Y.)--Reviews. I. Slide,
Anthony.
PN2277.N5S44   1986   792.9'5'097471   85-2266
ISBN 0-8108-1811-6 (v. 1)
ISBN 0-8108-1846-9 (v. 3)

CONTENTS

iii

iv

PREFACE

Selected Theatre Criticism: 1931-1950 collects contemporary
reviews, reprinted in their entirety on more than 140 New York stage
productions. The productions represented here include dramas,
comedies, musicals, and revues, and have been selected on the basis
of their contemporary and historical importance, both in terms of
critical and popular regard. Reviews relate to original productions
only; revivals have been included only if they were particularly
notable, such as the John Gielgud and Leslie Howard productions
of Hamlet and Orson Welles' production of Macbeth.

Reviews included in this volume were chosen from America,
The Commonweal, Cue, The Drama Magazine, Life, New Theatre,
The New Yorker, Newsweek, PM, and Rob Wagner's Script. Among
the critics/reviewers to be found in this anthology are Robert Bench-
ley, Oliver Claxton, John Gassner, Wolcott Gibbs, Walter Kerr, and
George Jean Nathan.

Productions are listed alphabetically by title. Following the
name of each production are given the name(s) of the author, the
theatre and the opening date. Additional credit information may be
found in the Best Plays and Theatre World series.

For help in the preparation of this volume I would like to thank
the staffs of the Library of Congress, the Los Angeles Central Library and the Doheny Memorial Library of the University of Southern
California. Special thanks to Alan Gevinson, who served as my re-
search associate in Washington, D.C.

Reviews from America are reprinted with permission of America
Press, Inc., 106 West 56th Street, New York, N.Y. 10019: © 1941,
1947 and 1948, All rights reserved.

Reviews from The Commonweal are reprinted by permission of
Commonweal Foundation and its publisher, Edward S. Skillin.

Reviews on pages 17, 18, 49, 58, 67, 69, 132, 139, 202, 210,
and 248 by Robert Benchley, Charles Brackett, and Wolcott Gibbs
reprinted by permission; © 1931, 1932, 1933, 1934, 1940, 1941, 1942,
1943, and 1949 The New Yorker Magazine, Inc.

Anthony Slide

ABE LINCOLN IN ILLINOIS (Robert E. Sherwood; Plymouth Theatre, October 15, 1938)

STORY--This is the story of Abe Lincoln's early days in New Salem, Illinois, to the moment when he boards a train at Springfield to depart reluctantly for the White House in 1861--with the odds in Richmond two to one that he will not live to get there.

It is a simple, bewildered, fearful Lincoln who is egged on by his friends and associates to get out in the world and fulfill his destiny. He loses his one true love, Ann Rutledge, and for the sake of his career marries ambitious Mary Todd, who is determined to wed a future President. Friends and wife see this man grow in stature beyond their fondest dreams for him. They, and the audience, watch him become the human, tragic Abraham Lincoln of history.

ACTING--For the third time in a week the stage has given us a great individual acting performance. Raymond Massey, as Lincoln, is superb. He never once falters in his portrayal of the man, whether sitting simply in the house of Mentor Graham, learning the niceties of the English language, or turning on his wife and damning her for the meddling shrew she was. The groping, the strength, the tenderness of the man are wonderfully performed.

Mr. Massey is ably supported. Muriel Kirkland, as Mary Todd, is close to perfection, and Wendell K. Phillips is excellent as the drunken Herndon, who understood his Lincoln. There are too many other players to salute them all in this space, but all do well.

PRODUCTION--The lighting, staging, and setting of the three acts and 12 scenes are equal to the writing and playing, which is high compliment. Elmer Rice staged and Jo Mielziner did the sets.

CUE SAYS--Robert Sherwood has written his best play in Abe Lincoln in Illinois. It is a magnificent piece of writing. It is, also, a glowing affirmation of the spirit and destiny of these United States.

Here is a play that you most certainly must not miss.
                              --Oliver Claxton in Cue, Vol. 6,
                              No. 52 (October 22, 1938), page
                              11.

*   *   *

Up to the last act the great charm of Robert E. Sherwood's latest play is the charm of recognition. We all know the stories of Ann Rutledge and Mary Todd and of Lincoln's early political successes, we all know them and are interested in them. Therefore when they are put before us on the stage the dramatist's battle is already half won. When they are put before us as sympathetically as Mr. Sherwood has done and above all with a Lincoln so magnificently "in his habit as he lived" as that of Raymond Massey, the victory is complete. There have been numerous Lincolns in the American theatre, but probably none who has so completely filled the rôle, not only visually but spiritually as has Mr. Massey. Yet had the play ended with the second act it would have been but another play of the young Lincoln, a play made chiefly memorable by the verisimilitude of its chief protagonist. It would have been lifelike but non-electric. And then comes the last act and Mr. Sherwood's drama suddenly moves into epic proportions, taking on body and imaginative power. In the opening scene of the Lincoln-Douglas debate, in the scenes of his candidacy for the presidency, and above all his final adieu to his fellow citizens of Springfield as he leaves for Washington, this final act is informed with a rare dignity, even a majesty. In these scenes Mr. Sherwood reaches heights as a dramatist he has never reached before.

He is of course magnificently helped here by Mr. Massey, but unlike the opening acts the triumph is not merely one of recognition, either on the part of the dramatist or the actor--it is the triumph of the creative spirit. It would perhaps be too much to say that Abe Lincoln in Illinois is the finest play ever written by an American, though it would have been that if the first two acts had equalled the last. But, after all, it probably could not have been otherwise, for great themes make great art, and the great theme of Lincoln did not appear until his debates with Douglas. Most of the performances besides Mr. Massey's supreme one are admirable. Special words of praise should go to Lewis Martin's Ninian Edwards, Everett Charlton's Bob Armstrong, Wendell K. Phillips's William Herndon, Muriel Kirkland's Mary Todd, Albert Phillips's Stephen A. Douglas and George Christie's soldier and to Elmer Rice's direction and Jo Mielziner's settings. The Playwrights' Company has made an auspicious beginning in theatrical management.

> --Grenville Vernon in The Common-
> weal, Vol. 29, No. 1 (October
> 28, 1938), page 20.

*   *   *

Robert E. Sherwood's biographical play, Abe Lincoln in Illinois, serves as the first production of the newly formed and widely publicized Playwrights' Company, and if this play is any harbinger of what Broadway may expect from the five playwright members, the American theater is in for a supremely happy season.

Abe Lincoln in Illinois is not only Mr. Sherwood's best play, but it is safe and only honest to record that it is one of the finest dramatic pieces any American author has written. It is a tragic and beautiful play, the drama of a lonely soul forced against his will into public service. Lincoln is introduced to us some time in the eighteen-thirties when he is studying evenings at Mentor Graham's cabin. Shy, ugly, indolent, ambitionless, he recognizes his faults and is quite content to do nothing about them. Out of his heart are "the issues of life," and with those and the whispers of the ghosts of the forest he is content to live. He is afraid of living people, for he has always held the fear that they may kill him. And then he loves and loses Ann Rutledge. In his grief he plans to turn pioneer and, with his friend Seth Gale, make the long trek to Oregon.

Then Mary Todd, with dreams of the grandeur that may be hers, enters, and the well-known and oft-told romance is told again, this time with growing pity and terror, for as Lincoln is pushed into social life, he retires more and more into the sanctuary within himself. The play concludes as he leaves Illinois to take up residence in the White House as President of the United States. But he has lost everything. His wife, with her spirited goading, has forced him to curse her; America has divided against itself; he knows the smallness, the lies, the chicanery involved in public service; and he knows that he is hated, for at the moment of his election soldiers have appeared to guard his life. He is alone, and now lonelier than ever before.

Mr. Sherwood has written with lyric feeling and the relentless, majestic, glowing sweep that fine tragedy must have. And his play, while of the past, interprets the present in terms of what is gone by. Problems troubled our forefathers even as they trouble us-- factory strikes, corruption in democratic politics, the idiosyncrasies of the Supreme Court, whose Dred Scott decision exasperated thinkers of the day. His Lincoln is a tragic hero, unable to battle or to find peace in the conflicting emotions at war both within and outside himself.

This Lincoln has the American passion that Drinkwater's Lincoln lacked; this is a more complex and a more satisfactory portrait than the Lincoln E.P. Conkle envisaged in last year's Prologue to Glory. And Mr. Sherwood has been unduly fortunate in having Raymond Massey portray Abe Lincoln, for Massey has not only the proper physical attributes for the rôle, but he is emotionally and intellectually right for the part. He begins quietly, colloquially, and with each scene his performance gains strength and clarity until by the end of the play he has built a veritable shining monument both to the memory of Lincoln, the man, and to his own power as an actor.

Mr. Sherwood has also been fortunate in having Elmer Rice direct his play, for Mr. Rice knows his theater, and he knows how to get simplicity from lines that are already strong, true, and beautiful. Jo Mielziner's nine sets are excellent, unobtrusive backgrounds for the play that is told in their bounds.

And the supporting cast is superbly chosen. Muriel Kirkland, as Mary Todd, offers a performance that is almost unbearably true in the complexity of its nature. Exquisitely lovely in her single scene is Adele Longmire as Ann Rutledge. Herbert Rudley's Seth Gale is virile yet gentle, and Howard Da Silva's town-bully is perfectly depicted. Lillian Foster is extremely good as Mrs. Bowling Green, and Albert Phillips, as Stephen A. Douglas, is a veritable master of impassioned rhetoric.

Abe Lincoln in Illinois is, I am confident, this year's Pulitzer Prize Play.

--DeWitt Bodeen in Rob Wagner's
Script, Vol. 20, No. 481 (October
29, 1938), page 28.

AH, WILDERNESS! (Eugene O'Neill; Guild Theatre, October 2, 1933)

Mr. Eugene O'Neill has finally emerged from miasmic adolescent bogs (and high time it is, at his age!) and given us a play not only without cancer, rape, paresis or arson in it, but one rich in humor and delightful in its realistic reflection of wholesome human life ... one of the best plays of the present decade ... and one serving as the vehicle for one of the grandest performances for many seasons ... by that ripened old trouper, George M. Cohan.

When the theatre gets as good as this, glory hallelujah!

At least three performances in Ah, Wilderness! will make theatrical history: that by Mr. Cohan as the tolerant, mellow, understanding father of a boy who is just discovering himself spiritually, mentally and biologically; that of Elisha Cook, Jr., as the boy; and that of Gene Lockhart (who is stepping forward as one of the country's foremost character actors) as bibulous Uncle Sid.

And what a relief it is to find O'Neill admitting that, after all, the human race isn't going to pot. Most of his plays since Anna Christie have seemed to me like so many sophomoric stomach aches. But I'd say now that the boy has a future.

I came as near crying as I ever have since Sonny Boy, when George Cohan was trying painfully, falteringly, to tell his son some of the facts of life and discovered that he didn't have to ... when there was flashed between father and son that signal of mutual understanding which is the biggest thing in the world to a father or son when it comes ... if ever.

George Cohan, former song-and-dance man, producer, playwright, patriarch of tin-pan alley, here registers as about the top

actor of his time. I've been reluctant to admit it completely before;
I couldn't unreservedly join the chorus that went up over his Pigeons
and People last season; I thought that he blew up and went a little
song-and-dance before the end of that; but in this instance, he remains quiet, thoughtful, lovable to the finish, a calm captain of his
own artistic soul and of his audience to the final curtain, and, in
the part he plays, the steady pilot of his family through a momentarily tempestuous sea. What's all the shootin' for? Why simply that
his boy, Richard, full of thoughts too big for his head and emotions
too big for his heart, thinking that his girl has thrown him over,
goes off to get on his first drunk and to touch pitch.

And for once, Mr. O'Neill does not make this the cue for un-
loading a trainload of pitch.

As the young boy sat, dejected, on that old boat at the beach
in the moonlight and soliloquized (yes, we have to forgive Mr.
O'Neill a couple of soliloquies in this show) "Life is a joke and everything works out wrong in the end," I thought what a perfect picture Mr. O'Neill was drawing of himself of years gone bye.

But Eugene O'Neill has at last earned his long pants.

He has learned that profundities inferred are ever so much better than profundities dictated in so many words to Miss Dimple.
                                        --Don Herold in Life (November
                                        1933), page 42.

ALICE IN WONDERLAND (Eva Le Gallienne and Florida Friebus,
     adapted from Lewis Carroll; Civic Repertory Theatre, December
     12, 1932)

     After Dear Jane, I vowed I wouldn't go back to the Civic Reper-
tory Theatre for a long, long time ... maybe never.

     But I did go back to Alice in Wonderland, expecting to stay
about 20 minutes. I stayed until 3 a.m., hoping they might repeat
it if they caught me hanging around.

     If I had only one show to see in New York this Winter, I be-
lieve I'd make it Alice in Wonderland.

     The same Josephine Hutchinson who drove me away from Dear
Jane, tearing where my heart used to be, plays Alice beautifully, sin-
cerely, charmingly. (She probably didn't like Dear Jane any better
than I did.) Adaptation, playing, and everything are pleasing, and
the costumes and scenery by Irene Sharaff in the pen-and-ink manner
of Tenniel, and the masks by Remo Bufano, are marvelous.

The whole mad Alice affair seems so much more rational than this normal life that we live. Again I am convinced that the ulti- mate destiny of mankind is some sort of saving craziness which we have not yet glimpsed. With Fred Astaire's* permission, I'd like to enlarge our administrative staff to include not only the cast of Shuf- fle Along, but also Tweedledum and Tweedledee.

                                               --Don Herold in Life (February
                                                  1933), page 30.

ALL MY SONS (Arthur Miller; Coronet Theatre, January 29, 1947)

    With his second Broadway play, Arthur Miller seems to me to stand easily first among our new generation of playwrights. This, to be sure, is not saying anything very tremendous, since almost none of our newest playwrights have any real standing at all. But what is striking about Mr. Miller is that he seems to stand apart from the others rather than merely a cut or two above them. It is not sheer writing that accounts for the difference. Harry Brown can write rings around him on the stage, and as a matter of fact the writing in All My Sons is fairly uneven. It is not quite sheer play- writing either--though, on the whole, All My Sons is very effectively put together. It is rather that Mr. Miller has a personal intensity that charges what goes on with noticeable power; and that he has social and moral perceptions that permit his story to vibrate and ex- pand. The really disappointing thing about most of our "promising" playwrights is the awful mediocrity of their minds, the too great sim- plicity of their aims. Mr. Miller is more interesting than they, so that even his faults seem more interesting. If All My Sons creates an effect of congestion, it is because it has some notion of complexity. If matters sometimes get overheated, it is because they are not born of cold calculation. Even what is unconvincing about his people is partly due to their not being cut from whole cloth.

    But, faults or not, All My Sons is on the whole a compelling play. Mr. Miller has brought to it three things very vital to a seri- ous stagework: he has a dramatic sense, he has a human sense, and he has a moral sense. And these things converge upon a situation in itself provocative. The story of All My Sons is not easy to tell; it has many--probably too many--strands which are only slowly woven together. But it concerns an airplane manufacturer who, with two sons in the war, had allowed defective parts to be shipped out and cause the death of a score or more fliers. Joe Keller had, moreover, allowed his partner to go to prison for this act; and has convinced

---

*A reference to Herold's review of The Gay Divorce, in which he suggested that Congress be comprised entirely of Fred Astaire, his co-dancers and trained seals.

Chris, his surviving son, that he had no part in it.   The other son,
missing for three years, had been engaged to the partner's daughter.
Now she and Chris want to marry, but the stumbling-block is Chris'
mother, who refuses to admit that Larry is dead.   We gradually see
that her refusal is based on her knowledge of her husband's guilt;
and in time the idealistic Chris also learns that his father is guilty.
Upbraided and denounced, Keller--after agreeing to go to prison--
kills himself.

     Mr. Miller's approach to all this is not so simple as you might
suppose.   He is not just another playwright angrily shaking his first
at greed and unscrupulousness.   Indeed, his tone, though passionate,
is not at all polemical.   He is dealing with the complex problem of human responsibility, and dealing with it in very human terms.   He
gets at men's morality through their psychology.   Joe Keller has
rationalized his misdeeds by a callous acceptance of the American gospel of "practicality"; and he has discounted any responsibility toward
society by stressing his responsibility to his family--to seeing that it
gets ahead in the world.   And others, too, in the play are beset by
guilts and divided loyalties, with the moral compromises that result
from them.   Far from creating any villains, Mr. Miller shows how
close "villains" are to normally self-interested people.   Not cruelty
and hate, but self-interest and even self-preservation, prove the
greatest menaces to society--if only because they forge the most
plausible sanctions for acting irresponsibly.   More than at first it
seems to, All My Sons slashes at all the defective parts of our social
morality; but most of all, it slashes at the unsocial nature of family
loyalties, of protecting or aggrandizing the tribe at the expense of
society at large.

     Mr. Miller does not formulate any of this intellectually.   Far
from it; once All My Sons gets going, it is completely theater.   It
is full of tensions, of keyed-up people, of big hard-hitting climaxes.
As a serious work, the play undoubtedly suffers from being too theatrical.   But if Mr. Miller's personal intensity cannot save some of
All My Sons from being high-pitched, it does keep it from seeming
hollow.   The more serious flaws of the play are some imperfect characterizations and rather needless minor characters, a rather too
elaborate plot, and a certain amount of bad writing that Mr. Miller
has let get by him.

     But it remains a play of marked force, and it has been given
a very good production.   Mr. Kazan's staging retains the impact of
the play, and at times supplies the modulation that it lacks.   In the
roles of the father, the mother and the son, Ed Begley, Beth Merrill
and Arthur Kennedy are all highly effective--Mr. Kennedy in particular; and Lois Wheeler gives a good account of herself as the young
girl.   Mordecai Gorelik's backyard set is an additional virtue.
                       --Louis Kronenberger in PM (Janu-
                       ary 31, 1947).

                     *   *   *

A promising play of indignation at war profiteering, expressed in terms which approach classical tragedy, is upset by devices and confusions. Arthur Miller's All My Sons, presented by Harold Clurman, Elia Kazan and Walter Fried, attempts to show how slow but relentless fate overtakes a family whose head is guilty of causing the deaths of a score of flyers by selling faulty material to the Army. His theme is timely, and his script is not altogether lacking in the ominous grandeur of impending catastrophe. There is more weak craftsmanship than pent-up force in the gathering of his dramatic storm, however, and when it breaks it merely scatters rather than explodes.

The foreboding quality of the drama is at first sharply focussed in a mother who refuses to believe that her flyer-son is dead, although he has been missing for more than three years; and her almost vengeful opposition to those who disturb her pipe dream promises to be a direct line of mounting tension. The author loses his way, however, about halfway through the piece in an involved, though impassioned and justified, protest against such men as the father of this family, who has sacrificed honor to his own narrow selfishness. The play has wandered so far from its course at the end that the final news of the flyer's death produces a mere elaboration of the playwright's message rather than an emotional crisis of mixed pity and fear. Also, once having left his original track, Miller has to resort to such tricks as a chance word, a letter and a suicide to bring his curtain down.

The best element in the script is an accurate sense of character, and it is matched in the performances. Beth Merrill as the mother, Ed Begley as the father and Arthur Kennedy as a son who learns to hate his father are all excellent; and Karl Malden stands out in a small role as the son of another father who was victimized for a crime he didn't commit. Mordecai Gorelik's setting is a fine one, but Elia Kazan's staging, usually expert, in this case merely accentuates the script's own uncertainty of dramatic values. All My Sons has stature only occasionally yet it indicates that playwright Miller will probably do better next time.

--Cue, Vol. 16, No. 6 (February
8, 1947), page 16.

* * *

All My Sons, it says in the playbill, was produced by Harold Clurman, Elia Kazan and Walter Fried, in association with Herbert H. Harris. That's too many names to include in a brief review. Why couldn't they just call themselves Clurman & Co.?

Anyway, they have brought an interesting play to the Coronet, but one that is not original in subject or point of view. Arthur Miller, the author, is indignant because during the war many business men were not as honest as they might have been in their deal-

ings with the Government. His specific villain, one Joe Keller, delivered a consignment of defective airplane engines to the Army, and
was therefore morally responsible for the death of several pilots. He
was smart enough to escape legal blame, however; he continued to
prosper in business and retain the respect of his neighbors, and
was even exonerated by his conscience.

It is not difficult to understand why Joe Keller thought well
of him. He was a good family man, a protective husband and provi-
dent father and, as a patriotic citizen, he had willingly given two
sons to the war, one of whom did not return. In his opinion he had
not committed a wrong, but only made a mistake, and similar mis-
takes were being made in scores of plants every day. A feeling of
guilt did not catch up with him until his surviving son discovered
why the defects in the engines were not detected before they were
shipped out of the plant. Even then Keller did not actually feel
guilty, but wilted into a sort of King Lear dejection, crushed by the
scorn of what he felt was an ungrateful son. A pleasant love story
is involved in the plot, but the author is best when portraying character. The people in All My Sons are as admirable, pathetic, jovial
and despicable as one's various neighbors across the street.

Mr. Kazan's direction is adequate, and Mordecai Gorelik's set
is a nice suburban backyard.

--Theophilus Lewis in America
(March 1, 1947), pages 613-614.

THE ANIMAL KINGDOM (Philip Barry; Broadhurst Theatre, January
12, 1932)

Sacred and Profane love are waging their eternal battle in the
new hit by Philip Barry. The Animal Kingdom, however, reverses
completely the role in this apparently inexhaustible theme. Instead
of the siren outside the home who lures the husband by her starkly
physical appeal and the wife by the fireside who holds him through
less specialized virtues we have the two women precisely opposed to
this firm and convenient arrangement. It is the mistress who offers
intellectual companionship and sympathy in addition to the qualities
which surround "love among the artists" and it is the wife who uses
her physical charms to defeat the hero's quest for integrity. The
keynote is given with the last curtain line where the husband, in
final revolt against his spouse's bargaining with the key of her bedroom, remarks resolutely "I'm going back to my wife" and dashes out,
back to the studio.

There are moments of obscurity in the writing of this peculiar-
ly arresting idea and serious defects, I thought, in the casting.
Leslie Howard brought his usual sensitive, subtle understanding to

the role of the husband but while Frances Fuller was sincere and
believable as the mistress the characters of the two women lacked
the force of the contrast is so necessary to the theme. On the whole,
however, it is one of the most absorbing plays of many seasons and
achieves the almost incredible feat of contributing a new angle to
that triangle which is so irrevocably stamped as "eternal."

--Alison Smith in Life (March 1932),
pages 40-41.

ANNA LUCASTA (Philip Yordan; Mansfield Theatre, August 30, 1944)

Anna Lucasta is not a great play, but it is certainly exciting
theatre. It is the story of a girl whose first slip gets her thrown
out of her home, who returns to it under dubious circumstances, only
to fall in love with an innocent country boy whom she marries and
leaves on her wedding night because she thinks he will suffer from
the facts of her lurid past. It was written by Philip Yordan and
presented by the American Negro Theatre in Harlem, before John
Wildberg and Harry Wagstaff Gribble saw fit to bring it into the Mansfield.

And despite its slipshod and foolish story structure, Mr. Yordan has managed to create some substantial and interesting characters, and a cast from the American Negro Theatre turns in some performances that you are not going to be able to forget for a long, long
time. All the acting is excellent and some of it (four performances,
anyway) is just about the best, the most exciting you can see. While
Hilda Simms is a beautiful, provocative and tender Anna, it is Alice
Childress as a broken-down Brooklyn prostitute who will make you
sit close and breathless with the knowledge that you are seeing not
just good acting, but great, great acting. Frederick O'Neal, credited
with being the founder of the American Negro Theatre, plays a kind
of crafty minor Gildersleeve with expansive ease and innocence, and
Rosetta Le Noire, as his vitriolic wife, Stella, does a job that is like
a match being struck into fire across the audience. Canada Lee,
Georgia Burke, Earle Hyman (who brings warmth and credibility to
the country boy character), and everyone else concerned are superb
... but any one of the first four performances is worth an evening
in the theatre. When you learn that, though each has been interested and working in the theatre for years, this is the first professional appearance of O'Neal and Alice Childress, you can't help wondering if perhaps the conditions which lead to such a fact mightn't
be one of the things wrong with the theatre.

Let us assure you that you do not need to bring an interest
in the American Negro Theatre with you in order to find Anna Lucasta a stimulating experience. Mr. Wildberg, Mr. Gribble and the

cast are certainly people who have some idea what the theatre can
be like. You will, too, after seeing Anna Lucasta.

> --Irene Kittle in Cue, Vol. 13, No.
> 37 (September 9, 1944), page
> 18.

ANNE OF THE THOUSAND DAYS (Maxwell Anderson; Shubert The-
    atre, December 8, 1948)

Maxwell Anderson, who is certainly a most likely contestant
for the title of number-one-boy of the American theatre, has a way
with historical dramas. In the past he has enriched the stage with
such distinguished investigations of the Tudor period as Mary of
Scotland and Elizabeth the Queen. In Anne of the Thousand Days
he has returned to the same historical epoch to retell the tale of how
Henry VIII fell in love with Anne Boleyn and how their romance set
in motion events more significant than themselves and far more significant than they dreamed.

And he has employed poetic eloquence and dramatic perception
in his retelling of this oft-told tale. Furthermore, the Playwright's
Company has had the taste and judgment to employ Rex Harrison and
Joyce Redman to project Mr. Anderson's poetry in the roles of the
lusty monarch and his wilful queen. The resulting combination of
writing and acting talents adds up to an impressive piece of theatre.

Captious though I may be, it seems to me, in retrospect, that
Shakespeare's Henry VIII, as presented by the late and still lamented
American Repertory Theatre a couple of seasons ago with Eva Le Gallienne as Catherine of Aragon and June Duprez as the ill-starred
Anne, was a more engrossing spectacle. And perhaps I shouldn't
remind you that Henry VIII is considered one of Shakespeare's
less felicitous historical dramas.

As they are brought vividly to life by Mr. Harrison and Miss
Redman, Henry and his Anne are credible human beings. But, somehow, to me they are not at all sympathetic. I have never been anything but repelled by this romance which was consummated in a sea
of blood. Mr. Harrison, in the breadth and scope of his characterization of the faulty, uncertain Henry, achieves the same sort of
tour de force that another cinema actor, Charles Boyer, has achieved
at the Mansfield in Sartre's Red Gloves. Both these actors, heretofore unseen on the American stage, prove that there are better actors in Hollywood than the screen would sometimes let you believe.
If Joyce Redman seems a mite shrill as the ill-fated Anne Boleyn, it
is perhaps due to the incidents chosen by the playwright to highlight
this whole violent and bloody era.

The roles, of course, are rich in histrionic potentialities. And, as has been indicated, Mr. Harrison and Miss Redman make more than the most of them. Their lust for each other and for power creates many enthralling moments and there are several speeches which have hardly been surpassed in the theatre. The total of all these separate virtues does not, however, add up to the great tragedy that Maxwell Anderson must have intended to write, although his play as a character study of the younger Henry gives you a pretty fair psychological insight into those components that turned the older, bestial Henry into what he was.

As you may have gathered, Henry and Anne are by far the most important characters in Anne of the Thousand Days. But they are by no means the only ones. A large supporting cast helps to recreate the splendor and the barbarity of the Tudor Court. Naturally, Cardinal Wolsey looms large as ever in the proceedings--and Percy Waram contributes a lifelike picture of the wily, wise and too-worldly Prince of the Church. Wendell K. Phillips is appropriately despicable as the conniving Cromwell. John Merivale paints a vivid picture of one of the young men who were tortured into admitting adultery with the Queen. Charles Francis, Viola Keats and Louise Platt, enact members of the Boleyn family.

The sets, a difficult assignment inasmuch as the script wanders willy-nilly here and there in time and space, have been designed by Jo Mielziner. His solution to the almost insuperable problem depends pretty much on a sort of toy castle and spotlights that roam dramatically from place to place and face to face.

Motley did the costumes. Which is tantamount to saying they're magnificent. Altogether Anne of the Thousand Days is a major theatrical event.

> --Thomas Brailsford Felder in Cue,
> Vol. 17, No. 51 (December 18,
> 1948), pages 22-23.

ANNIE GET YOUR GUN (Book by Herbert and Dorothy Fields, Music and Lyrics by Irving Berlin; Imperial Theatre, May 16, 1946)

A handsome musical, particularly fortunate for the presence of the beautifully comic Ethel Merman. Whether she is slew-footing around through a straight scene or singing one of the many, many numbers she deigns to dish out, she is fine and funny. And the cast and production surrounding her add up to a good strong background.

The book by Herbert and Dorothy Fields might be called a little slow in less expert hands (and feet) than those of Miss Merman ... but since it was fashioned for her, you don't have to worry.

Richard Rodgers and Oscar Hammerstein 2nd produced this pleasant
business and Irving Berlin has given it music and lyrics which, while
not in the knockout class, are engaging for their very unpretentious-
ness.

It's all about Buffalo Bill's Wild West Show, his great two-fun
stars, Frank Butler and Annie Oakley, the show's rivalry with
Pawnee Bill's show, its travels and troubles--and its Indian braves.

Indeed, the Indian element gives Annie Get Your Gun the one
exciting production sequence it can boast of. This is a ceremonial
Indian dance, quite exciting to my taste, conceived by Helen Tamiris
(as are other dance sequences) and most dashingly performed by
Daniel Nagrin and a good company of expert dancers. The occasion
for this is the acceptance of Annie Oakley as a daughter of the Sioux
tribe, and it concludes with some wonderful Merman antics in lo, the
poor Indian fashion.

Ray Middleton as Frank Butler is a big, good-looking cowboy
type who can, as you probably know, sing. It is certainly a refreshing change from other male musical comedy leads, to hear a
baritone that doesn't get lost somewhere between the singer's throat
and the first three rows. Mr. Middleton sings just as loud and clear
as Miss Merman, and you know how loud that is.

Marty May, Lea Penman, William O'Neal (the tallest, most impressive Wild West impresario you ever did see), George Lipton, Harry Bellaver and what looked like hundreds of cowboys, Indians,
dancing girls, debutantes and what all ... help out. Lubov Roudenko
does some expert leg-twirling and Betty Anne Nyman and Kenny Bow-
ers perform some more or less routine dance numbers.

Jo Mielziner's sets are colorful, though not spectacular. I
was a little disappointed by Lucinda Ballard's costumes, which did
not, it seemed to me, take full advantage of the period possibilities.

Annie Get Your Gun is not in a class with Oke, Carousel or
Bloomer Girl (though it might have been), but in its own class it
does very well. It is Ethel Merman's show, and since she is most
generous with her presence, her performance and her voice, I don't
think anybody has a kick coming. I haven't.

> --Irene Kittle Kamp in Cue, Vol.
> 15, No. 21 (May 25, 1946), page
> 66.

* * *

Its original opening postponed, its advance publicity tremendous,
Annie Get Your Gun finally came to the Imperial Thursday night. The
news about it is cheerful, but very far from overpowering. It's a
big Broadway show, in all ways professional, in many ways routine.

But it has, for which its producers and patrons can alike be intensely grateful, Ethel Merman.

Miss Merman is in fine form. She is in fine form as a contralto, giving to ditty after Irving Berlin ditty her celebrated sand-blast treatment. She is in fine form as a comedienne, pining (mouth ajar and eyes a-goggle) with amorousness; making her body talk and her stride talk back; raising an oak of a laugh out of an acorn of a joke. She is in fine form as a personality--tough, rowdy, gusty, outstaring and outsnooting anybody who gets in her way. Moreover, as Annie Oakley--the blazing sharpshooter of Buffalo Bill's Wild West Show, whose aim never faltered till love made it fail--she is very happily cast.

For me, Annie is mainly Miss Merman's show, though the rest of it is competent enough of its kind. It knows its formula, and sticks to it like a well-raised baby. If the show hasn't a trace of style, at least it hasn't a trace of artiness. It has size, a primary-colors picturesqueness, the kind of organized activity that can pass for pep. Mr. Mielziner has done pleasant sets, and Miss Ballard bright costumes. Miss Tamiris' dances are of the lively, likeable pre-de Mille days, before Broadway tried for something better and generally came up with something worse. Herbert and Dorothy Fields' book spins a yarn that has Annie in love with a male sharpshooter she can lick: some of it is lively and perhaps more of it is not.

Irving Berlin's score is musically not exciting--of the real songs, only one or two are tuneful. But Mr. Berlin has contrived a number of pleasant ditties and has laced them with lyrics that, if seldom witty, are almost always brisk. Miss Merman makes the most of her numbers; and Ray Middleton who--as the rival gun-toter--has the right voice and looks does a very good job with his.

Annie is a musical put together for the greatest happiness of the greatest number. For a long time to come, no one will be handed any Annie Oakleys to see Annie Oakley perform.
                                        --Louis Kronenberger in PM (May
                                          19, 1946).

ANOTHER PART OF THE FOREST (Lillian Hellman; Fulton Theatre,
       November 20, 1946)

Lillian Hellman has reversed the usual order of sequels. In Another Part of the Forest, which Kermit Bloomgarden presents at the Fulton, she shows us the immediate forebears of the nefarious Hubbards, whose acquaintance we made several seasons ago in The Little Foxes. They are a bad lot, it seems.

In tones of sheer, gaudy melodrama, Miss Hellman depicts a Southern clan marked by drunkenness, insanity, black mail and as many cardinal vices as you can shake a stick at. Old Marcus Hubbard of Snowden, Ala., grew rich by bootlegging salt to his neighbors at fabulous figures during the Civil War. Rumor said that he was responsible for a massacre of Southern boys by the Union troops. His wife is insane. His daughter, Regina, has been having an affair with a seedy aristocrat. He swindles a family out of cotton holdings and arranges for his indolent son to wed the fluttery Miss Birdie.

Another Part of the Forest is composed of exaggerations. You don't believe in or care about any of the stencilled characters. The author has stacked the cards as in the cheapest sort of outmoded paperbacked novelette. Good people of the South may very well resent Miss Hellman's deliberate lampoon and question where she got her material.

The only excuse for the play is its cast. Percy Waram, as old Marcus Hubbard, dominates the play with subtle humor beneath his outward show of craftiness and venom. Mildred Dunnock is appealing as the demented mother. Leo Genn, as the elder son, is a portrait of restless unscrupulousness. Patricia Neal, as Regina, is bewildered and well mannered.

Jo Mielziner's sets of a rambling vine-covered exterior and a cluttered living room of the eighties give the play an air of ominous grandeur.

> --Russell Rhodes in Script, Vol.
> 33, No. 746 (January 4, 1947),
> page 19.

* * *

In Another Part of the Forest, Lillian Hellman has gone back to the world, to the very characters of The Little Foxes; and Broadway itself must go back to The Little Foxes for a play of equal tension and striking power. Once again the monstrous force of villainy is redoubled by the implacable drive with which the author projects it; once again there is a sense of explosion.

The play takes us back to 1880, 20 years before the period of The Little Foxes, when the father of Regina, Ben and Oscar Hubbard was very much head of the business and the household. Marcus Hubbard is quite their match in baseness, but a far more complex and interesting character. A pariah in the town he dominates, Marcus is ruthless, sardonic, cruel, with that responsiveness to art so often found in cold, cruel natures, and that sense of pretension so often born of the responsiveness. Married to a woman driven half loony by his treatment and by a sense of guilt about his past, he is jealously indulgent toward Regina, deliberately nasty to Oscar and Ben.

The household seethes with hatreds and frustrations, with trickery
and treacherousness; for the young Hubbards are not shown becoming little foxes through impact of circumstance, but as vulpine by
nature.

The major conflict in the play is that between Ben--with his
furious drive for power--and the father he hates for blocking the
way. Foiled and frustrated again and again, Ben stumbles on his
mother's guilty secret--something that can make his father the victim
of a lynching party; and with this as a whip, brings the old man to
his knees. Ben takes over, and Oscar and Regina quickly salute
the rising sun.

Of all this Miss Hellman makes driving theater, and something
more than driving theater--something more purposeful, more provocative, more talented. It is just because the play reaches higher
ground that one wonders why it does not have quite the stature it
should have. The answer, possibly, is that Miss Hellman's fable is
not adequate to the force behind it. You cannot write off Another
Part of the Forest as simply melodrama, for it is the people in the
play that stay with us, not the plot. They are vigorous people, and
Marcus is perhaps the most interesting character Miss Hellman has
ever drawn. Yet to some extent melodrama has been permitted the
last word, and the operations of villainy crowd out the inner nature
of villains.

Though the third act, where Ben turns the tables on his father,
has theatrical punch, it has a kind of dramatic inadequacy. For it
works things out at the diamond-cut-diamond level of knaves where
interest centers in a contest of wits. But for two previous acts we
have been involved in much more than a contest of wits; we have
been concerned with a passionate conflict of wills. Hence we can't
help feeling that the play should be resolved by something from
inside these people, by an eruption of character rather than a twist
of circumstance. All this might well make the play even more violent
than it is, but it would sustain the pitch at which Miss Hellman
seemed to be working. As it is, one merely has a sense of overload-
ing.

Told as Miss Hellman had told it, Another Part of the Forest
has more than a little in common with those sombre Elizabethan
"comedies" swarming with cheats and knaves and evildoers. But,
by lacking their simpler emotions and by being charged with Miss
Hellman's angry heat, it necessarily flows over into the world of
drama. The play, compared with The Little Foxes, seems less effective but more interesting, less controlled but more complex. And
by thinking of the two plays together, one begins to think of Miss
Hellman's writing as a whole, of that body of work which, far more
than single examples, is the key and criterion for assessing a writer.
What we find in such a view, beyond the sense of theater and the
technical skill, is a massive force animated by strong personal and

moral emotion. It never has yet found its exact trajectory; it has frequently collided with this or that obstruction. But it is there and when it finds just the right object to be exerted upon, it will create something tremendous in the theater.

I have not space to write as I should of an admirable production. Miss Hellman's staging is firm and incisive, and much of the acting is excellent. Percy Waram is close to superb as Marcus Hubbard, and Mildred Dunnock notably good in the difficult role of his wife. Leo Genn has real force as Ben, and Patricia Neal considerable, if too unmodulated, force as Regina; and there is a beautiful performance of the young Birdie by Margaret Phillips. Jo Mielziner has created outstandingly handsome sets, and Lucinda Ballard some extremely fine costumes.

> --Louis Kronenberger in PM (November 22, 1946).

ANYTHING GOES (Book by Guy Bolton, P.G. Wodehouse, Howard Lindsay and Russel Crouse, Music and Lyrics by Cole Porter; Alvin Theatre, November 21, 1934)

The musical shows are slow in coming in, but when they do come, they come good. Anything Goes was worth waiting for. Mr. Vinton Freedley has what might be called a "honey" on his hands at the Alvin, and things around town seem brighter than ever because of it.

He has taken the precaution of enlisting the services of several people who seem unable to displease the public. If there is anyone who does not love Victor Moore, he has the good sense to lie low. Mr. Moore is about the only comedian we know who is 100 per cent sure of his laugh, no matter what he says. As "Public Enemy No. 13" in the present opera (he is shattered when he learns that the government has finally dropped him entirely from the Public Enemy list as being too harmless. "I don't understand the present administration," he complains), we have Mr. Moore at the peak of his pathos.

William Gaxton, too, seems to be pretty well established as a sure bet, and it is difficult to decide whether people have a good time watching him because he himself seems to be having a good time, or vice versa. Anyway, everybody has a good time.

To complete his trio of safe plays, Mr. Freedley, who used to be a quarterback himself, has sent Miss Ethel Merman around the end into what is evidently an open field. Enough of Miss Merman is what people do not seem to get, and while I could wish that sometime soon she might be sent on without an evangelical "Hallelujah" number, I never let it interfere with my general appreciation of her talents.

Miss Bettina Hall has always exerted a good influence over me, and never more than here, for I do not quite believe her when she sings that she has a touch of the gipsy in her. She is an excellent antidote for the crass, bestial man-about-town influence of Mr. Moore.

Any show which has Cole Porter writing its music and lyrics need hardly try out in the provinces. Mr. Porter is in a class by himself, and by "class" is meant "class." In "You're the Top," he has exceeded even himself as a writer of original lyrics, and unless I do not know my theatregoers, the town will shortly be driving itself crazy trying to memorize the sequence of items indicating "top." In this one song, he has summarized American civilization better than any symposium of National Thinkers has ever been able to do.

The book was originally by Guy Bolton and P.G. Wodehouse, standard hit-makers, and I rather imagine that Howard Lindsay and Russel Crouse have aided considerably in making a standard hit of Anything Goes. Whoever made it, it is made.

--Robert Benchley in The New Yorker (December 8, 1934), page 36.

ARSENIC AND OLD LACE (Joseph Kesselring; Fulton Theatre, January 10, 1941)

The two little old ladies from Brooklyn were as batty as the Borden sisters, and their descendants weren't much better off. One nephew was a homicidal maniac, with victims scattered from here to Singapore; another imagined he was Theodore Roosevelt, with all that implies; the third was a dramatic critic. Out of these materials, Joseph Kesselring, abetted by Russel Crouse and Howard Lindsay, has created one of the best comedy melodramas you ever saw. To appreciate the special quality of Arsenic and Old Lace, at the Fulton, you probably ought to have a couple of aunts of a charitable and fluttery disposition who nevertheless have poisoned twelve men and buried them in the cellar. Since it is more or less unlikely that you are related to any such girls as these, I can only say that Abby and Martha Brewster have the kindest dispositions in the world and brew their arsenic-and-elderberry cocktails only for gentlemen who have passed their prime and seem destined for a lonely and vacant old age. At one point, indeed, Abby pauses to remark that one subject, sipping his last drink this side of paradise, had commented very favorably on its flavor. "It's delicious," he said, and expired merrily.

Nothing, perhaps, would come of all these rather bizarre cocktail parties if it weren't for the appearance of a nephew, with his face whimsically lowered by his physician to resemble Boris Karloff's,

who announces that he, too, has bumped off his even dozen. The
ladies, after all, have their professional pride and this is not a
challenge to be taken lying down. "Jonathan always was a mean
boy," says Abby petulantly. "Couldn't bear to see anybody get
ahead of him." So it is that one Mr. Witherspoon, the innocent
proprietor of a bughouse, sips his hemlock and goes to join the other gentlemen in the cellar, giving the ladies the victory by the
close score of thirteen to twelve.

These cheerful goings-on (when you have four lunatics and
some twenty-five corpses, you are a long way past the boundaries
of the gruesome) are supplemented by occasional bugle calls from
Theodore Roosevelt, the entrance and exit of a Brooklyn police force
which does a lot to explain how Murder, Inc., got along as well as
it did, and a love affair considerably less bothersome than most. If
I wished to complain, which I don't, I might say that a dramatic
critic, or even a composite of several dramatic critics, is hardly a
suitable romantic lead for any play, and also that the trade secrets
of this glum profession are apt to seem either dull or incomprehensible
to the average audience. However, Arsenic and Old Lace could easily survive worse handicaps. There could even be a character in it
supposed to represent Dorothy Thompson, and I would still think it
was wonderful.

Boris Karloff (in person) is theoretically the star of the evening,
and does very well, too, but Josephine Hull, as the odder of the Brewster sisters, is my girl. Miss Hull does so many remarkable things
that it is hard to say when she pleases me most, though it may be
when she murmurs vaguely "Now, who can that be?" on being confronted with an unexpected stiff in the window box. Jean Adair, as
her sister and the one usually responsible for blending wine, arsenic,
strychnine, and cyanide into one appetizing whole, is also very
charming, and so is John Alexander, who not only behaves like the
hero of San Juan Hill but looks like him as well. Allyn Joslyn, com-
bining some of the more picturesque qualities of Mr. Watts, Mr. Atkinson, and Mr. Nathan, cooperates with Helen Brooks on the love
story, and there are useful bits by Edgar Stehli and Anthony Ross.
Raymond Sovey, who did the set, seems to know exactly what a
Brooklyn house looks like on the inside, God help him.
                              --Wolcott Gibbs in The New Yorker
                              (January 18, 1941), page 33.

*   *   *

Joseph Kesselring, author of the new thriller, Arsenic and Old
Lace, has accomplished something of a tour de force in this work
which is now shocking and rocking New York. (We are divided as
to whether to call it a farcical horror play or a horrible farce.) The
playwright has managed to make Brooklyn, the city of churches, seem
gruesome. Those who have lived there, especially on Sundays, know
that this is not beyond the realm of possibility. But he has gone

further and made it appear laughable at the same time. Of course,
this appendage of Manhattan has been chortled at before. But to
orchestrate the laughs with shudders is something different.

As one who has lived there, this chronicler is compelled to
say, however, that murders in Brooklyn are not really so entertaining as this play makes out. This is typical of the strain on the
probabilities imposed by some of the outlandish turns in the story,
such as the disclosure that one of the cops in the play wants to be
a playwright. We always thought policemen secretly yearned to be
firemen, and vice versa. Also, murders are not done on quite the
wholesale scale in Brooklyn that is represented in this play, no less
than a dozen corpses occupying the cellar at one time, just like a
subway jam even in death. After all, Brooklyn is more conservative
than that.

But one forgives a lot of this, even the curtain call at the end
when the dozen corpses parade out of their graves for a bow. The
only thing one minds about this is that one wonders if one isn't look-
at a musical comedy (without music), and this parade seems merely
the procession of librettists taking a bow.

The play is the initial producing venture of Howard Lindsay
and Russel Crouse, who majored in the drama by writing Life With
Father, still fuming along pleasantly on Broadway. The producers,
with the assistance of the author and the stage director, Bretaigne
Windust, have managed to invest this piece with the same charm as
their earlier offering. One would imagine one was present simply at
an agreeable Brooklyn tea party, but for the persistent suspicion
that there is a lot of wholesale poisoning going on around the old
mansion. Even that is made to seem quite nice, so that nobody is
really bothered by it except the victims.

The local critics obviously enjoyed the new play because its
hero is a theatrical critic who doesn't care much about his drama-
tasting, and would rather write about a down-to-earth subject like
real estate. There were a number of amiable jokes about stage criticism which the Broadway death watch could take without hurling a
review at the play in riposte. And there were also some gags about
the movies, which always please the Eastern reviewers, especially
after inspecting a flock of plays about Hollywood.

One of the chief spoofs about the screen is that Boris Karloff,
who returns to the Main Stem after some years in filmland, portrays
the chief menace, and is called upon to murder one or two people
in the play simply because they tell him he looks like Boris Karloff.
That is the only reason advanced for these murders. In the eyes of
Gotham audiences, it seems to be sufficient. Boris is still Karloff
and revolting even though he is somewhat prettied up from his
Frankenstein phase, his hair actually being parted in the middle.
He plays the role very effectively, working his undershot jaw back

and forth with all the fluency but none of the blitheness of Elsie
the cow.

Other excellent performances are turned in by Josephine Hull
and Jean Adair as the two maiden aunts who are so good-hearted,
though arsenous, that one would hardly mind being liquidated by
them as long as they did it with their elderberry wine.

One of the chucklesome performances is that of John Alexander as the addle-noggined brother who believes himself to be Teddy Roosevelt, wears Rough Rider costumes, yells "Charge!" every
time he goes upstairs, and says "Bully!" on the slightest provocation. The critic is adroitly played by Allyn Joslyn, who, like Karloff, is a ticket-of-leave man from the movies. Edgar Stehli and
Helen Brooks are commendable but unreal, since they play sane folks
in a dippy cast.

With a good deal of ingenuity and astuteness Arsenic and Old
Lace travesties the usual mystery play without seeming to do so.
But at the end as we were bosomed out into the lobby by a freshet
of dowagers, we couldn't help wondering how long this current hit
would really appeal to the women, who might revere the same kind
of maiden aunt they see ladling out lethal doses coyly in this work.
Probably till the first spring freshets.

> --Frank Vreeland in Rob Wagner's
> Script, Vol. 25, No. 584 (Janu-
> ary 25, 1941), page 20.

AS HUSBANDS GO (Rachel Crothers; John Golden Theatre, March 5,
    1931)

Mr. Atkinson of the Times, writing about As Husbands Go,
said of Miss Rachel Crothers something which most dramatists would
rather have said of them than take Quebec on the morrow. He mentioned her wisdom, her serenity, her sense of humour, and her
sympathy with ordinary people. Nothing much more than that could
be done for Shakespeare. Miss Crothers deserves this high praise.
In As Husbands Go, she has given us the liveliest manifestation, to
date, of those cardinal qualities, and I, for one, after sitting through
a series of dramatic atrocities, feel like thanking her mother, her
father, and John Golden. The theme is the second blooming of two
attractive middle-aged women who become so spellbound by what they
think is the glamour of Paris that they return to American completely
determined to reorganize their lives along romantic lines. The older one, a widow, must return to face the wrath and criticism of a
débutante daughter. The younger, who has been the pink of propri-
ety in Dubuque and its suburban circles, is prepared to renounce a
hitherto satisfactory spouse for the English poet who has awakened

her to depths in her nature of which she had not dreamed until she
met him, etc., etc. We have all seen such things start in Paris,
and have also seen them finish there. Few of us have been able to
follow them to the hilarious conclusion which Miss Crothers provides.
The appearance of the chosen cavaliers upon the Iowan scene es-
tablishes that incongruity which is the basic essence of humour,
and the ladies do not find things as easy and natural as they seemed
in France. Catherine Doucet, who gives a superb performance as
the nit-wit widow, tangles their web of deception into knots which
bring howls from the audience, but the young poet finds the husband
more to his taste than he finds his inamorata, and the cementing of
their friendship over several bottles of Scotch, which also meets
with approval, foreshadows the satisfactory conclusion for which we
had trusted the author all along.

> --Baird Leonard in _Life_ (March 27,
> 1931), page 25.

* * *

Rachel Crothers has been writing for twenty-five, or is it
thirty years? She is one of our three or four women dramatists who
are worth their salt. She has never tried to be profound, for the
very good reason that she has nothing profound to say in the theater, and on occasion she has (like all good playwrights) given us
silly plays. But she knows how to mould her plays into agreeable
forms, and in even her inferior plays I can detect a fine balance,
an intellectual clarity that I'll call classic for want of a better word.
Her work is of the tradition of English comedy, and that means it is
well-bred, witty and wise. Miss Crothers at her best is interested
in human beings. _Mary the 3rd_, _Expressing Willie_, and even the
slighter _Let Us Be Gay_, are all plays about people. So is her latest,
As Husbands Go, now firmly settled into what is going to be a long
and successful run at the John Golden Theatre.

Lucile Lingard, married to an agreeable Babbitt, and Emmie
Sykes, widow, both from Dubuque, leave Paris with regrets that life
in the American middle west is neither so exciting nor free as it is
in Europe. An elderly admirer, Hippolitus Lomi, accompanies Emmie
home, and a young English writer, Ronald Derbyshire, follows Lucile
a few weeks later. Despite the opposition of Emmie's daughter, Emmie decides to marry Hippie, but Lucile's affair is not so successful.
To begin with, her husband, Charles, is not only decent and generous, he is far more intelligent than anyone had given him credit for
being, and when he gets drunk with Ronald (one of the best scenes
Miss Crothers has ever written) the truth pops out; he's not good
enough for Lucile. What is more, Lucile realizes it, and Ronald returns to England.

There's nothing so very exciting about this, as you can see;
but it's quite enough for a playwright who knows how to use it.
The result is a compassionate, amusing, pleasantly worldly comedy.

It is neither so brilliant as Susan Glaspell's Alison's House, nor so full of passion, but it is written with restraint and in the grand manner.

> --Barrett H. Clark in The Drama Magazine, Vol. 21, No. 7 (April 1931), page 11.

AS THOUSANDS CHEER (Book by Irving Berlin and Moss Hart, Music and Lyrics by Edward Heyman and Richard Myers; Music Box Theatre, September 30, 1933)

As Thousands Cheer yips assiduously and acidly at the heels of current (and sometimes not-so-current) events, and I rather like that in a review. It was the intention of the old Ziegfeld Follies to do this--in fact, that is why they were called the Follies--but Mr. Ziegfeld could find no one smart enough to keep up the kidding for him, and, besides, he, himself, was really more interested in glorifying the American gal.

"Revue Bites Foibles" might be an appropriate headline for a discussion of As Thousands Cheer, because the show is interspersed with newspaper headlines throughout, and the opening sketch concerns a man who has been bitten so repeatedly by his wife's feisty little peke, that he finally retaliates.

Some of the chapters are pretty harsh, I feel. For example, that one picturing the departure of the Hoovers from the White House. This one is, in reality, just another and an elongated Hoover joke, and Hoover jokes aren't exactly the newest thing in the world. And I rather hate to see Mrs. Hoover dragged in, for no President's wife ever did a better job of remaining the innocent bystander. (Now, if Mr. Roosevelt flops, the sketch writers may go for Mrs. Roosevelt plenty, for she has had no hesitancy about putting her oar into the public puddle.)

Any show which Moss Hart writes is sure to have plenty of sharp barbs, and the thrusts are certain to be worth anybody's evening. And any show for which Irving Berlin writes the music is sure to be worth wiring home about (Postal Telegraph, please).

Our pet, Helen Broderick, is in the thing, playing everybody from the Goddess of Liberty to Queen Mary. Marilyn Miller is back, as graceful and charming and devoid of voice as ever, and without much to do, except an excellent imitation of Lynn Fontanne and one of Joan Crawford, plus a funny-paper number which, it seemed to me, belongs in Barnum's circus rather than in this otherwise pretty adult entertainment. Clifton Webb is there, and I like him much better than usual because he does less dancing (it's good dancing, I

know, but it always makes me want to bite my nails and scream)
and because he has more chances as a comedian, as which, I have
decided, he is a card. (See his John D. Rockefeller and Mahatma
Gandhi.) But the show is made for me by Ethel Waters, colored
warbler soop-erb. She's as rich as a chocolate layer cake, as full
of personality as a carload of chimpanzees, and she must use a Fuller
radiator brush for a toothbrush. By the way, what a show an all-
colored Irving Berlin show would be!

It invariably embarrasses me when anybody tries to look like
Hoover, Teddy Roosevelt, Washington, Lincoln or Wilson on the stage.
I wish they would do that with mirrors.

--Don Herold in *Life* (November
1933), pages 42-43.

AS YOU DESIRE ME (Luigi Pirandello; Maxine Elliott Theatre, Janu-
    ary 28, 1931)

Pirandello's As You Desire Me is full of sound and fury, and
signifies almost nothing. But, being a characteristic blend of mystery,
melodrama, and metaphysics, it gives to Judith Anderson a rôle of
which actresses lie awake at night and dream. She comes in soused,
she suffers and suffers, she wears slinky, skintight gowns, she
walks up and down a staircase and poses on its landing, and at moments neither author nor audience is certain about her identity. And
she does it all extremely well. (In this connection, Marie Doro, one
of the most intelligent and cultivated women of our theatre, once told
me that she had been given mousy, saccharine parts for so long, that
the high moment of her career came when she was assigned in an all-
star revival to a rôle which allowed her to beat upon a door. And
how she did whack it!) The story of As You Desire Me concerns a
woman who, violated by soldiers marching by her husband's villa,
had disappeared through shame at her experience, and sunk to unbelievable debauchery in the cabaret life of Berlin. She is discovered
twelve years later by an old family friend and persuaded to return
with him to Italy and resume her rightful place in life. But time
has worked such ravages in her appearance and constitution that
there is grave doubt amongst her relatives as to the justice of her
claims, a doubt which is not decreased by the appearance of another
woman with similar intentions. After considerable Pirandelloish hem-
ming and hawing, the real wife gives up the struggle and returns,
unregenerate, to the scenes of her downfall. There is a general
opinion, which I share, that the author is not at his befuddling best
in this piece. On the night I saw it, Jose Ruben did not appear
as the painter, and because of the long waits and ignorance as to
their cause, I entertained for a moment the mean and grim hope that
for the first time in my life I should hear from a stage that famous,

pregnant inquiry, "Is there a doctor in the audience?"
--Baird Leonard in <u>Life</u> (February
20, 1931), page 18.

* * *

While Miss Judith Anderson is neither so brilliant nor so talented as Miss [Katherine] Cornell, I feel that in this Pirandello play
she is trying not so much to show off Miss Anderson as to interpret
Signor Pirandello, but perhaps that is because Pirandello is an artist
and Besier only a journeyman. At all events I was held by the
Italian play, and most of the time bored by the English one. In
fact, As You Desire Me reminded me a little of Barry's Hotel Universe, though it lacked the poetry of the American work. It closely resembles Pirandello's own Right You Are if You Think You Are,
another dramatization of the problem of human personality. It is no
more than the presentation of a composite viewpoint, and as such it
cannot possess that fullrounded and wholly satisfying effect that we
demand from a playwright who is content to present his human prob-
ings simply as he sees them; but within the limitations of the Play
of Ideas formula it is a superb thing. The plot has to do with a
woman who returns to her husband and family after ten years, a
victim of the war, who was supposed to have been ravished by the
invaders. But there is some question as to whether she is, after
all, the woman she is at first taken for; and from the moment her
husband sees her the entire interest is focussed on the mystery of
her identity. She is, however, precisely what each person desires
her to be, and so far as the "proofs" are concerned she may or may
not be the woman who disappeared ten years before. The mystery
is never cleared up, and realizing that no one has sufficient faith in
her she disappears. Then, you ask yourself, Who was she? Pirandello answers, As You Desire Her.

This is just another way of expressing the old philosophical
idea that nothing is except as we think it. Does God exist? If you
believe He does, He does, and that's as far as we can go. In his
play Pirandello has managed to sustain his thesis and yet to arouse a
good deal of plain human interest without falling into easy sentimen-
talities. The man's sheer technical equipment as a contriver of dramatic fables is amazing, but I take the liberty of disagreeing with
several Continental and a few native critics by proclaiming again that
Pirandello is no more than an extremely ingenious playmaker with a
good mind.
--Barrett H. Clark in <u>The Drama</u>
<u>Magazine</u>, Vol. 21, No. 7 (April
1931), pages 9-10.

BABES IN ARMS (Book and Lyrics by Lorenz Hart, Music by Richard
   Rodgers; Shubert Theatre, April 14, 1937)

Babes in Arms is as fresh as the burgeoning spring, rushing in with a whoop and a youthful exuberance which is irresistible to this weary old department, busy these last two months counting our gray hairs, one for each turkey production. Shall we say twenty new sere strands?

This gay and bouncing new show is one of the most vital, refreshing pieces of youthful hokum to come this way in a long, long time. The cast is juvenile as you have heard, but professional as you have not. The music is young and stirring and exciting and the costumes dashing and primavera and full of novelty and verve. The whole affair is as gay as a yacht in a fresh breeze and as cunningly ordered in its captivating conniptions as a bunch of Lambs cavorting to order.

That old shepherd, Dwight Deere Wiman, has taken his courage in both hands and tossed it into the laps of Richard Rodgers and Lorenz Hart, the musician and plot master responsible for the greenward goings on among the children of the dispossessed vaudeville community of Sea Port, Long Island. Those two sophisticated gentlemen, responsible for the bedroom observations of On Your Toes and numerous other au courant shows, have diverted from their usual primrose path with a tremendous and, it must be admitted, unexpected success.

How any one could expect to make a go of a show which requires nothing but kids, how they could expect to present a large scale, expensive musical comedy without the usual star is no longer a problem. Here is that daring venture and here it is as an enormous success.

Rodgers and Hart deserve the credit. They invented the idea and they have carried it through, aided only by Mitzi Green and a host of talented youngsters. They are the ones who have provided the hit songs. Nearly every tune in the show seems to have the requirements which will endear it to the radio audiences as well as the showgoers. Put in your memory book such items as "Johnny One-Note," "Way Out West," "Where or When," "The Lady Is a Tramp," "I Wish I Were in Love Again" and "Imagine." Those are the gay things on which Babes in Arms has arrived at the Shubert Theater and they are the songs which may keep it there indefinitely.

Not that the show is entirely without a star. Surely Mitzi Green fits into that category. A youngster indeed, but a trouper by now. The veteran child actress has become an engaging performer, sure of herself, with a fair voice and with an agreeable stage presence. She carries the burden of the plot and does the work usually assigned to someone of high calibre in the theater. It would seem that we are witnessing the debut of an important future entertainer.

Others notable in the bouncing company are Ray Heatherton,
Duke McHale, Wynn Murray and the inescapable Nicholas Brothers.
These are the children of vaudeville who stage a show to foil the
sheriff and come out on top of the town. They cavort in some of
Raymond Sovey's gayest settings and they are costumed with Helene
Pons' usual flair for the unusual. Add up the people, the songs,
the backgrounds and the clothes and they all spell a gay time in the
theater.

> --Herbert Drake in Cue, Vol. 5,
> No. 26 (April 24, 1937), pages
> 13-14.

*   *   *

Those who are in the mood for a frolic in the form of a good
song-and-dance show will find it in Babes in Arms. It is cuddly,
has freshness and a certain distrait quality that charms. A crowd of
youngsters cavort with all the energy of a catnip-tight litter of well-
fed kittens. Here is a piece of property the movies will snap up, or
I miss my guess ... again.

Babes is about a crowd of younkers who are broke; their parents are vaudevillians. Threatened with the Poor Farm, the kids
decide to put on a show but end with selling the old homestead as a
flying field. The sets and costumes are no more pretentious than the
kids could actually run up on a spare Singer and, except for the tag
scene, there is, mercifully, no lavishness anywhere. The Rodgers
and Hart score is uniformly top-flight. My favorite song happens to
be "That's Why the Lady Is a Tramp." Possibly the reason is the
way the now grown-up and now blonde Mitzi Green sells it. Her vo-
calizing lacks the depth and quality it once possessed, but her acting technique is just as certain. So, too, is her gift for mimicry;
she does a superb impersonation of the Luise Rainer telephone lament.
"Way Out West," "Johnny One-Note" (watch that, proofreader!), and
"Where and When" all measure up to the best in Tin-Pan Alley's out-
put.

A good portion of the last act is given over to "Peter's Jour-
ney," an artful, but not seriously arty ballet. Duke McHale abets
the superb Balanchine choreography, enters lithely into fantasy without making it Fantasy, into whimsy without making it Whimsy. The
Nicholas frères, more chocolate drops, are grand. Best line: "You've
got to have a name for everything. Y'know, like the Federal Theater
is called entertainment."

> --Herb Sterne in Rob Wagner's
> Script, Vol. 18, No. 429 (Septem-
> ber 18, 1937), pages 14-15.

THE BAND WAGON (Book by George S. Kaufman and Howard Dietz,
Music by Arthur Schwartz; New Amsterdam, June 3, 1931)

Elaborating on the advice of the poet to hitch your wagon to a
star, Max Gordon has hitched his Band Wagon to a constellation, the
light from which will be causing loud cheering at the New Amsterdam
Theatre for months to come. Advance notices from the outlying dis-
tricts on this show convinced the writer that the critics in the hin-
terlands had been outlying each other, but no such thing. The
Band Wagon is the most brilliant eyeful of color, talent, showmanship
and intelligent writing that the New York musical stage has seen in
many seasons. It is, in short, if we may coin an expression, a step
in the right direction.

The show gets away to a flying start with a burlesque of all
the hackneyed routine material seen in the average revue, and having
begun by making fun of the usual, it proves its point by proceeding
to be unusual. Beginning with the "Hoops" number by Fred and
Adele Astaire, the stage presents a succession of settings that are
nothing short of inspirational. Albert R. Johnson will now come forward and take a flock of bows. He created them. And how much
simpler it makes the work of the actor when he performs against a
background that has the audience all excited before he does a thing.
We use the word excited advisedly. In the "White Heat" number
the dancers, dressed in black with white gloves treated with radium,
do a fast routine on a stage that revolves around a huge black
cylinder. The first-night patrons were so excited that they practically had fits.

Honors for individual merit go to Fred Astaire whose work es-
tablishes him securely as our most accomplished dancing actor. There
may be a number of young men along Broadway who are better hoof-
ers than Fred from a standpoint of mechanical intricacy, but that is
just the difference. You never think of Fred as a hoofer. He is an
accomplished actor who uses his feet as an extra added attraction.
While other tap dancers are working themselves into a frenzy with
difficult acrobatics you will find Fred bidin' his time as he walks
through a comparatively simple little jig and makes you feel like standing up and shouting in appreciation of his smooth style and delightful personality ... and as a matter of fact quite a few people did
shout their approval at the completion of his "Beggar Waltz." Mrs.
Fredric March's comment to the writer was a perfect description.
She said it had the grace and charm of a painting by Degas. We
also call your attention to Fred's makeup in the Southern sketch.
It's a classic. In our opinion Mr. Astaire now occupies the position
held by Jack Donahue at the time of his untimely death. If there is
further praise we would not know how to express it.

Other musicians on the Band Wagon whose music is more or
less drowned out while Fred is present, but who toot their own horns
convincingly when placed in the spotlight are sister Adele, Frank Morgan, Helen Broderick and Tilly Losch. Of these Mr. Morgan is most
important. This versatile farceur has previously proven his ability
as a dramatic actor and screen star. Now that he is scoring in a

revue it only remains for him to take up the flying trapeze and har-
monica, after which he can challenge Joe Cook for the decathlon title.

Adele complements Fred's dancing with her own nimble feet,
and acquits herself commendably in the sketches. Her makeup in
the "Louisa" number is a masterpiece. Miss Broderick is consistently
amusing, and particularly so in "Where Can He Be," a travesty on
the musical comedy ingenue who always does a cute little song, the
sentiment of which is always where-can-he-be, in which she is always
billed as "Miss Glutz and The Boys." Miss Broderick's satire iso-
lates the germ and presents it in such plain view that producers of
musical shows in the future will probably recognize its presence more
readily--a circumstance which may eventually result in stamping out
this saccharine irritation.

The audience seemed to respond readily to Miss Losch's sinuous
dancing, but, frankly, we do not share this great enthusiasm. For
instance in her number "The Flag" we were left not only unmoved,
but practically in the dark. Maybe she's right. She writhes gracefully enough in "Dancing In the Dark," and deserves her ovation--
which doesn't alter the fact that the set and costuming are the big
thrills.

This brings us, a bit confused, to the authors of the book:
George S. Kaufman and Howart Dietz. The cause of the confusion
is this. These two very talented gents have written a series of
sketches that are characterized by smart satire, clever wit and original comedy. To which you say, so what? Well, so this: The ideas
behind the sketches are more amusing than their exploitation. It
may be the aim of George and Howard (and a worthy one) to revolu-
tionize revue formulas, but there is one rule they cannot toss out the
window. A sketch should end on its highest note. Several of the
ones in this show (unless they have been retouched) end in a bit of
a slide. The lines are amusing, but they occasionally overstay their
welcome. This may seem an unjust criticism inasmuch as the Kaufman-
Dietz sketches are consistently amusing, whereas the usual revue
blackout is padded to frame one clever gag ... but bits of entertainment like "The Pride of the Claghornes," "The Great Warburton Mystery" and "Pour le Bain" are too rare to be left with rough ends
sticking out to mar their potential value.

The musical score by Arthur Schwartz offers two tunes you
will hear a lot--"Dancing In the Dark," (it will remind you of "When
Your Lover Has Gone.") "New Sun In the Sky" and "High and Low."
The other ditties are unimportant except for Mr. Dietz's consistently
clever lyrics. The "Tra-la-la" thing is not good enough to close such
a marvelous show, and something should be done about it. And here's
a tip. Don't get up and leave when the principals start this song,
because at the finish the curtains are drawn back to reveal the entire cast in a ball-room scene that is a knockout.

You'll probably say this is the best revue you ever saw in
your life. Put in your ticket order now and you may get in by early fall.

> --Baird Leonard in Life (June 19,
> 1931), page 18.

THE BARRETTS OF WIMPOLE STREET (Rudolf Besier; Empire Theatre,
    February 9, 1931)

Somebody, probably Bugs Baer, has said that the business of
living results mainly in the personal proving of the platitudes about
life. As children, we wrote in copybooks innumerable repetitions of
statements which meaning little to us at the time beyond the achievement of a Spencerian slant which, if a defection in individuality had
permitted its formal aspect to stamp our chirography, would subsequently have made us suspects of being cum laude night school
graduates. As the shadows began to lengthen, we learned that many
of these homely, uninteresting precepts were true. Honesty being
the best policy, for instance. All of which is preliminary to the flat
pronouncement that we take to the theatre, as well as to life, exactly
what we have ourselves, and when you take as much as I took to
The Barretts of Wimpole Street, you need a bucket.

Mrs. Browning has long been for me the world's outstanding
heroine. Compared to her, even after reading De Quincey, Joan of
Arc was a piker. It is all very well to have a fine steed, a bevy of
soldiers, and a neurasthenic conviction that God has spoken to you
in arboreal retreats through a medium which Lee De Forest would
dismiss today as entirely void of commercial value. It is quite another thing to be racked by illness, and to maintain, throughout a
physical anguish which is literary history, a spirit which prompts you
to set down so much as a simple declarative sentence. What Mrs.
Browning set down, in spite of childhood memories of padded editions
for the parlour table, is what we all know, and what few of us, in
this age of Texas Guinans and Belle Livingstones, have the courage
to admit to ourselves. Nobody has ever written about love as she
wrote about it, although she was constrained in the middle of the last
century by an obligation to a form which makes some of her pronouns
and verbs sound a little out of place to the modern ear. (And that,
if you please, for the modern ear!) Before I go completely maudlin,
it may be wise to quote what a wise man once said of her: "When
she failed, it was because she missed her foothold--never because
she funked the leap." (If Guthrie McClintic is reading this article,
I want to reassure him that I thought The Barretts of Wimpole Street
was swell. And also remind him about the buckets.)

I began to bawl in Thirty-ninth Street where, because of a
traffic congestion superinduced by the opera line, there was time

and opportunity to quote "Sonnets from the Portuguese." I got
through "When our two souls stand up erect and strong" rather creditably, and even managed "Accuse me not, beseech thee," but when
I came to "Go from me. Yet I feel that I shall stand," etc., the
tears were so unrestrained that the gentleman beside me, who hap-
ened to be my husband, and who had maintained a manly and calm
politeness up to the moment, was fearsome that casual observers might
suspect me of a splendid afternoon in a speakeasy, and ushered me
into the Empire with a fine disregard of late diners and the portraits
of the Frohman stars. (If Guthrie McClintic is <u>still</u> reading this
piece, I want to tell him that I think Katharine Cornell gave a beautiful performance as Elizabeth Barrett.)

We all have our own ideas about the Brownings, and I think
we are entitled to them. Many of our memories, gathered during
adolescent days, are inaccurate, but disregarding Robert, with his
lemon-colored gloves and unflattering conversational references to
Shelley, about the plain vision of whom he had previously inquired
in verse at a publisher's rate, there is no denying the validity of
their affection, just as there is no denying the quality of the woman
who fulfilled his spiritual need. Miss Cornell plays Elizabeth Barrett splendidly in this connection, and if the play to which her family has given its title seems at moments to be more concerned with
the tyranny of a father under whose influence she lived out most of
her earlier years, she manages to project the personality which
causes many of us oldtimers to break down. Mrs. Browning brought
to love exactly what many of us would like to think we bring to life,
and to the theatre. We don't speak much about it, because we are
inarticulate. Mrs. Browning said plenty, and said it with almost incredible beauty. And Miss Cornell, for the first time in several seasons, has a part which is worthy of her exquisite sense of interpretation, and plays it, with very little conversation on her part, up to
what a thorough unacademician would call the hilt.

--Baird Leonard in <u>Life</u> (February
27, 1931), page 18.

* * *

Gilbert Miller has gone to the English writer Rudolf Besier to
find a vehicle for Katharine Cornell. As a vehicle <u>The Barretts</u> is
certainly adequate, but I see no reason at all why an actress needs
a vehicle. If she's a good actress it is her business to place her
talent at the service of the playwright. Miss Cornell has rarely
done this. She prefers to act in plays that reveal her own very considerable talents. Mr. Besier's play is a workmanlike dramatization
of the love story of Robert and Elizabeth Barrett Browning, with
which he has taken a few pardonable liberties. Aside from a couple
of delightful scenes carried almost entirely by the star, the play is
negligible.

--Barrett H. Clark in <u>The Drama
Magazine</u>, Vol. 21, No. 4 (April
1931), page 9.

BELL, BOOK AND CANDLE (John Van Druten; Ethel Barrymore
     Theatre, November 14, 1950)

     John Van Druten habitually works a very shallow vein, but he
refines it carefully and sometimes makes it glitter. His newest play,
however, seemed to me to run dry too quickly, and while I admired
the polish which the author and actors have given it, I didn't really
get an awful lot of fun out of it. There were only three or four
emphatic laughs over the evening, and a fair amount of pretty obvious punning. The piece is about a modern-dress witch who gets
her man by casting a spell over him, and the actors made a number
of remarks, sometimes making the same one twice, about being "spellbound" or finding the situation "enchanting." Lilli Palmer is a devastating witch, and Rex Harrison is adroit as her victim, and you may
find the evening rewarding enough just watching them work. They
skim the surface of an amusing idea very neatly, but after awhile
you become aware that there isn't much under them and start yearn-
ing for a headier brew.

                              --Walter Kerr in The Commonweal,
                                Vol. 53, No. 8 (December 1,
                                1950), page 197.

                         *   *   *

     When he writes this sort of comedy, which is his good sort,
John Van Druten can be as daft as he is deft. And when he has
the largely good luck of Lilli Palmer and Rex Harrison in its leading
parts, he can afford to stretch it to three thin, increasingly gaspy
acts. He still has a hit on his hands.

     Here happens to be the first time when this glistening couple,
each a bright particular star of previous plays, have appeared in
the same one. They should make a habit of it. Our more or less
monogamous stage, which oughtn't expect Mr. and Mrs. Lunt to do
absolutely everything, will be only too grateful to have Mr. and Mrs.
Harrison hitched up and highjinxing together, too.

     About the play, itself: regretfully, I'll retire to a rear rank
where, muttering to myself, I shan't disturb the general jubilations.
Mr. Van Druten did have a delicious idea. But he also had, for once,
a pretty listless wrist at cooking it up. For all the extras of fine
clothes and fashionable pleasantries which he has stirred into it, his
soufflé seemed to me to subside into a half-inch pancake at the end.

     In Murray Hill's handsomest apartment lives a witch. A young
witch, beautiful but bona fide. She takes a willful fancy to the manly publisher who lives upstairs. Learning that he is betrothed to a
girl she'd disliked at college, her conscience--or whatever witches
have for consciences--is clear. She incantates the gentleman straight
to her couch. Let that be a useful lesson to all the Misses Lonely

Heart. As demonstrated by this demon and her victim, a highly ornamental one, too.

So far, here is sheer Thorne-Smith-in-dress clothes with much of the same amusing mixture of the supernatural and the sub-moral which made that late literary faun so famous. But Mr. Van Druten has a gentler side, a sentimental zigzag in him which must prove that love conquers all, witches, wizards and publishers included. The lady loses her powers but, of course, she ends up by winning her man.

Mr. Van Druten has his old, ever-easy knack here of furnishing blissful lines, both conversational and sartorial, for his two chief performers. Quite as he had it in The Voice of the Turtle. As he had it, even longer before, in There's Always Juliet. Nor does he neglect some weirdly light moments for helpers like Jean Adair, Scott McKay, Larry Gates and a real, live Siamese cat. The cat keeps its baleful green eyes unblinkingly open looking almost a critic, appearing almost to agree that Mr. Van Druten's slowness seldom mars his smoothness, only draggles it a bit.

Lots of helpful first-nighters, departing up the aisles, announced that they had livelier notions of how to solve the pretty piece. But every one of their alternate endings would yet have included the lovely Lilli, the conquering Rex--and so no harm could have been done.

> --Gilbert W. Gabriel in Cue, Vol.
> 19, No. 47 (November 25, 1950),
> page 22.

BIOGRAPHY (S.N. Behrman; Guild Theatre, December 12, 1932)

A million dollars' worth of Ina Claire, is my review of the Theatre Guild's Biography. If Earle Larimore hadn't made the young radical such a nature-in-the-raw character, I might have liked the play a whole lot better. I just couldn't sympathize with Miss Claire's affection for this unbearable fire-eater. And though Jay Fassett did a good job of the politician, there was not much in the part to indicate Miss Claire's tolerance of him. Maybe if I had more of the mother in me, I could be more generous with these intolerable men with whom women fall in love on stage.

> --Don Herold in Life (February
> 1933), page 32.

BLITHE SPIRIT (Noel Coward; Morosco Theatre, November 5, 1941)

Noel Coward, whose delightful comedy of the hereafter joining the present has been amusing London for quite some time, seems to have touched the risibilities of American audiences as well. His Blithe Spirit is sending the cash customers at the Morosco into an assortment of hilarious merriment, ranging in quality and volume from quiet chuckles to positive gales of laughter. It's grand fun.

It is Mr. Coward's whimsy that the departed and jealous spirit of a British novelist's first wife returns to her relict's fireside to haunt, annoy, irritate and otherwise make unbearable the life of her ex-husband's second and current wife. The playful shade sets about her pranks and succeeds in creating considerable comic confusion and marital chaos before the third act curtain resolves the astral and mundane difficulties of those concerned.

The comedy--gay, witty, amusing and pixieish in the best Noel Coward fashion--is played for all it is worth by a first-rate cast: Clifton Webb as the bewildered astral-bigamous husband, Peggy Wood as the much put-upon wife, Leonora Corbett as the lovely, if malicious, ghost, and Mildred Natwick as the bouncing, bustling medium responsible for the ghostly intrusion. John C. Wilson produced.

--Jesse Zunser in Cue, Vol. 10,
No. 46 (November 15, 1941),
page 28.

* * *

There is only one way in which a spectator with religious convictions can enjoy Blithe Spirit. This is to ignore those religious convictions, and to regard the play as the gambol of a brilliant pagan mind.

Mr. Noel Coward has indulged in this gambol tactfully, from his viewpoint. Though it deals with the reappearance in this world of those who have died, it is concerned only with that reappearance and the earthly experiences which accompany it. Its sole suggestion of the lifted veil is the intimation that the dead Elvira, first wife of our hero, has been hovering about in some misty half-way point between the two worlds, awaiting her chance to return to this one. She gets it through the efforts of a medium who is holding the séance in the home of "Charles." He was Elvira's first husband, but he has married again and is living happily with his second wife, beautifully played by Peggy Wood.

All this is set forth in Mr. Coward's so-called "improbable farce," put on at the Morosco Theatre by John C. Wilson and featuring Clifton Webb, Peggy Wood, Leonora Corbett, and Mildred Natwick. The description, selected by Mr. Coward himself, certainly classifies his offering; but that does not prevent happy audiences from filling the Morosco Theatre at every performance, and chortling over the improbable situations. Happy audiences are doing exactly the same thing in London. And now for the plot.

Clifton Webb (Charles) is an author. He takes himself seriously and engages Mildred Natwick (Madame Arcati) to conduct a séance
in his home that he may see how such an enterprise is carried out.
Madame Arcati goes into a trance and Elvira, the dead wife of Charles,
appears. She is very effective in a misty gray ensemble which in
itself is a high work of art, and she is exquisitely played by Leonora Corbett, a young English actress who has come to us for the
first time and is already accepted with great enthusiasm.

I doubt if any other actress could put into this characterization
more effectiveness than Miss Corbett is giving it. From the top of
her gray hair and gray coif and gray eyes and gray face to the tips
of her gray shoes, she seems more a spirit than a living body.
She is not an admirable spirit. She is elfish, selfish, mischievous,
and finally malignant in her determination to kill Charles and get him
into the spirit world.

When she arrives, Charles alone sees her. This scene departs
abruptly from farce except in the acting of the medium. Miss Natwick holds throughout the play to the strongly farcical note. All
the others, except Miss Corbett, who rightly holds to her elfish mood,
fall into moments of seriousness which lie in the text of the offering
but which are confusing to the general mind. For we are puzzled
by a situation which is not farcical. It is the determination of the
dead wife to remain in the home of her living husband until she can
lure him away. In her effort to do this by killing him, she kills
the second wife. He is thus rid of them both and very glad to be;
and the third act dénouement is pure farce.

There is no question that audiences like the play. Mr. Coward
has put into it many of his brightest lines and the acting of the entire cast is among the best this season gives us. Indeed, the acting
has to be perfect to carry the erratic twists and turns of the play
from drama to comedy, from comedy to farce.

To my taste Mildred Natwick overstresses the farce note, but
the play must stress that note, or even its splendid company could
not hold it together. Mr. Coward has given his players a stupendous
task. They are equal to it, however, and they will continue to prove
this to us during the remainder of the winter.
                              --Elizabeth Jordan in America (No-
                              vember 22, 1941), page 192.

BORN YESTERDAY (Garson Kanin; Lyceum Theatre, February 4,
    1946)

Garson Kanin's play is as light as magnesium metal, as modern,
timely, and just as durable. A provocative business, it is graced

with Kanin's superb, muscular direction plus acting which sheds an almost actinic light on the dialogue. You may doubt some of the possibilities but in the very moment of doubting, Judy Holliday's performance as a post-war and so political Galatea will kindle a sharp answer to your doubt.

The play is extremely simple. Into the $235-a-day suite of a Washington hotel moves big, loud, aggressive and successful Harry Brock. Dealing in big-time junk, Mr. Brock buys a Senator for some $80,000, for the promise of the kind of legislation which will make him an international junk king. In Brock's suite are his mistress, Billie Dawn; his cousin, a kind of secretary-valet who keeps his hat on at all times; his lawyer, now a shady, slightly drunken character, but once an Assistant D.A. of the U.S. ... and, from time to time, a young writer for the New Republic. While Brock is the type who removes his shoes as soon as his feet hit carpet, he feels that the blonde Billie may not be up to the big time his deals now call for (cartels take finesse, it seems). So he employs the New Republic fellow to teach Billie a few things. Billie's learning is fast, funny, and often startling. There is a particularly sweet impact to the epithet Fascist once she searches her mind to find it. Lovely satire (a gin rummy game will turn you inside out), a fast, sure pace, makes this another State of the Union kind of thing, though, we suspect, its versatility gives it an even broader appeal. Judy Holliday as Billie and Paul Douglas as Brock are terrific ... but Gary Merrill, Frank Otto and Otto Hulett are pretty wonderful, too.

> --Irene Kittle Kamp in Cue, Vol.
> 15, No. 6 (February 9, 1946),
> page 15.

* * *

The news from the Lyceum is cheerful. With his first play, Garson Kanin has made a brighter Broadway. He is also, along slapdash comedy lines, trying to make a better world. Born Yesterday is fun at the expense of what is anything but funny; an angry theme turned into an entertaining evening. Mr. Kanin is pursuing one of the more dangerous enemies of society with a barrage of gags; he is preaching human rights with flippant humor. There are far more forcible ways of making people think, or act, or alter; but there is certainly no smarter way of making people listen.

Mr. Kanin's target is a big-time, roughneck racketeer who has gobbled up thousands of junkyards. He has come to Washington, where he keeps a Senator on his payroll, with a postwar itch to gobble up--all over the world--thousands more. While he is deep in skullduggery, he has the "dumb broad" he is living with tutored in the social and intellectual graces suitable to the capital. Unfortunately for him, his choice of a tutor is a bright young liberal on the New Republic staff. It need scarcely be added that, in terms of

teacher and pupil, the plot becomes a New-Deal Pygmalion story;
and, in terms of the roughriding plunderer, a modern-day Frankenstein.

Mr. Kanin's pursuit of his theme is a good deal less than classical; in fact, much of Born Yesterday appears to have been fished
up out of the grab-bag. Mr. Kanin gets off to an extremely exhilarating first act, in which the big shot and his blonde, installed in
a $235-a-day hotel suite, have an unforced vitality and achieve a
very amusing relationship. But once the plot takes over, much in
the way of characterization is lost. So (without any real gain in
seriousness) is much in the way of solid entertainment. Mr. Kanin
still squeezes fun out of one thing or another--particularly the lady's
bouts with book learning; he plugs up holes with gags; he works in
some melodrama when the racketeer tries to get tough. But as a
straight show that also tries to get something said, Born Yesterday
shows none of the tidy workmanship of a State of the Union. After
the first act, it lives pretty much from hand to mouth. Thanks to
enough funny cracks and to some admirable acting--of which more in
a moment--Born Yesterday manages to be diverting. But in terms
of how it opens, and what it opens out on, it is fairly disappointing.

It would be worth seeing, however, just for Paul Douglas'
and Judy Holliday's acting. Mr. Douglas' racketeer is a pretty ugly
customer whose baboon ways and roughneck ignorance are also highly entertaining. Miss Holliday is often quite wonderful--particularly
before her education sets in, and she can make the most of her flat
voice and high-styled floozie walk. Just watching her sort her
cards at gin rummy is a treat. The other performers are of no great
importance, though Gary Merrill is pleasant as the New Republic man.
But Mr. Kanin's direction is lively and ingenious, and Donald Oenslager's classy, cluttered set just right for its inhabitants.
                              --Louis Kronenberger in PM
                              (February 6, 1946).

THE BOYS FROM SYRACUSE (Book by George Abbott, Lyrics by
     Lorenz Hart, Music by Richard Rodgers; Alvin Theatre, No-
     vember 23, 1938)

STORY--Maurice Evans may be giving us the best Hamlet of
all time, but up on 52nd Street you'll find the best Comedy of
Errors of all time, to boot. Mr. Abbott has tossed away the Master's
dialogue, kept the plot and put it where it belongs--in a musical
comedy.

It is all there--the separated twins and their equally separated
twin slaves, and all the rigamarole they go through on the streets
of Ephesus; likewise, sundry misconceptions in the home of Antipholus

of Ephesus. Mr. Rodgers has written his best music for the affair,
and Mr. Hart has fitted it out with seemly lyrics.

ACTING--Jimmy Savo heads the cast, and I'll warrant that no
one, ever, any place or time, has succeeded in fusing pixiness and
lewdness as successfully as Mr. Savo. It is a startling and satisfactory combination. Savo is one slave boy, Dromio; Teddy Hart is
his twin brother, Dromio, and he does not lag far behind Savo's performance. A very fine pair of comics. Eddie Albert and Ronald
Graham are the two Antipholuses, and Albert contributes a little more
zest and nonsense to his part than does Graham. They both sing
well. Wynn Murray, as the wife of one Dromio, contributes good nature and a powerful voice that falls pleasantly upon the ear. Marcy
Westcott is a pretty Luciana, and Muriel Angelus does well as Mrs.
Antipholus of Ephesus. Betty Bruce contributes some good dancing
as the courtesan.

PRODUCTION--The show gallops along at the usual rapid Abbott pace, and it is well set by Jo Mielziner. Irene Sharaff has designed colorful costumes for the boys and girls of Ephesus, and
George Balanchine has devised some excellent dancing. The first
scene is particularly engaging.

Cue SAYS--This is the gayest prank to hit town in the memory
of the oldest inhabitant. You will like the comedy, the acting, and
the pretty, tuneful score. If you contemplate taking the kiddies,
be warned that The Boys from Syracuse is well drenched in good
humored bawdiness. If they are not up on the Facts of Life, they
will be well along that road to knowledge when the curtain comes
down.

> --Oliver Claxton in Cue, Vol. 7,
> No. 6 (December 3, 1938), page
> 12.

* * *

The most honest compliment one can pay The Boys from Syracuse, which is what George Abbott has done to Shakespeare's The
Comedy of Errors, is to note right at the start that Shakespeare
would have an awfully good time watching it. The Comedy of Errors,
as Shakespeare wrote it, may have been funny to Elizabethan audiences, but to us it is definitely lesser, unfunny Shakespeare, undistinguished by any lyrical passages and complicated by an overclassic
plot.

George Abbott, however, has made it into a really laughter-
provoking, often downright raucous comedy. He has simplified the
plot, cut out, with the exception of two lines, all the Shakespearean
verbiage. Rodgers and Hart have provided him with one of their
most lilting scores. You may have been whistling some of the songs
yourself--"Sing for Your Supper," "This Can't Be Love," "O Diogenes,"

"The Shortest Day of the Year." Irene Sharaff has costumed the
show brilliantly, and the ease with which Jo Mielziner's practical
sets roll off and onto the stage affords delight.

Best of all, The Boys from Syracuse has one of my favorite
cut-ups, Jimmy Savo, who, with his spitting-image partner, Teddy
Hart, makes up the Dromio team. When the two remaining lines of
Shakespeare are recited--

> The venom clamours of a jealous woman
> Poison more deadly than a mad dog's tooth--

Savo pokes his head out from the wings, and solemnly gives the
Bard his due credit. Eddie Albert and Ronald Graham are the handsome twin heroes, and Marcy Westcott and Muriel Angelus are the
beautiful but perplexed heroines. Best and bawdiest singing is done
by Wynn Murray, of "Johnny One Note" fame.

The audience at The Boys from Syracuse are not the least of
the fun. Nearby me a lady with a scrawny backbone and an up-
swept hair-do remarked to her escort, "This is awfully funny. Are
you sure it's Shakespeare?" "Oh yes," he assured her, "it's something they've made out of The Merchant of Venice."

--DeWitt Bodeen in Rob Wagner's
Script, Vol. 21, No. 505 (April
22, 1939), page 21.

BRIGADOON (Book and Lyrics by Alan Jay Lerner, Music by Frederick Loewe; Ziegfeld Theatre, March 14, 1947)

Past mid-season, and the best musical in this or many another
theatrical year has arrived. You Californians contemplating a trip
to New York, put Brigadoon on your list for required playgoing.
Not that there's any especial hurry, for the show will be at the Ziegfeld for years, or, at any rate, as long as Producer Cheryl Crawford wants to keep it there.

Brigadoon is the sort of production that used to make the late
Alexander Woollcott dance in the streets and fling his cap for joy.
No rooters for the theater are more enthusiastic than professional
critics when show business unfolds a work of talent that clicks in
every department. Brigadoon does it. It brings a thrill in direction,
acting, singing, design and color not sparked since Oklahoma! or
Carousel, or through the magic of such a charming non-musical as
I Remember Mama.

Alan Jay Lerner is telling the story of the ancient Scottish village of Brigadoon which the Lord, in answer to the local clergyman's

prayers that it be saved from a plague of wicked witches, caused to
vanish in 1747, but with the privilege of returning to the world for
one day every century. Tommy Albright and Jeff Douglas, two
young Americans, lost in the Highlands, stumble upon Brigadoon as
it rises out of the misty glen. It is Fair Day in MacConnachy Square
and Jeanie MacLaren is wedding Charlie Dalrymple, while Harry Beaton, who also loves her, looks blackly at the groom.

Under the spell of the legend, Tommy, like his compatriot in
Berkeley Square, falls in love with a maid from another century.
As the mists gather to lock Brigadoon in another one-hundred-year-
old sleep, Tommy, frightened by doubts, rushes back to New York
with Jeff. Haunted by Fiona, who walked with him 'mang the heather
on the hill, he returns to Brigadoon to be greeted by Mr. Lundie,
the village dominie, who knew that to love well one must give all.

A company of gifted young actors and singers, new to Broad-
way, plays with zest and great appeal. As Fiona, Marion Bell, a
Los Angeles girl, who sang leading roles with the San Francisco Opera
Company, is a bonnie, Highland lass. In a voice of great beauty
she sings some of the best compositions of Frederick Loewe, such
as the solo, "Waitin' for My Dearie," and, with David Brooks (Tommy),
"The Heather on the Hill," "Almost Like Being in Love," and "From
This Day On."

Mr. Brooks (who made his Broadway debut in Bloomer Girl
two years ago) reminds me of the early Glenn Hunter. Lee Sullivan
as Charlie Dalrymple is a typical Irish tenor, singing the lilting "I'll
Go Home with Bonnie Jean" and the lovely "Come to Me, Bend to Me"
in fine romantic style. Comedy is in the capable hands of George
Keane as the flippant Jeff, and Pamela Britton as the lass who wants
him for a while.

James Mitchell, a Hollywood boy, alumnus of Los Angeles City
College, takes laurels in his first speaking role as the dour Harry
Beaton, as well as leading dancer with Lidija Franklin. As Mr. Lundie, the philosophical schoolmaster, William Hansen contributes a
splendid characterization.

Agnes de Mille's choreography is rich in color and imagination;
Mr. Loewe's score, brilliantly conducted by Franz Allers, suggests
old Scottish airs; David Ffolkes has made full use of colorful tartans
in costumes and Oliver Smith's settings are like a breath from the
Trossachs; staging by Robert Lewis makes a vibrant production at
all times.

Brigadoon has courage to tell a poignant love story for its own
sake. It has not forgotten the skirl of the bagpipes and its handling
of fantasy is done with considerable delicacy and restraint. Ay, lad-
die, 'tis a bonnie, brave show, a daisy.

--Russell Rhodes in Script, Vol. 33,
No. 752 (April 1947), page 40.

* * *

A title so attractive as Brigadoon is something to live up to;
but Brigadoon lives up to it. And the musical fantasy at the Ziegfeld not only has charm; it shows a good deal of independence. It
calls its own tune; in the very act of making Broadway seem brighter, it makes it seem a touch less Broadwayish. It is true that I was
fingering larger adjectives at the end of the first act than I was at
the end of the show--for after a time Brigadoon loses some of its
lure, and at the last it flops down to a banal Broadway level. But
all in all it is a very engaging evening.

Brigadoon is so successful because it has hit on a very pleasant fantasy for a musical, and then known what to do with it. To
be sure, Brigadoon is imaginative at the Barrie level, not the Blake,
it is wistful and whimsical, sentimental and faraway. But Mr. Lerner's tale of two young Americans who stumble on a vanished Scottish
village that comes miraculously to life for one day every 100 years
is thoroughly appealing on its own terms. Brigadoon has realized,
moreover, that its charm must lie less in any story it tells than in
the general mood it creates; and it has created that mood by fusing
a number of theater elements as densely as possible. The music,
dancing, scenery and costumes surround the story rather than merely
set it off. In fact, Brigadoon is most alluring when these things
really are the story--when we are given the look and feel of 18th-
century Brigadoon, its customs and ceremonials, the details of a wedding, a funeral, a fair. There is a romantic love story, of course;
but it is Brigadoon itself that is really romantic.

In staging Brigadoon, Robert Lewis has fused its various elements with authority and spirit; and each separate element is pleasant or better. Musically, Mr. Loewe's score has no particular distinction, but it maintains a rather charming mood without becoming
monotonous, and it offers some likeable sentimental tunes. Agnes de
Mille's dances, if a little trademarked, are particularly clean-cut and
animated; the best of them, perhaps, being a sword dance that has
great style. Oliver Smith's sets are nicely evocative, and David
Ffolkes' costumes quite handsome.

The cast, too, is an attractive one. I especially liked Marion
Bell, who plays the heroine, and William Hansen, the old Brigadoon
schoolmaster. David Brooks' voice is as good as ever, and James
Mitchell's dancing is excellent; while Virginia Bosler, Lee Sullivan,
Pamela Britton and others come off well, too.

Mr. Lerner's book and lyrics are further pleasant items; in
fact, Brigadoon shows so much desire (as Finian's Rainbow didn't)
to make Broadway keep its distance, to avoid shoddiness, to hold
to a superior and stylish level--and so generally succeeds--that one
feels a little cranky even mentioning its weak points. The second
act does, however, let the mood partly dissolve and the charm rather

peter out; and the last two scenes are an outright blunder. Whether _Brigadoon_ was to have a bittersweet ending or a happy one was of very little moment, but it should not have slapped one ending on top of the other--and in the corniest Broadway fashion. As for the final ending, even in fantasy one good miracle doesn't deserve another. Even worse, shows like _Brigadoon_ should run like hell from those gauze-curtain visions of one's lost love standing forlornly on a hill top.

But even that can be forgiven in what is so obviously the season's freshest musical.

--Louis Kronenberger in _PM_ (March 16, 1947).

CABIN IN THE SKY (Book by Lynn Root, Lyrics by John La Touche, Music by Vernon Duke; Martin Beck Theatre, October 25, 1940)

Story--"Little Joe" Jackson finds himself dead after an argument during a dice game in which he sustains seventeen slashes with a razor. Lucifer, Jr., comes for him to carry him away to Hell, but Petunia, Joe's wife, has prayed so fervently that Joe gets another chance. The Lawd's General tells Joe that he will live again for six months and if he behaves himself he will enter Heaven. He also informs Joe that he will not remember during those six months that he is out under bond, so to speak.

Between a world of gambling and a beautiful woman named Georgia Brown, an amiable fellow like Joe has tough going to stick to rectitude. On his side are Petunia and the Lawd's General; opposed, Lucifer, Jr., and the fleshpots.

Acting--Ethel Waters heads this all-colored cast and heads it with the best performance of her career. Right at the start she hits the top when she uncorks a number called "Taking a Chance on Love" and with that, let me assure you, you hear something. From this moment on she dominates the show--and the cast that goes with her takes very high class domination.

Dooley Wilson plays a perfect Little Joe, and Katherine Dunham makes a right plausible temptress. Rex Ingram and Todd Duncan, as Lucifer, Jr., and the Lawd's General are fine.

The rest of the excellent players contribute most handsome support.

Production--A lot of forthright ingenuity went into the staging, directing, and costuming of this affair. Vernon Duke's music has a catch and a bang to it ably abetted by John La Touche's lyrics.

The dancing is grand, with Miss Dunham the striking leader of an excellent chorus. George Balanchine has tucked plenty of imagination and zip into these numbers.

Cue Says--Any way you take this you get plenty. The book, the score, the dancing, the acting all measure up one hundred per cent. Call Cabin in the Sky the perfect musical performance that colored players have been promising for years.

Roundly recommended.

--Oliver Claxton in Cue, Vol. 9, No. 45 (November 2, 1940), page 31.

*   *   *

Cabin in the Sky is an obvious attempt to capitalize on the popular interest in negro fantasy which put The Green Pastures into the hit class and Marc Connelly into a top hat. It has a story much concerned with heaven and hell, de Lawd and dat old debbil de Debbil. It has music added to it, moreover, so that a prancing colored chorus can put a kick in its religious atmosphere. In fact, out of an obvious fright that some of the customers might snore through the more pious phases, the show is liberally garnished with wickedness. But it doesn't really need the wickedness as long as it has Ethel Waters.

With that rich and pliable voice of hers, and her kaleidoscopic personality, she plays a faithful wife who stands well with the higher-ups of heaven. So when her shiftless, crap-shooting husband dies, her personal worth wins him a probationary second chance of six months on earth again, during which he is to show whether he can make the celestial team. He barely manages it in the face of various high-yaller temptations. Apparently he is accepted into grace in the end because Miss Waters sings "Taking a Chance on Love" vibrantly enough to win the heavenly big shots. Thus is a bridge established between the supernal regions and Tin Pan Alley, with Waters flowing under the bridge.

This parole of a scapegrace from purgatory is so reminiscent of Ferenc Molnar's most famous play that one gets the impression that Lynn Root, author of the book, really set out to do a sepia version of Liliom, plus Father Divine's Harlem heaven. It begins to appear that Vinton Freedley, co-producer with Al Lewis of the new offering, revived Liliom with Burgess Meredith last season to get a running start on this black-face variant. And Dooley Wilson, who plays the lovable rascal, gives you some idea of how Meredith might look in burnt cork. Maybe the next time Meredith does the Molnar play he might well black up for it.

The story gives the impression of a lot of whites trying to

"think black," and still remaining a bunch of palefaces. Even Vernon Duke's tantalizing music isn't always the equivalent of Roark Bradford and Marc Connelly. But there is a high-spirited darky crew, beautifully drilled in dance numbers by George Balanchine, who inject plenty of Senegambian zip and zow into the proceedings. And they do a boogy-woogy number that stirs the audience as vigorously as a revival meeting--and just about as religiously.

Katherine Dunham dances the husband almost into backsliding again, and sings torridly "Honey in the Honeycomb," to lyrics by John La Touche, recently elevated from the W.P.A. into the songwriting peerage. Rex Ingram, who eventually portrayed de Lawd in The Green Pastures, now acts Lucifer's insidious son, which shows a liberal tendency to play both ends against the middle aisle. The production is just as lavish a gesture toward Harlem as the pre-election distribution of hams in New York's colored belt, and likely to prove as popular. But just to balance the theatrical budget, we wish someone would now revive Othello in white-face.

> --Frank Vreeland in Rob Wagner's
> Script, Vol. 24, No. 574 (November 9, 1940), page 27.

CALL ME MADAM (Music and Lyrics by Irving Berlin, Book by Howard Lindsay and Russel Crouse; Imperial Theatre, October 12, 1950)

There are two ways to write a musical comedy. One is to get an idea, the other is to get people. Rodgers and Hammerstein have been making history with the idea method, and currently Howard Lindsay and Russel Crouse are making hay with the other. Their Call Me Madam is a throwback to an earlier form in which the authors start with a star, fashion book and songs explicitly for the star, and then employ skilled help in all other departments to make sure the star is not needlessly interrupted. What is surprising in this day of "integrated" musical comedy, fully developed ballets, and at least better coordinated plots is that the older method pays off so well.

Call Me Madam does pay off. In presenting Ethel Merman as a Perle Mesta-style ambassadress to Europe, Lindsay and Crouse have written her characteristic lines rather than a character. Irving Berlin has composed songs for Miss Merman to sing, rather than a score for a show. George Abbott has kept the stage from getting cluttered up around her, and Jerome Robbins is present only to back and fill with occasional dancing. The point is that Miss Merman is well worth all the attention given her, and the other talents involved, even though they are not asked to make fresh and personal contributions, have so much intelligence and so much skill that they are able to make an entirely pleasant evening out of an entirely calculated one.

This is mass collaboration on a bread-and-butter plane. If it doesn't provide you with the most original or exciting musical comedy you ever saw, it also spares you any over-ambitious bungling. The people all know what they are about, and they go about it conscientiously.

Of the collaborators, Ethel Merman naturally comes off best, and Jerome Robbins, who is a product of the newer school of musicals, naturally comes off worst. Miss Merman is lusty, emphatic, and irresistible. Mr. Robbins probably ought not to have taken the job. The indifferent plot structure gives him no opportunity to dance any part of the narrative, or even anything related to it, and while he makes a peasant dance in the village square about as good as a peasant dance in the village square can be, this is work for a lesser talent. Irving Berlin falls somewhere between the two. Several of his numbers, particularly "It's a Lovely Day Today" and "You're Just In Love" are the best Berlin, but the body of the score seems mechanical and sometimes monotonous. Of the secondary people involved, Paul Lukas does some difficult monologues very well, and Russell Nype is a real discovery as the juvenile.

My only objections to the evening were two: Miss Merman's ungenerous deportment in not sharing the "You're Just In Love" bows with Mr. Nype; and a straight campaign song called "They Like Ike." This last seemed to me in such gratuitous bad taste that I would have sworn it would kill either the show or Mr. Eisenhower's chances. So far it hasn't hurt the show. I am waiting to see what happens to Eisenhower.

> --Walter Kerr in The Commonweal,
> Vol. 53, No. 4 (November 3,
> 1950), pages 94-95.

* * *

They keep wishing for hundreds of millions of American dollars throughout this musical. Believe me, they're only fooling. They know that they already have those millions all wrapped up in their Ambassadress to Broadway, Ethel Merman. They've plenty of other causes to be cocky, but the lady insures them a lien on the whole U.S. treasury.

No show's birth had probably ever been so loudly, so lovingly, proclaimed--or so long in advance. Call Me Madam was due for royal salutes from the day when it was just a gleam in the Lindsay-Crouse typewriter and a very first glissando on Irving Berlin's keyboard. Well, it turns out to be a huge and handsome spoof, and--to nobody's surprise--a hit. A very glad hit.

You all know what and whom it is about. It is laid, says the
program, in "two mythical countries," one of which is ours. An extra note warns you that, "Neither the character of Mrs. Sally Adams,
nor Miss Ethel Merman, resembles any other person alive or dead."
Thus presenting Mrs. Pearl Mesta to posterity with impeccable grace
and humor, and no doubt pleasing the President, the State Department et al, as well.

You are introduced to the diplomatic dame while she is taking
her oath of office. You follow her from her three-ring drawing room
in Washington, D.C., where she is famous as "The Hostess With the
Mostes' on the Ball," to the little Grand Duchy of her middle-aged
romance. You watch her glitter with diamonds distilled from family
oil-wells. You hear her booming out her benevolent wisecracks like
a Brunhilde Oklahoma-born. She becomes a sort of female Paul Bun-
yan, taking all protocol in her Mermadam's stride.

She falls in love with a Foreign Minister whom her money can't
buy. Her young secretary fills up any chinks in the plot by falling
in similar love with a young Princess. It's pretty collegiate, the
plot. Lots of operetta plots are apt to be. This one stays chary
and often charming. There's a rowdy dignity to all the political
sideswipes, almost a majesty to Miss Merman's climactic tail-spin before the throne.

The songs? Better, much, than those which Mr. Berlin manufactured for Miss Liberty. Many of these new ones have the knack
of getting encores: tunefully sure-fire, eminently singable sentiments like "It's a Lovely Day Today" and "The Best Thing For You
Would Be Me." Then there's a pet duet, semipattering the tidings
that "You're Just in Love," which is bound to ripen on every radio
for the next five years.

Who sings them? Miss Merman the most of them, of course,
and you won't have to be told how. How with that funnily faultless
diction which she has, I mean, and that deep-throated, tough-hurling
tone she owns alone.

But there's another singer-actor to help her who is rather a
rare find. Russell Nype is his name, and he's such a serious young
skeleton, you almost feel you're looking at him through a fluoroscope.
The minute he starts to pipe any least lyric, however, your chuckles
become doubly fond, for he has the voice of a Groton boy gone
straight to heaven.

All directed in the George Abbott spirit, fast and colorful.
The lasses of Lichtenburg, with Raoul Pene du Bois' scenery surrounding them, belong on the best postcards. So see it for Christmas. This Christmas, the next or the next.

--Gilbert W. Gabriel in Cue, Vol.
19, No. 22 (October 21, 1950),
page 22.

CARMEN JONES (Book and Lyrics by Oscar Hammerstein II, based
on Meilhac and Halevy's adaptation of Prosper Merimee's
CARMEN, Music by Georges Bizet, adapted by Robert Russell
Bennett; Broadway Theatre, December 2, 1943)

A base canard running about Broadway these days, fostered
by those who know nothing about it, is to the effect that Carmen
Jones, the brilliant adaptation by Oscar Hammerstein, II, of the
Meilhac-Helévy-Merimée opera, is a swing Carmen. Nothing could
be further from the truth. Under the gaudy auspices of Mahatma
Billy Rose, this opus is New York's latest and most consummate hit
which gives those who are sick and tired of all these fabulous tales
about Oklahoma! something new and entirely different as a conversation piece.

Aside from elimination of the recitatif passages (which were not
included in the original) Carmen Jones offers the famous Georges
Bizet score as any Metropolitan Opera Company would sing it and
Mr. Hammerstein's lyrics prove him a splendid collaborator with the
French composer. The adaptation shows us life among parachute
factory workers in a Southern town. The entire cast is Negro and
the story is still that of Don José (Joe) and Micaela (Cindy Lou) the
gal he left for Carmen (Miss Jones) who threw him over for Escamillo,
the toreador (Husky Miller, the prizefighter).

Hassard Short, a genius in lights and staging, has never been
better than in this production which clicks along with marvelous
tempo from curtain rise to fall. The dazzling splendor of Raoul Pene
du Bois' costumes, with daring imagination capture Negro social life
in its amusing and super-duper imitation of white folks' café society.

The finale, with Carmen dying in Joe's arms, while we glimpse
the George Bellowes-styled background of Husky Miller's battle with
Poncho ("de panther from Brazil") is superb. Humor runs gaily
throughout, not only in the unmannered acting of the cast, but in
the sets, such as those of Billy Pastor's garish night club and the
Meadowlawn Country Club in Chicago, a vision of evening blue, in
the wild tom-tom of Cosy Cole, Swing Alley's great drummer, and
the gay Spanish dancing burlesque choreographed by Eugene Loring.

When all is said and done, it is the company of sepian performers collected from switchboards, factories, cleaning establish-
ments, jive-jazz bands, concert halls and even the New York police
department that gives Carmen Jones the works. They sing the
famous Bizet score with fervor. Give a great big hand to Muriel
Smith and Muriel Rahn who alternate as Carmen, to Carlotta Franzell
and Elton J. Warren who share Cindy Lou, to Luther Saxon and Napoleon Reed who sing the rôle of Joe and to Glenn Bryant, a strap-
ping giant, as Husky Miller, the pug. If all opera were performed

with such zest and imagination, no hats would have to be passed for
the Metropolitan.

                              --Russell Rhodes in Rob Wagner's
                                Script, Vol. 30, No. 670 (Janu-
                                ary 8, 1944), page 29.

CAROUSEL (Adaptation by Benjamin F. Glazer from the play, LILIOM,
    by Ferenc Molnar, Music by Richard Rodgers, Book and Lyrics
    by Oscar Hammerstein II; Majestic Theatre, April 19, 1945)

      This is a very rich dish with plenty of seasoning in the form
of music, dancing, new personalities, elegant production, etc. For
people who like a little more meat on the table it may prove a trifle
disappointing, since the Yankee shrewdness and saltiness often seems
wasted on a kind of watery brew in the way of premise and structure.
Perhaps it is simply the fact that the Molnar play Liliom is a trifle
too romantic for these times ... and this fact manages to show itself now and again throughout the very robust production at the
Majestic. But make no mistake, Carousel is deft and entertaining,
full of the light, engaging rhythm of authentic Americana ... handled
with the Theatre Guild's usual impeccable taste. Richard Rodgers'
music is a heady brew; and Mr. Hammerstein, two, has produced an
extremely adult book, and lots of amusing lyrics ("June is Bustin'
Out All Over"; "There's Nothin' So Bad for a Woman as a Virtuous
Man"; "You're a Queer One, Julie Jordan" ... are some of the
sprightly songs). Agnes de Mille's ballets have all the sly native
wit and expert structure you expect of her; Rouben Mamoulian's direction is dramatic but uncomplicated; Mielziner's sets (particularly
Nettie Fowler's Spa on the ocean front) are wonderful, and as for
Miles White's costumes ... well from little buttoned boots to lavender
printed muslins--they are almost too good to be true.

      The story? Well, a scapegoat of a fellow, one Billy Bigelow,
barker for a carnival, wards off girls or woos them in a small New
England seacoast town in the year 1873. Like all such glamorous ex-
troverts, once married, Mr. Bigelow is no great shakes as a steady
provider. Spurred to greater efforts by the knowledge that his wife
is going to have a child, he settles for the dangerous short cut to
wealth ... murder and robbery, and gets himself killed. Half of
Carousel leads up lightly to this by way of spectacular scenes ...
carnival, clambake, etc. The other half deals with Bigelow's heaven
from which he views the life down below of his wife and daughter.
Unfortunately, sandwiched between is Bigelow's deathbed scene, with
his wife and friend standing beside the not-yet-cold corpse, singing
their heads off. The sort to give you the willies.

      The cast is excellent. As the heroine, Jan Clayton is a deli-
cate spring reed of a girl with a refreshing personality, and a sweet,

sweet voice, who has reversed the usual procedure to come to Broadway via Hollywood. For our money she is the best new musical
comedy star of the season. Mervyn Vye is a terrific wayward sailor
villain in the Humphrey Bogart manner. Bambi Lynn dances and
acts Bigelow's young daughter superbly. And special mention should
go to John Raitt as Bigelow; to Jean Darling, Jean Casto, Pearl Lang,
Eric Mattson, and Russell Collins.

--Irene Kittle in <u>Cue</u>, Vol. 14, No.
17 (April 28, 1945), page 12.

THE CHILDREN'S HOUR (Lillian Hellman; Maxine Elliott Theatre,
    November 20, 1934)

Twelve years ago this month, first-nighters, distributed in
unexpectant attitudes around Maxine Elliott's Theatre, gradually
found themselves straightening up and cupping their ears. Something was happening on the stage that they had not looked for.
One of the decade's most dramatic pieces was being unfolded, without so much as a word of warning. As our own Nero would say,
"And that play was called <u>Rain</u>!"

It is a compensation for routine firstnighting that one always
stands a chance of experiencing, at unexpected intervals, the thrill
of gradual discovery that what is going on up there behind the footlights is the very thing that one has been going to the theatre hoping
to see.

It usually begins with the realization that one has been sitting
in the same position for twenty minutes without knowing it, head
cocked uncomfortably on one side and feet pressed firmly against the
floor. Then comes the excitement of being present in an absolutely
silent audience. Finally the whole truth dawns. This is it!

For the second time in Maxine Elliott's Theatre, we experienced
this excitement when, last week, <u>The Children's Hour</u> came in, without one initial fanfare, and quietly set itself up as the season's dramatic high-water mark. Along toward the end, it turned out to
have its flaws, but they were flaws of overproduction rather than of
quality. It has two too many endings, any one of which would have
sufficed.

In <u>The Children's Hour</u>, Miss Lillian Hellman has written a fine,
brave play, and has written it cleanly and, up until the last quarter,
so tightly that there is not one second when you can let your attention wander, even if you wanted to.

It tells a story which would have been impossible of telling in
public in the days when <u>Rain</u> was considered daring and <u>The Captive</u>

was being banned by the police. A monster of a child, a pupil in
a girls' school, deliberately concocts a malicious tale of Lesbian relations between the two young head-mistresses, with the result that
their school is broken up, their lives ruined, and one of them driven
to suicide. Their suit for libel against the girl's grandmother, who
spreads the lie, is dismissed, and the young woman who is left to
face the world does so alone without even the refuge of the marriage
which she had planned.

The language is frank, franker than we have yet had on the
subject, but it is immaculate. I doubt if there will be any giggling,
even at nervous matinées. Certainly there can be no offence to the
adult mind. On the contrary, the effect should be highly salutary
in the horror aroused at the enormity of irresponsible slander in
such matters.

Aside from several minor objections toward the end, such as
the one that the engaged young woman made it a little unnecessarily
hard for herself by sending her fiancé away, and that of the almost
O'Neill piling up of tragedy on what was tragedy enough already,
there might also be a feeling that such a dire situation would be
faintly impossible, and that a young child of such obviously pathological deviltry could not gain credence in a court of law, unsup-
ported by reputable evidence.

In case this worries you, it may be pointed out that Miss Hellman has court records to substantiate her story, records on which
she must have based it, so identical are the main circumstances.

In Edinburgh, in 1810, two school-mistresses, the Misses Woods
and Pirie, were similarly accused by a girl pupil, who had even less
to recommend her than the young villainess of Miss Hellman's play.
A suit for slander was instituted (and, by the way, shouldn't this
one have been for slander instead of libel? It was all done by word
of mouth) against the girl's grandmother, and after ten years of
losing, appealing, winning, appealing, and endless legal haggling,
with no evidence other than that of the already discredited viper,
the case came finally before the august House of Lords. Here a
technical verdict was awarded the school-mistresses, but further
legal haggling set in and there is no record of their ever having received a shilling for their ruined lives.

So, to doubters, Miss Hellman may offer as evidence (as she
already must know) pages 111-146 of a reputable volume called Bad
Companions, by William Roughead, published in 1931 by Duffield &
Green. Or even just point to Tom Mooney.

In producing The Children's Hour, Mr. Herman Shumlin has
shown not only courage but a fine sense of casting and direction (it
is a marvelous job of direction he has done). As the two unfortunate
teachers, Katherine Emery and Anne Revere lend a credibility and

dignity which are indispensable. Katherine Emmet plays the grandmother with just the right contrast of patrician righteousness and
eventual humility, and Robert Keith, as the sole, unhappy male, has
never been so convincing. The school children are all good, especially Barbara Beals as the tortured stooge for the young hell-cat,
and no greater compliment could be paid to the amazing performance
of Florence McGee than to say that at times the impulse is almost irresistible to leap upon the stage and strangle her. Our one regret
is that we are denied the sight of her humiliation.

The Children's Hour is possibly not for the children, but for
any grown-up with half a mind, it is almost obligatory.
> --Robert Benchley in The New
> Yorker (December 8, 1934),
> pages 34 and 36.

* * *

In contrast to Pride and Prejudice, the Broadway success,
The Children's Hour, is something to write home about. One fact is
simply undeniable--the play is powerful in every aspect of good theatre. The characters live, the drama is gripping and believable, and
the cast does a splendid job, particularly Florence McGee, who plays
the pathologic-kid, and the two school teachers, played by Ann Revere and Katherine Emery.

I might say, though, that I can find plenty to quarrel about
in the contents of the play. At the risk of being considered a wee
bit intolerant, and an advocate of singing the International during
all intermissions, I suggest that there are other themes far more important than that contained in this play. The Children's Hour tells
the story of how a mentally lop-sided little squirt of a school girl
ruins the happiness and lives of two teachers by spreading lying rumors that the two ladies in question have been playing house together
in a slightly fairyish fashion. Perhaps a lot of folks think such things
are more important than the fact that machine guns are beating a
tattoo against strikers in steel towns, or that the anguish of millions
of unemployed is not quite comparable to the grief of a school teacher
accused of Lesbianism, but I can't agree with them.

Perhaps such things really are more important in certain circles
of society. And, leaning over backward to be fair about the matter,
maybe this writer has seen very little of Lesbianism, and too many
police clubs. Thus it is possible that I am prejudiced from mere ignorance of the fact that sexual problems and resulting scandal are
a major social problem. But Children's Hour, as I say, is swell,
worth while paying to see, and something to write home about.
> --John Mullen in New Theatre,
> Vol. 3, No. 5 (May 1936), pages
> 25-26.

CLAUDIA (Rose Franken; Booth Theatre, February 12, 1941)

Story: David and Claudia Naughton, a suburban couple, have been married a short time. Their wedlock is marred by two items: Claudia's dumbness and Claudia's excessive devotion to her mother.

The first two-thirds of the play devotes itself to the comical effects proceeding from Claudia's lack of brain. She can't balance her check book, she kisses a total stranger, she sells her house to an opera singer and generally demonstrates considerable mental confusion.

The last act shows Claudia's adjustment to the inevitable death of her mother.

Acting: Dorothy McGuire gives a superb performance as Claudia, with a deft rendition in the shifting of her part from comedy to tragedy. Donald Cook does well as her husband and Frances Starr gives an effective and restrained performance as Claudia's mother.

In the supporting parts, John Williams, as the stranger who gets kissed, and Olga Baclanova, as the opera singer, do well. Adrienne Gessner and Frank Tweddell ably handle the minor parts of servants.

Production: Miss Franken has directed her play smoothly and Donald Oenslager designed a pleasant set.

Cue Says: The first portions of this scattered play, dealing with Claudia's stupidity, struck me as somewhat routine comedy. The change to tragedy at the end of the second act comes abruptly. The third act I found very moving and effective.

It struck me that Miss Franken did not make any too clear her course when she started the play. The comedy is bright enough, but lacking in relevance. The heroine remains an intangible character through most of the action.

However, I recommend Claudia because, with the excellent performance by Miss McGuire and the restrained pathos of the third act, you will find the play worth while.
                                        --Oliver Claxton in Cue, Vol. 10,
                                        No. 8 (February 22, 1941), page
                                        30.

*   *   *

In Claudia, now making headway as one of the real hits of the theatrical season despite its belated start, it seems as if the authoress, Rose Franken, set herself the arbitrary exercise of whittling a

comedy out of the most unlikely materials. Within this latest production by John Golden there is a wife with a mother fixation and a
desire to find out how much sex she has; a mother who wants to
shield the daughter overmuch from life, and who herself develops
cancer at the end; a philandering Englishman who threatens to dis-
rupt this quite attractive home, and a couple of servants with a dark
past that includes a criminal son. Sufficient, you'd say, to make
any German film producer smack his lips at the chance to play with
so much morbidity.

Stated thus baldly, you'd imagine that such premises would
lead to a couple of murders and maybe a suicide or two, including
some by the audience. And yet spectators (including this one) have
a most rollicking good time at the play. You laugh even while the
mother is facing sure death in the last act. And such is the magic
of the dramatist that you feel your mirth is quite sympathetic and in
good taste. That is because Mrs. Franken infuses into her play
more than enough genuine charm to satisfy Emily Post and Margery
Wilson.

Claudia is a far more entertaining piece than even The Silver
Cord, which it distantly resembles on the umbilical side. Doubtless
that is because Mrs. Franken does not have quite the standpoint of
the late Sidney Howard; namely, that the fate of that institution, the
family, hangs in the balance through the over-affectionate devotion
of a single grown child toward the parent. (This used to be known
as the Oedipus complex, in case you want to get technical.) Mrs.
Franken seems to take the cheerful view that the family will still
survive the isolated instance of her play, and that her heroine will
grow up and learn better, even if the playwright has to hit her over
the head to larn her.

This girl-wife is the outstanding character who raises the
comedy above the ruck, and who knows less about matrimony after a
year than does a hill-billy child bride. That is, you gather she
doesn't--but you can never be quite sure. She is one of those remarkable personalities whom most of us have encountered at least
once--the kind who says unexpected things, often amusing, always
breath-taking. And the innocent bystanders are never quite certain whether these startling gems are intentional and acute, or simply
spasmodic and excruciating. For instance, this girl restrains a man
from helping the hired hand fix a flat tire by saying the hired hand
"is a perfect nymphomaniac about flat tires." Apparently she doesn't
grasp what nymphomaniac means--it just popped out--and yet the next
moment she does. Hence audiences are delightfully baffled, and male
spectators go away making bets about her and looking speculatively
at their own cute wives.

She does obviously learn a great deal about life in the end,
through her own expectant motherhood and the discovery of her
mother's doom, and she learns particularly that she must face pain

gallantly and stand on her own feet, instead of just treading on other people's corns. It is a masterly portrayal of the sort of damsel
whose thoughts shoot out like meteors, but never follow any pre-
scribed orbit. Apparently this type of youthful femininity is growing either more prevalent or dramatists are becoming more noticing.
Besides this play, this type cuts a wide swath this season in Mr.
and Mrs. North, My Sister Eileen, and Out of the Frying Pan. It
is just as if the famous baby vamp of Upstairs and Down many years
ago has at last grown up and learned to talk about sex instead of
just acting it out.

Mrs. Franken has depicted her with infinite insight, and almost as much loving care as the girl's own stage mother might ex-
pend on her. The play is notable as establishing this writer more
than ever as a stylist whose style is never obtrusive. Her dialogue
is succinct and pungent without any sense of having been laboriously
hand-tooled. This play is a great advance over Another Language,
which rather annoyed us, especially in its screen version. The
people here are much easier to live with, on either side of the footlights. There is continuous talk about expectant motherhood, that
extends even to cows and chickens. Yet one never feels that it is
in bad form, perhaps because the action takes place in an artistic
colony in Connecticut. And the authoress achieves a high spot with
an egg, not only using it for casual jokes but making it stand for
a necessary symbol, sex in all its shining white simplicity.

Dorothy McGuire as the young wife gives a beautifully faceted
performance that stamps her as a memorable prodigy in a season of
young finds. Hers is a true Cinderella story of the stage, for she
is the understudy who made good, following Martha Scott in Our
Town and weathering a Chicago season with the ebullient John Profile in My Dear Children. In looks and voice Miss McGuire is a
choice blend of Betty Fields and Helen Hayes, and you can almost
see where one actress leaves off in her and the other begins.

Frances Starr, returning to the stage after some time as the
mother, gives a finely rounded performance, and Donald Cook is also
excellent as the husband, being something more for a change than a
handsome young man with a stock frown. Olga Baclanova, erstwhile
of the films, is a temperamental Slavonic prima donna to the life, and
John Williams likewise gives a sterling account of himself as the og-
ling Englishman who finds himself entangled with the child bride
when she tests her sex appeal, much to his astonishment. Mrs.
Franken is credited with the suave direction, but we refuse to believe that John Golden just sat by and chewed gum while this was
going on. Not unless it was a kind of gum that would glue his jaws
together.

                         --Frank Vreeland in Rob Wagner's
                           Script, Vol. 25, No. 594 (April
                           5, 1941), pages 24-25.

THE COCKTAIL PARTY (T.S. Eliot; Henry Miller Theatre, January
    21, 1950)

This season, which has seen some small rebellion amongst the
literati against the poet, T.S. Eliot, also sees him reasserting his
distinction--his supremacy, indeed--as a playwright. For this same
season must be indebted to him for a piece of infinite provocation,
exhilaration, of intrepid lingual and mental march, and of that ultimate quality, beauty, besides. I don't care whether many will mob
it. I'll go on contending that The Cocktail Party stands splendid
treat.

Here is that comedy, so-called, which Mr. Sherek, the English
producer, and Mr. Miller, American, put to a world premiere's test
at the Edinburgh Festival last August. It won a huge ovation there.

Mr. Eliot of Missouri, now of London and Nobel Prize fame,
has gone contemporary this time. Gone with a vengeance, the very
expert vengeance of a mystical surgeon upon all the bores, cads and
frustrates in his modern ken. He purposely makes puppets of them,
mere windpipes for his eccentrically flashing thoughts. But, as he
smiles and slices them open, these puppets display insides of almost
cathedral size.

I borrow a best possible summation of his theme: "the selfishness of human relationship, the isolation of the unloved and unlov-
able, the meaning of marriage and the way of martyrdom." All that
on a plot which extends only from the drawingroom cocktail party
to the analyst's office and back again.

Mr. and Mrs. Chamberlayne are at soulful and sexual odds.
Sir Henry, a scientist of superhuman influence, helps them back to
happiness. He sends one of their trouble-makers to death on an
African ant-hill, the other to Hollywood--but such is the persuasive-
ness of Mr. Eliot's fine cutaway words, both of these grim fates seem
godly right.

It is a little as though Noel Coward were being called to order
by the late Virginia Woolf. Or, when some of the richly imagist
speeches roll out of the characters' subconscious, as though Eugene
O'Neill had put on a monocle and begun to argue heaven and earth
with the angels on their own level, in their own golden tongue.

And it does, in addition, bring us some most brilliant acting
of the current British kind, not only by Mr. Guinness but by Cath-
leen Nesbit, Robert Flemyng, Eileen Peel, Irene Worth and their fel-
lows. All are as polished and letter-perfected as Director Martin
Browne could make them--and as such a play among plays demands.
                                    --Gilbert W. Gabriel in Cue, Vol.
                                        19, No. 4 (January 28, 1950),
                                        page 18.

COME BACK, LITTLE SHEBA (William Inge; Booth Theatre, February
    15, 1950)

Two magnificent performances are worth the price of admission
to this new play--even if such price includes blood, sweat and a
skull-splitting hangover. Two lifetime performances, terrifyingly
effective, pitiful, next door to wonderful, by Shirley Booth and Sidney Blackmer.

Because of such players, it is almost hard to see the play. As
presented by the Theatre Guild, it turns out to be a dogged, sometimes rather desperate enlargement of a short story into Freudian
vaudeville and full-length Alcoholics Anonymous tract. It has its
lags. It has a final letdown, maybe. But, even in the face of these,
it adds up to deep and quite continuous engrossment, semi-humorous
sympathy, sharp individuality: to all that could be asked of such an
intentionally wince-giving study of the chronic slovenliness, drunkenness, sex-bewilderment and success frustration which do mark our
Mean Street, America. Hand me the Alka-Seltzer and I'll say hooray.

William Inge wrote it. Mr. Inge--this is not to be held against
him--is an ex-critic. He is also a specialist, evidently, in the ways
and woes of gritty city life in the Middle West. He writes deftly,
pointedly. He achieves anyway that rapid-fire realism which the
stage allows and welcomes for whole truth.

He gives us the small household of Doc, otherwise unidentified,
and wife Lola. Doc had wanted long ago to be a genuine M.D., but
marriage--that sort of marriage--has made him just a chiropractor, a
bored but outwardly gentle husband, and a reformed souse, besides. In short, one of those queasy, greasy livers of the oft-
quoted life of "quiet desperation."

Wife Lola is a monument of good-hearted stupidity. She has
long since run to slattern's fat, fantasy and the radio. She keeps
dreaming about her little lost dog, Sheba. Sheba, that probably
repellent pup, is her symbol for youth gone, hope, happiness,
bridal strength and first flush, all gone. Somewhere between a
jeer and a wail, this recurrent call for the mongrel's return. It is
none the less poignant. It belongs to the grubbiness. It sums up
the grief.

There's a young girl boarder, bobby-soxed and alluringly be-
sweatered. There are the girl's young boy friends, and a disturbing
reek of rampant, cheaply gratified flesh. The bungalow can stand
it, and Lola [can] love it, but Doc breaks down. He flings away all his
meek morning prayers, his couple of years of dumb sobriety, and
starts off--berserk for fair or foul--on a terrific binge. He lurches
back retching gobbets of abuse, all his hatred of his wife, his usually hidden urge to treat her to a murderous hatchet-stroke in place

of monogamy's reluctant kiss. He has to be lugged off to a hospital.
He comes home again a few days later as subdued as ever, even more
dependent, shaken by that frightfully touching maudlinity of his kind
... and that's that.

That, and, in the midst of it, several scenes which are nearly
shattering, they are so riddled with pathos--a pathos which appalls
as much as it appeals. A short telephone speech of the wife's, for
instance, to her parental farm-folk who so obviously don't want to
have her on their hands while her husband is "sick." And the climax, the revolting but fascinating violence which makes Doc's worst
behavior an inevitability and therefore a relief. No, it hasn't all
this much smash. It couldn't have and live. Some of it is still as
loosely surfaced as when I first saw the play in Westport last summer. But it rates a fond and full respect.

While, as for those two chief performances--indeed, the performances by all the cast, including Joan Lorring, Olga Fabian, Lon-
ny Chapman, Daniel Reed, John Randolph and the rest--these are
beyond cavil, all along the line. Such acting must logically thank
the staging. A new, young director, Daniel Mann, has done this.
He has done it with a steadfast sensitivity, with complete, illuminating
care. But let's rename that theatre the Booth-and-Blackmer.

> --Gilbert W. Gabriel in Cue, Vol.
> 19, No. 8 (February 25, 1950),
> page 18.

CONVERSATION PIECE (Noel Coward; 44th Street Theatre, October
     23, 1934)

Conversation Piece is a comedy with the faint sweet smell of
decadence about it. It is set in England in 1811, and tells of the efforts of an impoverished French nobleman to marry off a charming
French girl to any English lord with money--a nobleman pimping, as
it were. It was written as a vehicle for the French actress Yvonne
Printemps by the everlastingly English Noel Coward, whose knowledge
of and contempt for the decadent upper class world in which he moves
creeps into his creations.

The production is perfect in its way. Clever oh-so-minor
lyrics and music, good acting, swell costumes and magnificent out-
door sets by G.E. Calthrop. Much of the dialogue is in French.
Ideal bourgeois theatre--and how the evening-dressed orchestra patrons lapped it up! No ideas, no vitality, everything just pretty-
pretty. What more could your little heart desire?

> --Ben Blake in New Theatre, Vol.
> 1, No. 11 (December 1934),
> page 20.

* * *

A feeble, so-called romantic comedy with so-called music, prettily staged and participated in by the bubbly Yvonne Printemps.
                              --George Jean Nathan in Life
                              (January 1935), page 4.

THE CORN IS GREEN (Emlyn Williams; National Theatre, November
     26, 1940)

So many critical hosannas have gone up about The Corn Is
Green, with Miss Ethel Barrymore, that I am embarrassed to say that
it didn't seem to me a flawless drama, or even an especially important
one. In this almost solitary dissenting opinion, the play at the National is earnest, worthy, handsomely acted and directed, and more
than a little old-fashioned. The fact that it looked wonderful to so
many people may easily be a comment on a terrible season in general
rather than a tribute to one play in particular. Compared with the
recent Hollywood cycle, Horse Fever, and one or two other exhibits
whose names I forget, any performance in which the characters be-
have like endurable human beings is a relief and a blessing, but I
can't believe that it is automatically a work of genius.

According to one of those mysterious Broadway rumors, Emlyn
Williams, the author, went back to his own past for the framework of
his story, though not necessarily, of course, for any of the details.
It deals, as you have probably been told much too often, with a
middle-aged woman of a literary and philanthropic disposition who
tutors a young Welsh miner so efficiently and relentlessly that within
three years he is able to win a scholarship at Oxford, although still
inclined to spell "water" with two "t"s. She has, I am glad to say,
no improper designs on her pupil; she merely wants to turn him at
first into a great writer, like Tennyson, and then, abandoning this
trifling project, into the savior of the working class. In the course
of this campaign, she is subjected to a good many annoyances. There
is a Tory mine-owner who sees no reason for shipping artistic miners
off to college--"Why can't he be just as clever at home?" he asks
callously--and there is a local girl called Bessie Watty whom the hero
seduces, largely as a protest against having his grammar corrected
every time he opens his mouth. Bessie, of course, has a baby
(someday a play will be written in which the girl does not have a
baby under these circumstances, but it will not be in my time or
yours) and naturally this presents something of a dilemma, since the
faculty at Oxford appears to have a prejudice against enrolling the
parents of illegitimate children. Well, Miss Barrymore and various
other members of the cast get their heads together and Bessie is more
or less sidetracked, thus permitting the young man to go to college,
where, I'm sure, his reminiscences brightened many a dull evening
in the Common Room.

I have the greatest respect for Mr. Williams' sincerity, not to
mention his mastery of the soft and lovely Welsh dialect, but I wasn't
really altogether happy at his play. It always seemed much too easy,
to employ a phrase I learned at my grandmother's knee, to guess
which way the cat was going to jump. Nothing, on the other hand,
can possibly be said against the performance given by Ethel Barrymore, who makes a serene, humorous, dignified, and very moving
woman out of a character who might easily have seemed an exasper-
ating old busybody. I have no idea how this was done, but it was.
Incidentally, I had never hoped to see Miss Barrymore in a gent's
straw hat, pushing a bicycle, and it is an experience I shall always
cherish. On the whole, I thought the others caught at least a part
of their star's remarkable vitality. I admired especially Richard
Waring, as the young miner hopelessly baffled by the subjunctive;
Thelma Schnee, as the far too amiable Miss Watty; and Edmond Breon,
as the Squire, who was able to enjoy the works of Alfred, Lord Tennyson, only because, after all, the fellow had been a gentleman and
a student at Cambridge. Herman Shumlin's direction was, as usual,
practically perfect.

> --Wolcott Gibbs in The New Yorker
> (December 7, 1940), page 47.

* * *

The Welsh appear to have a habit of erecting monuments to
themselves while still alive. In Carnarvon some years ago we saw a
statue to Lloyd George, among the living now. We remember it because we copied the Welsh inscription thereon and mailed it to a girl
of Welsh descent in this country. She had forgotten the ancestral
speech and thought it was merely another of those dirty foreign post
cards.

In view of this predilection no surprise is occasioned on learning that Emlyn Williams's new vehicle for Ethel Barrymore, The Corn
Is Green, is largely autobiographical. And no better monument could
be devised for any man. It's very much alive itself, and it's in good
English, instead of Welsh. (Except for a few chopped-up speeches
by the Welsh natives.) And it's one of the finest plays of this generation, in content, casting, and direction. Not even the baggy,
late-nineties costumes worn by the star and the supporting players
can disguise that.

It is somewhat akin to Young Woodley of blessed memory, being
once again the story of a schoolboy and an elder woman, this time
his teacher. But it is less romantic and lyrical than the Van Druten
play, more realistic and dramatic, concerned with the development of
a soul instead of the calf-love of adolescence.

The play is quite in contrast to Williams' previous macabre work,
Night Must Fall, in which Robert Montgomery more than justified his
existence on the screen. It gives people a message of hope--provided

they are educated. This, of course, applies to the readers of tabloids as well.

That implication of stretching out a hand to the benighted and
helpless, of being as it were a mother to all hapless and struggling
humanity, makes of Miss Barrymore a truly heroic figure, bulging
skirts and balloon sleeves and all. An English school-teacher, one
of the vanguard of emancipated females then appearing, decides to
open a free school for Welsh miners, finding, like others who have
seen the Welsh at home, that they are a strangely endearing and
pathetic race.

Against the opposition of the local squire the teacher persists,
primarily because she has discovered a young miner who shows a
flash of literary genius in his first crude school composition. She
spruces him up, mentally, socially and sartorially, and points him
like a beagle for an Oxford scholarship. Just as he seems on the
eve of winning it, there comes an echo of a night of passion amongst
the Greek verbs. He has had a momentary affair with a sex-ignited
servant girl, on the rebound from his teacher when she is strict and
lacking in affection toward his spirit, sensitive from newly adventur-
ing among masterpieces. The servant dangles her expected baby
over his head, but the teacher grimly promises to kill her if she
spoils the protégé's chances for Oxford by this flourish of disrepute.
He is thus enabled to win the scholarship, and the servant departs,
dumping the baby in the teacher's lap as a foundling.

On this foundation Williams has reared a play that is universal
in time and appeal, with its modernized variant of the Pygmalion
theme, that of the statue which craves tenderness from its sculptor.
Williams not only bears down on education as a solvent for many human ills, but also stresses the need for sympathetic understanding
between instructor and pupil--the fact that enlightenment does not
consist of learning to parse alone. The work is that rather remarkable rarity among plays; an outline of character development over
three years, not only amongst the leading figures, but also with such
minor types as the squire, described by the teacher as "wearing his
stupidity like a halo." But don't get the notion that this is stuffy
preachment. Williams himself has enough understanding of his people
to chuckle at them, and if the average sermon were as abundantly
salted with humor, it would play to standing room only.

Miss Barrymore is matchless, sinking her personality in the role,
making no effort to do a flute obbligato with her voice, and giving
no sense of a glamour girl trying to evade middle-age by hiding behind a beauty mask. She is particularly superb in the final scene
when she convinces her protégé to give up his conventional impulse
to turn toward the protection of his unforeseen child, persuading him
instead to continue with his work of serving his people as a shining
star. The star's charm is vitally helpful in keeping the part from
being just an order of prunes and prisms.

As the protégé, Richard Waring gives an unsurpassable performance, varied, incisive, and truly emotional. He achieves the uncommon feat of making you believe, when the other characters call
him "brilliant," that he is actually so, instead of just another actor
straining to look intelligent. Williams himself probably did no better
with this role in London. In the part of the servant Thelma Schnee,
a recruit from radio and summer stock, proves herself the acting find
of the season. She wins a derisive sort of sympathy for the little
opportunist, despite some vixenish lines and a get-up that belongs
with Alice in Wonderland. Rosalind Ivan as her blandly amoral
mother--almost the feminine counterpart of the father in Pygmalion--
Rhys Williams as a stodgy solicitor, Edmund Breon as the squire--
in fact, the whole cast, are a memorable credit to Herman Shumlin
as producer and director, and they might well stand transmigration
to the screen in a body.

> --Frank Vreeland in Rob Wagner's
> Script, Vol. 24, No. 580 (Decem-
> ber 21, 1940), pages 12-13.

COUNSELLOR-AT-LAW (Elmer Rice; Plymouth Theatre, November 6,
1931)

A criminal lawyer who marries above his station, enacted by
[Paul] Muni with a better-than-Dietrichstein technique. A thrill for
the palate.

> --Louise Bascom Barratt in Life
> (May 1932), page 43.

THE COUNTRY GIRL (Clifford Odets; Lyceum Theatre, November 10,
1950)

Clifford Odets has taken a very small and very familiar situation and, by the simple process of being patient with it, found it to
contain more dramatic interest than anyone could have supposed.
His story is that of the actor who has drunk himself downhill and of
the wife of the director who pulls him back into shape for a performance. The trouble with clichés is that people treat them as
clichés; they slap them onto a stage in their baldest outlines, without taking the trouble to think them through again. Odets has
thought this one through, down to the last detail, and it comes out
with the reality it must have had the first time someone used it. He
has been particularly successful with his actor: the man's moral weakness, superimposed aggressiveness, and natural talent are blended in
a dimensional character which is not at all attractive, but is command-
ing because it is true. Paul Kelly plays it brilliantly. Mr. Odets

has been less successful, I think, with the wife, the "country girl"
of the title, but Uta Hagen plays her with such skill and force that
it isn't until you leave the theatre that you realize the character has
never been adequately explained. The role of the director is an old
Odets standby: the biting, restless egocentric, and Steven Hill
makes him as effective as ever.

The play is well balanced: passages of quiet, careful motivation are followed by inevitable and satisfying flare-ups; nothing is
tacked on; everything moves with easy confidence. If it is all a little clinical, if you do not become much attached to any of the figures,
and if the author's passion for the theatre sometimes approaches
naiveté, it is nevertheless an impressive evening in the theatre, both
as a play and as a production.

--Walter Kerr in The Commonweal,
Vol. 53, No. 8 (December 1,
1950), pages 196-197.

* * *

Two fine plays at last. Your faith in the theatre may have
been battered down into mid-autumn martyrdom, but--here are your
endurance prizes, full sanctions for your optimism, after all. The
Christopher Fry play from abroad, the Clifford Odets one from right
here and now, and both of them well worth their weight in sell-outs.

Mr. Odets has done a deeply effective little job. He has done
it on that subject which has always hitherto been the theatre's pet
bugaboo, the theatre's own backstage. And when I call it little, I
do so with increased respect and fondness for the portability, the
personal familiarity, to which he has managed to reduce even its bit-
terest and most moving moments.

It tells about the seamy preludes to a Broadway success. It
tells the pitiful whole of a dipsomaniac ex-star, his enduring wife,
his young director. It illuminates their lives with the lurid smears of
a next-door's Neon lights. In that taut tongue which is Mr. Odets'
forte for dialogue, in a string of almost Chekhovian anecdotes which
have been secretly building up, coral-wise, to its minor tragedy of
unfulfilled desire between the wife and the director, it hurls its parcel of intensely human beings emotionally high. But it ends honestly,
inescapably. It gives them back without shatter or even shudder to
the humdrum where they belong.

These three chief characters Mr. Odets has written under a
tireless microscope. They have to be acted with care, plain conse-
cration, and they are. Uta Hagen, Paul Kelly, Steven Hill--it is
as impossible to think of this trio of roles being better performed
than it is to imagine any other players in them. The same sense of
felicity, nearly of inevitability, clings to the several smaller, semi-
humorous parts and their interpretation. The Boris Aronson settings

are so similarly good and suited. Perhaps this rightness on all sec-
tors is something inherent in the play itself. Something freshly re-
kindled by the author who staged it, too.

They say Mr. Odets' first version had grimmer things about
it; the wife, for instance, was riddled with sickness. I'm glad she
no longer is. This is ten times truer to the peeled-paint life which
she must go on living. Every episode rings now with that brisk-
clappered realism which is the best voice of our modern stage.

They also say, without thinking, that Mr. Odets has here
abandoned his former efforts to playwright all the wrongs of the
world. Rot. They probably patted Shaw on the head like that for
composing Candida--and The Country Girl, by the way, has quite a
bit of an Eighth Avenue Candida in its veins. That, and its own
brand of excellence, besides.

> --Gilbert W. Gabriel in Cue, Vol.
> 19, No. 46 (November 18, 1950),
> page 20.

DEAD END (Sidney Kingsley; Belasco Theatre, October 28, 1935)

Sidney Kingsley's Dead End presents only one phase of social
wrong, but the picture it paints is uncommonly effective, and the
larger implications of the scene are clearly present. Once again
Kingsley has selected a relatively routine central action, but to a
much greater extent than in Men in White he has not only handled
the situation with notable expertness but has permeated the play with
vital inferences. On the surface, Dead End is the story of a gangster who returns to his boyhood neighborhood to see his mother and
his first girl before disappearing somewhere. He finds bitter disillusionment and death on the waterfront which had started him on
his blood-bestrewn career. This situation is superficially melodramatic,
and is made more so by the fact of his betrayal by a childhood friend
who covets the reward money in a vain attempt to win a rich man's
mistress. However, the parallel story of the young boy who is being
driven into a similar career of crime and murder by the cumulative
effect of poverty, bad example and the callousness of the law, not
only makes the older gangster's career understandable, but places
the blame where it rightfully belongs. Supplementary details like
the jostling of the poor and the rich on the same waterfront and the
plight of the architect on relief, for whom society has even less use
and more contempt than for the criminal, also widen the scope of the
play, which becomes a pointed indictment, as well as a poignant
tragedy. Here and there the dramatist's writing had trembled quite
a little. Thus the picture of the rich is less fully dimensional than
the treatment of the poor, the romance between the unemployed
architect and the rich man's mistress is incompletely realized, and

the apparently happy ending is hardly conclusive. But in every
other respect Kingsley's drama is a credit to the stage.

Its authentication is greatly abetted by Kingsley's own forceful direction, Norman Bel Geddes' ominous setting, the acting of the
adult principals and the vivid performance of the child actors who
comprise the most dynamic group of youngsters the stage has har-
bored within our memory. Here and there the realism seems to be
a trifle gratuitous and self-conscious. Thus the dock which projects
into the orchestra may be a valid solution of one of the production
problems (the appearance and disappearance of the boys who are
constantly in and out of the water), but inspection of this part of
the set, which is open to the audience, reveals its make-believe
character. A stage gully is not a river. The ultra-realism of the
setting thus becomes rather fraudulent and unsatisfying. However,
one would be guilty of inexcusable obtuseness if one seriously identified Dead End with routine Belasco productions. The difference
leads to the whole question of realism in the theatre. Realistic art
must understand of course that it too is only a form of illusion on
the stage, and that its problem is to convince and not to describe.
But the objection to Belasco realism does not, as generally supposed,
relate to the means but to the end. If all the realistic drudgery--
genuine escalators, elevators, bric-à-brac, etc.--produces nothing
more than a picayune bedroom tragedy or a torrid romance there is
good reason for damning the realism as pretentious. The trouble
with the Belasco productions was that the plays did not warrant the
treatment. If, on the other hand, the realism authenticates a scene
which is trebly effective because it has been authenticated, as in
Dead End, the effort is neither superfluous nor pretentious, even if
the same immediacy might have been achieved by expressive simplifi-
cation. Dead End, it will be seen, illuminates dramatic, as well as
social, problems.

> --John W. Gassner in New Theatre,
> Vol. 2, No. 2 (December 1935),
> page 12.

* * *

The unwontedly rosy report of things theatrical that was
merchanted in this place last month and that radiated at least three
hogsheads of Grade A Angels' Teets seems to have been a bit pre-
mature. When it was confected, everything looked lovely and promised to be a deal more so. But in the meantime someone seems to
have got in some dirty work. Very little of even approximate dramatic merit has since appeared on the scene, the overwhelming majority of exhibits being the kind that have confounded the ardors of
even their paid press-agents. In many instances these exhibits have
been backed by motion picture money and have converted the theatres
into so many projection rooms, minus only the aroma of Hollywood
cigars and the garter-snatching. Their quick failure has been gratifying and is a tribute not only to the critical Ku Klux, which promptly

smeared them with tar and feathers, but to the public which sympathetically supported reputable drama by remaining away from them.

As a relief from the pervading dramatic blues we were tendered
Dead End, by Norman Bel Geddes out of Sidney Kingsley. As a
play, it amounts to little more than a basically eloquent theme in-
sufficiently embroidered with the colored silks of imagination and
skilful dramaturgy. But as a show maneuvered by Geddes it sweeps
up an audience with a very considerable theatrical force and tricks
the benignly uncritical into seeing it in virtues that Kingsley only
dreamed of. Taking a scenario placing in juxtaposition the squalid
poor and the gimpy rich and indicating in the former the soil from
which criminal impulses must inevitably spring, Geddes, with his art
catching a note of realism plus, has fattened the scenario into a
visual stage piece of high and vigorous kick. So vigorous, indeed,
that certain susceptible critics have been bamboozled into mistaking
his impressive scenery, lighting and stage generalship for an impressive sociological document.

Here and there we note other criticians who, while admiring
Geddes' realistic production, at the same time deplore it, dubbing it
a throwback to the Belasco day when the ultimate in art in West
Forty-fourth Street was considered to be the wafting over the footlights of recognizable coffee fumes from a pot actually boiling on a
real stove in an unmistakable reproduction of a Childs restaurant.
Such laments customarily emanate from those who in turn believe that
the ultimate in stage art, whatever the nature of the particular
dramas, are sets that look like something thought up by a hophead
full of aquavit and suffering slightly, in addition, from hereditary
insanity and an attack of jungle fever. Thus, a production of even
Pillars of Society that doesn't closely suggest a free-for-all fight between Cubists and Vorticists on the one side and Dadaists and
Fauvists on the other, with several designers of Bali travel-cruise
posters horning in, is displeasing to their aesthetic sensibilities.

That there must always remain a place for production realism
in the theatre, despite the patent fact that it was worked almost to
death and became a little ridiculous in the Belasco era, should be
plain. What made Belasco realism nonsensical was its constant visita-
tion upon fake-realistic plays. It was the old maestro's habit of taking a manuscript that cheaply romanticized fact and truth and lodging
it in settings that sought to conceal the sophistication that made him
a critical laughing stock. All the realistic tenement streets and
Childs restaurants and ranch houses that he ever threw upon his
stage couldn't conceal the adulterated and unrealistic dishes of dramatic tripe that he produced before and within them. George Bron-
son Howard and Wilson Mizner did the backward criticism of the day
a service when they showed up, for once and all, the Belasco fraud
by writing an honestly realistic version of The Easiest Way, producing it without obfuscating thousand-dollar Tiffany lamps, door-locks
that enchanted the nitwits by clicking loudly when keys were turned

in them, and cigars containing small electric batteries that gleamed
in the darkness, and proving that there was a very great difference
between truthful drama and merely truthful props.

Dead End, whatever its deficiencies as a dramatic script and its
occasional lapses into the romantic hokum of the old House of David,
is basically and essentially honest in its realism and Geddes' production is accordingly the only right and proper kind of production for
it. Now and again the wafted smell of cubeb cigarettes (surely
those gutter kids would walk a mile for a Camel) or something else
of the sort invades the authenticity of the realistic picture, but on
the whole the job is a thoroughly admirable one. And, speaking of
those kids, never before, I believe it safe to say, has the stage revealed so remarkable an aggregation of youngsters. There are a lot
of them and not one but what--in look, in pitch of voice, in gesture,
in comportment, and in that nebulous thing sometimes still referred
to by hamfats as the art of acting--is perfect. In brief, a first-
rate show if only a second-rate play.

--George Jean Nathan in Life (January 1936), page 18-19.

DEATH OF A SALESMAN (Arthur Miller; Morosco Theatre, February
    10, 1949)

Death of a Salesman has originality, authenticity, imagination
and a genuine pathos which lifts it far above any other play of this
season. Besides all these qualities, it has magnificent performances,
staging and direction. Arthur Miller, in Death of a Salesman, proves
what his prize-winning play, All My Sons, only implied; that he is
a prominent and significant new voice in the theatre.

Perhaps the thing that is most wonderful about this study in
futility is that Mr. Miller has created a little group of human beings
whose reality in no way depends on any specific situation. The fate-
ful progression of Willy Loman to his doom is as majestic in its inevitability as a Greek tragedy. Briefly, the plot is concerned with
a salesman, in the twilight of his life, who finds his usefulness is
over. The illusions by which he has lived and the mold in which he
has cast his sons, particularly the elder son, have proved false.
And, when forced to face a reality which he has always managed to
ignore, Willy Loman cracks under the strain.

As in All My Sons, Mr. Miller has a preoccupation with the
father and son relationship, but it is handled here with considerably
more sensitivity and vastly more pity. To convince his audience
that love and pride can destroy what they intended to build up, he
has created a completely benevolent husband and father, in whom a
lifetime of economic frustration engenders a well-intentioned but

destructive ambition for a son who, in his eagerness to believe in
his father's illusions, wrecks his own character. The torture which
these two inflict on each other and on the wife and mother is the substance of Mr. Miller's play.

Lee J. Cobb, as Willy Loman, defeated by inner and outer
forces, gives a magnificent and heartbreaking performance. His
range of tone is extraordinary and his portrayal of the baffled and
beaten salesman is unforgettable. Mildred Dunnock, as consistently
capable a character player as is currently about the stage, is splendid as the understanding wife who tries to save her husband from
his ultimate destruction. As the son in whom the father's hopes
are concentrated, Arthur Kennedy contributes much to the taut effectiveness of the play through his sympathetic performance. Cameron Mitchell does well by the happy-go-lucky other son whose world
is bounded by dolls, bars and dreams of a convertible. Jo Mielziner's multi-leveled, multi-lighted, semi-surrealist set, though a bit
reminiscent, is a good background for this play which moves back
and forth in time without the drop of a curtain, except at the
entr'actes.

Elia Kazan's direction is so much a part of the goings-on on
the stage, it is only after you leave the theatre that you realize
how really good it is.

Death of a Salesman, as few plays do, lived up to its advance
reports, and is an extraordinary worthwhile addition to this or any
other season.
                              --Thomas Brailsford Felder in Cue,
                                Vol. 18, No. 8 (February 19,
                                1949), pages 26-27.

                          *   *   *

Though it seems to me that Arthur Miller still has a tendency
to overwrite now and then, his Death of a Salesman, at the Morosco,
is a tremendously affecting work, head and shoulders above any other
serious play we have seen this season. It is the story of Willy Loman, a man at the end of his rope, told with a mixture of compassion, imagination, and hard technical competence you don't often find
in the theatre today, and probably the highest compliment I can pay
it is to say that I don't see how it can possibly be made into a moving picture, though I have very little doubt that somehow or other
eventually it will. The acting, especially that of Lee J. Cobb, as
the tragic central figure, Mildred Dunnock, as his loyal wife, and
Arthur Kennedy, as a son whose character he has lovingly and unconsciously destroyed, is honest, restrained, and singularly moving;
Jo Mielziner's set, centering on the interior of a crumbling house
somewhere in Brooklyn but permitting the action to shift as far away
as a shoddy hotel room in Boston, is as brilliant and resourceful as
the one he did for A Streetcar Named Desire; Elia Kazan, also, of

course, an important collaborator on <u>Streetcar</u>, has directed the cast
with the greatest possible intelligence, getting the most out of a
script that must have presented its difficulties; and an incidental
score, by Alex North, serves admirably to introduce the stretches of
memory and hallucination that alternate with the actual contemporary
scenes on the stage. Kermit Bloomgarden and Walter Fried, to round
out this catalogue of applause, are the fortunate producers of <u>Death
of a Salesman</u>, and I think the whole town ought to be very grateful to them.

    The happenings in Mr. Miller's play can hardly be called dra-
matic in any conventional sense. Willy is sixty-three years old, and
he has spent most of his life as the New England representative of a
company that I gathered sells stockings, though this point was never
exactly specified. Recently the firm has cut off his salary and put
him on straight commission, and the income from that is obviously
not enough for him to get along on, what with a mortgage, and insurance, and the recurring payments on an electric icebox, an ancient contraption about which he remarks bitterly, "God, for once
I'd like to own something before it's broken down!" In addition to
his financial troubles, his health and his mind are failing (he has
been having a series of automobile accidents, basically suicidal in
intent), and his two sons aren't much comfort to him. Long ago,
he had had muddled, childish dreams for them both--the elder, in
particular, was to be a famous football star, greater than Red Grange
--but things didn't work out, and now one is a stock clerk, not interested in much except women, and the other, when he works at
all, is just an itinerant farmhand. Willy's deep, hopeless recognition of what has become of him, of the fact that, mysteriously, society has no further use for him, has reduced him to a strange border-
land of sanity, in which fantasy is barely distinguishable from reality. The only remaining hope he has, in fact, lies in some crack-
brained scheme the two boys have for making a fortune selling sport
goods in Florida, and when that collapses, too, there is clearly
nothing left for him but to kill himself, knowing that at least his
family will manage somehow to survive on the money from his insurance.

    That is the rough outline of Mr. Miller's play, and it doesn't,
I'm afraid, give you much idea of the quality of his work, of how
unerringly he has drawn the portrait of a failure, a man who has
finally broken under the pressures of an economic system that he
is fatally incapable of understanding. There are unforgettable scenes:
the interview in which he is fired by the head of the firm, a brassy
young man, who plays a hideous private recording in which his little
boy names the capitals of all the states, in alphabetical order; a sequence in the Boston hotel, when his son finds him with a tart and
his love turns to hatred and contempt; a dream meeting with his
brother Ben, who has made a fortune in diamonds in the Kimberley
mines and stands, in his mind, as the savage, piratical symbol of
success; and, near the end of the play, a truly heartbreaking mo-

ment when Willy at last comes to realize that he is "a dollar-an-hour man" who could never, conceivably, have been anything more.

Death of a Salesman is written throughout with an accurate feeling for speech and behavior that few current playwrights can equal. It may not be a great play, whatever that means, but it is certainly a very eloquent and touching one. The cast, besides Mr. Cobb, Miss Dunnock, and Mr. Kennedy, includes Cameron Mitchell, Thomas Chalmers, Howard Smith, Don Keefer, and Alan Hewitt. They are all just what I'm sure the author hoped they'd be.

> --Wolcott Gibbs in The New Yorker
> (February 19, 1949), pages 54
> and 56.

DESIGN FOR LIVING (Noel Coward; Ethel Barrymore Theatre, January 24, 1933)

Mr. Noel Coward's design for living, as set forth in his play of that name, is an extremely freehand drawing of delightful line and aspect, regardless of its practicability as a blueprint. (And who is to say whether it is practical or not?) We may wonder a little just what would happen in a possible fourth act, after the two young men and the one young woman have gone back to living together again. We may speculate over the housing scheme and try to figure out just who would get whom, and what the tertium quid would do during those long spring evenings in Paris. (And stranger things have happened than that it should turn out to be the young lady who was out of luck.)

But, whatever goes on after the play has ended, there is one thing certain while it is going on: everyone, including the Messrs. Coward and Lunt, Miss Fontanne, and the audience itself, has been having a simply marvelous time of it.

In its light and airy way, Design for Living tinkles delicately at a more or less revolutionary note in human relationships. Revolutionary for the theatre, that is. When we stop to think of it, we realize that Mr. Coward has relegated that little imp Dan Cupid (at least in his more brutish moods) to a place among the minor prophets and has made him something of a nuisance into the bargain. Sex, as we were taught it in Sunday School, is seen as a "small enchantment," something which intrudes itself, like a charming but drunken friend who rings up at four a.m. for a party, spoiling the well-ordered routine of three people who would otherwise have been having a perfectly good time just fooling around together. Perhaps those long spring evenings in Paris do not hold so much treachery after all, provided the two young men have learned their lesson. But Miss Fontanne must give up wearing those yellow negligees if the thing is ever to work out properly.

That Mr. Coward has been told quite enough about the quality
of his own dialogue is shown in the scene in which his playwright
hero reads aloud the newspaper reviews of his latest success. "Witty," "provocative," "polished," "nay, even brilliant" are words which
apparently irk Mr. Coward by now, especially when used in conjunc-
tion with the qualifying adjective "thin." (He forgot "brittle.")
But the fact remains that his dialogue is witty, provocative, polished,
nay, even brilliant. Even dearer to this reviewer than the "brittle"
quips are the little words and phrases used in quite matter-of-fact
connections, chosen as evidently only an Englishman can choose
words and used here as only Mr. Coward among Englishmen can use
them. "Squirming with archness," as Miss Fontanne describes herself in her fine speech in the first act. Brandy "hurtling down" on
astonished insides. "You must be here to lash me with gay witticisms." And, to me one of the funniest lines in the play, when the
neophyte maid is unable to find anyone at the other end of the telephone after a long barrage of "'Allo"s and Mr. Coward says: "Never
mind, Mrs. Hodge. We mustn't hope for too much at first." It is
all very discouraging to one who has a working vocabulary of eighteen words, six of them being "swell" and "lousy."

There is, in fact, almost a plethora of amusing lines in Design
for Living. The outstanding ones in several of the scenes would
be even more outstanding if some of the lesser ones were cut. Even
the incomparable drinking scene, in which Messrs. Coward and Lunt
destroy a whole quart of brandy, with chasers from the sherry bottle ("real old Armadildo"), without once descending into the sordid
routine of such scenes—even this could be cut to advantage, although
I do not want to be the one to decide what should be cut. The lines
should not be thrown away, but wrapped up in tissue paper and
saved for another comedy. Design for Living just doesn't need them,
that's all.

But who are we, in this day and age, to cavil at too much of
a good thing, when good things are so scarce? And who are we to
feel vaguely uncomfortable at Mr. Coward's third act and final curtain, as if three people whom we had learned to like very much had
suddenly gone slightly bad on us? (The decision they came to was
logical and right enough, but it seemed as if they might have gone
about it with a little less ruthless touch, considering that they were
such pleasant people really.) These quibblings are more or less beside the point when we consider that Mr. Coward has not only given
us himself, Miss Fontanne, and Mr. Lunt at their very best (I didn't
like the character of Gilda very much, what with her intolerance of
success and comfortable hotels, but Miss Fontanne made everything
all right) but has also supplied us with food for thought and an evening of practically uninterrupted delight.

                                        --Robert Benchley in The New
                                          Yorker (February 4, 1933),
                                          pages 24 and 26.

DINNER AT EIGHT (George S. Kaufman and Edna Ferber; Music Box
    Theatre, October 22, 1932)

        You get everything but an elephant act in Dinner at Eight.
You get a little George S. Kaufman, Edna Ferber, Shakespeare, Al
Woods, Lincoln J. Carter, Eugene O'Neill, B.F. Keith and Frederick
and Fanny Hatton.

        The first two are the authors, but they have set out to pro-
duce a sort of Whitman's Sampler of Slices of Life. There is a suicide and there is a man who keeps putting his hand over his heart.
There is even a trick tea table which folds up its legs when it is
lifted, and produces a laugh. There is not enough George S. Kaufman.

        A clinical peek is taken into the home life, love life, business
life and soul life of each of several couples invited to a forthcoming
dinner party.

        My feeling about the whole thing is that it is awfully well done
but that so is the Encyclopedia Britannica.
                                        --Don Herold in Life (December
                                        1932), page 35.

DODSWORTH (Sidney Howard; Shubert Theatre, February 24, 1934)

        Maybe I had just the slightest chip on my shoulder when I
went to see Walter Huston in Sidney Howard's dramatization of Sinclair Lewis' Dodsworth.

        A few days previous, I had seen in a New York bookstore win-
dow a display of Mr. Lewis' voluminous preparatory notes and preliminary drafts and revisions behind a page of his Work of Art--
the suggestion being that because Mr. Lewis had done all this hard
work it must of necessity follow that his book is a good book. I
resented this Babbittian inference with a snort. I might as well
argue that because I remake each of my drawings ten times and chin
myself on a horizontal bar preceding each remake, my drawings are
of necessity good drawings. And I had an impulse to rent a com-
peting window across the street and stage an exhibit showing, with
displays of cups and strong coffee and alarm clocks and similar goads,
how much work it was for me to read Work of Art. The consumer
should sometimes be allowed to fire back.

        But I don't think it was this chip which caused me to feel that
without Walter Huston, Dodsworth would be a rather dull show. The
play breathed when he was on stage, but even that could not keep

me from thinking that Mr. Howard had documented the novel into a
play rather than dramatized it. Documented it honestly and intelligently, but without any great inspirational impetus. Maybe Mr.
Lewis' efficiency-engineered straight production-line methods don't
result in novels which result in great plays.

> --Don Herold in Life, April 1934,
> page 32.

*   *   *

*Sidney Howard has dramatized Sinclair Lewis's episodic novel,
Dodsworth, with almost complete success. As played by Walter Hus-
ton, Fay Bainter, and numerous other good actors at the Shubert
Theatre, New York, it has continuous interest.

Samuel Dodsworth (Mr. Huston) is a successful automobile
manufacturer and a genuinely fine person. For twenty years he and
his wife (Miss Bainter) had dreamed of a long trip abroad to see all
the places they had read about.

When the trip materializes, it serves to show up Mrs. Dodsworth's shallowness and Dodsworth's real worth. She, about 40 and
still physically attractive, collects a crowd of foreign admirers whom
Dodsworth correctly assumes to be second-raters.

She asks for a divorce in order to marry one of them. When
the marriage falls through, Dodsworth rushes back to her assistance,
but the final curtain finds him leaving her forever. She is too empty, and he has regained his self-respect.

Thirty-five speaking parts and fourteen colorful quick-changing
settings by Jo Mielziner are used to tell this story of the stage.
But it is Walter Huston, absent five years in the fleshpots of Hollywood, and Miss Bainter who are helpful in illuminating an occasionally hazy script with clear-cut acting.

Dodsworth is a triumph for the leading players.

> --Newsweek (March 3, 1934), page
> 34.

DU BARRY WAS A LADY (Music and Lyrics by Cole Porter, Book by
    Herbert Fields and B.G. De Sylva; 46th Street Theatre, Decem-
    ber 6, 1939)

Story--Louis Blore, washroom attendant at the Club Petite,

---

wins $75,000 in a sweepstake, and endeavors to get the leading sing-
er of the spot to marry him. She says no. Louis drinks a Mickey
Finn and dreams he is Louis XV. The lady becomes Du Barry, and
what's more she still spurns him. As for her other fancies, if the
original Du Barry were still alive she could undoubtedly sue for
libel.

Acting--I'll warrant that no two entertainers other than Bert
Lahr and Ethel Merman could carry on this plot, plus the songs they
sing, without driving the audience into the street screaming for the
morals squad. They have a way with them. I recommend particularly their singing together an item about friendship--a clean item.
They also do nicely with "But in the Morning, No!" This one is sort
of soiled. You will find plenty of Miss Merman at her best, and that
goes for Mr. Lahr.

Johnny Barnes and Harold Cromer contribute some swell tap
dancing. Benny Baker makes a funny Dauphin, and Betty Grable
is better than capable.

Production--The costumes and scenery by Raoul Pene DuBois
are the absolute tops in opulence and beauty. The colors and designs of the clothing are a treat to look at.

The chorus prances earnestly and well to Cole Porter's excellent score.

Cue Says--The subject of sex is belabored mightily throughout
this opus, with no suggestion of kid gloves. If you can deal with
that, you'll find Du Barry Was a Lady a swell musical show. Frequently hilarious, always beautiful, and most skillfully performed,
it ranks as one of the best of its kind.

> --Oliver Claxton in Cue, Vol. 8,
> No. 25 (December 16, 1939),
> page 53.

EDWARD, MY SON (Robert Morley and Noel Langley; Martin Beck
        Theatre, September 30, 1948)

After a depressing series of failures the New York Theatre
came alive the other night at the Martin Beck. Oddly enough, the
Prince Charming who awoke the sleeping beauty was your old (Oscar Wilde, Louis XVI) friend Robert Morley, who might at first glance
seem an unlikely candidate for so romantic a mission. But he demonstrates in Edward, My Son a knowledge of the theatre and its ways
which makes the recent efforts of our local bigwigs seem slightly
naive. Edward, My Son is a literate, beautifully acted play.

The season's first importation, it is also the season's first
dramatic hit. There will, apparently, always be an England. And
the excellence of this particular London product is a somewhat embarrassing lesson to New York.

Edward, My Son, which Mr. Morley co-authored (with Noel
Langley) and in which he co-stars (with Peggy Ashcroft and Ian
Hunter), is the story of a baby-happy lower middle class English family and of how they allowed their parental ambitions to destroy themselves and the ghastly object of their affections. The audience is
mercifully spared any face-to-face contact with the titular hero. So
Edward becomes a sort of dramatic amalgamation of Rebecca and Harvey, as sinister as the former and not half so simpatico as the latter.
But he's a remarkably effective theatrical device. Because of him,
his parents compromise with their standards. As their moral disintegration keeps pace with their economic and social ascendance, one
is never quite sure whether it's genes or indulgence which make invisible Edward a louse.

There are elements in the play which suggest Macbeth (there's
even a sort of Banquo's ghost). But here is tragedy on a more
humble, understandable plane. Mr. Morley as Arnold (subsequently
"Sir," ultimately "Lord") Holt is a bad, bad man. But his nefarious
deeds are all motivated by one sweet objective--Junior must have
nice things. He's so intense about this that he even abandons the
tastiest dish seen hereabouts in years (a blonde fascinator improbably
named Leueen MacGrath) so that his sprout's name shall remain un-
sullied.

Naturally, you know what happens to the best laid plans of mice
and Morleys. Edward meets an early end in the recent war--which is
probably for the best. But he leaves one (legitimate) heir, who is
the excuse for a final scene that would have been better omitted. Between curtain's rise and fall, however, there are thick slices of pathos
and of wit. Mr. Morley is a showman enough and, I fancy (see how
British one can get under the Morley influence), self-confident
enough to allow Miss Ashcroft to steal scene after scene as the mother whose inner integrity never quite succumbs to outward pressure.
In the early scenes, she's subtly right as an underprivileged wife
and mother. In the later ones, she is spectacularly superb as a
Mayfair peeress who finds small solace in tea gowns and blonde rinses,
vast solace at the bottom of a bottle. Not since Patricia Collinge
played Birdie in The Little Foxes has New York been treated to so
magnificently pathetic a lady lush. Ian Hunter is completely satisfying in the less spectacular role of the family physician and friend.
Edward, My Son is a welcome stranger.

--Thomas Brailsford Felder in Cue,
Vol. 17, No. 41 (October 9, 1948),
page 20.

FINIAN'S RAINBOW (Book by E.Y. Harburg and Fred Saidy, Lyrics
by E.Y. Harburg, Music by Burton Lane; 46th Street, January 10, 1947)

Finian's Rainbow, arriving at a time when Broadway was already bountifully supplied with first-rate musicals, immediately surpassed all competitors and established itself as best of its kind. It
is imaginative, melodious, humorous, colorful and grand. If my
superlatives are showing, it is because the recent arrival in the 46th
Street Theatre gives me an irresistible urge to say it's swell and
build up to a climax.

Finian's Rainbow has everything a well-made musical comedy
offers, plus the extra payoff of a serious theme; which makes its
humor mature as well as diverting. Taking the structure of the
familiar boy-meets-girl romance, E.Y. Harburg and Fred Saidy clothe
it with a blend of Irish folklore and Southern folkways and a fusion
of American ideals and conflicts. The latter materials have formerly
been considered too refractory for the purposes of musical comedy,
which must above all be entertaining. But in this production they
yield to a discipline that molds them into a unified and triumphant
pageant of the American Dream.

The story begins with Finian McLonergan showing up in the
not-so-mythical state of Missitucky, bringing along with him his
comely daughter and a stolen pot of elves' gold; and hot on his heels
comes Og, a leprechaun, anxious to recover Finian's loot. By various formulas of higher mathematics and dead reckoning, Finian has
developed the theory that planting gold in the ground causes lodes
of the precious metal to grow alluringly in adjacent lands.

When he plants his pot of gold, split seconds before the leprechaun catches up with him, the poor whites and black sharecroppers
living on surrounding farms suddenly get rich, proving his theory
correct. Finian's adventures and those of his associates make an
hilarious tale, full of delicate fantasies, flashes of satire, bursts of
melody, bits of low comedy, which do not degenerate into the vulgar,
and all sorts of delightful surprises.

Albert Sharpe, imported from Ireland, is an ingratiating Finian,
while Ella Logan, as his daughter, Sharon, is a colleen as fancy as
any you will lay eyes on between St. Patrick's Days. Miss Logan,
according to a program note, was born in Scotland, but there's a
lot of sweet Carolina in her voice. Donald Richards, Anita Alvarez
and Sonny Terry contribute handsomely to the melody and rhythm of
the production. David Wayne is appealing as the leprechaun who is
both wistful and impish.

The direction, by Bretaigne Windust, is all that could be desired. Jo Mielziner's sets and lighting form a poetic background for

the action, and the costumes by Eleanor Goldsmith are as original as
the story. In one scene, "When the Idle Poor Become the Idle
Rich," the costumes, separately and ensemble, are as humorous as
the Royal Nonesuch episode in Huckleberry Finn. Burton Lane wrote
the effervescent score.

Lee Sabinson and William Katzell are the producers. A merry
laugh, the Bible says, is like a medicine. The firm of Sabinson &
Katzell has made a huge contribution toward improving the moral and
physical health of the nation. Finian's Rainbow keeps the audience
roaring, with no scruples about it, from curtain rise to finale.

> --Theophilus Lewis in America
> (February 22, 1947), page 585.

* * *

"New York, New York, it's a hell of a town." Particularly at
show time. On the Pacific coast, one forgets how exciting the theater really can be. Tired original casts, inferior replacement casts,
too frequently make the touring troupes a parody of the show that
appeared on Broadway. Most delightful entertainment, the musical,
Finian's Rainbow. Charmingly fresh book, lyrics and music by E.Y.
Harburg, Fred Saidy and Burton Lane, which has been whipped into
admirable form by Bretaigne Windust. It's a salty show, with sharp
satire, lusty humor and enactments by David Wayne as the Leprechaun and Albert Sharpe as Finian himself. Ella Logan is pretty,
striking, despite an Irish brogue that is quite the same as the Scotch
brogue she used in previous seasons, bad legs which she emphasizes
by going pigeon-toed for coyness, and an attempt to seem fey, which
the lady seeks to put over by staring wide-eyed at the place from
which the spotlight emanates in the upper reaches of the auditorium.
The Michael Kidd choreography is dazzling, as is the dancing of
Anita Alvarez. The scenery of Jo Mielziner is superb, and reaches
its peak in a draw curtain of silhouetted trees. Best numbers:
"When the Idle Poor Become the Idle Rich," "The Begat" and "Necessity."

> --Herb Sterne in Rog Wagner's
> Script, Vol. 33, No. 749 (Febru-
> ary 15, 1947), page 12.

* * *

A combination of talents has merged into a tuneful, fanciful
musical entertainment at the Forty-sixth Street. Finian's Rainbow
has not only an excellent score by Burton Lane and crack staging by
Bretaigne Windust; its E.Y. Harburg lyrics, Michael Kidd dances, Jo
Mielziner settings, Eleanor Goldsmith costumes and enthusiastic performances also are part of its smooth blend of showmanship. Its book,
by Harburg and Fred Saidy, about happy Irish superstition and unhappy prejudice in a back woods state called Missitucky, is only
mildly whimsical, but it is not as weak a link as most musical comedy

librettos. Though it fails to be uproarious in the humor department, Finian's Rainbow has much more than enough elsewhere to charm the eye and ear.

The general mood of Lane's music is a plaintive one, but its harmonies range all the way from the Irish-tinted, sentimental "How Are Things in Glocca Morra?" to the rowdy "The Begat," whose lyrics about the word "begat" as used in "Abraham begat" are funny enough to be encored as many times as there are stanzas. Ella Logan, as a colleen just off the boat, and Donald Richards as a share-cropper have fine voices for love songs like "Old Devil Moon" and "Look to the Rainbow;" and even the ensemble puts across the Lane-Harburg concoctions with energy and coordination. The score has variety, melody, a fitting accompaniment of words and no deadwood at all; and Miss Logan and her collaborators sing it with the care and ability that it deserves.

If the caricature does not quite match the music in quality, it is principally because it contains a few too many privy jokes and a rather obvious cartoon of a southern senator. David Wayne, goodness knows, is superb as a leprechaun with an arch sense of humor, a pixie who has journeyed from Ireland to recover his stolen pot of gold. Albert Sharpe, an actor borrowed from the Irish stage for this occasion, is also just right as an elderly conniver who thinks he can make the gold grow by planting it in the ground near Fort Knox. Robert Pitkin is well cast, too, as "Senator Billboard Rawkins," who hates everybody; but the material in all cases lacks the subtlety of the performances, and it suffers in comparison to the rest of the musical's excellent doings.

Windust has put the show on with movement that is both smooth and colorful, and with sustained exuberance and visual interest. The ensemble dances are not the least of the attractions, being both imaginative and smartly executed; and Anita Alvarez makes a very good premiere danseuse, particularly in the moody solo called "Dance o' the Golden Crock." This Lee Sabinson-William R. Hatzell production has been given the finishing touches by Mielziner and Miss Goldsmith in the scenery and costumes. Finian's Rainbow has been mildly bewitched, to be sure, by that commonest of all show business devils, by name "book trouble." But in the end it is the show's good leprechauns who wield the most influence and set it up at the top as the most bewitching new musical entertainment of the season.

> --Cue, Vol. 16, No. 3 (January 18, 1947), page 15.

FRENCH WITHOUT TEARS (Terence Rattigan; Henry Miller Theatre, September 28, 1937)

It is the habit of Gilbert Miller to take a silly piece of nonsense, dress it up with all the perfections at his command and deceive the public into thinking it is being entertained. Such a soufflé
is French Without Tears which, while amusing enough in its mild, pat-
terned way, has all the meatiness of a hollow laugh. Perhaps we
shouldn't quarrel with Mr. Miller's ability to make much of little, for
he represents the commercial manager functioning at his best. His
works are uniformly urbane, dignified, gilded and essentially trashy.
I can't think of anything of his, except perhaps Victoria Regina,
which will mean anything except a name in the files a few years
hence.

While it is distinctly ungenerous to be captious with Mr. Miller
he must suffer the indictment and on the score of this latest show,
admit he is being more sketchy than usual.

French Without Tears is the title of an old text book, a volume
supposedly containing a method whereby the French language could
be eased into children without the accompaniment of tears. In the
play the language is being inserted into the muddled heads of a number of pleasant young Englishmen gathered in a small house in the
south of France. The house is run by a Monsieur Maingot and is
patronized by aspirants to the diplomatic service and other learned
professions, such as a European traveling man and a fellow who
wants to interpret in the Royal Navy. One of the youths has the
misfortune to bring his sister, a latter-day mass-production Delilah.
She introduces some curses, if not tears, into the discussions of the
French language.

The terrible young woman, an attractive ingenue named Penelo-
pe Dudley Ward, has a self-confessed ability to cause men to fall in
love with her. This she does for two acts, working out principally
on Frank Lawton, who finally escapes. This is all a bit of fluff,
don't you know, and the author has not tried to make it more than
that. For some people it might be enough for an evening's entertainment but not for me. Mr. Lawton is alternately charming and
sardonic; he doesn't have to act very much. Miss Ward is a refreshing newcomer, a tall dark blonde, a bit on the thin side but with an
air of belonging on the stage and definitely a good actress in this play.

The champion of all the assembled pleasant company of actors
is a Frenchman, Marcel Vallée, who, while never speaking an understandable word of English (his role is principally in French) convinces you that here is a master of technique. The playbill says he
is duly celebrated on his native shore. Of the other performers no
one can be said to stand out especially--fine actors all, they work
well as a team. In fact the whole production is a perfect thing--as
neat a bit of side-stepping realities as has been committed in some
time. It should have a long run.

--Herbert Drake in Cue, Vol. 5,
No. 50 (October 9, 1937), page
14.

THE GAY DIVORCE (Book by Dwight Taylor, Musical Adaptation by
Kenneth Webb and Samuel Hoffenstein, Music and Lyrics by
Cole Porter, Ethel Barrymore Theatre, November 29, 1932)

What this country needs is more good hoofing.

You don't think there was any sense or salvation in anything
that Hoover or Roosevelt said in the last campaign or that there will
be any heads-or-tails to anything anybody says in the next session
of Congress, do you?

I've just come from Fred Astaire's show, Gay Divorcé, and
I'm convinced that the greatest mistake we human beings ever made
was when we started to think with our heads instead of with our
feet. We build complicated structures of business and government
which we don't begin to understand and which topple over on us
every few years and make us look like saps.

It is my conviction that we won't get anywhere at all until we
go back to some of the simple animal accomplishments that God gave
us--such as our ability to hoof and warble.

Let's dismiss Congress, scrap the navy, can our diplomats ...
and turn things over to Fred Astaire and his co-foot-workers.

Gay Divorcé is an "intimate" musical comedy, which usually
means that the producer has saved himself $40,000 on the production,
but in this case nothing is missing, and Fred Astaire is present. I
may be a raving maniac, but for me any show with Fred Astaire in
it is, at the moment, the best show in town. Every dance he does
is (for me) another Lincoln's Gettysburg address.

The play itself isn't always as sophisticated as it hopes to be,
but I don't care about that. It has, besides Master Fred, Claire
Luce (and by the way, they're far too precious a pair of tootsie-
wafters to risk their necks nightly in that trip over that sitting room
table), Luella Gear (grand!), G.P. Huntley, Jr., and Betty Starbuck.
Quit asking!

Even a trained seal is a finer work of the Lord than any Ambassador we ever sent to London. And the man who first discovered
that a seal can balance a rubber ball on its nose may be a bigger
man than Columbus. ('Cause America would have been discovered
eventually, anyway--worse luck!)

Yes sir, what this country needs is more dancing and more
trained seals.

                              --Don Herold in Life (February
                              1933), page 30.

GENTLEMEN PREFER BLONDES (Book by Joseph Fields and Anita
    Loos, Music by Jule Styne, Lyrics by Leo Robin; Ziegfeld The-
    atre, December 8, 1949)

    No doubt about Blondes being on the preferred list. It is just
such a luxury stock of the show world as the Loreleis love, and they
and most every other middlebrow will rush to buy.

    Large, flesh-colored and peroxide-tipped bonfires are already
burning all around Times Square in honor of this huge new hit. I
can only toss in my own small lucifer. Maybe then I'll be allowed to
add that, for all its funniness, it isn't the ultimate of wit and polished plot, the whitest rose of musical romance.

    Anyway, welcome back to Anita Loos' hardy old bedtime clas-
sic in this different and deluxe edition, replete with ribald song,
much handsome dance and multiple scenery. Properly pagan salutes
to the rebirth of Miss Loos' latternight Venus in the big, weirdly
sumptuous person of Carol Channing who certainly does arise from
waves of fresh applause.

    You'll recall Lorelei Lee--you particularly ought to in this nos-
talgic issue--as that digger into the mother-lode of our Tippling
Twenties, who always wanted diamonds and got two million readers
and endless audiences, as well. Time and Joseph Fields, co-librettist,
have been kind to her. Her midriff and her humor have broadened
space. In the day of the atom bomb, she packs a couple of them
right in most effective spots upon her person. Miss Channing makes
her over into a whole mountain of glassy-eyed grotesqueness.

    Story? It's still all about Lorelei and her friend Dorothy, the
semi-innocents abroad--with a harvest of tiaras, Olympic team choruses, shipboard clutterbucking and swingtime in Paris. Lorelei still
ends up with a button business and no great zipper of a husband
on her jeweled hands. It just couldn't be funnier for one act.
There are two acts.

    A strong cast, however, and a very stylish, sometimes stun-
ning lot of John C. Wilson staging. Miss Channing's fellow-earring
from "Lend an Ear," Yvonne Adair, is here to play patient straight-
woman. Alice Pearce is present with her celebrated burp and giggle.
Messrs. McCauley and Brotherson head the males who at least sing
along. Give me my choice of loveliest things about it all, and I'll
vote for Anita Alvarez's dancing--more vivid, expressive, than ever.

    A good thing, then, this Blondes. Maybe too much of one.
                              --Gilbert W. Gabriel in Cue, Vol.
                                18, No. 51 (December 17, 1949),
                                page 28.

GEORGE WASHINGTON SLEPT HERE (George S. Kaufman and Moss
    Hart; Lyceum Theatre, October 18, 1940)

Story--Newton Fuller buys a house in the country in which
George Washington is alleged to have once slept. The place has no
plumbing, no water, and no road. Mrs. Annabelle Fuller thinks the
idea a dreadful one. At the beginning of the play the house is a
mess. By the last act it has been fixed up.

A mild love affair flits sketchily through the yarn, as do a
rich uncle, a mean neighbor, a hired man, and a hired girl.

The problem involved has to do with a foreclosure of the mortgage and the acceptance by Mrs. Fuller of the new estate.

The crusty neighbor wants to drive the Fullers away and for
some unexplained reason he holds the mortgage. Mr. F., in the
meantime, has been spending all his spare cash on gravel, well-
digging, and other country matters.

Acting--A large cast performs this skillfully. Ernest Truex
plays Mr. Fuller and Jean Dixon the tart Mrs. Fuller. Dudley
Digges does well with the uncle, and Paula Trueman acquits herself
nobly as the hired girl. Bobby Readick deserves notice as a nasty
little boy.

Production--John Root designed the excellent sets.

Cue says--There are some highly hilarious moments in George
Washington Slept with the usual good Kaufman-Hart wisecracking,
but by and large the play labors. Its devices weigh it down and
the dull, I am afraid, offsets the good.

The play has none of the smoothness and glibness of the
usual product of this playwriting team. The wisecracks are all the
way, stemming not so much from the goings-on at hand, as from the
sheer desire to get a laugh. A large part of the third act kills
time with the ancient procedure of getting the characters drunk--in
this case all of them, not just one or two. You won't enjoy it.
                                --Oliver Claxton in Cue, Vol. 9,
                                No. 44 (October 26, 1940), page
                                36.

THE GLASS MENAGERIE (Tennessee Williams; Playhouse Theatre,
    March 31, 1945)

Anybody with an ordinary movie camera who could manage to

film Laurette Taylor's performance in this play would have a kind
of documentary contribution to the Duse-Bernhardt legends. Of
course, it would be simpler if Warner Bros. would just film the whole
play as it is. At any rate, some permanent record should be made of
The Glass Menagerie if only so that we will not have to beat our grandchildren in order to make them understand how wonderful Laurette
Taylor was--is.

For Miss Taylor gives a performance that will justify the existence of the theatre for a long time to come, that is the pure, distilled essence of great acting from the first to the last moment,
from the aborted gestures to the consummated ones, from rambling,
unemphasized monologues to distinct diatribes of frustration and
spite. When she wasn't on stage we found ourselves wondering what
she was doing back there in the kitchen ... and, you know, there
isn't any kitchen backstage at the Playhouse.

As for the play, it is the first New York production of the
work of Tennessee Williams, a young poet and playwright of enormous talent. It is a simple story of four people in a tenement flat
in St. Louis in the depth of the depression ... a mother (a faded
southern belle but ever valiant, talkative); a sensitive and terribly
frustrated son who wants some taste of life beyond the movies and
the drab job he must stick to in order to perpetuate the family's
drab existence; a sister who is a lovely, shy, gentle, crippled girl;
and a brash but kind young man who comes calling on one, only
one, Spring evening. The play is amazingly and boldly (we thought)
uncomplicated by situation or action ... but its searching preoccupation with the complication and contradictions within the four humans
gives it a first act as warm with life as a chapter out of Maxim
Gorky.

The brother becomes at intervals a merchant seaman narrator,
who, having somehow escaped, presents to you this small slice out
of his memory, against a highly dramatic and moving backdrop of a
hot band playing in a dance hall in St. Louis. The brother's narration gives you the time, the background, for the small inconsequen-
tial drama, and from it drop words like Guernica to slash at memory
with its picture of a world sitting by, watching bombs fall on the
women and children of Spain. But other than this narration, there
is no world problem or broad social sense in the play; because the
particular problems of the Wingfield family were not entirely a product
of the time they lived in. And the second act, in which the brash
young man tries to help the crippled girl face life is not very believable. But such is the incredible power of the production that
you do not even know this until you are away from its spell. And
anyway, you do not care. Because Mr. Williams has given us a
great thing, if not a great play.

Eddie Dowling (co-producer) as the brother is tremendous...
seems to shake with the same substance which might swim in Miss

Taylor's blood. Julie Haydon is a gentle lyric of soft, shining shy-
ness. And Anthony Ross as the caller is very, very solid. The Glass
Menagerie is the kind of play at which even the most timid will shout
Bravo, and turn to wonder who said that, who said that.

--Irene Kittle in Cue, Vol. 14,
No. 14 (April 7, 1945), page 16.

*   *   *

After creating a minor furore in Chicago, The Glass Menagerie
finally reached Broadway Saturday night. Here, too, it should create something of a stir. As a play, I think there is a great deal
wrong with it. But I recommend it without qualms, because it
makes interesting and sometimes absorbing theater, and because
Laurette Taylor is giving in it one of the most remarkable and fascinating performances in many seasons. She has always been one
of the few really distinguished actresses that we have; she has
probably never offered more convincing proof of her distinction.

The play which she dominates and enlarges is in essence a
fairly simple portrait of a family, though in effect rather a pastiche
of dramaturgical styles. Miss Taylor plays the mother of the fam-
ily--a Southern woman in late middle age who has come way down in
the world, been deserted by her husband and been left with rankling memories of a much-courted, magnolia-petaled youth. Her son
is a lackadaisical dreamer, fond of the bottle and fretting against
his home life; her daughter Laura is a shy, painfully withdrawn crip-
ple. The burning desire of the mother's broken-down life is somehow to get Laura married, and she is forever plaguing the son to
bring "gentlemen callers" to the house. At length the son brings
one--to a dinner full of Alice-Adamsish mishaps and desperate gaie-
ties, and an after-dinner session with Laura from which the caller
escapes as soon as he decently can.

Miss Taylor's acting aside, there is enough that is human,
touching, desolate and bitterly comic about this family picture to
keep one steadily interested. Moreover, Mr. Williams has told much
of his story in telltale little scenes that can be far more effective
than conventional "big" ones; he is capable, when he remains relatively straightforward, of very good dialogue; and far from senti-
mentalizing the mother, he has shown up all her nagging, her pretenses, her small snobberies, her Southern foolishness.

So far as this is true, The Glass Menagerie is unhackneyed,
unhokumed theater. But Mr. Williams has fancied things up in other
ways, has rather jumbled his technique and forced his tone. Eddie
Dowling commutes between being the son in the play and a narrator
who stands outside it: the second role seems to me both pretty
otiose and pretty arty. To be sure, Mr. Dowling acts as commentator because the play is conceived as a "memory"; and it is further
projected as a memory by much use of atmosphere music and dim

lights. All this may make, here and there, for unusual theater; but
beyond the fact that Mr. Williams isn't really master of his rather
showy (and derived) devices, I think he has asked oddity to do work
that simple artistry can do far better. If The Glass Menagerie aims
(rightly in my opinion) at something different from straight realism,
at becoming a kind of mood play, then the mood and tone must be
begotten from within it, not built up all around it. I have no desire to see anybody writing like anybody else; but instead of tinkling
at various little Saroyanesque, Barrie-esque, Wilderesque whatnots,
Mr. Williams might at least have found suggestive the whole method
of Chekhov. For in its mingled pathos and comedy, its mingled
naturalistic detail and gauzy atmosphere, its preoccupation with
"memory," its tissue of forlorn hopes and backward looks and lan-
guishing self-pities, The Glass Menagerie is more than just a little
Chekhovian. But Chekhov worked from within, as Mr. Williams does
not; and successfully on more than one level, as Mr. Williams does
not quite; and in such a way that his comedy and pathos coalesced,
where Mr. Williams'--except where Miss Taylor makes them blend--
emerge separately.

If Miss Taylor's Southerner is not quite a great characterization, it is because the materials do not exist for one. But hers is
at least a great performance, which out of many small bits contrives
a wonderful stage portrait. She nags, she flutters, she flatters,
she coaxes, she pouts, she fails to understand, she understands all
too well--all this revealed, most of the time, in vague little move-
ments and half-mumbled words, small changes of pace, faint shifts of
emphasis, little rushes of energy and masterfulness, quiet droopings
of spirit. It is so fascinating as acting that it hardly needs to be
(though it generally is) convincing as portrayal. It represents a
personal style, but it is never just that mark of lesser actresses--
"personality." It is acting.

Mr. Dowling always has a quiet ease on the stage, and he has
it here; but in neither of his roles does he seem to me quite satisfactory. Julie Haydon gets the shy, scared side of Laura, but little
of the locked-up intensity that the role seems to suggest. As the
Gentleman Caller, Anthony Ross hasn't an easy role to handle, but
on the whole does very well with it. Paul Bowles' music is agreeable, and Jo Mielziner's set and lighting do most effectively what they
are asked to do.

--Louis Kronenberger in PM (April
2, 1945).

GOLDEN BOY (Clifford Odets; Belasco Theatre, November 4, 1937)

Clifford Odets returns to us from Hollywood with his abilities
unimpaired, his talents freshened, his technique surer, and his play-

wrighting direction clearer than when he left. In Golden Boy he
gives us his finest play and the Group Theater accomplishes in its
production its supreme effort of direction, acting, and presentation.

In outline, Golden Boy is the story of a sensitive boy with a
desire to play a violin. He is ugly and cockeyed and wears his
soul on his forehead for all to see and hurt. His hurt convinces
him that he can conquer his adversaries by developing his flair for
prize fighting. The play is the story of his compromise with his intelligence. He throws away the thing that would mean completion to
him for the fierce pleasures of combat and a comet career in the
fisticuffs racket. "I'm a bullet," he cries, "all future and no past."
But he is pursued relentlessly by his ravished mind and soul and
brought to earth in an auto wreck which solves all his problems,
past, present, and future.

Odets writes with the most pungent style of our times. Without exactly copying speech, he nevertheless conveys the staccato
rhythm of the language of the tenements and the streets. It sings
in machine gun cadence, almost prose-poetry, alive, vital, lusty,
speech.

The play itself has a driving momentum, a pace punctuated
with drama. It moves almost inescapably to its logical conclusion
and in that it seems to skirt the fringes of pure tragedy. Not that
the play is a somber study of an unhappy character. It sings with
good humor, is bristling with laughter. To sit through it is an experience not to be duplicated at anything done this season.

Luther Adler grows in his part of the protagonist. He is
almost incredibly young and tender in the beginning and does not
begin to lash out in that stinging style of his until it fits the time
in the play. The result is an overwhelming performance. It is impossible that the role could be done better. Frances Farmer, a Hollywood import, is the girl in the case. She is a hard-headed but
unhappy blonde; young, neat, smooth, with a beautiful face and a
trim figure. She turns in a simple and honest portrayal, completely
in tune with the magnificent ensemble acting of the rest of the Group
performers.

This is a fine play. Odets has taken a piece of life out of
time and made it live again on the stage of the Belasco Theatre.
                              --Herbert Drake in Cue, Vol. 6,
                              No. 3 (November 13, 1937), page
                              13.

                    *   *   *

After writing pithy dialogue for the Gary Coopers and Made-
leine Carrolls of Hollywood, Clifford Odets returns to the Group Theatre with an extraordinarily gripping play about a sensitive boy torn

between a violinist's career for which he has been trained and a
prizefighter's profession which is suddenly thrust upon him. It is
true that after the first act, the plot-scheme of Golden Boy becomes
perfectly transparent; the automobile wreck motif has been planted
so definitely that one knows the hero is sooner or later going to
steal an Iris March.

Nevertheless, Odets has created some absorbing characters.
Dramatically he is at his best in the simple domestic scenes. No one
can surpass him when he is dealing with the changing order of life
among the middle class, when he is treating with the conflict of the
younger generation with the old. For that very reason I still think
Odets wrote his richest drama in Paradise Lost, but I am apparently
among the few who found that play shining and true.

To see the ensemble work of the Group Theatre is to see some
of the finest acting that New York has to offer, and the players
from the Group, under the spirited direction of Harold Clurman,
have given unstintingly of their talents in Golden Boy. Luther Adler, Morris Carnovsky, Lee J. Cobb, Jules Garfield, Elia Kazan,
Art Smith, and all their comrades offer superlative performances,
while Frances Farmer, on leave of absence from Hollywood, shows
that her work is every bit as sure on the stage as it is on the
screen.

Golden Boy is aglow with golden drama--a direct refutation to
those who have bewailed the passing of Odets with his going to
Hollywood. Alloy his play may have, but it is none the less solidly
wrought, a bright experience in this year's theater.

> --DeWitt Bodeen in Rob Wagner's
> Script, Vol. 18, No. 445 (Janu-
> ary 15, 1938), page 16.

THE GREAT WALTZ (Book by Dr. A.M. Willner, Heinz Reichert,
    Ernst Marischka, and Caswell Garth, Adaptation by Moss Hart,
    Lyrics by Desmond Carter, Music by Johann Strauss; Center
    Theatre, September 22, 1934)

Dr. Max Gordon's presentation of Hassard Short's production
of The Great Waltz, a tale of the two eminent Strausses, father and
son, is, aside from the latter's own sweet music, a large disappointment. The book is slow and heavy; the stage sets, what with their
many little fancily colored electric bulbs, periodically resemble a Lig-
gett drugstore at Yuletide; and Mr. Guy Robertson, in the rôle of
Johann Strauss, Jr., is enough to justify an immediate declaration
of war on the part of Austria. The melodies, of course, are among
the loveliest things in all music, but the actors, scenery and $300,000

production squat upon them like old Thompson and Dundy, Hippodrome elephants.

> --George Jean Nathan in Life (No-
> vember 1934), page 26.

GREEN GROW THE LILACS (Lynn Riggs; Guild Theatre, January 26, 1931)

Lynn Riggs' Green Grow the Lilacs recaptures a phase of
American Life with which most of us are unfamiliar. It is laid in the
Indian Territory in 1900, and is filled with homely characters and
traditional cowboy songs, and affords Helen Westley the opportunity
of adding another characterization of an old woman, Aunt Eller
Murphy, to her rapidly growing gallery. As one partial to the po-
liter drama, I am unable to share the enthusiasm which this play
has awakened in various circles, but the Theatre Guild has given it
a good production, and the author has written it with sincerity and,
I am told, authenticity. It will at least be a satisfaction for those
who, like the ancient Athenians, are always on the qui vive for
some new thing, and it has a salty, folk lore quality which should
establish it as a commendable contribution to Americana. June Walker gave a good performance as the orphan bride whose wedding night
was made so turbulent by the shivaree customary in that early, unsettled country.

> --Baird Leonard in Life (February
> 20, 1931), page 18.

* * *

The name of Lynn Riggs is familiar to anyone who has taken
the trouble to read these articles of mine during the past three or
four years. On occasion I have gone out of my way to drag in on
the flimsiest pretext some reference to him. He has been writing
plays for more than five years, but until a few weeks ago he was
a relatively obscure figure in the American theatre. I have been accused by critics of boosting "nonentities" and "writers without talent," and no longer than a year ago I was ridiculed for speaking
respectfully of Paul Green and Lynn Riggs, just as I was for saying
a good word on behalf of a man who used to sign himself "Eugene
G. O'Neill." The same reviewer who dismissed Mr. Riggs with a
contemptuous phrase has since devoted several columns to his praise.

There is some satisfaction in this, not for the small pleasure
of saying to myself, I was right all along (I know darn well I was
right) but of proving the other fellow wrong.

In the case of Mr. Riggs, he has justified not only the belief
of those who knew he could write, but he has proved that there is

a large public waiting for him. The Theatre Guild's production of
Green Grow the Lilacs has not proved that this young men has genuine talent--that was obvious before--but it has once and for all
shown that what Mr. Riggs was after is something that appeals to
a wide audience. So quite aside from my pleasure in welcoming a
brave and joyous thing into the theatre, I have the added pleasure
of realizing that both Mr. Riggs himself and others after him will
find it easier to use the theatre in new ways without having to con-
form too closely to the threadbare conventions that are known as
"good theatre."

It is only one more proof of the vitality of our native drama
that a young man who is both poet and playwright should be able,
with practically no knowledge of the so-called demands of the theatre, to walk into it with a manuscript that combines poetry, drama
and life, and not be forced to leave all the poetry and most of the
life at the stage entrance. While Mr. Riggs cannot be called a re-
former, he has always stuck to his guns; more than once he has
turned down offers that would probably have brought him material
success, simply because that didn't interest him. In the preface to
the recently published text of Green Grow the Lilacs he has explained his aims with modesty and an extraordinary clearheadedness.

"The dramatist, it seems to me, has no business to interfere
just for the sake of making a 'play,' in its present--and idiotic--
meaning. That he may be tempted to, is lamentable, but not surpris-
ing--the rewards are great. But if he takes his work seriously he
will face his problems in a limbo beyond the knowledge of applause.
His role will continue to be humility and abnegation."

This is from a man who knows what he is about, but what follows is the wisdom of a poet and seer:

"Some time, his characters may do stirring things he could
never have calculated. And some time, if he is fortunate, he may
hear from the people he has set in motion (as Shakespeare and
Chekhov often heard) things to astonish him and things to make him
wise."

From all I have said you must not imagine that Green Grow the
Lilacs is a ponderous thing; it's anything but that. It is a high-
spirited, winged, joyous dramatic song. Its poetry is part and
parcel of the whole--never an ornament, never an addition. You
could no more take from it its lyric beauty than you could separate
the style of Shakespeare from his ideas: the one cannot be conceived
without the other. Nor is it a deep and subtle document. Subtle-
ties there are, of course, but they are present because the playwright gave his people dimensions, not because he wrote the subtlety in.

Green Grow the Lilacs is really a dramatized ballad done in six tableaus with cowboy ballads between the scenes. The time is 1900 and the setting Indian Territory shortly before the State of Oklahoma was admitted to the Union. The story is of a young cowboy and a farm girl. A pathetically degenerate farmhand nearly precipitates a tragedy, but is accidentally killed just in the nick of time. The cowboy is technically implicated in the affair, but at the conclusion of the story there's not the least doubt that he will be released.

It was this simple and conventional plot that led the few critics who either disliked the play or made serious reservations upon it to declare that Mr. Riggs still had something to learn about playwriting. What they meant was something about one kind of playwriting. But they are wrong. Mr. Riggs does know a good deal about shaping a story within a conventional framework, and the play he wrote to prove it has been running in a repertory theatre for more than two years. He's not interested in plays that are merely plays.

I turn again to the preface I have just quoted, and find this: "... it seemed wise to throw away the conventions of ordinary theatricality—a complex plot, swift action, etc.,—and try to exhibit luminously in the simplest stories a wide area of mood and feeling. This could only be done, it seemed to me, by exploring the characters as deeply as possible, simple though they appeared to be, hoping to stumble on, if lucky, the always subtle, always strange compulsions under which they labor and relate themselves to the earth and to other people."

Since I have read an inordinate number of reviews about Green Grow the Lilacs, I feel that nearly everything has been said. I find it extremely difficult to add anything fresh. Perhaps I am so gratified over the impression created by the play I am not so much interested at this moment in stating my own reactions more precisely. Perhaps it will be enough at this time to say that Mr. Riggs has created effective drama out of the simplest and seemingly unpromising materials. The plot is extremely conventional and it might also be said that the characters are too, only that would imply conventionality of treatment. So let me say that while he has used characters that would in the hands of almost any other playwright seem conventional, he has nevertheless made them into real people. This was simply because he has been able to look at things with the clear eye of the artist.

One word about the singing interludes. Some of these most assuredly interrupt the action, and Mr. Riggs has been criticized by a few of the reviewers for killing his suspense after the third scene. This is one of the things I particularly like, because in the conventional sense, Green Grow the Lilacs is not a play with continuous interest in the action. In lowering his curtain and bringing out the cowboys and farm girls to sing their lovely ballads, Mr. Riggs says in effect, "Don't get too interested in the story, because this is not a story play." The play, of course, has its conventions, just as opera or symphonic music or the sonnet each has its conventions. The interludes are therefore in one sense a proclamation to the effect that the whole thing is to be regarded in the light of an art form with its own peculiar limitations.

So my report on this play is that Mr. Riggs has given us not only a glamorous and tender drama but made it possible for this kind of play not only to be produced but to be accepted by a large theatre-going public.

The Guild's production left little to be desired. It is to the credit of this organization that it saw in Mr. Riggs' script something well worth doing, and that it spared no pains to reveal in detail precisely what Mr. Riggs was aiming at.

> --Barrett H. Clark in The Drama Magazine, Vol. 21, No. 6 (March 1931), pages 11-12.

GUYS AND DOLLS (Music and Lyrics by Frank Loesser, Book by Jo Swerling, based on a story and characters by Damon Runyon; 46th Street Theatre, November 24, 1950)

Guys and Dolls is the kind of a show that frustrates your efforts to communicate your own pleasure with it. You are so eager to convince people of its real superiority to the average musical success that you start throwing superlatives around (Leonard Lyons has simply collapsed and called it the best musical comedy he ever saw) and with each superlative you realize that you are falsifying the actual quality of the show and gaining less and less conviction. The trouble is that, as a show, Guys and Dolls was too easy to anticipate. Damon Runyon's short stories would obviously make a likely book for a musical. The title was a natural. The show would be boisterous, slangy, and sentimentally tough. So it's a hit. What else?

Well, it might have been a lot else. It might have been hard, funny, and completely manufactured. It might have traded on sentiment about Runyon rather than sentiment about the characters. It might have been a hash of Runyon trademarks with just enough reminiscent humor, together with a couple of sock numbers, to get it across. But George Kaufman is back in form and he has put together a show that shows no signs whatsoever of having been put together.

Integration is a terrible word when applied to musical comedy. It usually means dream ballets and not very much humor. But if there is a virtue in the word, Guys and Dolls has it. Story, music,

and dances are all of a piece and, what is so rare as to be unbelievable, equally delightful. I suppose the book is the biggest surprise. Written by Jo Swerling and Abe Burrows under Kaufman's
direction, it is interesting in its own right, very funny, touching
when it should be, and never leaves you impatiently waiting for the
songs. The songs, when you get to them, are just as good. Frank
Loesser seems to me the most interesting of the newer composers
for musical comedy. He draws on his background in folk music without being self-conscious or purist about it, and there is no purist
like a folk purist. He makes use of his knowledge of serious music
to freshen the forms which popular music may take, without for-
getting that he is committed to writing popular music. And even as
he is keeping himself within the boundaries of Tin Pan Alley, he is
writing with both eyes on the show rather than on sheet-music sales.
Add to this the fact that he writes excellent lyrics, and it may be
necessary to pause for a moment while we admire Mr. Loesser.

Even when you grant that the show is integrated, that its book
has an internal logic worthy of a straight play, and that its score
is just about perfect, you still haven't explained the spontaneous and
unexpected charm which wins you over approximately one minute after
the curtain goes up and keeps you sitting there, happier and happier,
until eleven o'clock. This, I think, must finally be laid to George
Kaufman, who has directed a good company with such honesty and--
strange word for the surroundings--innocence, that you feel friendly
and paternalistic about the whole bunch all night.

If, apart from its tremendous entertainment value, Guys and
Dolls makes any contribution to musical comedy form, it is this:
where Rodgers and Hammerstein's advances have been leading them
into an increasing seriousness bordering on operetta, a consequent
abandonment of some musical properties (such as dance in South Pacific) and a tendency toward remote romantic locales, Guys and Dolls
dumps the whole thing back into the vernacular without losing a
single one of the gains.

                              --Walter Kerr in The Commonweal,
                                Vol. 53, No. 10 (December 15,
                                1950), pages 252-253.

                         *   *   *

Damon Runyon, who used to sit so far back and take so many
theatrical first-nights on his quiet chin, should have lived to be at
this one. This musical, I mean, which they've made out of his
menagerie of human weirdies, his steel-girdered and concrete hunting-
ground of hippo-sized buses, cannibal taxis and blazing billboards,
his own Broadway. He'd have loved it.

Everybody within either subway or airplane distance must love
it, too. Because they, its composer, its book-makers, ballet-stager,
settings-and-costumes designers, have all done a mighty Main Stem

job. So has its director-in-chief, George S. Kaufman. We haven't
had a brighter, brisker super-spoof hereabouts since the days when
Mr. Kaufman himself used to write them.

There's a special attraction, though, to these Runyon Funda-
dors whom you'll now find cavorting, crap-gaming and ballading
around the stage. They've been sieved through so many printed
stories and successful pictures, sure. Yet they come out not only
as fresh as ever, but even with an added coating of nostalgia on
them.

Damon's present Pythiases were Jo Swerling and Abe Burrows.
These learned gentlemen, guys to you, have triphammered the plot,
which is neither too big nor too little, too rowdy or too rare, out
like this:

Nathan Detroit, hero A, has a doll in a night-club. Sky Mas-
terson, hero B, has to find his in a Save-a-Soul Mission. Except
for one short, lurid laugh-flight to Havana, plus a stunning climax
for bones-rollers down in the nether reaches of the city sewers, it
all happens there--in the night-club, the mission, the mist-snaking
sidestreets, the grubby-made-magical kiosks and crowds of Times
Square. It may be only an opera-boop version of that old yarn of
"Salvation Nell" they've caught, but they've certainly caught it on
the roar.

The book is but half of it, nor the better half, necessarily.
Frank Loesser lets nobody's ears down with his tunes and lyrics.
He starts right off on a "Fugue for Tinhorns" which sets the key
for all his fresh goods to follow. He's fine at such burlesque numbers as "Take Back Your Mink." He has a bell-song to beat Lakme's.
This is an even happier score than he did for Where's Charlie?,
and that, to my way of remembering, is talking tops.

The cast? It's a large one, an entirely likable one. It looks
well, talks smart, and sings with more than its Adams-apples. There
are Robert Alda, Vivian Blaine and Sam Levene topping it, along
with a winsome newcomer named Isabel Bigley. Netta Packer and Pat
Rooney, Sr., bring in pleasant notes from yesteryear. B.S. Pully,
Stubby Kaye, Tom Pedi, Johnny Silver are all famous italic types,
right out of Runyon. The assembly of girls could have come from
Mahomet's idea of heaven, but would obviously rather remain here in
Runyonland--and so will you.

> --Gibert W. Gabriel in Cue, Vol.
> 19, No. 49 (December 9, 1950),
> page 20.

HAMLET (William Shakespeare; St. James Theatre, October 12, 1938)

Broadway's most exciting play of the moment is Maurice Evans'
production of Hamlet in its entirety. Of that there can be no doubt.
All those who suspected Mr. Evans of exceeding rashness in undertaking this rôle so soon after Gielgud's spirited performance have
seen their fears calmly dispelled and their values proportionately re-
estimated. The Hamlet of Maurice Evans has overnight become the
measuring-stick by which all latter-day Hamlets will be judged.

Playing the whole works may be hard on the performing actors,
but it is wonderfully easy on the audience. A performance of the
uncut version simplifies matters that had hitherto been not a little
hazy. I've often wondered how this play must seem to one who had
not previously read it. Certainly anyone interested in getting the
full enjoyment of the stage performance has usually had to read the
text carefully before seeing the play, for the machinations of the plot
are basely confused in the wholesale cutting of lines. When those
lines are left intact, the play is not only clarified but its pace is
magically speeded. The hours from 6:30 p.m. to 11:30 p.m. fairly
whirl by, and the only time that seems slow in passing is the dinner-
hour intermission.

Wisely, too, neither Maurice Evans nor Margaret Webster, his
director, are attempting to propound any academic theories. They
are interested primarily in playing the play for its drama. Hamlet
was the greatest of the Elizabethan tragedies of revenge. The Elizabethan audience, like any audience, delighted in blood-and-thunder
stuff. Murder, revenge, insanity, and a ghost that stalked the
palace battlements was just what their vivid imaginations most craved.
The blood-stained melodramas of the Elizabethan theater featured one
of three possible revenge motifs: private, public, or divine vengeance. In Hamlet Shakespeare combined those three motifs in magnificent cumulative fashion. Disregarding the incomparable beauty
of the poetry with which he cloaked the design of his play, he turned
out in Hamlet the theater's most sure-fire melodrama. And that is
exactly the element which Mr. Evans and Miss Webster have stressed
in their production.

Mr. Evans has confessed that he wanted to present a play,
not a study of a hero suffering from dyspepsia. "All I knew about
Hamlet," he has said, "was what I had learned from seeing it played
in the theater." With him the play has become the thing, and because of that willingness to give due evaluation to all characters,
his own performance has benefited enormously. His Hamlet has the
simplicity of an allegoric Everyman.

For the first time in this era at least, all the subtly phrased
wit of the play, expressed through the character of Hamlet, has
come to the front. This is a drama of sardonic humor--a veritable
comedy in Dante's more subtle sense of the term. Hamlet was never
so "sicklied o'er with the pale cast of thought" that he could lose
his keen sense of dramatic irony. His wit was sharp and it was

quick, and if there was a sneer in it too, it was because he could
see through the smiles of the king and his court and know them for
the villains they were. Mr. Evans also knows how to read blank
verse, making it at once natural, exciting, and majestic. He gives
full value to the rich poetry of the speeches, but he is never guilty
of making them meaningless. In other words, he may spit, but he
never rants.

Miss Webster and he have been happy in having their production sympathetically and beautifully designed by David Ffolkes, and,
together, they have selected a supporting cast of actors, some of
whom are brilliant and all of whom are competent. The lucid and
eloquent Claudius of Henry Edwards is particularly to be admired,
for Claudius is one of the worst sufferers in the mangled versions
of the play. The Polonius of George Graham is blessed with more
than its usual humor, and the same is true of the droll Grave-Digger
of Whitford Kane. Mady Christians makes Gertrude less of the wan-
ton voluptuary she is usually depicted, but she plays the Closet
Scene with Evans in superb manner. In fact, if one were to pick
the highlight of the evening, that one scene would be it, for it is
shot through with tense excitement and the human anguish of a
mother and son made aware of each other's latent perfidy.

I have saved a special paragraph for Katherine Locke's Ophelia
because it merits exactly that. It is that wonder of wonders, an
intelligent Ophelia! Miss Locke makes the customarily slighted heroine more than merely a doll with a single redeeming mad scene.
There are times, particularly in the beginning, when she betrays the
fact that iambic pantameter is new to her--moments when something
of the Bronxian wistfulness of Teddy Stern from Having Wonderful
Time creeps through--but by the time she has reached the celebrated "Get thee to a nunnery" scene with Hamlet, she has grown
into the part.

All in all, Maurice Evans in Hamlet in its entirety is the living
theater at the best.

--DeWitt Bodeen in Rob Wagner's
Script, Vol. 20, No. 488 (December 17, 1938), pages 20-21.

HAMLET (William Shakespeare; Columbus Circle Theatre, December
13, 1945)

One of the best shows on Broadway these nights is Hamlet in
the so-called G.I. version which Maurice Evans cooked up for the
Army out in the Central Pacific. Better in every way than the uncut, conventional production which Evans made for us here about
four years ago, this presentation by Michael Todd at the Columbus

Circle Theater is exciting melodrama with a pretty well balanced cast
and the star himself a better actor than he has ever before shown
himself to be on these shores.

The costuming by Irene Sharaff is nineteenth century, which
is still romantic enough for the gentlemen and attractive for the
ladies. There are bright uniforms for the king, courtiers and
soldiers, and there is even a special waltz composed by Roger Adams.
Staging is by George Schaefer, a former technical sergeant with Major Evans--as he was then--in the Pacific.

Perhaps our best male reader of Shakespeare, Evans, nevertheless, has a weak voice, which he pushes too hard. As a result,
he has been missing from the cast with laryngitis for several performances, just as he was while doing his Richard II a few years
ago. "Missing from the cast," in the case of Evans, of course,
means that there are no performances until he returns.

Hamlet, G.I. style, is a rather excitable young man, bent on
revenge for his father's murder. Gone is the poet and dreamer,
and in his place one beholds a man of the world, tough and only
occasionally hesitant. All the way through, the play is engrossing.
Only at the end does the star throw away what for me is the high
spot--the famous duel and death scene. In the fight with Laertes,
purposeless and absurd gymnastics clutter it up, while the death
scene is artificial and hammy. Hamlet's death is written in operatic
tragedy; perhaps it cannot be played simply, but certainly it needs
no exaggerations. Feeling that G.I.'s would never accept the
"corny" gravedigger scene, Evans ripped it out of his stage script.

Thomas Gomez makes a dignified King Claudius, not especially
worried by the behavior of Hamlet. Thomas Chalmers, as Polonius,
contributes an excellent characterization of an old fuddy-duddy which
combines reality with amusement. Frances Reid, an alumna of the
Pasadena Playhouse, gives a new interpretation to Ophelia that fits
the modern handling of the play. Walter Coy is Horatio and Lili
Darvas (Mrs. Ferenc Molnar) is a capable, though foreign Queen
Gertrude.

> --Russell Rhodes in Rob Wagner's
> Script, Vol. 32, No. 721 (Janu-
> ary 19, 1946), page 24.

HAMLET (William Shakespeare; Empire Theatre, October 8, 1936)

After the curtain has been up five minutes at the Empire it becomes excitingly obvious that you are face to face with a fine Hamlet.
John Gielgud's interpretation of the stormy young man of Denmark is
splendidly conceived and brilliantly carried through to the inevitable

climax. It is an intellectual portrait, a strong, vibrant Hamlet, exceedingly bitter, bent indomitably on revenge. But Mr. Gielgud always seems an Englishman, direct, forceful, without recourse to Freud. He is a very nice fellow, indeed, puzzled, ever a thoughtful, pondering gentleman. Because of that his Hamlet is a more quiet, considered person than the passionate avenger of the usual portrayal. As such it carries a power of its own; a clearer-singing role, developed on a cleaner line of drama than your declaimer would be inclined to give the part.

Thereby Mr. Gielgud misses much of the glorious poetry of the lines, preferring to argue with himself rather than to intrude passion on the refined mental stage he has made of Elsinore. Lest this should sound as though we have a pedant in our midst, be assured that here is no stilted reading of immortal lines, no library dusting over of the finest drama in the English language. Mr. Gielgud offers us action, quick, clear and thorough. His Hamlet has more in it than is usually seen, more of the Fortinbras story and a little less of many scenes. A few words were cut here and there, a handful of lines (omitted, for instance, was "Something is rotten in the state of Denmark").

The production is by Guthrie McClintic, who is also the director. He has bought from Jo Mielziner some settings which, though superior, are below the fine standard we expect from that distinguished designer. Hamlet deserves only the best. The direction has a varied quality, not knit up with the central character at all times. Some of the players obviously go their own way, getting the richness out of the lines and ignoring the McClintic fetish for physical movement. The imagery is often in the words of the play and all the worried scurrying of actors on missions from wings to wings are of no aid to celerity. The drama compels occasional pauses while its words flow over the mind. A notable departure from tradition uses a twentieth century aid to the Ghost. His words come out of a microphone in tinny sepulchral sounds, a jolting accompaniment to a not too ghostly figure, which had, on the opening night, squeaky shoes. Perhaps we do protest too much but perfection is little enough to ask for Hamlet.

The Polonius of Arthur Byron is a measured piece of acting, rich, juicy and unctuous with the expertness of experience. A fine performance, by a splendid actor. The King of Malcolm Keen is a bulwark of Elizabethan flesh, a ruthless picture compact with proficiency. Judith Anderson's Queen is full-bosomed, constrained in her best scenes by Gielgud's quiet reading of his role. The tempestuous beauty of Miss Anderson is, we understand, a new note in Gertrudes, embodying the physical charms so necessary to make clear the incestuous nature of her union with Claudius. By the time most actresses are ready to play this role, time has conspired against them in all but technical skill.

For the rest, we did not care too much for the Ophelia of
Lillian Gish--but what actress can lend complete conviction to that
daffy role? It is probably an impossible task, although we prefer
the performance of Celia Johnson in the Bel Geddes version, three
or four years ago. Horatio is played by Harry Andrews who acquits
himself excellently in the few lines given him by Shakespeare. John
Emery is a fiery and hysterical Laertes, very fine in his duels.

For the others, there is nothing but praise, with small cavil-
lings here and there, to be expected by any player who essays a
role in Hamlet, even in such a generally fine one as this.

> --Herbert Drake in Cue, Vol. 4,
> No. 51 (October 17, 1936), pages
> 14-15.

HAMLET (William Shakespeare; Imperial Theatre, November 10, 1936)

Because Leslie Howard seemingly has a holy horror of "sawing
the air: and "tearing a passion to tatters" in the good old traditional
Shakespearean style, his performance of Hamlet gave the critics a
severe jolt. They, in turn, gave him an unmerciful drubbing. Gielgud's Hamlet, preceding Howard's by a few weeks, had brought forth
unanimous paeans of praise, so of course comparisons were obvious.
And the critics made them very odious; downright sadistic and un-
civilized. Conduct deplorably unfair, for actually Mr. Howard's fine
intelligence has given us a production almost sublime in perception
and beauty. To see it is one of the exciting privileges of our the-
ater--and I believe that is still an understatement.

Fortunately the public has rallied to his support. Each night
the curtain descends on applause so thunderous that Mr. Howard, in
a simple speech of gratitude, thanks the audience for "this recom-
pense for the suffering." But make no mistake; the audience knows
that the gratitude is theirs, that they are the beneficiaries. The
gesture of attendance may be given in a spirit of sportsmanship "to
help a distinguished artist, who has taken a licking, carry on," and
"because I like Leslie Howard,"--as I have heard a number of persons say--but they come away filled with genuine enthusiasm for his
enrichment of a glorious work. He has surrounded himself with an
excellent cast (the Polonius of Aubrey Mather being a particularly
joyous and satisfying interpretation), and Stewart Chaney has given
it an eleventh-century setting which for taste and beauty is incomparable. Virgil Thompson has composed some pleasing incidental music. Agnes de Mille's mime of the Players' scene is delightful and
unusual. The whole is colorful and brilliant, and Mr. Chaney's particular triumph is the magnificent prow of an old ship with which he
fills the stage in one scene. Comedy scenes are high-lighted and
tragic scenes subdued. It's a good show even when Hamlet jabs his

sword into mischievous old Polonius' embonpoint, abruptly curtailing
his eavesdropping. And it's grand theater when the last, murderous
scene resembles a current battle in Spain. They've done mighty well
by Mr. Shakespeare.

Leslie Howard is best in the comedy scenes. Here he plays
lightly, with grace and finesse. A successful Hamlet must have a
subtle sense of comedy. (Therein lay John Barrymore's success.
May he rest on past laurels!) By nature Hamlet was not a "melan-
choly Dane." He was a joyous young college lad overtaken by tragic
circumstances. But even in deep suffering he was ready with quick
and witty "come-backs," and the scene in which he kids Polonius (it
was kidding then and it's kidding now) into believing he is a bit
cracked, or balmy, is the highest form of sparkling comedy. Howard
and Mather do this superbly.

Leslie Howard, regrettably, is weakest in the soliloquies and
the scene with the Queen Mother. Here he errs on the side of re-
pression. He fails to develop the turbulence traditionally associated
with these emotional passages.

But, no matter. We of this generation--and particularly those
young persons who have only a reading knowledge of Shakespeare,
and will be seeing Hamlet for the first time here and on tour--should
salute Leslie Howard as a fine spirit and sensitive artist.

> --Essey Oppey in Rob Wagner's
> Script, Vol. 16, No. 392 (Decem-
> ber 5, 1936), pages 12-13.

HARVEY (Mary Chase; 48th Street Theatre, November 1, 1944)

We will all now please join in playing Harvey ... all of us, that
is, except those who think that a swig of buttermilk, coke, ginger
ale or such means making whoopee. Playing Harvey consists mainly
in your belief in the game's namesake--a white rabbit, six feet one-
and-a-half inches tall, usually found leaning against a lamp post,
who never speaks to you unless he likes you and then calls you by
your right name. Harvey can stop clocks. You can go away for a
long time and when you come back the clock still says the same time.

I met Harvey the other night. Frank Fay introduced us in a
play called Harvey, dreamed up by Mary Chase and enshrined by
Brock Pemberton at the Forty-Eighth Street Theater. Try to get in
between now and the Fourth of July. I was quite comfortable on the
left prong of a chandelier.

Harvey starts off in the screwiest manner, enough to frighten
anybody who's ever been bitten by a whimsy. But, hold tight; it,
as the saying goes, grows on you.

Elwood P. Dowd, a gentle tosspot who spent his first forty years being smart and then decided it was better to just be pleasant, is a problem to his widowed sister. After making the nightly rounds of several grogshops, he keeps bringing Harvey home with him. Nobody else can see Harvey except Elwood. Sister wants to have Elwood committed to the booby hatch, but the psychiatrist locks her up instead because she admits that once she thinks she saw the rabbit—and she who never took a drop in her life!

Out of what might have been mere farce or, at worst, treacly fantasy, comes an evening of sheer delight in the theater, thanks to an excellent cast and especially to Frank Fay as Dowd and Josephine Hull as his sister. For the remarkable performances of these two, the author and producer should rub Harvey's foot every night in gratitude. Even if he is a pooka. (Look that one up whenever you're talking to Harvey. You won't find it under any other conditions.)

Too long connected with unsuccessful exhumations of vaudeville, Mr. Fay is at last emancipated by a capricious profession to prove that as a master of genuine comedy acting he is second to none. He has that rare touch of casualness and charm that sweeps across the footlights, creating the illusion of close relationship between audience and player that marks a clicking acting job.

Miss Hull, as featured actress, is in equally varied key, surpassing her excellent work as one of the two homicidal old maids in Arsenic and Old Lace and as the looney mother of loonies in You Can't Take it with You.

And now, if you'll excuse me, I have to dash out and buy Harvey a quickie. He and I have an early curtain to make.
                              —Russell Rhodes in Rob Wagner's
                              Script, Vol. 30, No. 694 (De-
                              cember 16, 1944), page 24.

* * *

Harvey, for all its shortcomings, gave me the pleasantest theatrical lift I have had in a long time. The play itself is often wonderfully funny, and occasionally touched with something that goes deeper than fun. Beyond that, it contains two performances that it is difficult—and, for that matter, not at all necessary—to speak temperately of. Josephine Hull is as delightful as only Josephine Hull can be. As for Frank Fay, playing his first straight part since he was a shaver, and playing as tricky and perilous a part as any one could be assigned, he is superb. To say that nobody else could have done it better is to say nothing; so far as I can see, nobody else could have done it at all.

The kind of idea that Harvey rests on has led in the past to

more harrowing evenings than any other kind known to the theater.
For the play deals with nothing other than a man whose constant companion is an imaginary rabbit 6 ft. 1 1/2 in. tall. By every rule of
the game, this would seem to be whimsy with a vengeance. But
Mary Chase has turned it, for the most part, into wackiness with a
verve and flow and ability to fly up and kick the beam that makes
me temporarily tolerant even of leprechauns. She has given something funny to the theater, and something fresh. On that score
she can be forgiven some pretty serious sins--a first act that keeps
going way too long, and a last act that, in a sense, can't keep going
at all.

Elwood P. Dowd, an old bachelor given to sociable drinking,
has traded the reality of the world, which irked him, for the reality
of a rabbit; and he has no regrets. But for his widowed sister and
her eligible if elongated daughter Myrtle Mae, Elwood's companion
has its distinct social embarrassments; and driven once too often,
Sister decides it is time to enroll Elwood in a sanatorium. Sister,
who isn't so unlike Elwood that she hasn't had glimpses of Harvey
the Hare herself, winds up being confined in place of her brother.
From then on, madness really takes over, reaching its height during
an excellent second act.

What is specially good about so frequently funny a yarn is
that it carries out the classic theme of humorists that in wackiness
lies the greatest wisdom and the truest happiness. En route, also,
Miss Chase finds time to spoof the psychiatrists. But her best job
is her creation of Elwood himself.

Elwood, as Frank Fay plays him--timing everything faultlessly,
and giving his screwiness the effect of drollery--is immense. Mr.
Fay's job is a tightrope walk over Niagara, in which one false move
could easily be fatal. But every move is right, and a few seem magical. There is a long scene at the end of the second act where Elwood, questioned by the psychiatrist, talks about himself and Harvey, and sometimes only sits and looks. It introduces a new and
dangerous mood, and it could be awful. Somehow Fay manages to
transfix the audience and touch them.

All this is not to slight Miss Hull. Her performance is delight-
ful, but it is easier. And as the gangling, beau-barren Myrtle Mae,
Jane Van Duser does a good job too. In view of all this, Antoinette
Perry obviously deserves credit for her direction.

Harvey, as aforesaid, has its decided weaknesses, and it's not
for the literal-minded. But on a Broadway so given to staleness, it
is so refreshing as to make one hope one really did see Harvey
Wednesday night--and not just Harvey.
                                    --Louis Kronenberger in PM (No-
                                         vember 2, 1944).

THE HASTY HEART (John Patrick; Hudson Theatre, January 3, 1945)

On furlough back home from the American Field Service with
the British Eighth Army in Africa, Italy and the East, Captain John
Patrick turned out a honey of a play, called The Hasty Heart, which
Howard Lindsay and Russel Crouse are presenting to packed houses
in their newly acquired Hudson Theater.

From an old Scotch proverb, "Sorrow is born in the hasty
heart," comes the title. It is the story of a dour sergeant in the
Cameron Highlanders turned loose in a convalescent ward of a British general hospital behind the Assam-Burma front. A kindly medical officer didn't tell Lachlen MacLachlen that he was doomed to die
within a month or six weeks. He felt the lad should have his last
days cheered by a goodly company of men.

In the ward are an American, a cockney, an Australian, a
New Zealander and an African tribesman who can't speak or understand English. The men are advised by the colonel that their job
is to keep the Scot happy. But it turns out a pretty tough assignment.

MacLachlen hates the world and all in it. He insults his new
friends and rebuffs their attempts at cordiality. In fact, for most
of the time I wouldn't have blamed their ganging up on him and
tearing him to pieces. The attendant nurse arranges a birthday
party for the new patient in which the men give him a smart highland uniform, complete with kilt. This breaks through to the sentiment in the heart of every Celt and MacLachlen softens up.

All is well until the colonel, according to military code, has
to tell the Scot the truth and offers him the choice of staying at the
hospital or a flight back to Scotland for the time left him. En-
raged at the idea of men being kind to him, as he thinks, through
pity, MacLachlen turns on his friends. This is about the last straw
for the American who bawls him out in just about the choicest tongue-
lashing you'd want to hear.

The stubborn Scot with his leave papers in his hand, drags
his duffle bag toward the waiting plane. Realizing how he has hurt
real friends, however, he has to jump probably his greatest hurdle
and, for the first time in his life, admits he was wrong.

Capt. Patrick has handled the theme extremely well, balancing
humor and pathos neatly. I am very much afraid, however, that he
has pictured his central character with too straight strokes at the
danger of losing all sympathy for him. The Scotch are a reticent
race, assuming a gruff manner to protect them from intrusions on
their privacy. I have known many both in this country and on their
native heath. But I doubt strongly that anybody would give a hoot
for them if Lachlen MacLachlen is typical.

An odd thing about the cast is that, with the exception of J. Colvin Dunn, each of the actors playing British parts is American and, therefore, their accents are phoney to acute ears. Richard Baseheart (Lachlen) is out of Zanesville, Ohio. He does a pretty good job of Scotch brogue and burr, but it would never fool a studious observer as anything but counterfeit. The Scottish accent is probably the most difficult to assume in the world.

By the way, remember when all the best parts on the American stage were being played by Englishmen? Lots of Americans can imitate a British accent and fool producers, but if they told the truth to managers and admitted American birth, they lost their jobs, The Hasty Heart is turnabout and, probably, fair play.

One of the best performances is that by John Lund as the Yank, a thoroughly believable and refreshing impersonation.

> --Russell Rhodes in Rob Wagner's Script, Vol. 31, No. 697 (February 3, 1945), page 10.

* * *

The Hasty Heart is an interesting and now and then compelling piece of theater that gets 1945 off to a nice start. But though I enjoyed the play and think many other people will also, I can only regret that Mr. Patrick--by too often succumbing to the obvious and the sentimental--let slip the chance to write something of far larger stature. For The Hasty Heart provides a familiar theme with not only a timely setting and a special circumstance; it also takes an unfamiliar turn, it also has the opportunity to achieve a higher than usual level. As it is, what might have been an ironic human tragedy has been sheared away to nothing beyond effective popular theater.

The play concerns a young Scots soldier who--unaware that he has but a short time to live--is brought into a British convalescent ward in Burma. Having fought for everything he has got in life, he is sore at the world; and being consumed with terrific defensive pride, he is surly and distrustful toward every one he meets. The men in the ward, and the ward nurse, knowing Lachlen's fate, do everything they can--in spite of his behavior--to be friendly. Only after many rebuffs and mighty efforts do they win him over. Won over, he exults in the friendship he has always craved. Then his Colonel is compelled by Army regulations to tell him of his real condition. In a flash Lachlen grasps that all this friendliness has sprung from pity; his pride reasserts itself, and he bitterly slams the door on his companions. But in The Hasty Heart it once again reopens.

One knows that it will--for the whole tone of the play premises a sentimental rather than tragic ending; indeed, the play itself revels in all of its sentimental opportunities, and even the character of Lachlen is projected for its theater values rather than its really hu-

man ones. Though you instantly guess his loneliness and stubborn
pride, Lachlen is introduced as almost a freak, and for quite a while
permitted to display his misanthropy in stock joke-book Scotch terms
of thrift, opinionativeness, and contempt for all other nations. It
is the pathos of his fate and the reality of his type, rather than the
character itself, that give Lachlen his human appeal.

And since Mr. Patrick fails to characterize Lachlen with any
unusual perceptiveness, it is no surprise that he cannot face up to
the tragic implications in the Colonel's disclosure; that he refuses to
throw Lachlen back on himself, the victim of his own character and
the senseless cruelty of life; and the more tragic a victim from
being plunged back into the wilderness after reaching the Promised
Land. Though Lachlen is brought round in the end with some
plausibility, all the real sinew goes out of the story; and the
Colonel's disclosure, instead of effecting a termination, becomes
merely a dramatic device to stretch out the story. Certainly audiences, almost to a man, will prefer Mr. Patrick's ending; but all
the same The Hasty Heart has in it the seeds of a much bigger play.

What, in addition to the interest in its story, makes The Hasty
Heart attractive is its background. Lachlen's ward-mates--a Yank,
a Tommy, a Negro colonial, an Aussie and a New Zealander--are
lively and colorful stage people. Their talk has a natural ring to it;
their humor, even its very lameness at times, springs out of themselves; their attitude toward Lachlen, their pranks and their kidding, have something human about them. They are much better
soldiers than the theater generally provides us with.

The production also has considerable merit. Bretaigne Windust
has given the play life, color and movement, and brought the acting
--itself uneven--into some kind of unity. Richard Basehart, given
the limits of Mr. Patrick's characterization, makes a very good Lachlen. John Lund makes an extraordinarily good American; and John
Campbell, Earl Jones, Victor Chapin and Douglas Chandler are all
adequate or better as the other soldiers. As the nurse, Anne Burr,
though rather lacking in flexibility, is generally effective. Raymond
Sovey has designed an attractive and serviceable set.
                                    --Louis Kronenberger in PM (Janu-
                                      ary 4, 1945).

THE HEIRESS (Ruth and Augustus Goetz; Biltmore Theatre, Septem-
     ber 29, 1947)

September was a rather barren month in the theatrical world,
bringing only five productions, two of which were too puny to survive critical disapproval and public indifference. The last four days
of the month, however, brought along with them three specimens of

respectable drama: Our Lan', reviewed here last week, The Heiress
and How I Wonder. Broadway clairvoyants are predicting that the
second of the trio, The Heiress, will go into the record as the season's first hit.

Borrowed by Ruth and Augustus Goetz from Henry James' novel, Washington Square, The Heiress is certainly a delectable theatre
piece. The title character is a rich young woman whose father, disappointed because she falls short of his ideal of a young lady of
fashion, continually harps on her lack of social poise. The more he
badgers her, of course, the more self-conscious and awkward she
becomes, a sitting duck for the first itinerant fortune-hunter willing
to flatter her stunted ego. A gentleman with a nose for money appears quickly enough, and the girl succumbs to his blandishments,
but her father, while caring little for his daughter's happiness, is
determined that her inheritance shall not fall into prodigal hands.

As presented in The Biltmore by Fred F. Finklehoffe, with
Basil Rathbone and Wendy Hiller starred in the leading roles as
father and daughter, The Heiress is a conflict of interests and emotions that never lets down or deteriorates into sentimentality, but
marches forward toward a logical conclusion with the inevitability of
taxes. Miss Hiller is brilliant as the suppressed daughter and Mr.
Rathbone shines as the austere father, which is fortunate for them;
otherwise Patricia Collinge, coming up with her usual sparkling performance in a secondary role, would steal the show.
                                    --Theophilus Lewis in America
                                       (October 18, 1947), page 82.

                          *   *   *

If a literate evening in the theatre is your dish you will like
The Heiress but don't fritter it away as an incidental entree in an
entertainment menu that begins with three cocktail parties and ends
at the Stork Club. In it the spacious, leisurely and circumlocutory
world of Henry James has been recreated by Ruth and Augustus
Goetz to whom it was suggested by James' short novel Washington
Square and the result is good news in the theatre.

The Heiress, like an inhaler of old brandy is something to be
slowly savored. Character is gradually but thoroughly developed
and although the entire action takes place in the drawing-room of a
dignified residence on Washington Square in the circumspect 1850's
it frequently mounts to moments of dramatic intensity, never sacri-
fices reality for melodrama. The situation is anything but new. A
wealthy ugly duckling is wooed by a charming heel, her father op-
poses the match. It's as simple as that but on this slender framework Mr. James and his adapters have woven a fascinating web of
subtlety and nuance that is penetratingly interpreted by the skillful
performers who have been assembled for the New York production.
Wendy Hiller, as the woman who wants to be loved for herself, Basil

Rathbone as the father who thinks he is acting for her own good,
Peter Cookson as the engaging rotter and Patricia Collinge as the
concupiscent aunt all create characters whose timeless humanity in
no way depends on the elaborate Victorian trappings of the play.
This after all is the difference between contrived trumpery and genuine theatre.

>   --Thomas Brailsford Felder in Cue,
>   Vol. 16, No. 41 (October 11,
>   1947), pages 17-18.

HELLZAPOPPIN (Ole Olson and Chic Johnson; 46th Street Theatre,
    September 22, 1938)

    ACTING--Olsen and Johnson, ex-vaudeville headliners, have
little to offer in their revue other than routine capability. Vul-
garity is part of their stock of tricks. They are surrounded with
dancers; singers, and a flock of quaint artists who do almost everything but train seals. Hardeen, brother of Houdini, practices
legerdemain; Walter Nilsson rides on an odd assortment of bicycles
and unicycles; Hal Sherman is a comic dancer; Bettymae and Beverly
Crane stand out as a dance team; Billy Adams does some nice tap-
ping; Barto and Mann are effective acrobatic dancers; the Char-
ioteers offer good singing.

    PRODUCTION--Hellzapoppin is without doubt the noisiest pro-
duction ever to assault the ear drums. Likewise it is the most
spraddled out contrivance ever to rattle around in a theater. Performers bob out of seats, rush up and down the aisles, scream at
the people on the stage from boxes and balcony. When you leave
the theater you have to search your pockets to be sure that you are
not taking some of the show home with you.

    The sets are nothing much and the lighting is bright.

    CUE SAYS--There are moments when you wish someone would
come in and spray a hose on the joking to clean it up. Other times
you are bored. And at other times you rock in your seat as the
bombardment of low comedy hits you from all angles. What goes on
offstage is largely very funny indeed. If you like the kick-in-the-
pants school of humor, go to Hellzapoppin. Otherwise steer clear.

>   --Oliver Claxton in Cue, Vol. 6,
>   No. 49 (October 1, 1938), page
>   11.

HIGH BUTTON SHOES (Book by Stephen Longstreet, Music and Lyr-
    ics by Jule Styne and Sammy Cahn; Century Theatre, October
    9, 1947)

For a musical that's not very good, High Button Shoes is a
very good musical indeed. Some of it is wonderful, much of it is
gay, and the rest has the merit of being bad without being boring.
It's an upsy-downsy evening, but certainly as much sky as swamp;
and if you'll frankly accept it for better or worse, I think you'll
enjoy yourself. I did. I've seen shows with twice as much class
that weren't half as much fun.

Delving into the past, as has every show this week, High Button Shoes turns up in New Brunswick, N.J., in 1913. Thither
comes Phil Silvers as a rather harassed conman; and there he and
his stooge, Joey Faye, start some spangled real-estate operations
that implicate one of the most respected families in the town. Since
Rutgers is also in New Brunswick, Rutgers is also in the show--as
a place where football is played and romance is popular.

An amiably uninspired book provides Mr. Silvers, who can be
a very funny fellow, with about an equal number of opportunities
and obstacles. When the book is doing right by him, Mr. Silvers is
a riot; and when it isn't, Mr. Silvers--like most of his brethren in
the business--sweats to little avail. Joey Faye, I fear spends most
of the evening as merely a likeable tag-along; but on the other hand
Nanette Fabray, who has always been entitled to get by on her looks
alone, emerges in High Button Shoes as a real and thoroughly viva-
cious personality, of great use in song, dance and story. She is
one reason why the show so often is gay.

But Jerome Robbins is the reason why the show at its best is
wonderful. He has created a Mack Sennett ballet, a period fandango
of bathing beauties and Atlantic City bath-houses, of Keystone cops
and robbers and all the rest, which as it keeps gaining in speed
and growing in size and gyrating in all directions, becomes one of
the comic glories of the age. Mr. Robbins has a hand in the show's
No. 2 exhibit as well, a delightful song-and-dance number called
"Papa, Won't You Dance With Me?" wherein Miss Fabray and Jack
McCauley do some fine period whirling.

Beyond this show-stopper, Mr. Styne's score is pleasantly un-
sensational--or somewhat better than Mr. Cahn's lyrics, which are
agreeably third-rate. But Mr. Abbott has staged the proceedings
with a tonic and cheerful air, and the cast works as though it likes
what it is doing. What I think High Button Shoes most needed was
more time, rather than more talent; some things in it are straight-
out lousy, but others look as if they just weren't allowed to come to
a boil. If they had been---; but the show's worth seeing, as it
stands, for what Mr. Robbins has to offer alone.
                                    --Louis Kronenberger in PM (Octo-
                                      ber 12, 1947).

* * *

There are a good many moments of high hilarity in this brassy musical recreation of life in 1913, notably a Mack Sennett Ballet in which the bathing beauties of yesteryear, the Keystone cops and all the other impediments of film fun in the World War I period including a large gorilla come amusingly to life. Phil Silvers is the star of the show and is fairly omnipresent. All of which means that if you like Phil Silvers you'll probably like High Button Shoes.

The music and lyrics, by Jule Styne and Sammy Cahn, are of the loud bouncey variety to match the energetic capers of the cast. The book concerns a slick operator (played by Mr. Silvers) on the loose in and around the Rutgers campus, Atlantic City and elsewhere. Nanette Fabray, to our mind one of the more engaging soubrettes currently to be seen on the musical stage, puts over her songs with considerable charm.

Ballet's Jerome Robbins (Fancy Free, On the Town, etc.) has provided dances that are artistic without being arty. Mark Dawson makes a personable and convincing juvenile lead as a singing football hero. Other capable contributors to the good-humored goings-on are Jack McCauley, Joey Faye, Lois Lee.

High Button Shoes, though hardly the greatest musical ever to reach Broadway, is genial, slapstick fun much of the time.
                                        --Thomas Brailsford Felder in Cue,
                                            Vol. 16, No. 42 (October 18,
                                            1947), page 21.

HILDA CRANE (Samson Raphaelson; Coronet Theatre, November 1, 1950)

In at least one notable respect, Samson Raphaelson's Hilda Crane brings the drama of Ibsen full circle. The Ibsen heroine, whether in the Norwegian's own plays or in those of his imitators, was a rebel against the conventional social code, particularly as it defined her role as wife and mother. When the restrictions imposed upon her became intolerable, she was likely to assert her freedom and bring down the third-act curtain by committing suicide. Hilda Crane, heroine of Mr. Raphaelson's play, finds herself in revolt against all the freedoms which the Ibsen girl finally won. Wanting only to be a wife and mother, and discovering that too many freedoms have made this impractical, she asserts her conventional femininity and brings down the third-act curtain by committing suicide.

In some ways this is a cheerful note. It may be that we are through with the underprivileged woman, and are ready to take up the underprivileged man. It may mean that, as husbands, we are coming to a time when we can stop throwing our used socks into

wastebaskets and turn them over to wives who really yearn to mend
them. I doubt it, but Mr. Raphaelson thinks we may hope. At
the very least, if we are in future to be spared Hedda and the vine
leaves and Nora and the check-book, our evenings in the theatre
may become more bearable.

It would be even more encouraging to report that the form,
as well as the content, of the Ibsen-style play had undergone a
change. But in every other respect Hilda Crane remains pure Ibsen.
Here is the same careful but earthbound prose. Here is the same
attention to a social problem rather than to persons, or to an action
for the sake of its own interest. And here, above all, is the effort
to write tragedy without the conditions of tragedy being present.

Hilda Crane, like the Ibsen heroines, is the victim of environ-
mental pressures, rather than of any failure within herself. It is
Mr. Raphaelson's point that society now pushes its well-meaning wom-
en into the full use of their freedoms, and so denies them the unified and productive life they might have had in a valid and lasting
marriage. But society is the villain, as it always was with Ibsen.
Hilda is no more responsible for her own plight than Nora or Hedda
or Mrs. Alving were. And tragedy is unthinkable without personal
responsibility. It is always a matter of self-destruction, rather than
destruction by impersonal forces over which one has no control.
When the victim is wiped out by a purely external force, whether it
be a social pressure or a careening truck, the result is pathetic,
not tragic. Mr. Raphaelson has not been able to alter the Ibsen
formula enough to keep Hilda out of that classification.

The result is that the final scene, Hilda's suicide, is too much
for what has gone before. She has not the stature as a person to
put us through the enormity of her final act. She has not been sufficiently responsible for her own failure to make us feel that her
ending is due her, and was inevitable from the beginning. Because
it does not follow from a necessary dramatic logic, the conclusion
of the play is merely depressing, and tends to make us forget some
of the good things which have gone before it.

Actually, the play is a far more than competent example of its
kind. If we are to continue to have the prose problem play, with its
substitution of journalism for poetic insight, Mr. Raphaelson has this
time handled it as well as any. The author does not dawdle over the
exposition of his thesis but keeps the action moving at an absorbing
clip and is able to deliver the necessary big scenes with considerable
impact. With the exception of the last scene, you will probably find
the evening consistently interesting. It is further well directed by
Hume Cronyn and sharply played by a good cast. Jessica Tandy
may have been ill-advised to follow her role in Streetcar with one
having so many surface similarities to it, and she still has not developed an emotional top, but she is attractive and skilful. Frank
Sundstrom is exceptionally good as the libertine who helps destroy

her, and Evelyn Varden does a remarkable job of finding the precisely right tone for an extremely difficult scene. Cast as a dom-
ineering mother-in-law, and having got her share of laughs early in
the play, she is asked, at a climactic moment in the second act, to
feign illness. If the illness is too obviously feigned, it will become
comic and destroy the dramatic tension of the scene. If it is not
feigned at all, but entirely real, it will destroy sympathy for the
heroine who is at that moment giving her a tongue-lashing. Miss
Varden has been able to balance herself between these two pitfalls,
and without underplaying, and the scene becomes a minor triumph
in the art of acting.

You will not be bored at Hilda Crane, even though it falls
short of Mr. Raphaelson's intentions.

--Walter Kerr in The Commonweal,
Vol. 53, No. 7 (November 24,
1950), pages 171-172.

* * *

That beautiful embodiment of shining sorrows, Jessica Tandy,
appears here in what evidently started as a woman's serial, but
ends exceeding grim. She and some others of its dedicated cast
are far and away the brightest things about it. The tears it draws
are still too thickly mixed with soap for a good, lively lather.

Samson Raphaelson wrote it. Mr. Raphaelson has written several successful, several most amusing and companionable plays. Nobody usually knows better than he does how to wed acts one and
three and insure them a happily-ever-after. But now he would very
soberly atone for such easier hits. Now he'll try to scrape away the
surface and show us this tragically mutinous process of a present-
day girl's secret heart, instead. For so serious an intention, so
feelingful in mood and deliberate of motion, let's honor him. But
we'll then have to call his latest work more or less a dud.

His heroine returns home to Winona, Illinois, after two smashed-
up marriages and a Manhattan history of drifting from bed to boredom. She dreams of trying wedded life a third time with a romantic
young professor in the local university. She is shocked by that
disciple of Shelley, however, into a much more prosaic union with one
of those stout, stripe-suited manufacturers who are the pillars of
all Winonas. She does her two-year best to be a model wife and
mother. But the poet-professor comes back, sighs and conquers.
She spends a single happy, if tawdry, night with him and straight-
way solves everything--to Mr. Raphaelson's satisfaction, anyway--
by taking a lethal dose of sleeping pills.

All this in an atmosphere which the author strives to keep
conscientiously ordinary, in a convocation of kith and kin who, despite his fidelity to their petty commonplaces, seldom ring true. All

this with a wording which never even grazes the border of such beguiling stuff as Tennessee Williams'. And that comparison must be made. For Raphaelson's play has plenty of the same plot, same people, as Streetcar had. It has them dunked in prose.

Miss Tandy, directed by Hume Cronyn in the bosom of the family, gives the piece whatever distinctive stir it can sometimes summon. She is made wholly of warm light, this moving and lovely young actress. The manufacturer John Alexander, is sincerity itself, about two hundred pounds of it, and altogether good. The lover, Frank Sundstrom, slinks and quotes as intelligently as the text allows. Beulah Bondi and Evelyn Varden are back, presenting the older generation's arguments with large authority ... and seeming almost to bay for deeper, bigger things to say.

Here and there, yes, a scene of it manages to drip a certain pity. Yet the source of that moisture still looks like a microphone, not a truly troubled human soul.

> --Gilbert W. Gabriel in Cue, Vol.
> 19, No. 45 (November 11, 1950),
> page 22.

I REMEMBER MAMA (John Van Druten; Music Box Theatre, October 19, 1944)

Whether or not you've checked Oklahoma!, The Voice of the Turtle or Carmen Jones off your list of theater musts, grab a pad and pencil right now and beg the management at the Music Box to give you a peek at I Remember Mama. By special invitation of Richard Rodgers and Oscar Hammerstein, 2nd, I was there opening night. This is one of those slick jobs that John van Druten, who authored Turtle for Margaret Sullavan, turned out as an adaptation between original works.

Based on Kathryn Forbes's little-known novel, Mama's Bank Account, I Remember Mama is about a Norwegian immigrant family in San Francisco at the turn of the century. Papa is a carpenter who hands over his wages every week for Mama to budget. One of the daughters keeps a diary and wants to be a writer. Dagmar, the youngest, nurses rabbits and Uncle Elizabeth, a tough tomcat. She also wants a horse in the house and dreams of being a vet when she grows up. The son will be a doctor. An old maid aunt marries the local mortician. Every night an old actor boarder reads Dickens or "The Ancient Mariner" in rolling syllables to the family.

Then there is great-hearted Chris, the "black Norwegian," with a thundering voice to disguise his sentiment and charitable deeds for the poor and deformed, and a clubfoot to make him swear

and drink from a flask. But first of all, there is Mama. She it is,
with a bank account that isn't there, who knits the little family together.

You will see Mama creeping into little Dagmar's hospital room,
when visitors aren't allowed, creeping in on her hands and knees,
pretending to be the scrubwoman; standing up to blustering Chris
and helping him through his last "skol"; trading her mother's brooch
for a celluloid dresser set to give Trina at graduation; curing Uncle
Elizabeth from his alley scars with a mild dose of chloroform: swap-
ping Norwegian recipes with a celebrated novelist in exchange for advice on how Trina may become a great writer. Mama runs everything
with determination and devotion.

First and most distinguished piece of genuine theater in the
new season, this play combines rare and prescient direction by Mr.
van Druten with as perfect ensemble playing as you are likely ever
again to witness. Built on one revolving stage with two small ones
at either side, the sets of George Jenkins by turns show the interior
of Mama's house, the hospital corridor and Uncle Chris's bedroom at
his ranch. By imaginative lighting, the exteriors are sketched in
cross sections which view the streets of San Francisco or the hills
outside the ranch.

It is a thrilling, exciting evening. The performance of Mady
Christians as Mama is a brilliant, thoughtfully worked out characterization through accent and behavior that stamps her as a really great
actress. Oscar Homolka makes Chris her equal in a wide variety of
moods and one especially powerful scene, his best dramatic work
since he came over from England a few years ago.

I Remember Mama has the sustained flow of a placid novel. It
is the work of the theater's most highly endowed artists. As they
say in Mama's family, "Iss good!"

> --Russell Rhodes in Rob Wagner's
> Script, Vol. 30, No. 694 (De-
> cember 16, 1944), page 24.

THE ICEMAN COMETH (Eugene O'Neill; Martin Beck Theatre, October
    9, 1946)

Absent from the world's stage since 1934, Eugene O'Neill, the
only living Olympian aside from George Bernard Shaw, returned to
New York, his native city, two weeks ago with the first performance
of his marathon play, The Iceman Cometh. Already discussion of its
pro's and con's has made lively dinner table battles and, although
the camps of those who like it and those who find it a bore are
sharply marked, majority opinion is in O'Neill's corner, hailing the

play as the absorbing work of a master craftsman and a tonic for
the current American theater.

Although the characters in The Iceman are cloaked in escapism,
nobody can accuse O'Neill of writing an escapist play. It is realism
and a true study of fundamentals in human nature. For another
point, if you insist on escapism for the playgoer, The Iceman is a
welcome relief from such poorly-contrived soap-box haranguing as
Maxwell Anderson's Truckline Cafe, for instance, or any one of the
agitated, one-sided and artistically dishonest plays by so-called
"liberals."

O'Neill's theme, apparently, is that you should never try to
play God and spoil illusions that have made people happy or, at least,
contented.

Reaching back to the youthful days when he was loafing and
drinking on the West Side waterfront of New York between long voy-
ages home from Cardiff and the Caribbees, O'Neill takes you to Harry Hope's Raines Law Hotel of 1912. Characterization of the proprietor and design of the setting are said to be directly inspired by
Jimmy the Priest and the hostelry that O'Neill knew thirty-four years
ago.

Harry Hope's is a last refuge for the drunken, damned men
who live on the rotgut he sells for fifteen cents a shot, and pipe
dreams straight from the bottom of the bottle. Hope humors them
with drinks and rooms they can never pay for. The drinks are
served at all times, in accordance with the Raines' edict, the sole
requirement being that you must have a "prop" sandwich on the table
after closing time.

Bolstered by boozy recollections of their past, the old soaks
flirt with dim hopes of straightening themselves out--tomorrow.
They are a one-time anarchist, now a sideline observer; an ex-
captain in the British infantry, suspected of purloining regimental
funds during the Boer War; a one-time leader of a Boer commando,
charged with desertion; a former proprietor of a Negro gambling
house; a Harvard Law School alumnus, whose father was convicted
of running a bucket shop, now afflicted with the DT's and babbling
of a brilliant career in the District Attorney's office; a has-been
Boer War correspondent, who kids himself that he became a drunk
because of his wife's faithlessness; an anarchist ex-editor; a light-
fingered former circus man; a police lieutenant fired from the force
for graft.

Added to these dregs in humanity's barrel is the night bartender who lives off the earnings of three prostitutes, but insists
that he isn't a pimp, just a business man; the day bartender, who
toys with the idea of marrying one of the streetwalkers; the three
tarts, who object to being called whores; a wild youth who sold his
mother to the police in an I.W.W. bombing.

As the play opens, they've been waiting all night for Hickey,
a hardware salesman, whose custom it is to show up once every year
and throw a party to get them all roaring drunk. Hickey is a card;
he makes them laugh; they can hardly wait till good old Hickey gets
there with his joke about how he left his wife safe at home in the
hay with the iceman. But Hickey arrives cold sober. He buys
champagne for everybody and a cake with candles for Harry's six-
tieth birthday. He cracks a few feeble jokes. But he's not the same
Hickey. He doesn't need the booze any more and he wants to free
the old soaks from their pipe dreams and make them face reality.
Once they've done this, he says, they'll be at peace with the world
the way he is.

Beginnings of a carefree drunken party turn into a wake. Under Hickey's needling banter, the bums grow morose, painfully spruce
up and go outside Harry's saloon for the first time in years to get
their old jobs back and straighten out. Harry himself, once a local
politician, begins the walk around the ward he promised himself after
his wife died twenty years ago.

But one by one, they all return, like poor pooches with their
tails between their legs, as Rocky, the bartender describes it.
They're broken men and they know it for the first time, worse than
they were before, because they've lost their pipe dreams, illusions
of straightening out--tomorrow. Old friends fight each other.
There's no kick in the fifteen-cent rotgut any more. They can't
pass out any more. They all curse Hickey because he's destroyed
their simple contentment.

Then Hickey, in a sixteen-minute speech, reveals his awful
secret. He's shot his wife because he couldn't stand her eternal forgiveness that made him feel such a heel. Now he can face death
(which is the iceman for all of them) with calm. They don't want to
hear his story, say he's crazy. Yes, he says, he must have been
and you feel that he says that because he's sorry for having spoiled
the dreams of his old pals. As Hickey is led away by the cops, the
bums drink up. There's kick in the rotgut now. Of course, Hickey
was talking nonsense. What could you expect from a guy who was
bughouse?

--Russell Rhodes in Script, Vol.
32, No. 741 (October 26, 1946),
page 24.

* * *

The Iceman Cometh would be a better play had it been written
for acting, under the four and a quarter hours it takes. The first
act takes an hour and fifteen minutes. But it is superb and is, in
fact, an excellent one-act play by itself. There is no action, as
such, throughout. It is all talk and some of it is repetitious, but
repetitious in the natural way, if you've ever listened to a stewbum

talk. Its subject matter is treated engrossingly and it is dramatically correct and disturbing to witness.

The important thing, however, is the uncanny craftsmanship
displayed by O'Neill, not only in his characterization, but in his
dialogue. Unquestionably, he is a master of theater. In The Iceman,
he lays bare the mind and soul of human beings to an extraordinary
degree.

One of the great things about O'Neill's plays is that they are
eminently actable. In an interview here he has said that rarely, if
ever, have actors exactly fitted the parts as he originally conceived
them. As I read the play after having seen the performance, I was
acutely aware that this is true. O'Neill describes his characters
with the pains of a fastidious novelist and, visually, some in The
Iceman cast do not quite fit his version.

This is by no means intended as criticism of the actors. Almost without exception, they acquit themselves admirably. Dudley
Digges as Harry Hope is superb, and remarkably fine jobs are turned
in by Carl Benton Reid as the reformed anarchist, Nicholas Joy as
the British captain, Frank Tweddell as the ex-Boer commando, Russell Collins as the former war correspondent, Tom Pedi as the night
bartender, John Marriott as the Negro gambler, Morton L. Stevens
as the old circus man, Paul Crabtree as the renegade who betrayed
his mother, and Ruth Gilbert, Jeanne Cagney and Marcella Markham
as the streetwalkers.

The leading role of Hickey is played by James Barton. It is
an unusually long one and at times seems to be too heavy a burden
for the actor, especially in the last act, when I found it almost impossible to hear him distinctly, as he dropped his voice in a mis-
judged use of variety. He was at his best in the earlier sequences.

In producing The Iceman Cometh, the Theater Guild deserves
the thanks of all true playgoers. The setting by Robert Edmond
Jones captures the atmosphere exactly and Eddie Dowling's direction
aids the mood.

> --Russell Rhodes in Script, Vol.
> 32, No. 742 (November 9, 1946),
> page 25.

* * *

When America's most celebrated dramatist offers his first play
in a dozen years, he may well become the victim of the too high
hopes he raises. But one can have gone to The Iceman Cometh
with more reasonable expectations, and still have come away more
than a little disappointed. Disappointment is relative, of course--as
achievement is; and to say that I do not find The Iceman very impressive is not to imply that a great deal of it is not interesting, is

not individual, is not expert, is not finely theatrical--or that in a theater where mere slickness is too quickly applauded and real seriousness is too seldom apparent, The Iceman is not worth having or seeing. It should be seen. One might well see it for the production alone, which is one of the best integrated in years, with many good performances and with sets by Robert Edmond Jones that are misleadingly simple but supremely right.

But The Iceman leaves me dissatisfied. The commonest objection that will be levied against it--its great length, its often static tone, its often repetitious incident--is not really the most crucial; or if it is, is only so in terms of theater rather than drama. The Iceman is much too long for what it says, but not necessarily for what it might have said. It deals, spaciously by intention, with a great many lives, most of them falling into one group, but three of them standing apart from it. All these need room. But though, in terms of theater, Mr. O'Neill has dealt fruitfully with all his people, in terms of drama he has not; and philosophically his play is more long-windedly explicit than it is in any way profound.

Mr. O'Neill has pictured a saloon full of drunken bums who hang on to life through the generosity of the proprietor, an old drunk himself. The boozers are of many kinds--a disillusioned anarchist, a Harvard Law School graduate, a Boer War Dutch general, a Boer War British captain, the former owner of a Negro gambling house, an old circus man; and for company, they have a pair of barkeeps and a trio of streetwalkers. The drunks are washed up and out-at-elbows, living only to cadge rotgut and quarrel more from habit than animus; but they are kept going by their "pipe dreams," their clouded illusions that tomorrow will change their luck or stiffen their characters.

Each year, on the proprietor's birthday, a traveling salesman named Hickey throws them a party, getting as drunk as they do. But this year when Hickey comes, he announces that though the party is on, he is out of it. Something has reformed him, he has found peace by facing reality, by discounting "tomorrow"; and he nags the others, who hate the idea and soon come to hate him, to pull themselves together and follow his example. They try, but they can't; they can't, and they are done for. But they have still to hear Hickey's own story, how he had killed the wife he loved because her forgiveness of all his transgressions bred an unbearable sense of guilt in him. Hence Hickey had resigned himself to death. The police lead him away, and the slobs go back to their drinking and their pipe dreams.

But Hickey the messenger and breath of death, has shaken two people: the old anarchist who had thought himself past illusions, and a newcomer, the young son of a woman anarchist who had squealed on her because, he finally confesses, he had hated her. He proceeds to commit suicide.

These are Mr. O'Neill's people, and he treats them with compassionate affection. He pumps color and humanity into his sodden derelicts and his whores, he lets them talk and curse, snooze and squabble, perform their little tragicomic bits of vaudeville. They are not probed very deeply (we know almost as much about them in the first act as in the last) they do not grow, but they grow beautifully familiar and hence fairly real: the four hours of The Iceman have the cumulative value of a very long novel, where abundance does well enough what art would do much better.

Hickey, of course, is in different case. He is someone with whom Mr. O'Neill creates suspense and contrives development: with him abundance is no substitute for art, and with him O'Neill fails. He fails, first, by keeping Hickey mysterious for three acts for the plot's sake, and then letting him pour out his story far too articulately; Hickey explains himself with a textbook clarity that robs him of a truly dramatic role in the play, or a really human complexity. Mr. O'Neill, who marred Mourning Becomes Electra by spreading Freud right over the surface of it like so much peanut butter, has done something like the same thing, with Hickey's explicit self-knowledge here.

But Hickey also comes off the shadowy figure usually produced when the symbolic side of a character precedes the organic side in an author's imagination. Neither as an enigma nor as a belated and extensive autobiographer does Hickey come off as a dramatic figure. Only theatrically does he have his uses.

As for Mr. O'Neill's "thesis," it would seem to be that men cannot live without illusions; hardly a new or very disputable idea. One would be less inclined to treat it with levity, however, had Mr. O'Neill let it seep into the story rather than build up four long acts to wave it like a flag at the end. Or, better still, had he given it (however truistic it was in itself) enough of what used to be called poetic truth; had he made it operate persuasively enough inside the play's own context, so that it shed new illumination, so that it provided a genuine experience. But a genuine experience is just what I failed to get from The Iceman Cometh. For all its fine scattered scenes of theater, it left me cold.

I haven't space to do justice to all the acting in The Iceman. Dudley Digges, as the old saloon-keeper, turns in another of his fine and expert performances, and James Barton, as Hickey, turns in a competent one. One must single out, too, Carl Benton Reid and Tom Pedi; and Paul Crabtree, John Marriott and Ruth Gilbert. And Mr. Dowling's direction.

--Louis Kronenberger in PM (October 11, 1946).

IDIOT'S DELIGHT (Robert E. Sherwood; Shubert Theatre, March 24,
   1936)

     Whatever else may be said of Idiot's Delight, Robert Sherwood's
latest play and the Theatre Guild's final production of the season, one
thing is clear: it is a smash. It is also a good show. It has color:
A hotel in the Alps bordering on four countries, a cast of characters
which includes a German scientist, a French pacifist, a munitions mag-
nate, a tantalizing Russian lady who is half mountebank, half sooth-
sayer; an articulate and racy American hoofer, a bevy of night-club
beauties. The play has literate lines and references that only readers of the better weeklies will properly appreciate: "Whoever wins
(the war) Austria will lose," quotations from Thomas Mann, gibes at
the stupidity of humankind, not unsympathetic allusions to radical
ideas, and a depreciation of jingoism. It is performed by a company
of smart and engaging actors. With all this, and above all, there
is the theme of war (the author is definitely against it), not any war
but the specific brand that nowadays we chew every morning with
our breakfast.

     Such a play cannot and must not be dismissed. Its appeal is
extremely broad. Its reflection of its fairly-well-to-do middle-class
audience, our dominant audience for higher grade best sellers and
S.R.O. successes, is almost perfect. Analyze and understand this
play and you will have learned much about a great section of our cos-
mopolitan public.

     Structurally Idiot's Delight is rather loose: there is not much
plot and very little conflict in the sense of a struggle of wills. Most
of the characters are caught in a situation over which they have no
control and to which they do not see their own relation except as
passive victims. The French "internationalist" is an exception, but
at the outbreak of war the author shows that he loses his pacifist
convictions and dies with a patriotic exclamation on his lips. (What
is this "internationalist?" A synthetic figure without sharp defini-
tion. If he were a Radical-Socialist he would not call for "revolu-
tion," if he were a Socialist he would not speak of Lenin as his leader, if he were a Communist he would not hope to stave off war simply
by an appeal to reason.) The German scientist is working on a cure
for cancer, but when his fatherland is threatened he decides to give
up his work, since humanity is not worth saving (although his country is apparently worth dying for). The Russian lady of doubtful
origin hates war, but she has been the mistress of a big munitions
manufacturer for some time. The hoofer apparently feels that if
makers of armaments were put out of the way most of the trouble
would be gone, but he never really encounters the villain (the munitions manufacturer) and the latter himself makes the presumably un-
answerable point that he is fulfilling a task which was not set by
himself alone. "Why are there no answers to my questions?" the
hoofer asks despondently. The truth is (a) the questions are not

properly put, (b) he doesn't ask the right people, (c) he isn't really a character, for a person as evolved as he is supposed to be might
come closer at least to some theoretical answers!

    Given these figures and circumstances there can be little drama.
Instead there is conversation: bright, wistful, sexy, cultural, like
an expensive steamship ad, and political in the intriguing manner of
a New Yorker editorial. To lend punch and pathos to the situation
we have the bing-bang and br-r-r-ing of an off-stage war. However,
the dish would lack intellectual piquancy if there were not some sem-
blance of social comment; so we have a chorus number done cutely
by Alfred Lunt and les girls which is interrupted by the sudden entrance of the internationalist who screams that Paris has been bom-
barded, that they are all dancing in a world in ruins. But it is to
be remembered that it is the dance number, with its lights, its bare
thighs, its playfulness, and not the interruption, which is applauded
and remembered by the audience.

    Where does all this lead? At the end of the play the hoofer
and the Russian lady alone in the hotel defy death that is being
hurled down on the mountain by bombing war planes. He plays the
piano and she clings to him. "We are the real people," she says,
"and we know that the deadliest weapons are the most merciful"--
and with that the curtain falls. In other words, these two (symbolical) artists who are the playboys and wantons of civilization express
the idea that in this crazy cruel, but rather nice world of ours
it is really best to die. There is no consistent intelligence, there is
no justice, there are no heroes, no valid fighters. If one dies then
let it be at least with humor, music, a dash of romance and philosophy. It is the spirit of sorrowful acquiescence. You shake your
head, sigh and permit what you deplore.

    Is it pessimism? Not at all: pessimism suggests pain and the
public in our theatre will not pay for that. Just as the play's action is loose and the characters only partly defined, so the tone of
the play never mounts to anything like a dangerous tension. The
quality is pleasant throughout without any palpable blood-pressure.
Art can arise from decadence, it can even arise from despair, hate
or mockery. But for art to arise from them they must be clear
through a certain degree of force, of completeness, of experience.
When ingredients of popular sentiment and prevalent notions are distilled and thinned down to fit the tastes of nearly everybody, you can
really concern nobody and you get at best only entertainment.

    A play of this kind might take on fresh meaning in a creative
theatre. The Guild production is on the level of the play, in an un-
differentiated way. It is a neat package. Mr. Lunt is an actor
(there aren't so many) and he has a certain spicy sense of characterization, though he fails to convey any complete person.... The
last moment in the show reveals the nature of the whole production:
positively and negatively. The air raid is raging and the two chief

characters are at the piano. What is the relationship of these two
elements? What impels the two people to go to the piano: fear,
defiance, desire to drown out the hateful noise, bravado? Nothing
is clear: the two characters simply sit there, a light shines up on
their faces, a pretty picture is made.
> --David Shepperd in New Theatre,
> Vol. 3, No. 5 (May 1936), page
> 9.

* * *

Offered as a brilliant argument against the folly of war, it
resolves itself into a mere box-office vaudeville show punctuated with
superficial philosophical meditations of the kind customarily encountered in the screeds of boiler-plate sydicate sages.
> --George Jean Nathan in Life (No-
> vember 1936), page 4.

THE INNOCENTS (William Archibald, adapted from Henry James;
   The Playhouse Theatre, February 1, 1950)

I'd rather have as little skin as one of Henry James' ghosts if
I only slithered past with an impression that this is a solid and entire, doubt-proof, hard-shelled play. It is not, and in that very
lack lies its character and--for me--its peculiar virtue. This, however,
I can hastily guarantee you: as fine a blend of the ancient willies
with modern stagecraft and amazingly good performances as you will
see from here to Gehenna and return.

Many a playwright has taken out James' little horror classic
The Turn of the Screw, and has wondered whether ... and then
shuddered and put it back upon the shelf without even trying. A
youngish one, bold beyond the rest, has anyway tried here, and has
in large part succeeded. He has managed to keep much of the loathsome beauty of the tale. He has made it groan with its original in-
tangibles and awful inferences.

Miss Giddens, Victorian governess, comes to an English country house to take charge of a parentless pair of youngsters. She is
soon clutched by some rottenness of the air around her--around these
juvenile twain, more so--and by that conspiracy of the insurgent
dead which has turned them from Kate Greenaway illustrations into
little imps of nameless obscenity, treachery and spite. It is evil
incarnate and contaminate, in the scarcely visible shapes of two departed servants, which she must fight.

A play of such mood will have to run a risk of tenuousness,
of too much creep and shadow. It will also be put to embarrassment

when its apparitions start their rubber-shoed parade and take on
opaque flesh and greasepaint. These demerits are there. These and
that general sense of indistinctness which the stage makes a habit
of abhorring. And yet--an extraordinary piece, recommendable to
those who like their chills especially well written, their poignancies
dark-tinged.

We've had a whole new Children's Crusade in the theatre, this
season. Extraordinary acting by shavers, pre-shavers and sheer
tots. Add these two: Iris Mann and David Cole. They play their
complex parts with a staggering skill. A couple of their scenes together ought to be put up in cellophane and preserved for some
sort of hellish hall of fame. But Beatrice Straight, governess and
star, is their adult equal--and handsome about it--and Isobel Elsom
makes them a suitable fourth. It has all had most sensitive direction
by Peter Glenville.

Two other immeasurable aids: the musical score by Alex North,
the setting by Jo Mielziner. I can't recall a room of more fearful
sweep and fungoid grandeur or lighting more fitted to the strange
spook-ridden lilt.

> --Gilbert W. Gabriel in Cue, Vol.
> 19, No. 6 (February 11, 1950),
> page 18.

AN INSPECTOR CALLS (J.B. Priestley; Booth Theatre, October 21,
1947)

Good entertainment, yet provocative stuff, is J.B. Priestley's
An Inspector Calls, an eloquent plea for the mutual responsibility of
one man for the other. Thomas Mitchell, a familiar face on Beverly
Drive, plays the Inspector with his special brand of Gaelic effectiveness.

> --David Commons in Script (Febru-
> ary 1948), page 60.

* * *

J.B. Priestley is always bursting with "interesting" ideas--
which may be why I so often find him an uninteresting playwright.
For the idea, the technical trick, the clever twist not only obtrudes
itself way past its bedtime, but it obliterates all sense of flesh-and-
blood, all our incentive to believe, all our capacity for caring. Anything so tricky can hardly help seeming, after a time, a little trashy.
Anything so tricky, again, is very likely to conceal something a little trite.

The trickiness, this time, doesn't even conceal the triteness--

though very likely it's not meant to. Very likely it's only meant to
give it a new sheen or gloss. Mr. Priestley has merely hung enough
bells on a tract to try to make it tinkle like a theater piece--and
come up with a quite unexpected, fairly catchy little tune at the end.
Mr. Priestley has merely done his best to make a serious subject
palatable. But in the course of being made (or not being made)
palatable, it comes to seem pretty piffling.

Mr. Priestley, who has a very real social conscience, is concerned in An Inspector Calls with everybody's involvement--and often
guilty involvement--in other people's lives. For a specific fable, he
has had a mysterious police inspector call at the home of a smug,
successful manufacturer and implicate everybody there in a young
girl's suicide. Father had once fired her from his factory; daughter
had later got her dismissed from a dress shop; mother had refused
her charitable aid; and the young son of the house, along with the
prospective son-in-law ... but perhaps we should leave their roles
undivulged. Be assured, however, that they had most of all to do
with hurrying the poor girl toward suicide.

In the thorough-going way in which this small family unit of
five--plagued quite as much, surely, by coincidence as by guilt--
drove one poor girl to her grave, there is much that smacks strongly of the Victorian morality play at its worst. Mr. Priestley, being
quite as aware of it as you or I, suddenly does a backflip on the
whole business, suggesting near the end that maybe the inspector
had been having the family on, or hadn't even been an inspector,
or ... but again I will leave something up Mr. Priestley's sleeve. I
would only say that all these final fillips, however momentarily en-
livening, came much too late to make up for the tedium in which the
play had been engulfed for a good act and a half. They largely,
too, destroyed any claims the play might have to being taken very
seriously. The tract had merely wound up a stunt; something pretty dull stood forth as also pretty trivial.

The production is pleasant enough without ever being very exciting. It brings Thomas Mitchell back to Broadway, after a number
of years in Hollywood, as the inspector; and Mr. Mitchell plays the
inspector neatly and quietly, without too much suggestion that he
may have spectral or supernatural affiliations. The family group--
Melville Cooper, Doris Lloyd, Rene Ray, John Buckmaster and John
Merivale--all acquit themselves very capably, and Stewart Chaney has
housed them well. But Mr. Priestley has left them rather dangling.
                                        --Louis Kronenberger in PM (Octo-
                                        ber 23, 1947)

                         *   *   *

There is unquestionably an idea for a fine play in J.B. Priestley's thesis that the actions of every human being in some way affect
the lives of every other human being. And it might even be that

Mr. Priestley has written that play in An Inspector Calls. But he
didn't know his own strength. He wrote about an act and a half too
much and, in consequence, there is a lot of dramatic dead wood that
might have been pruned out of An Inspector Calls to the infinite im-
provement of its unity and pace.

Mr. Priestley's story of a family celebration disturbed by the
visit of a soidisant Police Inspector who represents some nebulous
idea that might be called "Retribution" or "Conscience" or something
like that, is leisurely and contemplative rather than dramatically exciting. The lethargic tempo, although skillfully manipulated by Sir
Cedric Hardwicke's direction, leaves too much time for the rather
mechanical plot skeleton to show through the flesh of the dialogue.

A girl has committed suicide and each of the outwardly respectable characters onstage has contributed in some way to her death.
Unfortunately the audience is given ample opportunity to guess each
one's role in the tragedy long before it is exposed by the author.

Thomas Mitchell returns to Broadway as the omniscient inspector who strips the characters of their pretensions. Melville Cooper
contributes a lifelike portrait of a smug industrialist. John Buckmaster deserves special credit for making quite a lot out of the essentially wooden role of the daughter's fiance. Doris Lloyd, Rene
Ray, John Merivale complete the cast.

> --Thomas Brailsford Felder in Cue,
> Vol. 16, No. 44 (November 1,
> 1947), pages 18 and 20.

JOHN LOVES MARY (Norman Krasna; Booth Theatre, February 4,
    1947)

Nina Foch and William Prince, attractive refugees from B pictures, share the heart interest in John Loves Mary, farce by Norman
Krasna, author of Small Miracle and Dear Ruth, latest comedy hit to
stand 'em up at the Booth. The piece is presented in substantial
elegance by Richard Rodgers and Oscar Hammerstein, 2nd, in association with Joshua Logan, who has directed it to sprout two laughs
wherever one grew before.

Mr. Krasna has developed enough complications in his plot to
fatten up several anemic comedies. He is here concerned with Mary
McKinley, waiting in her parents' St. Regis Hotel apartment for the
return of Sergeant John Lawrence, absent in the war for the past
three years. Lawrence's arrival is signal for an immediate wedding
which Mary's father, an important Washington Senator, proceeds to
plan. Lawrence's hesitancy, it develops, unknown to Mary and her
parents, springs from his aversion to bigamy. Returning a favor to

Fred Taylor, a pal who saved his life on the battlefield, he has married the latter's English girl so that she can come to this country to join Fred.

But John's buddy, thinking his English sweetheart had been killed in the London blitz, has already married in New York and at the moment is expecting fatherhood. John loves Mary and tells her so. What he fails to do is tell her about his predicament. Hence, for two more acts of horsing around, simple misunderstandings are built into unbelievable situations before the final curtain is brought down with Mary and John taking the English girl to Reno for her divorce and their marriage.

Miss Foch has a way with comedy that should stand her in good stead for future stage plays and boost her stock for more variety than Hollywood has given her to date. Mr. Prince has little to do as the bedeviled G.I.

As Fred Taylor, fumbling, deadpan and hesitant, Tom Ewell is wonderfully funny, while Loring Smith, as Senator McKinley, gives rich, well-restrained caricature to the part of a pompous legislator. These two have the best lines in the play and fully account for their inherent hilarity. For the record, Pamela Gordon, Gertrude Lawrence's daughter, is making her New York stage debut as Fred's Cockney girl.

The first act of John Loves Mary is the best example of fast-moving, uproarious farce we've had in many a season. From then on, it runs mechanically downhill, despite excellent playing and shrewd direction.

> --Russell Rhodes in Rob Wagner's
> Script, Vol. 33, No. 750 (March
> 1, 1947), page 20.

* * *

It must be nice to know that the things you fill a play with will also fill a theater. Mr. Krasna, in any case, seems to know it. A hit for him would seem to be merely a synonym for a play, and rather easier, on the whole, to write. In John Loves Mary, as in Dear Ruth, Mr. Krasna knows his way about the stage. He is a trained popular psychologist in the field of laughter; a dealer in slick prefabricated parts in the field of construction. John will still be loving Mary at the Booth long after many other theaters have gone dark on more perplexing and less popular emotions.

Well, popular entertainment is all to the good, and Mr. Krasna is better at it than most. Some of John Loves Mary seems to me lively enough, and all of it seems innocuous. Furthermore, it has been given the very brisk production it requires. If this is pretty thin

praise, the answer is that for me the play is pretty thin fun. I
very often found it easier to understand why other people were
laughing than to laugh myself. There were too many jokes I had
done my share of laughing at in the past, or found far too pat to
be funny. There were stretches that merely seemed tedious, and
others that merely seemed complicated. And one trouble with purely
popular comedy, Broadway-style, is that it never seems to have a
really ingrained comic point of view. It never gets inside the characters or underneath the situations; it never subordinates the part
to the whole; it never creates anything. Everything is exploded on
you; nothing ever creeps up. Real humor squarely unites the most
heterogeneous audiences; gags and Grand Rapids farce-furniture
splits it at every turn.

John Loves Mary is predominantly farcical, and very much a
thing of plot. It vies, indeed, with Othello in hopelessly complicating a great many lives that could be straightened out by five minutes'
straight conversation. That, however, is very right for farce; what
alone is wrong is that the complications become tiresome. John,
as you know loves Mary, comes home from the wars to marry her.
But John's army pal, Fred, had come home earlier--without the English girl he loved. And since the girl could only get into the United
States by marrying a soldier, John had married her, expecting her to
divorce him immediately and marry Fred. Unfortunately, it turns out
that Fred has already married some one else and is momentarily expecting a baby.

With this for a starter, and with John and Fred trying to use
their wits instead of coming clean, the play piles complication on
complication and crisis on crisis. Some of these are entertaining,
but the plot, in the end, tends to get in the way (the more so as
it requires scenes that have to be played fairly straight). Things
are actually more fun when they partly depend on character--on
Mary's father, a tough baby of a Senator; on a heel who had been
John's lieutenant and is now a "major"--in the Paramount's ushering
corps; on a general who is very defensive about the Army. But the
best things, the genuinely comic things, are bits of pantomime prac-
ticed by the befuddled John and Fred.

As Fred, indeed, Tom Ewell is the funniest thing in the show;
and William Prince gets a good deal into the straighter-written part
of John. Nina Foch's Mary seems to me on the weak side; but Loring
Smith is excellent as her father, and Harry Bannister and Lyle Bettger are very helpful as the brass hat and the heel. And Joshua Logan's direction is perhaps the most helpful thing of all.

> --Louis Kronenberger in PM (Febru-
> ary 6, 1947).

* * *

A couple of expert farceurs under Joshua Logan's excellent

direction have made much laughter out of an adequate Norman Krasna script. John Loves Mary is one of those comedies of deceit,
with a small lie leading to bigger ones until the whole situation becomes overwhelmingly complicated. The central love affair which
causes all the trouble is, however, less important than the perimeter
of this play, which finds Tom Ewell as an ex-G.I. and Loring Smith
as a blustering Senator performing and projecting qualities of humor
very much similar to those which exalted Philip Loeb and Donald Mc-
Pride in the well-remembered Room Service. With Logan's manipulation timing these and other performances to perfection, this Rodgers
& Hammerstein production is by far the best new comedy of the season.

     Playwright Krasna has provided the company with a good point
of departure, but it remained for others to raise the doings into the
upper regions of hilarity. The idea is that John, a home-coming
soldier, really does love Mary, a Senator's daughter; but he has
previously married an English girl in order to get her into the United
States to rejoin John's best friend and wartime buddy, whom she
loves. To add to the difficulties, John's friend, despairing of ever
seeing the English girl again, has married someone else. The mounting discord of embarrassment and intrigue is the sort of shaky
dramaturgical fabrication whose card-house existence depends on delicacy of touch. Logan has put it together with such subtlety that it
never wavers until near the end, when it is high enough anyway.

     The director does not attempt to salt this script with such
obvious measures as gags, props or comic extravagancies of action.
The punch lines here would sound desperately normal if written down
alone; but they are all the more solidly funny because they arise
almost accidentally out of a situation, an attitude, a change in timing
or a twist of character. Logan's principal asset is Ewell's performance as John's buddy, a willing but diffident chap who, though never
made to be a plotter, is caught in the middle of these complex circumstances. Logan has directed Ewell into a habit of throwing away
lines inflected from plaintiveness to eagerness while at the same time
holding a pose or accenting with a gesture, a straight-faced farce
style which is immensely effective. In contrast there is Smith's
brusque lawmaker, who is played with an engaging representation of
rockbound authority.

     Also performing here with ease and assurance and having their
occasional moments of sparkle are William Prince as the embattled
John, Nina Foch in the rather thankless role of Mary and Ann Mason
as the Senator's wife; and among the other members of a polished
cast are Pamela Gordon, Lyle Bettger and Harry Bannister. The
script provided by Krasna for John Loves Mary is somewhere near the
level of his Dear Ruth; but it reaches the higher realms of amusement through a tour de force of execution.
                              --Cue, Vol. 16, No. 7 (February
                              15, 1947), pages 15-16.

JOHNNY BELINDA (Elmer Harris; Belasco Theatre, September 18,
    1940)

    Story--Up on Prince Edward Island lives Black McDonald and
his daughter Belinda. This unfortunate gal, known as The Dummy,
can neither speak nor hear. Her father uses her as a servant and
has never considered her with parental regard.

    Dr. Davidson, young and new to the community, demonstrates
that Belinda can be shown the sign language and educated. Her
eager learning awakens Black McDonald's affection and Dr. David-
son's love.

    This simple and frequently touching tale has an overlay of al-
most everything you can put into a play--sudden death, the mortgage, worse-than-death, an illegitimate child, prying neighbors,
murder, etc. Even a courtroom scene.

    Acting--Helen Craig, as the girl who cannot speak, gives a
genuinely excellent performance and handles the transition of her
character from drudge to a sentient person skillfully.

    Horace McNally, a newcomer, plays the part of the doctor
agreeably, and Louis Hector makes Black McDonald a living part.

    In fact, the efforts of these three give the play such life as
it achieves. Without their unassuming acting the affair would have
come to nothing.

    The rest of the cast do not offer much, but then, neither do
their parts.

    Production--The piece has been well staged by Mr. Gribble.
Frederick Fox's excellent sets are well lighted by Feder.

    Cue Says--The core of this play, the relationship between the
girl, the father, and the doctor, offers many effective and appealing
scenes. The elaborate plotting that accompanies this never intrudes
with enough force to obscure the main affair.

    You can call the whole thing melodramatic hokum, but you can-
not deny it a good gob of emotional content.

    I recommend Johnny Belinda.

                                        --Oliver Claxton in Cue, Vol. 9,
                                        No. 40 (September 28, 1940),
                                        page 39.

JUMBO (Book by Ben Hecht and Charles MacArthur, Music and Lyrics by Richard Rodgers and Lorenz Hart; Hippodrome, November 16, 1935)

      As an epitome of this type of variety show multiplied tenfold
with the resources of the circus, one could not find anything more
suitable than the present production of Jumbo. It combines every
conceivable adjunct of theatric art without ever approaching drama in
the strict sense. One cannot take the thin thread of plot spun by
Messrs. Hecht and MacArthur seriously. Their tale of a feud between two rival circus companies, along with the Romeo and Juliet
passion of two youngsters from the warring camps, is merely a convenient peg on which to hang an equestrian ballet, a parade of animals and saxophone players, headed by the still beaming Mr. Paul
Whiteman (this time on a white palfrey which bears up most wondrously), a docile pachyderm, a ten-reel circus, and a flood of wisecracking expletives from the comically raucous Jimmy Durante. We
pay homage to the latter's profundities ("They say an elephant never
forgets. But what has he got to remember?" or his brilliant reference to paper money as "government literature") and to a resonant
roustabout chant, "We don't know where we're going, but we're on
our way," which sounds perilously like a crack at the New Deal. But
Jumbo is innocent of meaning. It remains honestly and, except in
the inept bridal finale, successfully an orgy of the senses. One is
grateful for the pageantry, one is giddy with trapeze gazing, one
admires the performance of a super-juggler and the precocity of a
waltzing horse, and one leaves pleased and vacuous. Reflecting upon
the experience one wonders whether much of our present content-free
theatre wouldn't do well to pool its energies for the presentation of
gargantuan shows of this kind instead of continuing to dish out
picayune portions of entertainment like the pale fare of There's Wisdom in Women and Most of the Game. We would also be happy to
dispense with all further dissertations on the artistic temperament like
Play Genius Play that made such catastrophic recent appearances on
Broadway. We would be equally pleased to see Pirandello mercifully
interred and could leave the mysteries of play-writing decently confined to playwrights' cubicles instead of seeing them served up in
plays like On Stage. We prefer to eat our chicken without watching
the processes of decapitation, plucking and disemboweling....
                          --John W. Gassner in New Theatre,
                            Vol. 2, No. 2 (December 1935),
                            pages 10-11.

                          *   *   *

      As if Jimmy Durante weren't a circus in himself, Billy Rose has
supplied almost everything else you can think of. A whale of a show.
                          --George Jean Nathan in Life (Jan-
                            uary 1936), page 4.

* * *

If you have seen Jumbo, that brainstorm of Billy Rose, alleged master mind of Broadway showmen (as the program "admits"), don't bother to go to the circus the next time it comes to town. Jumbo is a circus minus the indelicate odor of Mamie the Giraffe, hamburger stands and sawdust. The only discernible difference between the circus and Rose's show is that Jumbo is played in an air-conditioned house. And, yes, I almost forgot--Jumbo has Jimmy "Mutiny" Durante and a clown who seems to be infested with bananas (he pulls three hundred out of one pocket). Jumbo is a lot of tinsel, tight-rope walkers, and girls who hang upside-down from the roof. It's just another case of Broadway making a lot of noise about nothing and being very entertaining while doing it.

--John Mullen in New Theatre, Vol.
3, No. 5 (May 1936), page 26.

KEY LARGO (Maxwell Anderson; Ethel Barrymore Theatre, November
27, 1939)

Story--King McCloud has led a band of friends to fight for Spain. Four remain when the action begins, and the fight is coming to an end. They are about to stage one final, hapless rear-guard action before the collapse of the loyalist regime. To McCloud this makes no sense--death without a reason seems to him illogical and inexcusable. He deserts after trying to persuade his companions to come with him.

McCloud eventually arrives at the home of the father and sister of one of his late companions. Here, on a wharf on Key Largo, Florida, he finds himself faced once more with the problem of death, honor, and logic. Gangsters have taken the place over and threaten the security of D'Alcala, the father, and the virtue of Alegre d'Alcala, the daughter.

Acting--Paul Muni, returned to the stage from the films, does a magnificent bit of acting as the harassed McCloud. With perfection of voice and gesture he gives reality to the harassed character. As Alegre, Uta Hagen reminded me somewhat of Frankie Parker playing tennis. She knows the technique, but knows it mechanically and without life or spirit. As her father, Harold Johnsrud plays with feeling and restraint.

In the short part of spokesman for the men who refused to leave the wars, José Ferrer brought depth to the part.

Production--The three settings have been richly designed by Jo Mielziner, and the direction of Guthrie McClintic is excellent.

Cue Says--Mr. Anderson writes theatrical dialogue of great
beauty. The highly poetic cast to much of the talk is a treat to
listen to, and the philosophical theme of the play a valid one. Unfortunately, the mechanics he has chosen to shape his point are not
up to the writing. Gangsters on a wharf are petty and false, and
the device employed for turning the climax has very little reason to
it.

The play, though, must be recommended for the beauty of its
writing and the fine performance of Paul Muni.
--Oliver Claxton in Cue, Vol. 8,
No. 24 (December 9, 1939), page
50.

* * *

Maxwell Anderson's latest play is a tragedy of the loss of faith
--not religious faith, but faith in any meaning or belief in life. King
McCloud is a radical who in Spain joins the Loyalists, realizes that
they are beaten, tries to persuade a group of Americans he has led
to desert and, when he fails, deserts himself, joining the Franco
forces to save his life. Stung by his conscience he returns to America to confess his act to the families of the men he abandoned. On
a Florida key he meets the father and sister of one of his comrades
and again shows his cowardice and lack of belief in anything by
knuckling under to a gambler. In the end, however, he regains his
manhood by realizing the nobility in the souls of two Seminole Indians and goes to his death by killing the gambler and being killed
by one of the gambler's satellites. But it is not the plot that really
counts; and to be frank the final tragedy is an utterly contrived and
unnecessary one. McCloud could have saved the sister of his dead
friend by other means than the one he takes. Mr. Anderson has
never been one of our most skilful masters of theatrical structure.
So let us turn to what he is really interested in--the study of a
tortured soul. McCloud is the center and focus of the play, is a
sort of modern Hamlet in so far as he is weak and vacillating, but
unlike Hamlet he has argued himself into the only belief he has, that
man is without meaning. The result is inevitable--this particular
man becomes a coward and a weakling.

I have said that Key Largo is not a tragedy of the loss of religious faith. What I mean is that Mr. Anderson has not visualized
it as such. In reality, however, the loss of any sense of religion is
implicit in all the actions of his chief protagonist. It is this, whether Mr. Anderson realizes it or not, which is the real basis of the
play. McCleod is logical and having no belief in anything beyond
this world, his logic leads to its inevitable sequel. Though the animal is not evil, because he lives by instinct alone, man by being
given reason becomes evil when he lives the life of instinct unhindered by a realization of anything higher than that instinct. Mc-
Cloud sees nothing beyond this life; and more logical than Mr. Ander-

son himself, he follows that logic to the end, or nearly to the end.
He denies in his words and acts that honor and integrity and faith
of soul exist, and when at the end he sees them at last in two poor
Indians, his ignorance comes to him as a sudden revelation. But the
real reason for that ignorance even then escapes him, as apparently
it has escaped Mr. Anderson himself. Mr. Anderson is a poet,
though he has written more eloquently than in Key Largo, and the
reason is perhaps that confusion of mind makes a confusion in his
words.

    The part of McCloud is magnificently acted by Paul Muni, with
variety of mood and voice and posture. Mr. Muni is indeed welcome
back from the fleshpots of Hollywood. He is an actor endowed both
with emotional warmth and intellectual power. Admirable too are
José Ferrer as Victor, Ralph Theadore as the rascally sheriff, Frederic Tozere as the gambler, and Harold Johnsrud as D'Alcala. Uta
Hagen acts the girl with great intensity, though one might wish for
more variety. Guthrie McClintic has staged the play admirably for
the Playwrights Company.

                              --Grenville Vernon in The Common-
                              weal, Vol. 31, No. 7 (December
                              8, 1939), pages 163-164.

KISS ME, KATE (Music and Lyrics by Cole Porter, Book by Bella
        and Samuel Spewack; New Century Theatre, December 30, 1948)

    The good news that rings out at the Century Theatre these
evenings is that Cole Porter is still the top. For Kiss Me, Kate,
Mr. Porter has wrought some of his most charming tunes, and the
wacky, witty rhyme schemes that his imitators have never really succeeded in imitating crackle brightly all over the place. It's nice to
have Cole Porter back in the groove and it's nice to have Kiss Me,
Kate on Broadway. It's the kind of big, sumptuous musical that
everybody will want to see--at any price.

    Bella and Samuel Spewack's book, based on, or rather, in-
spired by, Shakespeare's Taming of the Shrew concerns a separated
stage couple who are putting on the Shakespeare comedy in Baltimore.
The combination of backstage modernity and onstage period background allows Kiss Me, Kate to include a little bit of everything.
And it does--from costumed spectacle to old fashioned vaudeville.

    Alfred Drake gives a triumphant performance as the make-
believe Petruchio, who is doing a little genuine shrew-taming on the
side. Mr. Drake has a rare combination of voice, virility and stage
presence and the role is custom-tailored to his talents. He swag-
gers about with equal ease in Shakespearian costumes and a 1949-
model dressing gown, giving tongue the while to some of Mr. Porter's
pleasantest melodies.

Patricia Morison, as his real life ex-wife and stage bride, is pretty to look at and pretty to hear. She must also be a young woman of considerable stamina to withstand, nightly, the roughing-up she receives from her Petruchio. She's a welcome addition to Broadway.

Secondary on and off-stage lovers are Harold Lang, late of Look Ma, I'm Dancin! and Lisa Kirk, late of Allegro. I suppose it would be technically correct to describe Mr. Lang as a dancer and Miss Kirk as a singer, but both actually do both and walk off with several of the show's big moments while they're about it.

Mr. Porter has provided Kiss Me, Kate with such an embarrassment of musical riches that it's a little hard for me to say which songs I like best. But take my advice and don't be late for the second act curtain. The opening number, called "It's Too Darn Hot," is Cole Porter at his lilting best and it is also the occasion for some inspired dancing by Harold Lang and a pair of Negro youths named Fred Davis and Eddie Sledge.

Among the love ballads, I found "So in Love Am I," as warbled by Mr. Drake and Miss Morison, the most pleasing and, I think, "Always True to You (In My Fashion)" sung by Miss Kirk is probably the wittiest. But perhaps the most charming Porterisms are in the songs he has written for the Shakespeare scenes, in which he manages to employ the Elizabethan idiom with enchanting effect. Get thee to Kiss Me, Kate!

> --Thomas Brailsford Felder in Cue,
> Vol. 18, No. 2 (January 8, 1949),
> page 18.

KNICKERBOCKER HOLIDAY (Book and Lyrics by Maxwell Anderson, Music by Kurt Weill; Ethel Barrymore Theatre, October 19, 1938)

In Knickerbocker Holiday Maxwell Anderson, who apparently will try anything once, is taking an excursion into musical comedy. As a lyricist he displays a refreshing talent for natural rhythms and original rhyme-schemes; as a writer of a musical-comedy book he alternates between mocking, hearty wit, and plodding, forced humor. His book is particularly ponderous up until the middle of the first act when Walter Huston, as Peter Stuyvesant, makes his belated entrance. With Mr. Huston once on the stage, Knickerbocker Holiday recovers its festive spirit, and affairs proceed at a genuinely sprightly pace.

Mr. Anderson is writing of that feeling of democracy which pervaded the island of Manhattan in the year 1647 when New Amsterdam was threatening to become as big as Boston. His hero is a fictitious Hollander, Brom Broeck, who, because of his fantastic inability to take orders, is really the first American. The prospering town council, one of whose members is a stubborn Dutchman named Roosevelt, are rank amateurs at reaping individual profits from the harvest of democracy, and are suddenly startled into perturbed activity when their new governor Peter Stuyvesant proves to be a veritable professional profit-snatcher. Like Brom Broeck, Stuyvesant cannot brook orders, and the two clash, not only over the question of government, but as rivals for the hand of the lovely Tina Tienhoven.

Kurt Weill has written some immensely clever and melodic music for Mr. Anderson's lyrics, the best of which are "There's Nowhere To Go but Up," "Young People Think about Love," and a riotously funny lament, "Our Ancient Liberties." Mr. Huston's portrait of Stuyvesant is bold, roguish, and merry. He has two songs in which he is excelling good--a beautiful lyric about an aging man's love, "September Song," and a sly, roisterous ditty called "The Scars." Clumping gracefully around on one silver leg, he also goes through an effective dance routine with the maidens of New Amsterdam, kicking and pirouetting with the liveliest of them. Mark Smith is jocular and pompous as Papa Tienhoven, the head of the council, while Jeanne Madden, as his rebellious daughter, is charming both vocally and physically. Ray Middleton, playing Washington Irving, who from his 1809 study recasts the Knickerbocker past for us, sings in an admirable baritone, while Richard Kollmar, as the young hero, sings a splendid tenor, but the young man also manages to inject some of the more distressing qualities of Dick Powell into his performance. Joshua Logan has done a smooth job of directing, and Frank Bevan's Rembrandt-like costumes are especially to be admired, as is the Battery set of Jo Mielziner.

Knickerbocker Holiday, while not an important play as was the Playwrights' Producing Company's first offering, Abe Lincoln in Illinois, is rollicking good entertainment and a worthy follow-up for the company. I hope the next time Mr. Anderson responds to his Euterpean muse that he goes whole hog and gives us the joyous American operetta of which Knickerbocker Holiday shows us he is capable.

> --DeWitt Bodeen in Rob Wagner's
> Script, Vol. 20, No. 483 (November 12, 1938), page 31.

LADY IN THE DARK (Book by Moss Hart, Lyrics by Ira Gershwin, Music by Kurt Weill; Alvin Theatre, January 23, 1941)

Facile is the descent from the editorial chair of a fashionable women's magazine to the psychoanalyst's grim confessional. This is

the gospel, according to Moss Hart, whose Lady in the Dark has just
moved into the Alvin Theatre. To an old magazine man it would
doubtless appear that Liza Elliott was fortunate beyond the wildest
dreams of anybody in that unsavory racket. She had a fancy office
in which nobody threw cigarette butts on the floor or scrawled telephone numbers on the walls; there was a rich backer with no exas-
perating theories about how things ought to be run; there were no
disgruntled contributors or, as far as I could see, anything so vulgar as a typewriter in the joint. In fact, about the only professional problem confronting this lucky girl was the choice of what cover
to put on the Easter issue. Mr. Hart's play has been generally described as a fantasy. It is, indeed.

In spite of all these advantages, however, Miss Elliott wasn't
happy. Her case history, as outlined to the sawbones at twenty
bucks a throw, was full of frustrations. As a very little girl she
was plain, in embarrassing contrast to her beautiful mother, and her
school days were just one damn thing about another. They wouldn't
let her be the Princess in the Commencement play, for instance, and
then when the class elections came around she was chosen Best Student, a disgusting thing, of course, to happen to anybody. As
those of you who are familiar with the black magic of Vienna will
realize, such experiences as these can set up bothersome complexes,
and by the time Mr. Hart's heroine got to be an editor she was as
mixed up emotionally as Mrs. Ethan Frome. In the end, I am happy
to say, Dr. Brooks fixed everything, and Miss Elliott was able to
find peace with an advertising man called Charley Johnson. It is
obvious that the author classifies this as a happy ending, and who
am I to argue?

All this, I'm afraid, is a preliminary to saying that I wasn't
altogether carried away by Lady in the Dark. The plot of a musical play, as a rule, is immune to rational criticism, but Mr. Hart
clearly wishes his new piece to be taken seriously, as a dramatic
work as well as a spectacle. On this basis, I can only report that
Miss Elliott's wrestle with her subconscious, while spirited, would
scarcely be likely to make any professional list of fascinating cases,
and that, considered sheerly as a thing of beauty, the production
at the Alvin may easily remind the captious of certain goings on at
the Center Theatre, where giant turntables and similar miracles have
also been used to astound the unwary.

Psychoanalysis, according to persistent rumor, has long been
one of Mr. Hart's own best girls, beyond question or reproach, and
this may account for something rather wide-eyed, reverent, and perhaps a little old-fashioned that crept into the scenes describing his
heroine's conversations with her physician, as well as those dealing
with her numerous suitors. It is harder to say why the musical se-
quences--the patient's fantasies and childhood memories--weren't altogether satisfactory either. Kurt Weill's tunes were pleasant, if
not precisely memorable; Ira Gershwin's lyrics were always urbane,

and often witty; the dances, supervised by Albertina Rasch, were
brilliantly executed; and the costumes and settings, though stupendous, showed both imagination and taste. The total effect on me,
however, was an almost perfect balance between rapture and fatigue.
There were times when everything seemed wonderful, and there
were others when I simply wished to see no more scenery split and
dissolve, no more beautiful women rotate on turntables, no more
ballets, each as pretty and expensive as a pure white yacht. I
can't explain this peculiar reaction, except by saying that all this
magnificence seemed exactly the sort of thing that could have been
handled just as intelligently (and perhaps a little more magnificently)
in Hollywood.

None of the above, of course, has anything to do with Gertrude
Lawrence, who, in one carelessly chosen word, is superb, whether
prone on her consultant's sofa, running over her symptoms, or merrily singing a fine, tough song called "The Saga of Jenny." Of the
rest of the cast, I have only strength left to remark that Danny
Kaye, Bert Lytell, Macdonald Carey, Margaret Dale, and Victor Mature (courtesy the Hal Roach Studio, Inc.) all deserve your respect-
ful attention.

--Wolcott Gibbs in <u>The New Yorker</u>
(February 1, 1941), page 26.

* * *

Gertrude Lawrence's recent attack of influenza was nothing to
be sneezed at, as it resulted in a large dose of publicity for the
opening of her new play, <u>Lady in the Dark</u>. Columns were printed
about her condition, and the likelihood of when she would cease
gargling and resume gurgling. Columns more were printed about
the fact that Moss Hart, the author of this play with music, jumped
in and took her part on the night of the dress rehearsal, and had to
be led around by the stage manager's hand during the blackout
scene shifts, to avoid having a high-priced author bitten by his own
scenery.

This led to further columns about the elaborateness of the settings, and the fact that they were rotated on a whirligig mechanism
that virtually symbolized the fluttery whirligig of the heroine's mind.
This led again to further columns about the appropriate manner in
which the scenic designer had also redecorated Miss Lawrence's
dressing-room, throwing several star chambers, in fact, into one,
and fitting up a bedroom so that she could sleep there late o' nights,
or stay in the mood of the piece between matinée and evening performance, in case she felt her mood slipping.

The postponement of the opening, moreover, gave the cast a
chance to perfect themselves in their lines and in broken-field running to dodge the advancing scenery. So by the time Miss Lawrence
recovered from her grippe (no doubt stimulated thereto by the deco-

rations of her dressing-room), and the show actually opened without having a single actor, let alone an author, mashed by the stage décor, everyone concerned was ready to take a bow, including the press department. And they were enabled to do so, because the Broadway drama diviners practically abased themselves before this show. Even after having kissed their hands blithely to several good productions lately, the critics still had some appreciation left--enough, in fact, to shoot the works.

They hailed this as the outstanding achievement of Girlish Gertie's career. Most of them even hailed it as the high point of the season, entitling the reviewers to go fishing for the rest of the winter if they wished. A large part of that was undoubtedly due to the gifted author, still gifted despite the fact that his usual collaborator, George S. Kaufman, did not even lurk backstage amid the jungle of scenery. He depicted a frustrated woman editor of a feminine magazine, who takes all her thwarted longings to a psychiatrist, so that the latter interprets them in various kaleidoscopic scenes that might be a combination of Pirandello, Sid Grauman and Irving Berlin. As you might expect from such a combination, the editress is able to steer her way toward her true love, hooking him among three suitors after several long casts of the rod.

The resounding success of the new piece, which is a sensation even without borrowing the services of Ethel Merman from Panama Hattie, is also traceable to the trick turntable stage, which everyone on Broadway except stagehands loves. New Yorkers have not witnessed this kind of scenic merry-go-round since the Center Theater ceased to be dramatically significant and went into the refrigeration business with It Happens on Ice. Just to let a first-nighter have a peep at a lavish scene, and then whisk it away from him before he has a chance to sneer at it, is enough to make him say "Ah!" with surprise.

A lot of the success of the play is attributable to Kurt Weill, whose music was also ensnaring enough to make the reviewers toss adjectives into the air. And a lot of its success, believe it or not, is derivable from Freud. The late Sigmund's ideas are such outworn currency in many other places that they can now be turned into coin of the realm on the stage. The theater is generally so far behind the vanguard of contemporary thought in most cases that the intelligentsia love to frequent it, since it permits them to feel superior.

But the Freudian complex, as translated into dream action by Moss Hart (perhaps with a spiritual nudge from Walt Disney) makes capital entertainment, as far as the average theatergoer is concerned.

Theatergoers of the past generation may recall Molnar's The Phantom Rival, in which Leo Ditrichstein and Laura Hope Crews revealed a woman's innermost dream-thoughts when they went sidling

back to the love of her girlhood and played hooky from hubby.
Just as that was a hit, this big cousin of today was bound to be
even more so--for it has better machinery, and also Gertie Lawrence.

Miss Lawrence not only has a chance to exhibit all the shim-
mering comedy which has become hers by grace of Susan and God:
she also reveals the emotional quality which her previous works have
barely hinted at. As if this were not enough for one evening, she
reverts to some of the enchanting didoes in Charlot's Revue which
the old boys now treasure as part of their anecdotage. She sings
and dances, doing numbers in swing and in reminiscence of that
memorable Chinatown "blues" item, and also queens it at a wedding
looking like Marlene Dietrich and Gaby Deslys combined. What
more could any star want--or any audience, either?

Victor Mature has at last arrived on the Broadway stage, after
having virtually trekked here by covered wagon from Pasadena, making a detour on the screen through 1,000,000 B.C. Young Mr.
Mature is much more attractive when presented in modern dress,
without a bearskin rug. To make his crown of happiness complete,
he has just been picked by the Harvard Lampoon as the young man
least likely to succeed. (Ann Sheridan earned a quarter of a million
last year after achieving the same distinction.) But he says he finds
it good fortune enough to be able to kiss La Lawrence once nightly
and twice on matinées. Bert Lytell also shares honors with the principals, and with the scenery.

                              --Frank Vreeland in Rob Wagner's
                              Script, Vol. 25, No. 586 (Febru-
                              ary 8, 1941), page 20.

THE LADY'S NOT FOR BURNING (Christopher Fry; Royale Theatre,
     November 8, 1950)

For what time it plays here--even if I can't imagine that that
time will be forever--this romantic comedy by England's Christopher
Fry wants a fiercely partisan and loving audience. Wants and deserves it. Deserves and, so I pray, must have it. Because here
is the theatre's proudest but most perilous commodity, a thing of
beauty. Here also happens to be a joyful career-piece for those British twain, John Gielgud and Pamela Brown.

No subtraction from its acting if I advise you to read the
printed text first. Perhaps, like so many, you already have. In
such case you already know why London has been making the hullabaloo it has over Mr. Fry's extraordinary wealth of words, witticisms, lilts, glowing quilt-works of bravo sentiment and silken
laughter. In such case, too, the performance can be taken with that
surer appetite which literary epicures choose to use.

In "the Fifteenth Century, either more or less exactly," two
young people meet on the brink of death. One is a discharged, disillusioned soldier who trumps up his own charge of murderer and demands that the village authorities shall hang him. The other is a
girl who, snatched for a witch, is condemned to the stake. A day
of court-room idiocy, dungeon cruelty, followed by a night of insidious moonlight, merciful acquittals and sheer antic hay. They're
doomed to live and love. They escape arm in arm, giving each other
the dawn's greetings and a "God have mercy on our souls."

That's the mere outward story. Mr. Fry pours the elaborate
fascination into it, however, of glowing foolery, imagery, descriptive
delicacy. Don't let me discourage you by calling it verse. But verse
it is, and fine, nearly finest. Abroad, they compare Fry with Jon-
son or Marlowe. They ought, and I'd add that he seems sometimes
to edge the lyrical surge of these with the modern mental frostiness
of T.S. Eliot.

We'd had some unhappier Fry, last season. We can well see,
now, why we didn't enjoy it. If all his actors do is mouth him, he
is just a prodigous mouthful. The throb of so much cadenced, al-
literated language can become a dense tom-tom. It occasionally can
in this present play, too. Yet they play it, quite all of its imported
company, to its utmost. They give it its jewelled due.

Not only Mr. Gielgud, who staged the whole of it himself, and
who has found a precisely right medium of quiet scorn and mock
idealism for his main role. Not only Miss Brown, who looks and
speaks more lovely than ever, almost like a doe with a very human
libido. There are several others especially endearing: Eliot Make-
ham as an ancient Chaplain whom you'll want to take home and in-
stall on your library mantelpiece, Esme Percy in a rip-roaring drunk-
scene, and young Richard Burton among them. The Oliver Messel
setting is, all on its own account, a hymn to the sun.

So, see it. Read it first, but anyway see it, hear it--and let
it restore your faith in that most patrician sport, the poetic theatre.
For its writing is truly music set to words.

> --Gilbert W. Gabriel in Cue, Vol.
> 19, No. 46 (November 18, 1950),
> pages 20-21.

* * *

Christopher Fry has done one extremely important thing: he
has discovered a twentieth-century verse form for comedy. Matters
had got to the point where it was almost impossible to convince anyone that comedy could be written in verse, so strong is the strangle-
hold of prose upon our age. Lip service was still paid to the notion
of verse tragedy, because both verse and tragedy seemed equally
remote from our time; but prose comedy had been galloping along at

a successful rate and there seemed no reason to wish for anything
better. Mr. Fry has given us something better--has found an
imagery and a rhythm for comedy which increases the intellectual and
emotional range of things to be laughed at--and his work comes as
a stunning surprise.

Broadway has had to wait for Mr. Fry's second American production to take his work to heart. Last season's A Phoenix Too
Frequent was apparently so ruinously directed and acted as to conceal completely the quality of the play. On the printed page Phoenix
seems to me the most perfect thing of its kind since The Importance
of Being Earnest and, within its limited intention and shorter length,
superior to The Lady's Not for Burning. It has a sharply defined
narrative that is developed with alacrity and precision. By comparison, The Lady seems talky and meandering. But The Lady has its
own virtues and they represent an experimental advance for Fry.
He has tried for more complexity and got a richer texture out of it.
He has tried for more rounded characterization and picked up a little human warmth. Where the earlier play was a perfect joke, intellectual to the core, the new one is an imperfect but possibly more
appealing attempt to capture nature on its own vexing, complicated,
and fulsome terms. It keeps shifting gears, and pulling back into
first rather too often, but when it gets where it is going you feel
you have been with the people all the way. Phoenix is an exercise
in detachment, The Lady an experiment in participation. Fry asks
you to accompany the characters rather than observe them.

There is a danger here of becoming too fulsome. In one of
his plays Mr. Fry has a character settle back and sigh happily: It's
nice that anyone can say anything at all.

And it is nice, now that verse has made it possible. But
drama is still limited by the singleness of its action and the things
said must have some relation to this singleness. Occasionally Mr.
Fry forgets this and indulges himself in the pure delight of all that
can be said. I am so grateful for the method of saying it that I am
willing to indulge him his indulgence, but the audience isn't likely
to, and he will do well to brake his verbal exuberance every now and
then.

The effect of talkiness is accented by John Gielgud's performance in the present production. Where the rest of the company, under Mr. Gielgud's own direction, is reading contemporary verse as
though it were contemporary, Gielgud himself is frequently guilty of
chanting. The result is that Fry's verse has been compared to
Shakespeare's in some quarters, whereas the author's chief distinction is that he has found a new form instead of echoing an old one.
If Fry is like anything, he is like Shaw in verse.

In a still later play, Venus Observed, the stuffy Dominic is
informing his sister Perpetua that their charming father is a crook

and likely to go to jail. Dominic expects his sister to be shocked, but she is a pleasant realist:

> Perpetua: ... I was able to believe you at once.
> Poppadillo has the most beguiling
> Jackdaw look about him. But you think
> He wouldn't be happy in prison?
>
> Dominic: He wouldn't, but what
> Difference does that make? Would you be able
> To look anyone in the face, with a father jailed?
>
> Perpetua: Oh, yes, if he were comfortable.

That is like a dozen passages in Shaw, and Fry has much of the impudent love of paradox, the passion for plain sense, and the hopeful cynicism of his prose forebear. He has neither the romanticism of Shakespearian high comedy nor the lowness of Shakespearian bumpkin comedy. Even when, in The Lady's Not for Burning, he introduces two brothers who seem on the bumpkin side, they turn out to have the intellectual facility and emotional disillusionment of a couple of Shavian Caesars. Mr. Gielgud is unwittingly doing the playwright a disservice by letting himself lapse into recitation.

Mr. Fry is something very fresh and exciting in the contemporary theatre, and when he finally masters his plotting and brings himself to reject a few of the bright sayings which come into his head, he may well turn out to be of the first rank.

--Walter Kerr in The Commonweal,
Vol. 53, No. 8 (December 1,
1950), page 196.

THE LATE CHRISTOPHER BEAN (Sidney Howard, from the French of
René Fauchois; Henry Miller Theatre, October 31, 1932)

After a slightly abortive dash for distinction, during which fourteen new plays were hurled into the offensive in two weeks, the Season now seems to have withdrawn into a rather timid period of contemplation and prayer, doubtless to check up on the casualties and to count the house. On the whole, things seem to have gone pretty well. Out of the fourteen or so, we have Dangerous Corner, Dinner at Eight, the Irish Players, Miss Le Gallienne and her brave little band (with, I hope, a subdued Mr. Schildkraut), and The Late Christopher Bean, all of them distinctly worth an evening. Many a month in the old boom days came through with less.

The Late Christopher Bean is the only one which we have not taken up for study in our seminar, and, although more analytical seminars in the future will probably not devote much time to it, we may safely put it down for November, 1932, as what is known in academic circles as "good fun." Sidney Howard has taken Prenez Garde à la Peinture" from René Fauchois and has really more than adapted it into a New England setting, in which a dead and suddenly-appreciated Cézanne has been turned into a dead and suddenly-appreciated Christopher Bean, with New York art dealers, critics, and forgers invading a Massachusetts hamlet for neglected canvases, to the confusion and moral disintegration of the natives. As Mr. Howard has transformed it, the play verges on the farcical now and again, with mustard pickle and watermelon conserve obtruding themselves into the strictly satirical rhythm of what may or may not have been the original composition, and there are also moments when a good, practical-minded pusher could have cracked a whip over the heads of everybody concerned and startled them into a little less lethargy, but, as the evening progresses (and it does progress), the humor of the thing builds itself into an almost irresistible good time and as I understand it, a good time is what we go to the theatre for these days.

Here, also, we find Miss Pauline Lord back again in a part exactly suited to her peculiar talents, and, as the maid-of-all-work who finds herself the sole custodian of the Bean tradition, she gives to the part what probably no other actress on our list could give in comedy and tenderness. Whoever played it in Paris could, I am sure, watch Miss Lord's performance and lift a bit of it to her advantage. Walter Connolly is again perfect as a small soul harassed by big things, and is still, in topical parlance, one of the few remaining undefeated teams of the East. Beulah Bondi, too, turns a conventional New England wife into a character of entirely different proportions and, whether Ernest Lawford likes to be told it or not, he might step right from the stage into the job of art critic on a New York daily.

I must protest, however, against the stage convention which makes it impossible for New Englanders to speak correct English. According to our playwrights, the only residents of Massachusetts who do not employ the double negative are the Overseers of Harvard College and possibly a stray hermit in Concord. For a young lady of the evident education and sartorial taste of Miss Adelaide Bean (no relation to the title rôle) to go about saying "I ain't got no" and "like I was going" is a slur on the notoriously efficient public-school system of Massachusetts which I, as an old Massachusetts public-school boy, hotly resent.

> --Robert Benchley in The New
> Yorker (November 12, 1932),
> page 22.

THE LATE GEORGE APLEY (John P. Marquand and George S. Kaufman; Lyceum Theatre, November 23, 1944)

This is a very slick article. Which should be no surprise
since J.P. Marquand, who wrote the book from which a thin sliver
has been made into a play, is a very slick writer of chronicles of
defeat (Apley, H.M. Pulham, Esq., So Little Time); George Kaufman
who, with Mr. Marquand, did the adaptation, and who, all by himself, staged the whole business, has never been associated with a
gauche, ungainly, or particularly unsuccessful production; and of
Max Gordon, the producer, ditto. Thus, The Late George Apley
reflects this combination of expert craftsmanship, of knowing showmanship, in a neat brick-by-brick building of a slick, successful
play.

    In Boston, in 1912, George Apley is a smug, satisfied member
of one of Boston's best families. He is fairly erudite too ... if you
accept an acquaintance with Emerson, Thoreau, and other flowering
New Englanders, and later, even Freud ... as substantial evidence
of erudition. His wealth is inherited, needs no particular attention
from him, so much of his time is spent on charitable committees and
clubs like one called The Bird-Watchers (which is a tenuous thread of
pathos throughout the play). Like all Mr. Marquand's heroes, Mr.
Apley is the epitome of defeat. Social and economic security having
won out against a brain and a certain genuine warmth toward his
fellow men, Apley is settling like an old, inanimate house into the
staid, smug pattern of Boston Brahminism. The first act, reflecting
all of this, is an exquisitely ghastly picture of a Thanksgiving Day
family gathering. The Apley children, a young man who goes to
Harvard, a young woman who goes skating with brash young pro-
fessors, are in full revolt against the deadly hand of family history.
How one young Apley wins out, how the other is defeated is the
meat of the play, which, while full of engaging jibes at Boston, at
upper class fuddy-duddies, never quite lives up to the promise of
its first act. At one point there is a conflict between Mr. Apley and
an up-and-coming industrialist from Wooster which might have been
sharp and exciting but which never quite comes off. So, too, with
the rest of the satire, which is of the strictly comfortable variety,
allowing 1944 prototypes of an Apley to sit in uproarious judgment
on poor old George, without the slightest twinge of personal identification. The humor is very Kaufmanesque, though the preponder-
ance of Harvard-Yale jokes is a little on the heavy side. Unless you
went to one or the other institution you won't split your sides.
Judging by opening night laughter, everybody in the audience, including Hope Hampton, had been to either Harvard or Yale. The
Late George Apley, then, is a very amusing, very light satire, with
a very regional flavor. While nobody says Mr. Marquand, Mr. Kaufman and Mr. Gordon have a duty to produce a genuine social satire
... it is perfectly apparent from this play that they are the boys
who could if they wanted to. in George Apley, they evidently didn't
want to, are even prone to betray a faint admiration for the Apleys
of the world.

    The acting is generally excellent. Leo G. Carroll is superb

as Apley, making the man lovable, gentle, a really good man ... a
man you'd like to give a good push to. Janet Beecher is sweet, real
as Mrs. Apley. Catherine Proctor is incredibly good as a poor relation slowly going mad from too many years of Boston and Apleys.
In an epilogue in 1924, David McKay does a truly admirable job of
growing up into a typical Apley. Stewart Chaney's set of a Boston
drawing-room complete with Stuart portraits, books, and Brussels
lace curtains, is very handsome.

> --Irene Kittle in Cue, Vol. 13,
> No. 49 (December 2, 1944), page
> 19.

* * *

From J.P. Marquand's well-known novel Mr. Marquand and
George S. Kaufman have made a pleasant play that will also be an
extremely popular one. It has its quota of funny lines, of entertaining scenes, of Beacon St. atmosphere; and in Leo G. Carroll it
has an actor who can play George Apley with genuine perception and
superb finish. That is as much, perhaps, as one can expect of
The Late George Apley on the stage. Obviously it had to differ
from the book, and it isn't surprising that it is by no means so
good as the book. And even on its own terms it is a little thin, a
little too mixed up in its tone, and more than a little repetitious in
its humor.

There isn't much point in extensively contrasting book and play;
at least, the main object--of portraying a Boston Brahmin who was a
slave to code and a creature, not so much of thoughts and emotions
as of conditioned reflexes--is the same in both. The double-lens
method of the novel, which parodies, a fuddy-duddy biographer
while satirizing his subject, must naturally be lost. So, too (which
is more of a sacrifice) must the gradual development of Apley himself. Apley is presented to us in middle age, after his character
has congealed. He is presented, atmospherically, in terms of his
very small pursuits and tempest-in-a-demi-tasse crises; he is presented a trifle more dramatically in relation to his son and daughter,
both of whom are ready to break with traditions for love (as once
their father had been). Along with this goes a comedy of Boston
manners, as well as some broader comedy that must be pinned on
New York, where Mr. Kaufman barbarically resides.

What we most lose of Apley on the stage is the chance to watch
him harden into a mold; as we also lose some of those centrifugal impulses that Apley could keep in check but never quite kill. We only
see a man who has made privilege a synonym for duty, and bumbling
pursuits a symbol of Boston importance. Apley is permitted his wistful reminiscences and for a time is even prepared to let his children
go their own way; but the reminiscences fail of effect, as the sudden
parental dispensations rather fail of credibility. The authors' char-
acter-drawing is really not so good as Mr. Carroll's character acting;

it is Mr. Carroll who, with real artistry, makes Apley always walk
his own chalkline.

The fun in the play lies in variations on the theme of Boston
smugness and snobbery, and some of it is very good fun indeed.
Apley's bird walks, Cousin Hattie's tombstone, Harvard, Emerson,
the outer darkness of New York--these take turns supplying laughs,
and perhaps they take a few too many. By the third act, at any
rate, the fun is pretty well played out. And the epilogue, which
shows Apley's son well on the way to becoming father, is on the
whole not judicious.

The acting is generally good, though it is done in rather a
medley of styles. Only Percy Waram as Apley's brother-in-law and
Janet Beecher as his wife play along with Mr. Carroll in the Beacon
St. manner; their performances are consonant and good. Margaret
Dale is good in a broader way, and in her one real scene Margaret
Phillips comes through very well. The least happy characterization
in the play is that of Apley's son, and it allows David McKay little
elbow room. Most of the other characters are helpful, and Mr.
Kaufman's direction is good on the whole, though it countenances
some running exits better suited to farce. Stewart Chaney's set is
suitably handsome.

                              --Louis Kronenberger in PM (No-
                              vember 22, 1944).

LIFE WITH FATHER (Howard Lindsay and Russel Crouse; Empire
      Theatre, November 8, 1939)

        This is an altogether delightful comedy. Whether or not it
completely visualizes Clarence Day's well known book I am unable to
say, as I have never read it; all I can say is that it stands firmly on
its own feet as dramatic entertainment. For this Howard Lindsay
and Russel Crouse are to be heartily congratulated. They have magnificently placed upon the stage the pompous, overbearing Victorian
husband, his wife, who always manages to manage him, and their
brood of redheaded children. In a sense the play is not a play at
all, for the story is a thin one, having chiefly to do with Mother's
successful attempt to get Father baptised. The triumph of the
adaptors therefore is the greater that the audience's interest rarely
flags. It is a triumph of characterization, of the whimsical revealing
of tiny bits of human motive and action. Father is certainly master
in his own house, and probably everywhere else--when Mother
doesn't get into action. But when Mother does, Father is always
circumvented, and what is more he knows it, though protestingly.
To hear delighted feminine voices whispering in the audience, evidently to their spouses: "That's just like you!"--when Father makes
one of his Victorian gestures of superiority--would have pleased Mr.

Day were he still in the land of the living, and certainly pleased
Mr. Crouse, if he heard them. Mr. Lindsay wasn't in a position to
hear them, for he was impersonating Father on the stage, and impersonating him with rare relish and effectiveness. In this he was
superbly abetted by Dorothy Stickney, who as Mother gives the performance of her career, a performance whimsical, knowing, packed
with charm. Admirable too are John Drew Devereaux, Richard Simon,
Raymond Roe, Larry Robinson, Richard Sterling, and Teresa Wright.
Life with Father is one of the two or three musts of the season so
far.

> --Grenville Vernon in The Common-
> weal, Vol. 31, No. 5 (November
> 24, 1939), page 118.

* * *

Story--The play deals, in the main, with those momentous moments when Mother was trying to get Father baptized. You should
know, if you have not read the book, that getting Father to do anything was something of a problem, and leading him to the baptismal
font was an effort of major proportions. His attitude toward the
church was somewhat lacking in reverence.

Also weaving gently through the affair is young Clarence's
love affair with a house guest.

The story does not make the play. It's Father. It's Father
reacting to the New Haven Railroad, maids, household accounts,
kippers, the mayor, the ministry, and cabs. Father screaming "Oh
God" when confronted with these things highlights a good dramatic
season.

Laurence Sterne once complained mildly of the "whiffling vexa-
tions that come puffing across a man's canvas." There was no mildness in Father. He puffed right back at them.

Acting--You could not fit one word of criticism in here. Howard Lindsay plays Father to the hilt. Every rant, every glare, every ripple of outrage comes naturally from the part. As Mother,
Dorothy Stickney offers equal perfection. Teresa Wright, a pretty
and attractive newcomer, excels as the girl Clarence falls in love
with, and John Drew Devereaux does splendidly as Clarence. The
rest of the cast render grand support.

Production--Stewart Chaney's costumes and set will carry you
right back to 48th Street when that thoroughfare was way up town.
Here is a good clean breath of old New York right down to the
kilties of little Harlan Day. They ought to set a fashion.

Cue Says--Life with Father makes a most beguiling evening.
The play never lets you down, never hits a false note, nor goes out

of character in search of a wisecrack. It gives you no brittle
sophistication to laugh at and walk away, but a pleasant warmth to
take home with you.

> --Oliver Claxton in Cue, Vol. 8,
> No. 21 (November 18, 1939),
> page 37.

THE LITTLE FOXES (Lillian Hellman; National Theatre, February 15,
     1939)

STORY--The Hubbards, Oscar and Ben, have made a deal
with a Northerner to erect a mill in their small Southern home town.
To fulfill their part of the contract they need $75,000 from their
brother-in-law Horace Giddens, who is seriously ill at Johns Hopkins. Their sister, Regina Giddens, lures Horace back home. The
action of the play then resolves itself into an astonishing display of
theft, chicanery, and general overall cruelty.

ACTING--Tallulah Bankhead, as Regina, heads this capable
cast, and gives a grand portrayal of a selfish, greedy woman. Carl
Benton Reid and Charles Dingle are fine as the brothers, and Patricia Collinge is excellent as the frustrated, drunken wife of Oscar.
Frank Conroy is good as the harassed Horace.

PRODUCTION--Mr. Shumlin has staged this perfectly.

CUE SAYS--This is a tense picture of greed and social stupidity that will hold you from start to finish. Put The Little Foxes
down as a play for you to see.

> --Oliver Claxton in Cue, Vol. 7,
> No. 18 (February 25, 1939),
> page 41.

* * *

With The Little Foxes, Lillian Hellman moves out of the damnable
brackets of "promising playwrights" to take her place among the top-
ranking American dramatists. For The Little Foxes is as sound a
piece of dramaturgy as any theater season can boast. It is not a
pleasant play, but to the theater craftsman it is a flawless one, and
to the theater observer it is one of the most exciting experiences
the contemporary stage can offer.

It is more than a case-history which Miss Hellman is this time
recounting. It is the drama of the rise of the industrial tycoon, the
ruthless capitalist made possible by labor conditions at the turn of
the century. Stealing, lying, killing, this snarling pack of representative little foxes--the family of Hubbards--arrives at power.

And at the play's close the victor is the most cunning among them,
the sister Regina who cheats her cheating brothers and is responsible for the death of her husband. Goaded on to power, Regina
is allowed a final glow of sympathy. Like Lady Macbeth, her conscience begins to color her thoughts--and yet you know there will
never be a sleepwalking scene for Regina. Conscience-stricken moments, perhaps, but moments that she will dismiss with an I'll-think-
about-that-tomorrow attitude.

   The Little Foxes, however, is not a starring vehicle; it is a
powerful play with ten good acting parts, and Herman Shumlin has
assembled what is just about the year's most perfect cast. Tallulah
Bankhead, playing the vixen Regina, gets her chance to create a
role in a really first-rate play, and how she takes it! Selfish,
despoiling, coarse, Regina--as Bankhead acts her--will go down in
the gallery of great acting performances. No less brilliant is Patricia
Collinge's portrayal of Birdie, the poor, frustrated aristocrat, the
only one of the Hubbards with background and innate culture. I
think this year's theater provides no more pathetic moment than
that awful confession Birdie makes, how she has been able to bear
the horror of her situation by becoming a quiet drinker. Frank
Conroy's work as Regina's husband is excellent, and Charles Dingle,
Carl Benton Reid, and Dan Duryea are the triumvirate of Hubbard
men--a trio of as loathsome villains as you could hope to find. I
liked especially Florence Williams as the young daughter, and thought
Abbie Mitchell magnificent as the old faithful negress. Indeed, magnificent is the word for The Little Foxes.

                                   --DeWitt Bodeen in Rob Wagner's
                                     Script, Vol. 21, No. 510 (May
                                     27, 1939), page 25.

                          *   *   *

   * Lillian Hellman's new play, The Little Foxes, provides fresh
evidence of its author's high position among American women writers
for the stage. Both in The Children's Hour and in this exhibit--
even, indeed, in certain phases of her defective Days to Come--she
indicates a dramatic mind, an eye to character, a fundamental
strength, and a complete and unremitting integrity that are rare
among her native playwriting sex. Her dramaturgic equipment is
infinitely superior to Susan Glaspell's; her surgery of and grip on
character are infinitely superior to Lula Vollmer's; and compared
with her Rachel Crothers is merely a shrewd damsel in a box-office
dispensing prettily water-colored parlor tracts. Some of her other
sisters enjoy pleasant little talents but there is none in the whole
kit and caboodle whose work shows so courageous and unflinching
an adherence to the higher and better standards of drama. Once

she has succeeded in mastering her present weaknesses--a periodic confusion of melodramatic bitterness with suggestive tragedy, intensified and unrelieved acerbity with mounting drama, and a skeletonization of episode with dramatic economy--she will find herself occupying a really distinguished critical place in our theater.

Her latest play, admirably staged by Herman Shumlin and given the best performance of her career by Tallulah Bankhead, to say nothing of being further assisted on its course by a supporting company with hardly a flaw in it, is a scrutiny of social and economic changes in the South at the turn of the present century. Related in terms of a middle-class family of rapacious and conniving knaves bent upon outdoing not only one another but upon sacrificing all that is proud and fine in the tradition of the old southland to the new economic slavery and the new capitalistic greed, it may flippantly be described as a Dodie Smith nightmare. It may also be less flippantly described as the very best illustration of the difference between the current cheap and squashy family drama calculatedly manufactured by English female pastry cooks and the fond intention, at least, of American women like this Hellman to bring to the stage that inner inviolable dramatic vitality and thematic meat which London critics on brief excursions to these shores so offendedly and patriotically minimize and derogate. From first to last, The Little Foxes betrays not an inch of compromise, not a sliver of a sop to the comfortable acquiescence of Broadway or Piccadilly, not the slightest token that its author has had anything in her purpose but writing the truest and most honest play on her theme that it was possible for her to write.

The central characters are a woman and her two brothers who individually and apart brook no interference with their selfish determinations to get for themselves what they want out of family, community, finance, and worldly position. The woman is hard, disillusioned, and merciless to the point of contributing to the death of her invalid husband in order to perch herself on top of the heap. The brothers descend to perjury, theft, and even to veiled threat of murder accusation to dislodge her from it. In the handling of character, the ghost of Strindberg here and there peers over Miss Hellman's shoulder as in the treatment of theme the ghost of Ibsen--momentarily and paradoxically, too, the ghost of the Pinero of The Thunderbolt--here and there edges the spook of Strindberg to one side. The conclusion resolves itself into a temporary triumph for the wily, slate-hearted female but with the evil of the money-hungry brothers' machinations a cloud darkening her future. And out of the parable of boiling acid there emerges the disgust and defiance of a new, young generation that throws into the face of mankind the challenge of human decency, fairness, equity, and honor.

Where the play partly defeats its potential, proper, and full effect is in the grinding monotony of its emotional drive, in its periodic over-elaborate melodramatic countenance, and in its failure to

invest its explosion with that complete sense of tragic purge which
is the mark and nobility of the drama of Melpomene. It strikes the
note of bitterness so steadily and loudly that, when the moment for
purging exaltation comes, the psychic and emotional ear is too dead-
ened to hear it even were it there. But just the same it is a play
'way above the general and, though it must by its very nature prove
anathema to popular audiences, a credit to its author and to American dramatic writing.

> --George Jean Nathan in Newsweek
> (February 27, 1939), page 26.

LOST IN THE STARS (Book by Maxwell Anderson, adapted from
    Alan Paton, Music by Kurt Weill; Music Box Theatre, October
    30, 1949)

    No telling what this fine, affecting musical narrative by Max-
well Anderson and Kurt Weill will mean to those who have not read
the novel it came from. I think it beautiful. I join in voting it a
sympathetic transportation from print into libretto and distinguished
score--and a handsome thing to see, besides. The Playwright's
Company, presenting it, does mighty well.

    Lost in the Stars comes, of course, from Alan Paton's great-
hearted Cry, the Beloved Country. Its re-workers seem to have
kept as close, probably, as opera-makers ever can to much of the
word and deed; even more so to the book's epic spirit. They've
left out some memorable minor characters. They've reconditioned
some scenes to full-blast oratorio and decorative miming. But their
medium obviously made them do so. Their results are vivid, exciting. They turn a loving little trudge into a large, picturesque
parade.

    Forgive them for changing the name of the piece. Their title-
song, it seems, was left over from a former collaboration. Also,
they'd long ago wanted to wring a musical out of just such another
saga of an ancient, errant Negro--"Scipio Africanus," wasn't it?
Well, they are good, loyal conservationalists, these Messrs. Anderson and Weill. Loyal to the public, too.

    The tale still tells of a grey-haired, simple old Zulu pastor
who must leave his little African hinterland parish, travel down to
wicked Johannesburg and search for some slack members of his family. The search is sad enough, the finding worse. For his son has
murdered a white man, a famously good white man. The supreme
penalty, sorrow and disgrace. It ends with the white man's father,
a stiff-necked Britisher, breaking down, shaking hands and sitting
out the final vigil with the Rev. Kumalo, that bewildered old black
Rock of God.

I could wish Todd Duncan, the Kumalo, a more sharply shaded character. Yet Mr. Duncan sings him stirringly, and there are many rich voices the match of his which make Mr. Weill's songs stunning. Here, re-employing the ballad-chorus technique which he used in his recent Lemonade Opera miniature, the composer gives us of his absolute best--with just a dozen instruments, at that. Some of his effects are magical.

The Mamoulian direction, the imaginative scenic sweeps by one George Jenkins, the spoken dignity and definiteness which Leslie Banks' performance lends--all these things help. It is a generous evening in so many ways.

> --Gilbert W. Gabriel in Cue, Vol. 18, No. 45 (November 5, 1949), page 24.

LOVE ON THE DOLE (Ronald Gow and Walter Greenwood; Shubert Theatre, February 24, 1936)

From England comes the best play of this season, an exciting drama of the British working class, expressed in such terms of mounting tragedy as must startle our own hysterical exponents of the left wing drama out of their noisy futility. This play gets to the bottom of things, it is embedded in the solid truth of moral decay under poverty and casts up the shadow of an appalling future for the unemployed, the desperate jobless who are down in the muck along with their trampled and abandoned notions of why they are and where they are going.

The authors propose no nostrum for the disease, their job is to report and dramatize. What Walter Greenwood has observed is recorded in his novel, from which this play has been wrought with the collaboration of Ronald Gow. They have written a drama which lives and glows on the stage, surcharged with emotion, paced slowly at first, but soon growing into a crescendo of developments which leave you almost breathless at its completion.

The setting is a slum of Manchester, England, a manufacturing center; the house is that of the Hardcastle's, respectable, vigorous folk, who are reduced to penurious jobs and the dole. The father is a dumb beaten man, full of despair at the failure of his honesty to win him some security. He has a wife, and daughter. In this last character the play's chief expression is found. She is young, struggling for a place in the sun. But the inexorable pressure of poverty destroys her, a little at a time, until at the end she throws over everything she believes in for the sake of financial security.

This actress is twenty-one year old Wendy Hiller, who came

out of the Manchester the play is set in. She electrified London in
the part and here she is duplicating that success. She is stunning
of face and figure and equipped with expressive gifts which are
rarely found in combination. As the play is the most exciting of
the season, she is its most exciting actress.

There is a perfect supporting cast, no quibbles being ap-
plicable to Reginald Bach, the director and the father in the play;
to the three filthy old women who express so vividly the degrada-
tion and decay of the district, Carrie Weller, Marie de Becker and
Helen Strickland; to Alexander Grandison, the son; to Marga Ann
Deighton, the mother; and to those other actors who have gained
distinction by their association with a fine play, Brandon Peters,
Stanley G. Wood, Barry Macollum, George Bleasdale, Johnny Cort,
Selma Hall, Rita Davies and Ross Chetwynd.

--Herbert Drake in Cue, Vol. 4,
No. 18 (February 29, 1936),
pages 6-7.

*   *   *

Both Love on the Dole, by the Messrs. Gow and Greenwood,
and Sweet Aloes, by Joyce Carey, were considerable successes in
their native England. In the former I could detect very little of
merit, and in the latter I could detect none at all. Despite the generally warm local critical reception of the Gow-Greenwood exhibit,
its unquestionably pregnant theme of the pressure of present-day
economic ills upon the humble of the world seems to me to have been
treated with so cut-and-dried a literality, to say nothing of so theatrically stenciled an approach to character, that it often verged
nervously upon the edges of burlesque. This, due in part to the
unbelievably ham manner of staging, became particularly evident in
the scene showing the two romantic young lovers, perched on a
high rock on the moors beyond Manchester, suddenly doomed to
tragedy by news of the young man's loss of his job. If the writing
of the scene had been twenty times better than it was--and it could
have stood the improvement--the setting, a kind of valentine cut out
in the middle of a drop-curtain with a lot of changing colored lights
played on it by way of suggesting the setting sun, would still have
made it a ridiculously laughable illegitimate dramatic cousin to much
the same scene in the operetta, Alone At Last. As for Miss Wendy
Hiller, whom all the critical boys fell for, both histrionically and pic-
torially (and apparently also anatomically), with an enthusiastic plunk,
my own critical enthusiasm must remain in abeyance until she ceases
fondly to listen to and caress her speaking voice and until, further,
she learns to regard it as a funnel for pure dramatic utterance rather than as a solo marimba concert.

--George Jean Nathan in Life, May
1936, page 21.

MACBETH (William Shakespeare, adapted by Orson Welles; Lafayette
    Theatre, April 9, 1936)

In Harlem's opinion, the Federal Negro Theatre Project's production of Macbeth, at the Lafayette Theatre, was an eminent success. After years of playing distasteful stereotype and idiomatic
roles in the American theatre, the Negro at last was attaining the
status of an actor.

It is generally believed that the Negro is a "natural" in an
idiom part. Broadway producers and directors have therefore felt
that the Negro has no need of real direction or training. They only
think of the Negro portraying Negro roles, but not an actor in the
sense of interpreting universal emotions.

The Negro has become weary of carrying the white man's black-
face burden in the theatre. In Macbeth he was given the opportunity to discard the bandana and burnt cork casting to play a universal character. Here, the Negro played a role not essentially
Negro in text. Nor was his race designated by the dialogue of the
play. From the point of view of the community, Harlem witnessed a
production in which the Negro was not lampooned or made the brunt
of laughter. He attended the Macbeth showing happy in the thought
he wouldn't be again reminded, with all its vicious implications, that
he was "a nigger."

While the play was not strictly Shakespeare's Macbeth because
of its Haitian background and other minor changes, this proved unimportant to the audience, because of its broader implications. The
play was definitely a break from the dialect part assigned to the
Negro in the present inhibited American theatre.

The presence of Broadway and Park Avenue in the theatre on
the night the play opened might have added to the glamour of the
occasion, but such an audience could hardly be termed a particularly
sympathetic observer for a play in which Negroes were not Stepin
Fechits or polygamous wenches. The Broadway reviewers, writing
for this group, therefore journeyed to Harlem with the idea of seeing
a mixture of Emperor Jones and Stepin Fechit, with burlesque thrown
in to season a palatable opinion many of their readers have of the
Negro. This was best evidenced by their reviews the following morning.

Burns Mantle in the New York Daily News wrote, "It is a little as though O'Neill's Emperor Jones had re-established his kingdom
in his South Sea Island." John Mason Brown, writing in the sometimes liberal New York Evening Post, thought, "... it should be a
tale of Black Majesty and of murder and of fear besides which even
Emperor Jones would seem tame."

Throughout the reviews the stereotype opinions of Negroes strongly stood out. Brooks Atkinson contributed a "classic" when he called the production "an idealization of Negro extravagance." But unhappily for Mr. Atkinson the "bizarre" costumes were conceived by Nat Karson, white. The re-arranging of the play was done by Orson Welles, the white director. Negroes merely played the roles and did the stage work which is always denied them in Broadway productions. Later in his piece Mr. Atkinson referred to the "ferocity of Negro acting" and how "... with an eye to animalism ... they turned the banquet scene into a ball."

Ignorant of what the production meant to Harlem, Burns Mantle reported that the "audience applauded because of its natural gaiety." Arthur Pollock adorned his piece with the statement "It (Macbeth) has a childlike austerity ... with all its gusto." And Percy Hammond, thinking in the same vein said, "They seemed to be afraid of the Bard, though they were playing him on their own home grounds." But Arthur Pollock reached the high point here, when he said, "They play Shakespeare as if they were apt children who had just discovered him and adored the old man."

None of these reviewers, however, applauded the fact that the Negro had discarded the bandana in the theatre and that a Negro Theatre was in the making. In line with the Herald-Tribune's anti-project policy, Percy Hammond concerned himself with the political aspects of the production. In his lead he took a slap at the government's subsidizing the project: "The Negro Theatre, an off-shoot of the Federal government, gives an exhibition of de luxe boon-doggling ... being one of your Uncle Sam's experimental philanthropies." Grinding the political axe even finer he decried, in effect, the employment of workers on a theatre project. He said, "Washington spared no expense in making it (Macbeth) an ostentatious spectacle. The costumes and the scenery might cause an unendowed Broadway impresario to tremble at its apparent costliness."

Despite Arthur Pollock's implication that Macbeth was in the same class as a popular Harlem night club show, for Negroes to play Macbeth is a significant departure from a long line of stereotype and idiomatic roles in the American theatre. The result was a magnificent and spectacular production of a Haitian Macbeth, competently acted by a cast of 175 beautifully costumed players.

The title role was interpreted by Jack Carter, who will be remembered for his amazing characterization of the vital Lonnie in the Theatre Union's production of Stevedore, and again as Crown in the Theatre Guild's original production of Porgy. Edna Thomas played Lady Macbeth with skill, despite Percy Hammond's feeling that she was "daintily elegant."

--Roi Ottley in New Theatre, Vol.
3, No. 5 (May 1936), page 24.

THE MADWOMAN OF CHAILLOT (Jean Giraudoux, adapted by Maurice
    Valency; Belasco Theatre, December 27, 1948)

    Maurice Valency's adaptation of Jean Giraudoux' Paris hit, La
Folle de Chaillot is original, imaginative stimulating theatre. It is
also beautifully acted and magnificently staged in the sets and costumes designed by Christian Berard for the Paris production. Add
to all of this the fact that it has many moments of high humor and
it is easy to forgive the Madwoman her two faults. Her dialogue is
occasionally turgid and her solution to the world's problems is perhaps a mite naive. But she is a welcome and decorative addition to
the Broadway scene.

    Giraudoux' comedy-fantasy tells the story of an ancient and
charmingly daft Countess who saves the "little people" of the world
by luring the forces of capitalist exploitation into an oubliette. Not,
of course, without considerable assistance from a large cast of picturesque characters that includes three other ladies as mad as herself and almost as ingratiating.

    It is the author's whimsical conceit that the city of Paris is
built on top of one of the earth's richest oil fields and that a ruthless industrialist and a monomaniac prospector intend to substitute a
wasteland of oil wells for the city of light. All of this so that they
may promote a new world war.

    But the forces of evil reckon without the Countess. Striding
about the neighborhood in her tatterdemalion, turn-of-the-century
finery, she rallies to the cause the king of the Paris sewermen, a
ragpicker, a deaf-mute, a juggler and assorted denizens of the Paris
substrata. Then she and her fellow madwomen hold a gloriously insane trial and the offenders are fooled into a descent into oblivion
by a carafe of water flavored with kerosene.

    The Countess' purpose is greatly facilitated by the fact that
she resides in a cellar that opens, conveniently, on the labyrinthine
Paris sewer and the denouement is handled as pure fantasy, which
makes it merry rather than macabre.

    The English actress Martita Hunt, whom you probably remem-
ber as the mad Miss Havisham in the film Great Expectations, is
superb in the rich central role of the mad Countess Aurelia. But
Estelle Winwood more than holds her own as the number-two madwoman, while Nydia Westman and Doris Rich are right in there fighting as the other members of the folle foursome. The play reaches its
high point in a scene in which this quartette exchanges elegant
badinage about non-existent animals and people. It's the biggest
thing since the Mad Hatter's tea party and it's battier, if anything.

    Other performers who loom large in the large cast are John

Carradine, Vladimir Sokoloff, Martin Kosleck, Clarence Derwent, Le
Roi Operti.

> The Madwoman of Chaillot is interesting and expert theatre.
> > --Thomas Brailsford Felder in Cue,
> > Vol. 18, No. 2 (January 8, 1949),
> > pages 18-19.

THE MAN WHO CAME TO DINNER (Moss Hart and George S. Kaufman; Music Box Theatre, October 16, 1939)

Story--A visiting celebrity-lecturer to a small Ohio town ac-
cepts a dinner engagement, slips on the host's doorstep and breaks
his hip. The host is then saddled with his crippled guest, who is
a burden of no small proportions.

While sitting in his wheelchair he ruins the peace of the house-
hold--nearly breaks it up, in fact--and endeavors to prevent the
marriage of his secretary to a local newspaperman.

The fellow is vain, sadistic, rude beyond measure, sly, and
a monument of egoism. The model for this chap is stated by all
hands to be Alexander Woollcott.

Acting--Monty Woolley is superb as the lecturer. Edith Atwater as his secretary, and Theodore Newton as the newspaperman,
are excellent. In minor parts John Hoysradt, David Burns, and
Carol Goodner handle themselves with finesse. The rest of the large
cast are up to their standard.

Production--Grand.

Cue Says--This is along the mad pattern of You Can't Take It
With You and equally as successful. A very funny play, touched up
with a lot of ludicrous side issues, it is definitely one for your book.
> --Oliver Claxton in Cue, Vol. 8,
> No. 18 (October 28, 1939), page
> 28.

* * *

This is another Kaufman-Hart success. They seem to flow in
as regularly as the tides, and if they are unimportant in the realm
of literature or psychology, they are theatrical entertainment at its
height. It is not even a secret of Polichinelle that The Man Who
Came to Dinner is about Alexander Woollcott; it has been proclaimed
from the housetops and with no protests from Mr. Woollcott himself.
Sheridan Whiteside is a lecturer, wit, and friend of the great who

gets marooned in a midwestern town and proceeds to insult everyone about him. The plot of the play concerns his attempts to break off the engagement of his secretary to a young journalist in order that his secretary may remain with him. Whiteside is an egotist, as cruel in his tongue as he is selfish in his life, even though he does think Christmas is his own private property. But he is a master of invective, and it is this invective which is the backbone of the play. The play itself is a farce-comedy; the second act is a masterpiece of construction. The first and third acts are perhaps less well molded, and the introduction of the mummy-case just a little too much to swallow. If it were sound-proof it would also be air-proof, with the result that the last act ought to end in a tragedy for the actress immured in it. But then the play is a farce and we must let it go at that. It is replete with riotous situations and Woollcottian remarks. Moreover it is superbly acted by Monty Woolley as Whiteside, by Edith Atwater as the secretary, by John Hoysradt as a thinly concealed Noel Coward, by Ruth Vivian as Lizzie Borden alias Harriet Stanley, by Theodore Newton as the young journalist and by a young American actress who has returned to her native land after becoming one of the toasts of the London stage--Carol Goodner. Unless I am very much mistaken, Miss Goodner is of star material.

> --Grenville Vernon in The Common-
> weal, Vol. 31, No. 2 (November
> 3, 1939), page 47.

MARY OF SCOTLAND (Maxwell Anderson; Alvin Theatre, November 27, 1933)

I ought to have a step-ladder on which to get up and say my piece about Mary of Scotland.

I am the first to throw rocks when the Guild gets on one of its high horses and comes a cropper, so I must not neglect to rejoice all over the place when they do a Mary of Scotland. I must get out and ring doorbells about this, yea, even church bells and college chimes. Pardon an old fellow's ecstasies; I used to enjoy a moderately highbrow thing once in a while back in the ivy-clad days, and I thought I'd forgotten how. Surges that haven't surged in me for years surged the night I saw Maxwell Anderson's Mary of Scotland. There's been such a vogue for catching significance in mediocre things, these past few years, for sensing submerged meanings in comic strips and other excrementary by-products of our hurried times, that it is pleasant to know that there is genuine magnificence left in a contemporary pen or two.

Little Helen Hayes, whom I last saw in some driveling cinema, here comes to rank among the really great actresses of any time, with sweetness, dignity, strength and richness of diction, and now

and then a saving hint of humor. And standing toe to toe with her
in this woman-fight is hoarse, hard Helen Menken as the ice-cold,
crafty Elizabeth who is out for Mary's scalp. These two girls, Hayes
and Menken, give you one of the great evenings of your life. And
Philip Merivale, looking more like a bare skull than ever, is superb
as Mary's rough and gusty friend, champion, suitor once rejected,
and lover finally accepted when it is too late for his troops to help.

Mary of Scotland is a project in the grand manner, which does
not falter an instant in a long evening all too short. And I thought
I hated costume plays!

--Don Herold in Life, January
1934, page 38.

ME AND MOLLY (Gertrude Berg; Belasco Theatre, February 26,
    1948)

After some 16 years on the radio, the Goldberg family have
finally reached the stage. On the stage their picture of Bronx home
life has the warmth its devotees will be expecting of it, and the humor they will demand. It's a picture that calls for some comment.
Up to a point, it's not only plausible but real. Up to a point, it's
not only amiable but affectionate. The characters have been taken
from life, the only question being where they have been taken to.
For if Me and Molly doesn't offer much in the way of reality, it has
a good deal in the way of realism--the drip pan under the icebox; the
piano hoisted in through the window. And if Molly Goldberg is much
of the time a rather specious Malaprop, she's even more of the time
a quite undeniable mother.

As a picture of a Jewish family in what might be called the
second stage of struggle--a struggle not to survive but to get on
and get educated--Me and Molly follows so broad an economic, social
and cultural pattern that you have to go out of your way, you have
to milk it purely for tears and laughs, to make it seem false. In
the same manner, the Goldbergs' neighbors so little try to be human
beings that it would be silly to say that they fail to be; they are
pure comic types. And to accomplish this much of her job, Mrs.
Berg needs no more than an observant eye, which she has. I won't
even add a sensitive ear--for what her people talk is as often stage
dialect as human speech.

With the Goldbergs themselves, however, we look for something more--something that evidences insight as well as eyesight, a
writer as well as a reporter. And by getting absolutely nothing more,
we feel that we are getting a good deal less. Watching the Goldbergs struggle vainly to be real people rather than standardized
blobs of emotion and behavior, we would gladly, after a while, have

them less real in exchange for being more robustly unreal, more ex-
uberantly and outrageously comic. But always <u>Me and Molly</u> introduces some relentless symbol of realism like the drip pan under the
icebox; always, as it veers toward the absurd, it sternly yanks itself back to the average, under the impression that the average is
the genuine. But the average, as it turns out, is more often the
dull and the flat. For I'm afraid that warm-hearted and observant
as she is, Mrs. Berg knows neither how to write, nor how to write
a play; so that <u>Me and Molly</u> is never interesting for long, even as
theater.

Having gone thus far in analyzing a play that I might more
succinctly--and more sensibly--have described as a popular-style comedy that I happened to find quite dull, I am tempted to make two or
three comments more. "It's certainly true to life," I heard some one
say as I was leaving the theater; and it struck me, and not for the
first time, how if enough details in a play are recognizable, the whole
thing can pass for real. The characters needn't breathe so long as
the radiator properly hisses; the emotions can come canned so long
as the fruit on the table looks fresh; while, ounce for ounce, average-
ness is much more convincing than art. And more convincing, for
one reason, because it's so much more reassuring: it introduces
none of those really ugly or depressing matters that people don't
want to be reminded of. In every age people like the Goldbergs have
only to appear to be voted wonderfully real, while an entire society
denounces Madame Bovary as overdrawn, or Hedda Gabler as incredible, or Hardy's Jude as quite monstrous. Surely none of us would
blame them for finding the Goldbergs more fun; must they always
find them more real as well?

Miss Berg is much the kind of actress she is a writer: as
Mrs. Goldberg she has warmth and personality and very little skill.
But by just being natural in a well-greased role she comes off better
than the more professional members of the cast. So very resourceful an actor as Philip Loeb seems to me sunk in the much less ingratiating role of Mr. Goldberg; and most of the other performances,
like Ezra Stone's direction, seem routine. Harry Horner's set contributes a good deal to the true-to-likeness.
                                        --Louis Kronenberger in <u>PM</u> (Febru-
                                          ary 29, 1948).

                              *   *   *

Gertrude Berg's comedy of life in the Bronx in 1919 is, in
its own way, as regional as any of the offerings of the Dublin Gate
Theatre. Based on the old radio program <u>The Goldbergs</u>, <u>Me and
Molly</u> is essentially a story of warm family life, with a fundamentally
human quality, friendliness and backbone of the nation overtones
that should endear it to family-style theatre-goers. It is thoroughly
moral, full of smiling-through-tears schmaltz and its cast is orna-
mented by the largest gathering of ingratiating children yet assembled
on any stage.

So it is probable that the public will overlook the minor circumstances that the play lacks one witty line or one original idea.

The heroine is the "Mrs. Goldberg" of the radio serial and is played by authoress Berg. Philip Loeb plays Darby to Miss Berg's Joan and Eli Mintz, David Opatoshu, Margaret Feury are conspicuous in supporting character roles (all the roles are "character" roles). It would be nice to pat all the individual small fry on the back but we'll have to be content with deep bows to Joan Lazer and Lester Carr as the little Goldbergs. Ezra Stone has directed with sympathy and understanding.

Me, I'd rather remember <u>Mama</u> but you, and lots of others, may forget her for <u>Molly</u>.

> --Thomas Brailsford Felder in <u>Cue</u>,
> Vol. 17, No. 10 (March 6, 1948),
> page 17.

* * *

*<u>Me and Molly</u> is Gertrude Berg's stage version of her popular radio program about the Goldberg family. In theory, this should have turned out as perfunctorily calculated as another <u>Abie's Irish Rose</u>. Instead, Mrs. Berg's play is a warm, amusing, and often touching comedy of real people and their minor problems.

The time is 1919, and the scene is an apartment in the Bronx into which the Goldbergs have just moved with the idea of buying a piano for their daughter Rosie (Joan Lazer). The plot is only a little more complicated than that. Uncle David (Eli Mintz) gets the piano, and Molly Goldberg sees to it that the bashful Mr. Mendel (David Opatoshu) marries the resident piano teacher (Margaret Feury). The rest is concerned with Jake Goldberg's ambition to go into the dress business for himself, and with Molly's maternal coaching from the sidelines.

Ezra Stone directs these intimate matters with dispatch and, considering their identification with vaudeville, with surprising subtlety. The cast is uniformly good, from the Goldbergs and their relations to a drove of visiting neighbors. Philip Loeb fusses and fumes properly as the harassed head of the Goldberg ménage, but it is Gertrude Berg herself who sets the pace for the evening with a thoroughly likable impersonation of her own Molly Goldberg.

> --<u>Newsweek</u> (March 8, 1948), page
> 75.

THE MEMBER OF THE WEDDING (Carson McCullers; Empire Theatre,
    January 5, 1950)

    Only the living stage can soar like this, and sometimes it
does. Sometimes, by sheer felicity of writing, acting, directing, a
small, frail play manages to fling its broomstick arms out almost
world-wide and make a marvellous ascent into regions strictly reserved for the saints and cherubim. Carson McCullers' dramatization,
as acted by Ethel Waters, Julie Harris and the rest, and as staged
by Harold Clurman, is one of those few plays.

    It is a play written pretty much against the rules, and there-
fore all the rarer. It seldom amounts to more than half a play, but
this half has a sympathy in it so distilled that its essence should be
kept in sacred vessels. It is infinitely lovely.

    Miss McCullers, that lady of the lonely heart and the golden
eye who has been treating us to some of our most distinguished contemporary novels, seems to have determined to do her own theatre-
chores in her own way, at her own gait, with her own meanings and
meanderings left intact. She has, and they are also left alive. Often radiantly alive.

    Her story is the slight enough one of the young girl in a
small Georgia town whose growing pains include a crazy impulse to
accompany her brother and his bride on their honeymoon. She'll be
denied this, naturally. We grin at her, alternately want to whack
or cuddle her, give a curiously glad gulp when, in the end, she
breaks through her chrysalis of the awkward age and finds a new
life just around the corner.

    Wait, this isn't just one of those Elsie Dinsmore books which
I'm probably making it sound like. Nothing Pollyannaish about it,
either. This young Frankie is made of fierce stuff, her fantasies
as piteous as rebellious, her insecurity washed down with bitter
spittle and back-alley obscenities. And what actually happens to her
happens against a background of death, double-death, all that grub-
by terror and tragedy and quiet protest at which Miss McCullers has
proven herself such a specialist. For Frankie's two inveterate com-
panions--an old Negro cook, a little boy from next door--come to
griefs too cruel to be tattled here. Cruellest of all that, she emerges
from them as unscathed as most kids almost always will.

    They are very dear character studies, these kitchen three:
the lank of a girl, the little, bespectacled boy, and the Jimtown
Mammie. Maybe the last of them, particularly as Ethel Waters plays
her, has to be the best. Has to be the big, fat, battered old
cushion of humor and humanity on which the whole business rests.
If so, Miss Waters wants and gets the major praises. Her performance is faultless, rich, forever right. The final sight of her sitting

dignifiedly, dumbly alone there in that deserted cook-shack is something never to forget.

As for Miss Harris, here's the chance for which this young
hopeful--increasingly hopeful, every unluckier piece she has appeared
in--must have been praying. She takes it and makes it a triumph,
nothing less. She pours an apparently unlimited zest into it. But
that's only the base of her concoction: she adds such a secret taste
and tang, such rough-tongued tenderness, as should make the role
famous. All the gangly ecstacy and agony of your own teen years
come back with her.

They have a wonderful find, too, in pint-sized Master Brandon
De Wilde. They have a cast of others altogether admirable, and a
set by Lester Polakov which helps and heightens. They certainly
have, in Mr. Clurman's, the finest of this year's direction. Anyway,
the most genuine applause of the year up and said so.

                                    --Gilbert W. Gabriel in Cue, Vol.
                                    19, No. 2 (January 14, 1950),
                                    page 20.

MISS LIBERTY (Music and Lyrics by Irving Berlin, Book by Robert
    E. Sherwood; Imperial Theatre, July 15, 1949)

The great expectations which preceded the arrival of this much-
heralded fable-set-to-music were not, unfortunately, realized. Miss
Liberty has plenty of everything. All the ingredients of a hit musical
are present, but there was something wrong with the recipe. It's
big and beautiful but just a bit boring.

Miss Liberty has music and lyrics by Irving Berlin, a book by
Robert Sherwood, direction by Moss Hart, settings by Oliver Smith,
costumes by Motley, choreography by Jerome Robbins and a dazzling
cast. Under the circumstances, it could hardly miss. But it does.
By an inch rather than a mile, but the inch is enough to spoil what
might have been a wonderful party.

Miss Liberty has an involved and altogether typical musical
comedy plot. It tells, quite tediously, I thought, the story of how,
after Mr. Pulitzer of the World had gained kudos and circulation for
his paper by raising the money to build a pedestal for the Statue of
Liberty, Commodore Bennett of the Tribune tried to go him one better by importing from France a young lady who had been the model
for Bartholdi's torch-bearing amazon. The only hitch was that she
had done nothing of the kind.

There is the eternal triangle, composed this time of Allyn Mc-
Lerie as Miss Liberty, Eddie Albert as a young Tribune photographer

and Mary McCarty as a Police Gazette reporter. Boy meets McCarty, boy meets McLerie, boy ditches McCarty and that's all there is to that. Which isn't enough, somehow, to justify all the shenanigans that take place on the stage at the Imperial.

There are several pleasing songs, notably "Homework," a torchy ballad that is projected to perfection by Miss McCarty, "Only for Americans," a novelty number that is the high spot of the first act and a song I liked a lot called "Paris Wakes Up." The management did not, apparently, share my opinion, since they gave this particular tune only a brief once-over. These and a couple of others are potential hit paraders, but the Miss Liberty music is not, on the whole, as outstanding as Mr. Berlin's last contribution to Broadway, Annie Get Your Gun.

The presence of the brilliant character actress, Ethel Griffies, in the cast is, perhaps, Miss Liberty's single greatest virtue. When she is onstage the show awakens and sings. And, fortunately for everybody concerned, she is onstage quite a lot. Philip Bourneuf and Charles Dingle portray, respectively, the Messrs. Pulitzer and Bennett, and do so with their accustomed skill. Mr. Smith's sets are all they should be. Mr. Motley's costumes are customarily elegant and Mr. Robbins' choreography, though not quite as original as usual, is certainly pretty to watch.

But the thing that Miss Liberty hasn't got is that indefinable "X" quality that makes a smash hit.

> --Thomas Brailsford Felder in Cue,
> Vol. 18, No. 30 (July 23, 1949),
> page 24.

MISTER ROBERTS (Thomas Heggen and Joshua Logan; Alvin Theatre, February 18, 1948)

You will like the executive officer of the U.S. Cargo Ship AK601 the moment you lay eyes on him. You will admire his quiet virility, his casual efficiency and his unpatronizing friendliness with the crew. And when you learn of his feud with the ship's captain you will instinctively take his side.

The AK601 performs its indispensable but unglamorous service hundreds of miles behind the combat zone, and Mr. Roberts wants to get into the shooting war. Every week he writes a letter requesting a transfer to a ship in the battle area, and as regularly the captain forwards his requests to the Navy brass, stamped "disapproved." The captain has a triple motive for disapproving Mr. Roberts' requests. First, because he dislikes the man and takes delight in frustrating him; second, because he does not want to lose a capable

executive officer; third, because he is a selfish and misanthropic
individual who does not feel secure unless the personnel of the ship
are constantly aware of his authority. That Mr. Roberts, serving as
a buffer between the captain and the crew, sustains the morale of
the men, who are often on the verge of mutiny does not make the
captain like him any better. The contest between the two men grows
increasingly bitter until their smoldering enmity flares up in an explosion of hate, and you will be happy when Mr. Roberts comes out
on top.

While Mr. Roberts is an emotionally exciting conflict of anti-
thetical characters, adapted by Thomas Heggen and Joshua Logan
from the former's novel of the same title, it is also a consummate
theatre piece, lush with delectable humor ranging from flashing shafts
of irony to such delicious morsels of low comedy as hauling a quartette of inebriated crewmen aboard ship in a cargo net and the concoction of "Scotch" whiskey from grain alcohol, Coca-Cola and iodine.
Since there is but one female character in the story, there is little
room for sex, but that little inclines toward pornography; and those
who may harbor the belief that Tobacco Road reached the ultimate
in coprology just ain't heard nothing yet.

Henry Fonda, starred in the title role, makes the character
dignified and appealing, while William Harrigan, as the captain, reminds one of an elemental force of evil. Robert Keith is perfect as
a kindly and humorous ship's doctor, and David Wayne is good as a
young ensign with girls on the brain. Jocelyn Brando makes a pretty picture in her white lieutenant's uniform; and the ruck of the cast,
as individuals and ensemble, offers a performance that is a high
tribute to Mr. Logan's direction. Jo Mielziner designed sets that are
both realistic and imaginative.

The production, presented by Leland Hayward, is residing in
the commodious Alvin. Thousands will be cheering Mr. Roberts for
many months to come, most of them, unfortunately, titillated by the
gutter words in the dialog. A minority will appreciate the tense
drama and Fonda's brilliant performance.

--Theophilus Lewis in America
(March 13, 1948), pages 669-670.

* * *

Joshua Logan and Thomas Heggen have translated the latter's
novel of life aboard a navy supply ship during the recent war into
eloquent theatre. It is not, in the opinion of this reviewer at least,
the greatest war play ever written but it is a rewarding evening's
entertainment.

As people who have read the book will remember, Mr. Roberts
does not concern itself with the blood and thunder of combat but
rather with the nerve tensions that arise in a group of men who are
destined to play a subsidiary role behind the lines. Since war is

one-tenth glory and nine-tenths boredom, the subject certainly deserves attention.

The Logan-Heggen script is consistently fast-moving and suspenseful, skipping from high hilarity to touching pathos with never
a thought for the unities.

The title role is custom-tailored to the talents of movie star
Henry Fonda who was, appropriately enough, a Lieutenant (jg) in
the Navy at one point during the war. He plays the part of a genial,
humane cargo officer who acts as a buffer between the harried crew
and the horrid captain, an all too familiar epitome of the regular service officers who plague a hitherto free citizenry in wartime. The
Captain is played by William Harrigan.

The other principal elements in this counterpoint of personalities are a lethargic and girl-crazy Ensign who is played to the
hilarious hilt by ex-leprechaun (of Finian's Rainbow) David Wayne
and a disillusioned, caustic ship's Doctor etched properly in acid by
Robert Keith.

The four officers play out the drama while a numerous crew
serves as a sort of animated backdrop. Stripped of its trimmings,
Mr. Roberts is the simple tale of how the good officer buys a liberty
for the crew from the bad officer at the price of his own chance
for a transfer to combat duty, how the men discover this and forge
an application for their benefactor and how the latter is finally killed
in action on the eve of VJ Day.

But there's a lot of good theatre woven around this plot. A
rip-roaring fist fight, an entertaining scene in which the sailors are
returned in various stages of disintegration from their shore leave,
another in which their reactions to the brief appearance of Miss
Jocelyn Brando (the only woman in the cast) are portrayed with
risible authenticity.

Jo Mielziner's sets are photographically exact reproductions of
various parts of the U.S. Navy Cargo Ship AK 601, known far from
affectionately to her personnel as "the bucket," and Mr. Logan has
directed the piece for the maximum of fluidity.

The shortcomings that keep Mr. Roberts from being quite as
honest a play about men without women as either Command Decision
or Skipper Next to God are that it is a little too glib, a mite too
contrived, a touch too sentimental and that it never quite makes up
its mind whether it is broad farce or high tragedy.

But theatre-goers will, without question, make up their minds
that Mr. Roberts is well worth seeing.

--Thomas Brailsford Felder in Cue,
Vol. 17, No. 9 (February 28,
1948), page 18.

* * *

*Strangely enough, neither the United States nor England was able to produce a solid play about the Navy during the war or during the current, nervous peace. All that is changed now. It shouldn't be news to anyone in New Haven, Philadelphia, or Baltimore that Mister Roberts, based on Thomas Heggen's popular novel of the same name, and dramatized by the author and Joshua Logan, is the United States Navy's gift to the theater.

Mister Roberts is the hottest thing to hit Broadway in many shore leaves. It has guts and gusto. It is alternately ribald and sentimental. It is brilliantly acted and brilliantly directed. Most of all, it is almost too hilariously funny for its own good. And, oddly enough, although the dialogue is sometimes rough enough to make the first-world-war What Price Glory? sound like The Rover Boys in the Rockies, it is never offensive.

Author, Author! Although Heggen, Iowa-born and a graduate of the University of Minnesota, saw a lot of action in his four-year stretch in the Navy, you would never guess it from either his novel or his play. His frustrated heroine is the U.S.S. Reluctant--the Navy cargo ship AK 601--that sailed the Pacific without ever having anything more lethal fired at her than an empty brandy bottle. Obviously such ships as the Reluctant, plying the back areas of the Pacific loaded with "toothpaste and toilet paper," helped make the war possible. But as far as the crew was concerned, the "bucket" was committed to a regular schedule between Tedium and Apathy (about five days each way in the heat) with an occasional side trip to Monotony and, once, a 2,000-mile run to Ennui. Any heroism involved was equivalent to manning a ferryboat between New York and Staten Island for several years without shore leave.

The result, of course, was ineffable boredom and a mounting tension that bordered on shell shock. Every man on the ship would have given a month's pay to be transferred--although very few of them had any desire to get in the way of a Zero. All except Lieutenant (jg) Roberts (Henry Fonda), who quit medical school because he really believed in the war and wanted to fight in it. Instead, his battle is with Captain Morton (William Harrigan), and in this crusade the crew and the officers are behind Mr. Roberts to a man. (The more adequate descriptions of Captain Morton must be omitted from any magazine that goes into the home.)

Staunchly arrayed with Mr. Roberts against the Captain are the ship's doctor (Robert Keith), a wise man, cynical and given to tippling, but always willing to share a gallon of medicinal alcohol with

the crew, and Ensign Pulver (David Wayne), who depends on Roberts
for educational and spiritual guidance, sleeps sixteen hours a day,
and spends his waking hours either talking about women or con-
triving elaborate and ineffectual plots against the captain's peace of
mind.

Out of these four characters and more than a dozen other less
articulate victims of heat and boredom and global celibacy, Mister
Roberts distills a wealth of incident that results in a rich, rewarding
balance of hilarious comedy and a sobering reflection on the relationship of men at war. It would be difficult to pick out one scene as
superior to another. Joshua Logan stages them all with zest and precision: Mr. Roberts's impulsive revenge on the captain, a free-for-
all brawl that would take Hollywood several days of shooting to dupli-
cate, a shore-leave aftermath that is a triumph of broad comedy and
stage mechanics, and, finally, the climax in which young Pulver, having learned of Mr. Roberts's death off Kyushu, suddenly grows up
to take his hero's place.

Men Without Women: There are women in Mister Roberts, although only one of them ever gets on stage. These are nurses who
are within range of telescopes and field glasses while they think they
are alone and unobserved. One of them (Jocelyn Brando) visits the
Reluctant with a jigger of Scotch in mind, and leaves hastily under
somewhat embarrassing circumstances. Otherwise, this is an all-
male cast, and Actor's Equity can be proud of it.

It is reported that David Wayne, who could have stayed on in
Finian's Rainbow as long as there was a pot of gold at the end of
the rainbow, rebelled at the idea that the American public might regard him as a permanent leprechaun. Nothing could be less pixy-ish
than his role as Ensign Pulver, and he makes his point in a performance that comes off second only to Fonda's.

It is Fonda, of course, returning to Broadway after ten years,
who dominates the neurotically embattled U.S.S. Reluctant with his
calm, knowing impersonation of Mr. Roberts. The Hollywood actor
was perfectly cast in the first place, but his sensitive performance
is just what the play needed to temper its rugged realism in its brief
time out for significance.

Fonda willing, he will become a permanent resident of New York.
The advance sale at the Alvin Theater's box office, in excess of
$400,000, sets an all-time Broadway record for a "straight" play and,
considering the New York reviews, that's only pocket change. The
old bucket Reluctant is firmly anchored on 52nd Street and now is
the time to start thinking of ordering seats for next Michaelmas.
                              --Newsweek (March 1, 1948),
                                pages 65-66.

MORNING'S AT SEVEN (Paul Osborn; Longacre Theatre, November
    30, 1939)

        Story--A bare, quick recital of the plot of Morning's at Seven
cannot include the flavor, the quality that goes into its telling on
the stage.

        The Swansons and the Boltons live in adjoining houses in an
American town. Aaronetta Gibbs lives with the Swansons, and all
the ladies involved are sisters. The "young folks" included are
Homer Bolton, reaching forty, and his fiancé of twelve years standing, Myrtle Brown.

        Cora Swanson wants to move herself and her husband Theodore
out of the house and away from Aaronetta. Myrtle wants to get married. Esther Compton, another sister, is at odds with her husband.
Carl Bolton is having "spells" at an inopportune time, just when
Homer has brought Myrtle to meet the family. Carl is smitten by
futility and wishes he had become a dentist. When this mood is on
him he leans against a tree.

        Acting--You can call this company of elderly and skilled per-
formers perfection. They all ring the true note. The sisters are
Jean Adair, Dorothy Gish, Kate McComb, and Effie Shannon. Enid
Markey is wonderful as Myrtle, and John Alexander grand as Homer.
The men of the family are Thomas Chalmers, Russell Collins, and
Herbert Yost. Congratulations to one and all.

        Production--The set by Jo Mielziner is something to love and
cherish. It is the back of the two houses, and a faithful and hearty
reproduction of those architectural monstrosities that respectable
folk along Main Street built toward the close of the last century.

        Cue Says--This play has a quality and an inherent humor that
make it thoroughly delightful. The humor stems from the situations
and the natural dialogue, and not from any irrelevant wisecracking.
Morning's at Seven is hereby heartily and happily recommended.
                                        --Oliver Claxton in Cue, Vol. 8,
                                        No. 24 (December 9, 1939), page
                                        51.

MOURNING BECOMES ELECTRA (Eugene O'Neill; Guild Theatre, Octo-
    ber 26, 1931)

        Two portions of this come with one order. You get a 5:30
P.M. show with an 8:10 rain check whether you like it or not. Bargain hunters will rejoice that they are saving two bucks by being

late in the season. The new O'Neill play shows him at his best, which means that half the audience tells the other half that he borrowed the idea from the Greeks and the other half opines that he could teach the Greeks a lot. The Greeks were just amateurs at gloom in comparison with the real New England temperament so familiar to O'Neill and so meticulously depicted by old favorites like Alice Brady and the expressive-faced Nazimova. A sincere and truly great tragedy which the Theatre Guild may well be proud to offer.

--Don Herold in <u>Life</u> (May 1932), page 42.

MY SISTER EILEEN (Joseph A. Fields and Jerome Chodorov; Biltmore Theatre, December 26, 1940)

Story--Ruth Sherwood and her sister Eileen come from Columbus, Ohio, to make their way in the big city. Ruth wants to write. Eileen wants to act. Ruth is wisecracking and without too much feminine allure. Eileen has all a girl needs to have.

Mr. Appopolous rents them a sub basement apartment in his Greenwich Village rooming house, along with subway blasting, leaking pipes, and broken locks on the doors.

The play has to do with how the girls make out in their efforts to keep going with the small amount of money to hand. They could go home but they do not want to.

Acting--A large banzai to the entire cast.

Getting down to details, give a mark to Shirley Booth as Ruth Sherwood. Give her a mark chiefly for playing the part with restraint and understanding, a part that could have run strictly to type. Jo Ann Sayers, in her first Broadway appearance, both looks and performs like sister Eileen, who kept the men spinning.

Morris Carnovsky, a fugitive from the Group Theatre, does grandly with Mr. Appopolous. Mr. Carnovsky stands out as an actor who can project his lines with clarity and a feeling for their content.

In lesser parts take notice of Gordon Jones, as a lodger, and Eda Heineman, as a tenant looking for a landlord.

Production--George S. Kaufman staged the play and to perfection. Donald Oenslager's set is excellent.

<u>Cue</u> Says--<u>My Sister Eileen</u> tops the season's new plays. Gay, amusing, and clean, for a change, you should have a fine time at it.

The humor is light-hearted, the byplay of the plot very funny indeed, and the whole a delight. Go and see it.

--Oliver Claxton in Cue, Vol. 10,
No. 1 (January 4, 1941), page
22.

* * *

All through My Sister Eileen we kept thinking about Elmer
Rice, even before we'd seen his latest show. That was because this
new play, adapted from the popular stories by Ruth McKenney,
deals, like [Elmer] Rice's Two on an Island, with the struggle of
young folks to get a foothold on Manhattan, but is somewhat more
casual and often resembles a game of tag rather than a play. It
lacks the social background and novelty of presentation in Rice's
comedy of last season, but it is bursting at the seams with comedy
lines. First-nighters, worn out by several weeks of drudgery with
petrified plays--a sad lot, these premiere slaves!--embraced the new
work by Joseph Fields and Jerome Chodorov with delighted funny
bones. It caught New Yorkers in holiday mood, ready to laugh just
because their Christmas shopping was over. So the play jumped into the hit class overnight.

It also had a couple of presents in its stocking. One was the
direction of George S. Kaufman, which not only kept this Greenwich
Village merry-go-round going, but also insured that the critics
would look upon the piece with proper deference. The other gift
was the performance of Shirley Booth, ambling through the part of
the elder sister Ruth like a droll case of throbbing head and aching
bunions. Miss Booth held the show together by the sheer, casual
flipness of her performance, at times when it might have slipped
even lower than the Village basement where it was laid. And to
think that a few years ago no actress annoyed us more than this
player, who now makes us bounce in our seat! Miss Booth has im-
proved vastly--or else we've softened up.

At times we detected a story in the piece--about a couple of
sisters who set out to conquer the literary and theatrical world, and
who finally stumble upon the beginnings of success. There's a misunderstanding when one sister thinks the other is in love with the
young editor whom she herself pants for. This misunderstanding
lasts all of five minutes, and puts that much suspense into the play.
Also there's a galloping scene where half-dozen young Brazilian naval
cadets, amorously following one sister home from the Brooklyn Navy
Yard, switch their impressionable ardor to the younger sister and
do a snake dance with her through the streets that shocks even the
cops of Greenwich Village. This is technically known as the climax.
But mainly audiences don't really bother with such trivialities. They
just get set for the laughs.

A program note quotes Ruth McKenney as saying that after

viewing the harum-scarum proceedings in the play, she decided it
wasn't part of her life at all, but just a fairy-tale. It's the kind
that might have been written by O. Henry and performed by a
Charley's Aunt troupe. Patrons enjoy it so much that few think of
the pathetic footnote of actuality, that the original of the sister
Eileen died just a short time ago in a California motor accident.

Jo Ann Sayers impersonates this person with a naïve acceptance
of male admiration, and the lack of stage skill noticeable in this West
Coast recruit fits in well with the ingenuousness of the part. Morris Carnovsky shares comedy honors with Miss Booth as a Greek
landlord with painting aspirations. The producer, Max Gordon, has
supplied an excellent cast to depict the Village's frowsy mounte-
banks, including Bruce MacFarlane as a snide reporter and Gordon
Jones, once a football star himself, as an all-American ace reduced
to ironing clothes for the gal who's supporting him. The only members of the cast who didn't get their full share of honors were the
two dogs who are paraded on the upper street level of Donald Oenslager's excellent set, which enables two planes of action to proceed
almost like a double feature. We saw these pooches being hustled
homeward from the stage door while the rest of the cast were still
taking bows.

> --Frank Vreeland in Rob Wagner's
> Script, Vol. 25, No. 582 (Janu-
> ary 11, 1941), pages 26-27.

NATIVE SON (Paul Green and Richard Wright; St. James Theatre,
    March 24, 1941)

Richard Wright's searing novel has been brought full fledged to
the stage by himself, Paul Green, and the theatrical craftiness of
Orson Welles. It will give you a deeply moving, highly exciting
evening.

Played in ten scenes for two hours and without an intermission,
it holds you beyond the discomfort of sitting in one place, intent on
one subject for so long a time. Call it triumphant theatre.

Here is the presentation of a case, the lot of the Negro in
this White country, stated in terms of raw melodrama and at the end
special pleading, that will leave you thoughtful and shaken when you
leave the theatre. Go braced for a hard boiled evening.

The story deals with Bigger Thomas from the colored slums of
Chicago. Bigger is ignorant, resentful and lost. He gets a job driving the car of millionaire Dalton and in the course of his duties takes
young Mary Dalton on a tour of communist meetings and colored
night spots.

Trying to get the drunken Mary to go to sleep quietly he is discovered by Mrs. Dalton, who is blind. Or rather he is not discovered, but in fear that he may be, he strangles Mary to keep her silent. From there on he runs away from the law, and of course, is captured, tried, and convicted.

The somewhat overlengthy statement of Bigger's case in the book has been skillfully telescoped in the play.

Canada Lee plays Bigger to perfection. He brings out in full the ignorance, hope and the resentment of the character. As Mary Dalton, Ann Burr does splendidly in the scene where Bigger kills her. This scene is perfect in writing, acting and directing. In especially excellent support are Rena Mitchell, as Bigger's girl, Ray Collins, as his lawyer.

Mr. Welles' production gives the play a strength and a value it does not intrinsically hold.

--Oliver Claxton in Cue, Vol. 10, No. 13 (March 29, 1941), page 30.

* * *

We must confess that we have kept away from Native Son, the dramatization by Paul Green and Richard Wright of the latter's novel, because of a prejudice. Whenever a critic admits to a prejudice, that's news. But we have actually been reluctant to do an injustice to the authors and players in this drama of negro oppression.

One of our basic resentments, which we find it hard to overcome, is against the prevalent hullabaloo by adulators of the negro around New York. We regard it as spurious and hypocritical in a large degree. We know of women who professed to admire Paul Robeson, made a great fuss over that great artist at a social affair, and then, after dancing with him, went off in a corner and made remarks behind his back. We've seen people who grew very emotional about the plight of the poor colored man, but who humiliated their darky servants before others. We always got along without any trouble whatever with any colored workers we've encountered, but we never made a righteous to-do over them. It's just a current variant of the old missionary mothering of the benighted Africans, now out of date.

Lest our rankling conviction about this creep into a review of Native Son, we have decided to confine ourselves to a report that the local drama-tasters acclaimed the acting of Canada Lee, former negro pugilist champion, in the lead, and gave grudging but high tribute to Orson Welles' direction, hailing the play as a sensational hit in a

season that has suddenly awakened just when it was slipping into
summer hibernation.

> --Frank Vreeland in Rob Wagner's
> Script, Vol. 25, No. 596 (April
> 19, 1941), page 27.

NIGHT MUST FALL (Emlyn Williams; Ethel Barrymore Theatre, Sep-
    tember 28, 1936)

    In Night Must Fall Emlyn Williams cannot escape the fascination
of peering through the dark window of the soul of a criminal. His
play is set conveniently enough in a small English cottage, close by
the site of a recent murder. Outwardly the drama progresses with
the tense excitement of the excellent mystery show, but there is, in
addition, an almost morbid preoccupation with what goes on in the
mind of the protagonist.

    It is a familiar experience to have sudden glimpses of the sub-
personality one never receives in comfort, but usually with curiosity.
Mr. Williams' own curiosity is so intense, however, that it arouses
your own and in the safe anonymity of the dark theater you find
yourself travelling with him down unfamiliar paths.

    The wonderment follows you out of the theater and away from
the play which was, after all, offered strictly as entertainment.
Yet, there is some question about that, too. Mr. Williams is doubly
successful with his play because he not only entertains you with a
first class show but also infects you with the excitement of his own
inner probing.

    Through the progression of this well conceived and carried
out play you are recurrently seduced by the wedge-words of the
author to a more intense observation of what goes on in the mind
of one, Dan, a bellhop in a neighborhood hotel. There is little question that he has committed the butchery which was found in the back
yard of Mrs. Bramson's cottage. Yet only the audience, and the
girl, Olivia Grayne, are sure. The others live in their comic British
way, unconcerned.

    One of them, Mrs. Bramson, a wealthy widow, is cozened by
Dan, who intends to murder her at the end of his pleasurable cat-
and-mousing. He opens up the window of his mind, however, to the
girl Olivia, who finds strange fascination therein. Eventually, she
falls in love with the boy, and tries frantically to shield him from
the police at the last minute.

    Mr. Williams plays the leading role himself, giving an impres-
sive demonstration of the capabilities of a really first-rate actor.

His characterization is a magnificently conceived and acted piece of technical proficiency. The supporting company, while without the vibrating acting of its author-director-star, gives an admirable counterpoint performance. Mr. [Jed] Harris is to be congratulated on his first play of the season.

> --Herbert Drake in Cue, Vol. 4,
> No. 49 (October 3, 1936), pages
> 14-15.

NIKKI (Book by John Monk Saunders, Music by Philip Charig; Longacre Theatre, September 29, 1931)

The John Monk Saunders story of war flyers--with music. It should be gone before you decide not to see it.

> --Life (October 30, 1931), page
> 21.

OF MICE AND MEN (John Steinbeck; Music Box Theatre, November
   23, 1937)

My friends who have read the book tell me that this is a dramatization with the utmost fidelity in motivation and action to the novel from which it has been converted for stage purposes. That can be readily accepted, because the author was also the adapter.

This is a compressedly realistic play. It tells of two farm workers who tour the west. One is a pathological case, a sub-zero moron with the strength of a chimpanzee and the mind of a backward child. The other is a sympathetic fellow who protects and mothers the idiot. The story of their last job is told in their own language, which is to say the farmhands' version of gutter argot. On reflection, it appears that the words used are perhaps the strongest that the stage permits today but they are so essentially correct in their own atmosphere that the impact comes later, when the observer is not intent on the play.

The leading character is called Lennie. He has slight capacity for memory and when excited becomes extremely confused. Engaged in a fight he grabs and holds, crushing his opponents' hands without especially meaning any harm. Caressing a puppy, he overdoes it and rubs the thing to death. Another pet habit of his is to stroke mice, which promptly die. To make the tragedy, he comes to grips with the smooth hair on the head of a backwoods tart, snapping her neck when she grows afraid of his touch.

The play, whatever the intention may have been, emerges as more of a case history shocker than as a tragedy. It seemed to me that it is presented more with the intent of being sensational than anything else. Much of it is over-directed. The scene in which a dog is killed, for instance, has no necessary relation to the play.

In the first place, is it necessary that these observations be offered in the theater? Like the murder stories in the tabloids they are completely unnecessary to living or to art. This is morbidity, not tragedy.

Some very fine actors are in the cast. Broderick Crawford has the virtually impossible task of portraying the psychopathological case. He does his best but he reminded me more of a man drunk on top of a gigantic hangover than of an ill mind. Wallace Ford has the part of the over-sentimentalized keeper of the idiot. He is a fine actor in what he has to do but his task is not credible.

> --Herbert Drake in Cue, Vol. 6,
> No. 6 (December 4, 1937), page
> 13.

* * *

The first play of the year which can in all honesty be called flawless is John Steinbeck's dramatization of his own novel, Of Mice and Men. To those who read that simple, stark prose-tale, it must have been apparent that here was drama primarily elemental, ruthless, and inevitable. Steinbeck has preserved those same sterling qualities in his dramatization.

Of Mice and Men was and is remarkable in that it is one of the few psychopathic studies which embody both pity and terror. It is an American folk play containing those same dramatic elements which made the Greek stories of kings heartrending and awesome. Without apparently trying, Steinbeck has captured a classic quality that evaded Eugene O'Neill and Maxwell Anderson when they consciously sought to re-adapt the Electra and Medea legends. But more than that, this play is told so simply that, were it stripped of its hearty, naturalistic dialogue and acted entirely in pantomime, it would still tell its brutal tale with relentless intensity.

George S. Kaufman has performed his smoothest directorial assignment, and Donald Oenslager has conceived a series of strikingly beautiful sets. The cast comes as near to perfection as human actors can. Hollywood has never really done right by Wallace Ford; he has made supporting rôles in pictures like The Lost Patrol and The Informer outstanding portraits, but he has also been condemned to a series of half-baked wise guys completely unworthy of him. Now, as kind-hearted George, he plays the part of his life--a tender, earnest performance. Broderick Crawford, as poor Lennie who couldn't help killing the things he loved best, likewise plays with

174 Of Thee I Sing

compassionate understanding. John F. Hamilton as Candy and Will
Geer as Slim contribute superbly imagined performances, as indeed
does every masculine member of the cast. Claire Luce dresses over-
theatrically as the San Joaquin tart, but her performance is nevertheless sympathetically contrived.

Paste the season's first gold star opposite the name of Sam H.
Harris for his production of Of Mice and Men. This play is unique.

> --DeWitt Bodeen in Rob Wagner's
> Script, Vol. 18, No. 442 (De-
> cember 18, 1937), pges 32-33.

OF THEE I SING (Book by George S. Kaufman and Morrie Ryskind,
Music by George Gershwin, Lyrics by Ira Gershwin; Music Box
Theatre, December 26, 1931)

William Gaxton, a Jimmie Walkerish Presidential candidate--
running on a platform of love, pursued by a jilted Atlantic City bathing beauty, and baited by a timid stranger-to-everybody (resembling
a composite Hoover and Coolidge and turning out to be Vice-President)
--is ha-ha No. 1. Add the pineapple tartness of Florenz Ames who
sings, "She's the illegitimate daughter of the illegitimate son of the
illegitimate nephew of Napoleon" with as much vim as if he had been
told the understudy could do as well, and you have Laugh No. 2.
The third comes when the timorous Vice-President asks, "Don't you
think more people might read the Presidential speeches if they were
funnier?" and the President grimly retorts, "I don't think so. Some
of them have been very funny."

> --Don Herold in Life (May 1932),
> page 42.

OKLAHOMA! (Book and Lyrics by Oscar Hammerstein II, based on
the play, GREEN GROW THE LILACS, by Lynn Riggs, Music by
Richard Rodgers; St. James Theatre, March 31, 1943)

The Theatre Guild, bewhiskered oldster of the footlights, has
been kicking up its heels this season. Having first produced the
domestic fantasia Mr. Sycamore, it proceeded to collaborate with The
Playwrights in the Luntish musical extravaganza The Pirate, and now
is altogether on its own with another, Oklahoma!--a musical comedy-
drama as happily filled with melody and humor, skittish playing and
exuberant dancing as anything you've seen on the boards in years.

Oklahoma! is a musical and visual delight--an altogether enchanting show to which you can, and should, take the whole family.

Based on Lynn Riggs' Green Grow the Lilacs (1931), this beautifully
and expensively produced romantic opus (the love of a lovelorn cowboy for a neighbor ranch-girl) is set at the turn of the century in
the old Indian Territory. Richard Rodgers has written 15 or more
songs that are among his best (half of them will certainly be hitting
the hit parades for years); Russell Bennett's orchestration of Rodgers' lively score chuckles with melodic giggles and sly harmonic
whimsies; Oscar Hammerstein 2nd's spritely book and jolly lyrics are
as amusing as his tender love songs are captivating; and Agnes De
Mille's choreography sparkles with jocose satirical ballet, jaunty taps
and waggish dance improvisations.

The cast couldn't be bettered. Alfred Drake and Joan Roberts
in the leading romantic roles have lovely, fresh young voices, and--
what is more astonishing in a musical--they both can act, which is
equally true of the whole cast. Betty Garde, Joseph Buloff and
Ralph Riggs contribute enough comedy to fill half a dozen ordinary
shows--to which you can add Celeste Holm and Lee Dixon, complete
with comic ditties, and Howard da Silva, a chilling menace who can
also sing a doleful dirge with a juicy jive jingle.

There are dozens more--all contributing enthusiastically and
generously toward making this a gay evening in the theatre: Rouben
Mamoulian's frisky direction; Lemuel Ayers' rich, rangy sets; Miles
White's nostalgic costumes. They all say--and I add my voice, too--
go see Oklahoma! and lose no time about it!

--Jesse Zunser in Cue, Vol. 12,
No. 15 (April 10, 1943), page
26.

*   *   *

Oklahoma! is a little more than a musical comedy without being
pretentiously so. Based on Lynn Riggs' Green Grow the Lilacs, it
is a folk musical laid at the turn of the century, for which Richard
Rodgers has written one of his most charming scores, and into
which Agnes de Mille has introduced some picturesque and lively
dancing, and a very good first-act-finale ballet. The whole show
has just enough of an old-fashioned period quality to be pleasantly
refreshing.

The book, to be sure, is just one of those things, if that, and
the comedy is neither subtle nor extensive. But they play so minor
a part in the evening's business that they can play an equally minor
one in this review. Oklahoma!--for the record--tells of the trouble
a couple of nice guys in cowboy boots have in winning a couple of
pretty farm girls. A comic peddler and a villainous hired man provide the competition, and dutifully scram at the stroke of 11. For
regional color, there's a box social, Lemuel Ayers' very attractive
sets, and an assortment of ten-gallon hats.

Mr. Rodgers' score is agreeably varied, but the bulk (and the best) of it is well on the romantic side, with plenty of melody and warmth. "People Will Say We're in Love" and "Oh, What a Beautiful Morning" sing themselves rapidly into your memory, and "The Surrey with the Fringe on Top" has a gay and humorous lilt. Mr. Rodgers' ballet music is full of color: "I Can't Say No" is a good comic ditty; "Poor Jud" an amusing mock-mournful one; and "Oklahoma" is one of those lusty anthems that the whole cast rolls up to the roof. Mr. Hammerstein's lyrics have less crispness and wit than Lorenz Hart's at their best, but the songs in Oklahoma! call for less sophisticated words, and Mr. Hammerstein has found very likeable ones.

Miss de Mille's dances have style, and a personality of their own; and her ballet--though I wasn't crazy about the end of it-- has freshness and variety, and enough humor to keep it from turning fancy.

Joan Roberts is pleasant and pleasant-voiced as one of the heroines and Celeste Holm (though she can't sing) amusing as the other. As the more prominent of the two swains, Alfred Drake is engaging and capable, with the right voice for his songs. Joseph Buloff shows his comic skill by making the peddler amusing without much help from the book.

Oklahoma! is just different enough to add something special to Broadway's musical life.

> --Louis Kronenberger in PM (April 1, 1943).

OLD ACQUAINTANCE (John Van Druten; Morosco Theatre, December 23, 1940)

Story--Katherine Markham and Mildred Watson Drake, both novelists and both getting along in years, are friends. Mrs. Drake has a 19-year-old daughter, Deirdre. Miss Markham has a lover ten years her junior, Rudd Kendall. Rudd climaxes one of a long line, Miss Markham having plenty to say all through the play about the number of affairs she has had.

Rudd wants to marry her, and after proposing, falls in love with Deirdre.

Acting--Jane Cowl, as Miss Markham, and Peggy Wood, as Mrs. Drake have themselves an actresses' field day with this, and very fine they are at it. The honors are even.

Adele Longmire is pretty and capable as Deirdre, and Kent Smith all right as Rudd.

Production--Auriol Lee has staged the play skillfully.

Richard Whorf designed the sets, and with the apartment living
room in the second act has produced a masterpiece. Called on by
the script to design something horrible, he succeeds up to the last
color conflict.

Cue Says--Rate this an uneven minor comedy, redeemed by the
performance of the two stars. Some of Mr. Van Druten's lines are
bright, some duller.

This seems to be sex year and Old Acquaintance does not stray
too far from the beaten track.

> --Oliver Claxton in Cue, Vol. 10,
> No. 1 (January 4, 1941), page
> 22.

THE OLD MAID (Zoë Akins; Empire Theatre, January 7, 1935)

The Old Maid, dramatized by Zoë Akins from the Edith Wharton
story, is a tear-jerker that belongs to the drama's yesterdays, that
period so wistfully and affectionately recalled by oldsters who lustily
cry into their beer at the mere mention of the old Empire Theatre
and who spent most of their evenings at Krause's Music Hall. It is
as anachronistic as Samuel Shipman. (Incidentally, Sammie again appeared on the modern scene recently with a melodramatic something
called A Lady Detained, which belonged to a period antedating The
Old Maid, although it is impolite to the latter to mention it in the
same breath.)

> --George Jean Nathan in Life,
> March 1935, page 30.

* * *

Delia Lovell, loving and loved by a gentleman called Chet
Spender, whom the audience never meets, nevertheless marries Jim
Ralston. Cousin Charlotte Lovell also loves Spender. He and she
take a little walk together following Delia's wedding. The little walk
ends in Spender going to Europe, and without his knowledge, leaving
Charlotte in that certain condition.

Aided by a family physician, Charlotte, for a period of years,
is able to pass off her child as a deserted foundling. Establishing
a kind of day nursery for poor children, she is thus enabled to see
her own daughter daily. Circumstances, which arise out of her sub-
sequent engagement to Jim Ralston's brother, Joe, force her to confess her indiscretion to Delia. The first result is the breaking off
of her marriage plans.

Delia's self-frustrated love for Spender instigates in her an insatiable hatred for Charlotte and an intense love for Spender and Charlotte's offspring, Tina.

A clear thinking woman with the ability to make those about her see things her way, Delia sets her plans and succeeds in usurping Tina's affections from her own mother. Meanwhile, we see Charlotte sacrifice her whole life for a daughter who, in time, grows to loathe her....

This synopsis is the gist of Edith Wharton's novel The Old Maid. It is also the gist of the play, current at the Empire, which Zoë Akins fashioned from the novel. It is a drama to which you must bring the mood of old lace, and from which you may garner something of the incense of sweet lavender. In brief, its maternal phase makes it ripe for the season's finest cry.

To the drama Judith Anderson as Delia brings an overwhelming performance. All the more overwhelming for its sustained and brilliant underplaying.... In contrast, Helen Menken's Charlotte is at first somewhat simpering. Later it becomes a trifle too brittle, and wears its maternal instinct too much outwardly and too little inwardly. It gave me the feeling of Miss Menken's last season's Elizabeth, handicapped by the secretiveness surrounding an illegitimate child.

It was good to see the veteran George Nash as the family doctor. Good, too, to see Margaret Dale delightful as a wealthy aunt. Margaret Anderson's Tina was also in the right key.

Localed in old New York, this period play has the benefit of Guthrie McClintic's artful direction and is also enhanced by Stewart Chaney's utterly exquisite settings and authentic costumes. These may be gazed upon with respect and admiration.

The women folk will lead the way to The Old Maid. Where women go, men follow.

> —D. Frank Marcus in Cue, Vol.
> 3, No. 12 (January 19, 1935),
> pages 11-13.

ON BORROWED TIME (Paul Osborn; Longacre Theatre, February 3, 1938)

The engaging notion which is the mainspring of this play is that it is given to the very young and the very old to have certain perceptions and perhaps certain powers not vouchsafed to ordinary people. Old Gramps in this play, and seven-year-old Pud, are

equipped to deal with many things, including Death. That grim
spectre appears as Mr. Brink early in the play to take Gramps away,
but the old gent is too strong minded and chases him up a tree.

The fantasy is beautifully handled by Paul Osborn, who has
not made a single slip on either the whimsical or sentimental side.
His characters are real people, lusty, crossgrained, petulant, acidulous, or naughty, running down the scale of ages. The character
of Gramps, magnificently played by Dudley Digges, is a profane old
man, given to tobacco, drink, and reminiscent leering at the neigh-
boring women. The grandmother is sweet but occasionally sour, and
the little boy gives promise of being as full of hell as his willful
grandparent.

The play is about what happens to Gramps when he has Mr.
Brinks safely up the tree. The local doctor thinks he is crazy, and
there is some shooting, but no death. There is a funny scene where
the doctor tries to kill a fly and cannot. However, it is made very
clear that the Paul Osborn notion of Death is rather pleasant and
easy going, which makes it possible for the traditional ending in
this type of play, the death of both Gramps and Pud. The latter
was played by an engaging little boy named Peter Holden, whose
performance was almost as perfect as the brilliant playing of Dudley
Digges.

> --Herbert Drake in Cue, Vol. 6,
> No. 16 (February 12, 1938),
> page 13.

* * *

No more satisfying play has appeared on Broadway this season than Paul Osborn's dramatization of Lawrence Edward Watkin's
novel, On Borrowed Time, Dwight Deere Wiman's hit-contribution to
this year's theater. Like Our Town, it deals with a subject generally conceded to be taboo on the other side of the footlights--death.
More remarkable, however, is that the treatment is not only wholly
entertaining, but at times uproariously funny.

Death in On Borrowed Time is personified by an average, soft-
voiced, middle-aged gentleman named Mr. Brink, who looks for all
the world like an insurance salesman. When it comes time for anyone to quit this life, Mr. Brink quietly appears, and releases him
gently from earthly cares. But Gramps Northrup fights off Mr.
Brink. Gramps has the affairs of his grandchild Pud closest to his
heart; Pud must not fall into the hands of a tyrannical aunt ("whore
of Babylon" Gramps calls Aunt Demetria). Eventually, Gramps gets
Mr. Brink up a tree, and keeps him there until Pud's future is determined.

In essence, On Borrowed Time is a modern re-telling of a medi-
eval legend. But what Watkin did for the old tale of death on a holi-

day was to create two homely characters as protagonists--an old man
given to blasphemy and a small boy given to imitation. What Osborn
did was to transfer Gramps and Pud to the stage, losing none of the
essential joy of those characters in the transference. Osborn, whose
chief claim to fame has heretofore been that comedy of a modern
Malaprop, The Vinegar Tree, has not betrayed Watkin's story by any
addition of cloying sentiment, and he has done, furthermore, a remarkably concise piece of dramatic construction. The play's manuscript, in turn, has benefited by Director Joshua Logan's sensitively
guided and humorously touched direction.

        The actors are all to the good. Dudley Digges has, in the
role of Gramps, the part of his life, and he plays the profane old
man with unequaled charm. He will probably go on playing Gramps
as long as he wants, for On Borrowed Time is of the stuff that en-
dures in the American theater. Much has been written about that
miraculous seven-year-old, Peter Holden, who plays Pud. I can only
note awesomely that Master Holden knows more about the beauty of
naturalness on the stage than many a senior actor. Fond mamas
and papas with ambitious darlings might take a hint: Master Holden
has never seen a play from out front. Frank Conroy makes Mr.
Brink an utterly pleasant gentleman in sack suit and topcoat, and
Dorothy Stickney is to be especially commended for the skill of her
characterization as Granny.

        All in all, On Borrowed Time is a well-nigh flawless fantasy.
Actually, however, the play grows beyond whimsy and fantasy; it
is in the further realm of magic, for it invokes and sustains a proper
spell of sheer enchantment.
                              --DeWitt Bodeen in Rob Wagner's
                                Script, Vol. 19, No. 458 (April
                                16, 1938), page 12.

ON THE TOWN (Book and Lyrics by Betty Comden and Adolph Green,
      based on an idea by Jerome Robbins, Music by Leonard Bern-
      stein: Adelphi Theatre, December 28, 1944)

        A lot of new stars deserving of a lot of new adjectives got born
the other night at the Adelphi Theatre, when On the Town came into
town for what looks like a good, long stay. It is not, thank God,
like Oklahoma! and it doesn't make the slightest effort to be. It is
full of sprightly and sharply modern humor, so that laugh follows
laugh so quickly that you'll want to see it again to be sure you
haven't missed something. It is so young, so fresh, so much a
product of the time we live in, so brashly impertinent that it is probably going to annoy a lot of people. Like people who think Show-
boat was the last word in musicals, who need a long rest between
takes, to whom hot jazz has all the charm of a hornet's buzzing.

Sono Osato, dancing star of <u>One Touch of Venus</u>, dances with her expected hare-like grace, shows a lovely, natural manner in her acting. Nancy Walker emerges as a new comedienne, tiny, trigger-tough, full of a wholly modern, tense rhythm in her songs. Authors and performers Betty Comden and Adolph Green take part in their own routines with an engaging lack of inhibitions. And every smallest bit part is played or danced or sung to perfection. Particularly memorable is Susan Steell's portrayal of a tippling singing-teacher housed in Carnegie Hall, who hides her bottle of gin behind the metronome, sneaks nips at every opportunity. The dancers are, as might be expected, extraordinary.

Touted as an extension of the idea Jerome Robbins used in his ballet <u>Fancy Free</u>, involving three sailors on leave in the big city, the revue is much more than that. Takes you on a quick, slick, fun-packed tour of New York, from the Museum of Natural History, through familiar night clubs, to the subway and thence to Coney Island.

Written by Betty Comden and Adolph Green (remembered as the Revuers) it is full of the sharp, quick satire this team is famous for. Leonard Bernstein, better known for his classical music background, has written some of this year's most beautiful songs, all of them fine, but things like " Come Up to My Place," "I Can Cook," and "You Got Me" (and I'm free, Gabey, I'm free), of very definite hit-tune quality. Jerome Robbins' choreography and staging of the dancing and musical numbers ought to set some older hands who shall remain nameless (as the Theatre Guild, Mr. Billy Rose, etc.) to biting their fingernails. The sets run an imaginative gamut including everything from small, intime interiors to Coney Island, show Oliver Smith to be versatile as well as talented. As you may have gathered by now, we found <u>On the Town</u> the year's best revue. The only thing we won't go all out for, and this, in a small voice ... the costumes are not very good.

--Irene Kittle in <u>Cue</u>, Vol. 14, No.
1 (January 6, 1945), page 12.

ON YOUR TOES (Book by George Abbott, Lyrics by Lorenz Hart,
    Music by Richard Rodgers; Imperial Theatre, April 11, 1936)

Departing from the customary stew of pretentious skits and dances, the Dwight Deere Wiman production, <u>On Your Toes</u>, gyrates around the novel topic of balletomania. It essays rather successfully some mild satire at the expense of the classic Russian and the modernistic ballet, particularly in two travesties, the "Princess Zenobia" and "Slaughter on Tenth Avenue" ballets; it is even more entertaining in its spoofing of the aristocratic pretensions of devotees of the art: "Too Good for the Average Man," sung by the Diaghilev of the

play, is the best of this year's comedy songs. On the other hand,
this musical is not free from some pretentious artiness of its own,
while the mildness of its theme, along with a number of concessions
to sentimentalism, make the whole sedative at best. It is only fitting
that the season's musical offerings should end with a bromo-seltzer.
Among the performances, Luella Gear's acting makes a fine art of
sophistication, and Ray Bolger's is something to be grateful for.

> --John W. Gassner in New Theatre,
> Vol. 3, No. 6 (June 1936), page
> 9.

* * *

An intelligent musical show, but don't let that scare you. Its
travesty of art-ballet nonsense, while good criticism, is richly amusing.

> --George Jean Nathan in Life
> (November 1936), page 4.

ONE TOUCH OF VENUS (Book by S.J. Perelman and Ogden Nash,
    Lyrics by Ogden Nash, Music by Kurt Weill; Imperial Theatre,
    October 7, 1943)

With One Touch of Venus Broadway, which has been lurching,
stumbling and even walking crab-fashion for two months, has begun
to hit its stride. Whatever is wrong with it--and we shall come to
that presently--One Touch of Venus is an unhackneyed and imaginative musical that spurns the easy formulas of Broadway, that has personality and wit and genuinely high moments of music and dancing.
And among other things, it brings Kenny Baker to a Broadway that
badly needs another good juvenile, and brings Mary Martin back to
Broadway to prove that she is anything but a one-song girl. She
is, indeed, a fetching and accomplished actress who keeps going
through an entire evening.

Venus, like Oklahoma!, breaks with musical-comedy tradition.
But where Oklahoma! has the smell of new-mown hay, Venus is like
a trick perfume. I suppose the simplest way out is to call it sophisticated. S.J. Perelman and Ogden Nash have dandified the fanciful
plot with their cleverness and wit, and Mr. Nash has worked up some
smart and ingenious lyrics. Kurt Weill has composed all kinds of
songs with all kinds of orchestrations and Agnes De Mille has had
even bolder ideas about dancing than she had for Oklahoma! Nobody
concerned has been the least bit inhibited. Unfortunately nobody
has been completely successful.

Mr. Weill, I think, comes off best. His is a good evening's
worth of music, and on three occasions it is delightful. "I Am a

Stranger Here Myself," which Miss Martin puts over superbly, is the
high point of the show and one of the best musical-comedy songs in
years. "Speak Low," if less memorable, is also very taking, and
"The Trouble with Women" is a grand barber-shop quartet.

Some of the dancing that Miss [Agnes] de Mille has contrived
is remarkably fresh and original. The trouble as a whole, however,
is that it lacks lightness and seems to lack variety.

As for the book, its cleverness is often too strained, or at
least too literary. There is real wit in it, but much that would rate
an appreciative smile if it were read goes to pieces on the stage,
trying to fetch a laugh. Furthermore, this tale of a statue of Venus
that comes to life lends itself to mots of a carnal nature that have
something of a smirk about them. But if Messrs. Perelman and Nash
have had fairly tough going, at their best they have delivered themselves of subtler wit than has probably ever graced a musical comedy
before.

Miss Martin is worthy of her star part. She can do more than
sing, she has an air about her, she is good to look at--in fact terrific to look at in a Mainbocher black dress. John Boles does what
he can with a rather unrewarding role. Teddy Hart is once again
an amusing little man with a modified shriek for a voice. Paula
Laurence is funny where she can be, which isn't too often. But
Sono Osato's dancing is one of the big things in the show--I wish
there were space to say more.

Even though much of Venus doesn't come off, I found it an
unusual and very pleasant evening.
                              --Louis Kronenberger in PM (Octo-
                                ber 8, 1943).

                         *   *   *

The laggard theatrical season of 1943-4 last week shook itself
free of the turkeys, dead ducks and resurrected banshees that have
haunted it since August, and soared off into full flight with the first
solid smash of the Fall semester.

There is glee and dancing in the streets of Broadway, notably
on 45th in the neighborhood of the Imperial, and One Touch of Venus
is the immediate cause thereof. For here is a musical that has the
class, imagination and refreshing novelty of Lady in the Dark and
Oklahoma!--a show lively in idea and plot, bubbling over with melody
and song, kicking its way lightly and gaily through a merry evening
in the theatre.

It's the first thoroughly professional job of the season. The
roster of names on- and back-stage guarantees you your money's
worth, and more. Cheryl Crawford (Porgy and Bess) produced;

music is by Kurt Weill (Three Penny Opera, Johnny Johnson, Lady
in the Dark); book and lyrics are by S.J. Perelman and Ogden Nash;
Elia Kazan (Skin of Our Teeth, Harriet) directed. Agnes de Mille
(Rodeo, Oklahoma!), whose startling choreographic patterns have done
miracles in vitalizing the ballet in America, created some of her
most fascinating satirical and humorous dances for Venus. The costumes are by Paul du Pont, Kermit Love and Mainbocher, and the
sets by Howard Bay (Little Foxes, The Patriots, Something for the
Boys, The Merry Widow).

No amateurs, these. Nor in the cast assembled by the extravagant Miss Crawford: Mary Martin, on leave from Hollywood--breath-
lessly beautiful and graceful and expert in the ways of the theatre;
Kenny Baker, surprisingly adept in his first stage role; John Boles,
saucy Paula Laurence, pop-eyed Teddy Hart; and an astonishing
young dancer, Sono Osato, whose funny little ballet dance sketches
are gems of humor and ineffable grace.

The plot weaves lightly around a Pygmalion theme. An art collector brings to his museum a 3,000-year-old statue of Venus which
comes to life and falls in love with a barber from Ozone Park, L.I.
The collector is annoyed at the disappearance of his statue, assigns
private detectives to find it, or her, and complications ensue when he
sees Venus' affections fastened upon the somewhat dimwitted razor
wielder from the suburbs. The lady is pursued by her owner,
haunted by her Temple's guards, woos the hair-clipper lad, swooshes
her rival for his affections off to the moon, and winds up--well,
perhaps you ought to learn for yourself how true love finds its way
across the East River and Greenpoint to Ozone Park.

Despite the fact that there is more plot here than you might
normally find in a whole season of musicals, it doesn't get in the way
of songs, dances and other entertaining business. Several numbers
stop the show: Mary Martin's "I'm a Stranger Here Myself," "Speak
Low," "Foolish Heart;" Kenny Baker's "How Much I Love You;" a
hilarious barber shop ballad harmonized by Baker, Boles, Hart and
Harry Clark, entitled "The Trouble with Women;" "Way Out West in
Jersey," with Baker, Helen Raymond and Ruth Bond; and Miss de
Mille's dances, "40 Minutes for Lunch," "Venus in Ozone Park," and
a skittish Sono Osato romantic dance interlude with a sailor.

If the foregoing seems to suggest that you might do well to
hasten to the Imperial Theatre, that is the general idea of this piece.
Better hurry, for the line is reaching over to Eighth Avenue now.

                          --Jesse Zunser in Cue, Vol. 12,
                          No. 42 (October 16, 1943), pages
                          18-19.

OTHELLO (William Shakespeare, adapted by Margaret Webster, Music
    by Tom Bennett; Shubert Theatre, October 19, 1943)

It must be no news by now that Margaret Webster's production of Shakespeare's poignant tragedy of The Moor of Venice is one of the most exciting theatrical events in years. As staged by Miss Webster under the auspices of the Theatre Guild, as played by Paul Robeson in the role of Othello, José Ferrer as Iago, and Uta Hagen as Desdemona, the eloquent and stirring tragedy--never one of Shakespeare's best--attains a three-dimensional quality not readily found in the script.

Bemused by the skill of the staging and acting, one forgets the unexplained motivations for Iago's machinations; you come closer to believing that Othello might murder his suspected wife upon the flimsiest of hearsay evidence; you accept Roderigo as a fatuous fool and Cassio as a simpleton. For the first time you sense why black Othello, looking upon himself, might question the constancy of his wife's love; you see an Iago whose malevolence is logically and sardonically humorous, instead of merely villainous in the heaving bosom school of the Shakespearean drama. Robeson's giant Othello--primitive, majestic in his dignity, but bewildered by the effete products of 16th century Venetian civilization--is a perfect foil for the sly and murderously evil Iago, a startling and dramatic contrast to the fragile and lovely alabaster-skinned Desdemona.

The others in the cast are as perfectly attuned to its subtle beauties--among them, Jack Manning as catspaw Roderigo, Miss Webster as Iago's wife Emilia, Averell Harris as Desdemona's father Brabantio, James Monks as Othello's lieutenant Cassio, Edith King, Robert E. Perry, and others.

This Webster-Robeson Othello is a triumphant achievement--a pitiful and touching tragedy, a sad and lovely drama, rich in its sonorous beauties, mellow and musical in its cadences, breath-taking in the natural art of its staging. As you love the theatre, do not fail to see it!

> --Jesse Zunser in Cue, Vol. 12, No. 44 (October 30, 1943), page 14.

* * *

Broadway took a new lease on life this week when Paul Robeson came to town in Margaret Webster's staging of the Theater Guild production, Othello. Robeson got in the groundwork for Othello in London more than ten years ago and there was considerable criticism then, and at Radcliffe two seasons back, over a Negro's public love-making to a white Desdemona.

Few theater folk know their Shakespeare as well as does the talented daughter of Dame May Whitty and Ben Webster. She it was who supervised the latter appearances of Maurice Evans. She takes a much maligned work usually relegated to the libraries and makes it

a rip-snorting piece of live melodramatic theater. In this, of course,
she is aided by a handpicked cast that, in addition to Robeson, includes José Ferrer (best of contemporary Iagos) and Uta Hagen
(Mrs. Ferrer) as Desdemona.

The scholars may question if it is necessary to place a Negro
in the leading role of Othello. The Moors are not Negroes. However,
the device is an understandable collaboration between Miss Webster
and Master Will to emphasize a difference in culture and civilization
between the Venetians and the people of Othello's race. The current
production at the Shubert cannot be passed off lightly and your correspondent will reserve a future article to more comment on this
brilliant Broadway offering.

--Russell Rhodes in Rob Wagner's
Script, Vol. 29, No. 666 (November 4, 1943), page 27.

OUR TOWN (Thornton Wilder; Henry Miller Theatre, February 4,
1938)

This being the blank wall or sceneryless era in the theater,
the fashionable Jed Harris has produced for us a play without any
settings. Thornton Wilder conceives it as a rehearsal of a play,
using only chairs, tables, stepladders, and two garden arches for
properties. The stage manager is played by Frank Craven, who
explains the workings, acts a few parts, and is general narrator of
the evening.

The hero is the town. Nothing done by individuals is of much
importance, although there is a satisfactory romance and the inevitable procession of birth and death. Mr. Wilder's town is a little village of 2000 in New Hampshire. The action takes place between
1900 and 1913, with frequent lapses of years, explained by stage
manager Craven. The writing and, particularly, the extremely fine
acting, bring that small town to life on the stage.

Mr. Wilder has the ability to convince you that his actors are
echoes of real people, and so long as he portrays their daily lives
and keeps his personal philosophy of beautiful death off the stage,
the play is grand entertainment. Fortunately, the Wilder poetic conception of the dead grouped happily in the church yard and gos-
siping among themselves is not over-emphasized. Martha Scott, a
new ingenue who seems to have everything, turns in a stunning performance. Likewise stunning are both Frank Craven and his son
John, apparently following in the distinguished footsteps of his father.

--Herbert Drake in Cue, Vol. 6,
No. 16 (February 12, 1938), page
13.

* * *

Not so very long ago Thornton Wilder publicly stated that he considered the novel an outmoded medium for the contemporary writer and that he was therefore through writing novels. Henceforth he would devote his talents to playwriting, for he considered the drama the vital medium for this generation's expression. Mr. Wilder has accordingly been training himself carefully for his debut as a dramatist--a variety of one-act plays, a translation of Obey's Lucrece for Katharine Cornell, an acting version of Ibsen's A Doll's House for Ruth Gordon--and now his first full-length original play, Our Town, which Jed Harris has given the kind of production playwrights dream about.

Our Town is not only one of this town's best plays, but it is an admirable contribution to American drama. If it doesn't win this season's Pulitzer award, something is wrong with the judges' committee, for this is one of the few plays which fulfill the actual requirements set down by Mr. Pulitzer.

In the dramatic medium, Wilder works with that same lucidity of speech, that same succinctness of characterization that made his novels memorable. As a dramatist, he has not fully discarded the novelist's implements. He employs a narrator (played in friendly fashion by Frank Craven), using him as the property man is used in oriental drama; he paints his scenes with words, thereby exciting in the imaginations of his audience a far more realistic picture of his New England village setting than if he had been assisted by a corps of the theater's best set designers; he even uses something of the novelist's "reflecting mirror" method, for not all of his events take place in their sequence, and one is sometimes asked to reflect back to another date and another setting in order to get a picture of a scene in its entirety.

His story, like the stories of his novels, is simple. Laying it in Grovers Corners, a sleepy little New Hampshire village of 2,642 people, of which 86 per cent are Republicans, he is detailing a narrative of childhood, love, marriage, and death. On one side of the stage is the home of Dr. Gibbs, the town's doctor; on the other side of the stage, across the street, is the home of Mr. Webb, town's newspaper editor. George, who is Dr. Gibbs's son, falls in love with Emily, Mr. Webb's daughter; they get married. Emily dies in childbirth, and the play closes with George sobbing bitterly on the freshly turned earth of her grave.

It is in the last scene that Wilder lifts his play into the realm of sheer poetry. His scene is the hillside cemetery. On one side the dead sit in chairs; on the other is the funeral cortege huddled under black umbrellas, singing the hymns of their faith. Emily, in her bridal gown emerges from the mourners and takes her place among the dead. She wants to return to the living, and, although

the dead advise against it, she does return for the day of her
twelfth birthday, an unimportant but happy event. But she alone
has a knowledge of the future, and events to her seem to swim in
a rushing torrent of meaninglessness; the people she loves live oblivious
to the beauty and significance of their lives. Willingly she returns
to her grave, and when George weeps over her, it is in reality she
who is infinitely above and infinitely sorrier for him.

John Craven, as George, and Martha Scott, as Emily, play with
the utmost simplicity; they make the tragedy of young love unbearably real. The entire cast of forty-nine players is remarkably good,
but the Gibbses, portrayed by Jay Fassett, Evelyn Varden, and
Marilyn Erskine, and the Webbs, interpreted by Thomas W. Ross,
Helen Carew, and Charles Wiley, Jr., are the very kind of people
you know must have lived in Grovers Corners, New Hampshire.

--DeWitt Bodeen in Rob Wagner's
Script, Vol. 19, No. 452 (March
5, 1938), page 12.

OVER 21 (Ruth Gordon; Music Box Theatre, January 3, 1944)

Ruth Gordon has written herself a play and a part. The play
is first-rank comedy, and the part is an actress' heaven--a juicy
role filled with wit and whimsical drama and howling hilarity--a role
that any Broadway actress would give ten years of second-rate first-
nights to get her teeth into. She got Max Gordon to produce and
George S. Kaufman to direct it--and the result is a hit, one of the
few sure-fire comedies of the season, and a certainty to run on and
on through this new year of 1944.

The comic plot whips around a couple in their late thirties and
their trials and tribulations at Air Cadet School in Miami. The husband is a liberal newspaper editor who enlists in the Army because he
feels that is the most important contribution he can make to the war
effort. His wife, a Hollywood scenarist, comes to stay with him and
help him win his commission, despite the pleas and wire-pulling of
his millionaire publisher-boss to force him out of the Army and behind his editorial desk again.

Much has been said to the effect that this is a Young Man's
War, and the 39-year-old editor--with the aid of his wife--sets out
to disprove that statement. How he does it, and how he wins his
second lieutenant's bars--in spite of the comic hardships of Army life
in an auto court, a scheming publisher, a hard-boiled colonel, and
lures from Hollywood, is the substance of Miss Gordon's comedy. It's
thin, but so generously laden with laughs--good-humored, malicious,
satirical and plain howlers--that you don't mind in the least the slight-
ness of the story.

Miss Gordon's performance is a delightful lesson in the magic of extracting laughs, and the supporting cast plays up beautifully, gathering to themselves a full bouquet of lines and laughs in the skittish footsteps of their star. Among them: husband Harvey Stephens, publisher Loring Smith, Army couple Tom Seidel and Beatrice Pearson, Philip Loeb and others. All contribute to a thoroughly enjoyable play, unqualifiedly recommended, a welcome addition and an auspicious beginning for the New Year.

> --Jesse Zunser in Cue, Vol. 13, No. 2 (January 8, 1944), page 14.

* * *

Weary, no doubt, of poor scripts, or perhaps just to show that she can write her own ticket and match it with her acting talents, Ruth Gordon has brought to the Music Box the town's latest hit, Over Twenty-One, written by and for herself. Although Max Gordon (same spelling but no relative) is the producer, you can bet your last New Deal penny that it was Ruthie who was smart enough to wheedle him into it and lucky enough to have the celebrated George S. Kaufman to stage it.

They are saying along Forty-fifth Street that Over Twenty-One has its true-to-life touches. Well, anyway, everybody knows that Miss Gordon's husband, Garson Kanin, an old man of 39, is in the Army and that she chucked Broadway to be near him while he was studying for a commission at officers' training school. Everybody knows (or imagines they do) Dorothy Parker, the wit, Ralph Ingersoll, the editor, and Marshall Field, the aristocratic publisher of the decidedly unblushingly pink PM. Miss Gordon, some years ago in Here Today, played a Dorothy Parker and is probably much funnier than that remarkable former fellow townslady of mine in Hartford, Conn.

Miss Gordon has a field day, as is her right in a part by, with and for Ruth Gordon. Sometimes she is on stage all by herself. She has plenty of dry lines, such as her pathetic comment to a young Army wife who asks, "Is your husband really almost forty?" Answers, Ruthie, "Yes, he really is. We've been everywhere about it, but there's nothing we can do." And plenty of pantomime and shenanigans with the help of Philip Loeb, as a movie producer; Harvey Stephens, as the middle-aged editor; Loring Smith (very amusing) as the blustering publisher; Carroll Ashburn as a stuffy colonel; Dennie Moore, as his skittish wife.

As the lady writer, Actress-Author Gordon shows not only an unexpected awareness of the theatre's scope for comedy situations, but a brilliant interpretation of the play's humors. Only when she becomes serious does she fail, as a playwright, to do the right thing by herself as a player. Mainbocher costumes become her, and why

not? Kaufman's direction speeds <u>Over Twenty-One</u> for well deserved
standing-room only. Thanks, Miss Gordon for a swell evening.

--Russell Rhodes in <u>Rob Wagner's</u>
<u>Script</u>, Vol. 30, No. 671 (January
22, 1944), page 29.

PAL JOEY (Book by John O'Hara, Music by Richard Rodgers, Lyrics
     by Lorenz Hart; Ethel Barrymore Theatre, December 25, 1940)

Story--Joey--Pal Joey of John O'Hara's pieces in <u>The New York-</u>
<u>er</u>--lands a job in an obscure Chicago night club. Joey's approach
to women lacks any overtone of delicacy, truth, or honor.

Vera Simpson, rich divorcee, comes to the club and eventually
takes up Joey as a hobby. Mrs. Simpson's dealings with men pitch
to the same low plane as Joey's. She sets him up in business in his
own spot, but drops him when two crooks try to blackmail her.

Joe drops easy and bounces quick.

Acting--Gene Kelly, who came to notice last year as the hoofer
in <u>Time of Your Life</u>, plays the shallow, lustful Joey, and does an
excellent job of it. Most musical comedy parts don't need much in
the way of acting. This part does, and Mr. Kelly carries it off.

Vivienne Segal performs as Mrs. Simpson and does it with the
minimum smark, which is quite a trick.

As one of the crooks, and also a night club singing toughie,
June Havoc gives a swell performance. Jack Durant, as the other
crook, dances and sings to effect, and Leila Ernest, as a girl who
almost falls in love with Joey, also does creditably.

Jean Casto appears and sings one song, "Zip," about a strip
teaser, and gets a well deserved hand.

Production--From the standpoint of production <u>Pal Joey</u> comes
up as one of the best musical shows to come to town for a long time--
no small triumph in this year of good musicals.

The sets by Jo Mielziner are fine, and the dance direction of
Robert Alton swell.

Richard Rodgers has written an excellent score, the best songs,
to my mind, being "I Could Write a Book," "That Terrific Rainbow,"
and "Happy Hunting Horn." The capers that accompany "That Terrific Rainbow" are highly hilarious.

The lyrics supplied by Mr. Hart for "Bewitched, Bothered, and Bewildered" and "In Our Little Den" hit an absolute low of bad taste.

Cue Says--As far as acting, music, and staging are concerned Pal Joey rates as tops. But, for me, the bright edge wears dull as the tawdry story and the roundly indecent lyrics of the two songs mentioned come over the footlights. Mr. O'Hara's dialogue is crisp and literate, but his plot is barefaced.

Your own sensibilities will have to tell you whether to go or not.

--Oliver Claxton in Cue, Vol. 10,
No. 1 (January 4, 1941), page
22.

* * *

What a developer of talent George Abbott is--comparable to Maecenas, S.S. McClure and Leo the lion, that talent scout for M-G-M! The producer-playwright has never shown this gift to great-er advantage than in Pal Joey, his current saga of café society which is likely to outlive café society itself. This musical show continues to pack 'em in although there isn't a single featured or starred name on the program, the cast rating equal notice as pals of Pal Joey him-self, who outranks the others only because he's a rank heel.

Take the actor, Gene Kelly, who plays the titular role from head to toes, especially when it comes to dancing. Only Abbott would think of taking a young acting hoofer who'd played minor parts in Leave It to Me and One for the Money and handing him a part that might well entitle him to electric lights on the marquee, if the manager wanted to be extravagant with bulbs. Yet Kelly's perform-ance goes far to make the show remembered, playing the rat with an unaffected grace that almost makes him ingratiating, and dancing with easy verve and a lack of that panting effort in his twirls which makes audiences perspire rather than admire in the case of other dancers. It's a heel-and-toe achievement, you might say.

To be sure, Kelly registered strongly as the hopeful tap-dancer in the saloon of The Time of Your Life last season, so that some of the credit for his development belongs to William Saroyan, in case you want to quibble. We don't make too much about assigning credit in this respect, because somehow or other Saroyan always gets all the credit that's coming to him. And it should be remembered that Abbott is deserving of praise with regard to this, because other managers who are meanies might shy away from taking actors who had received the accolade of Saroyan recognition.

Then there's Vivienne Segal, the vocalist who made resounding progress some years back in The Chocolate Soldier, The Desert Song and The Three Musketeers, yet seemed to have been swallowed up by

the all-devouring mike of radio lately. Abbott brought her back to
the stage and made Miss Segal her own mouthpiece again. Not only
is the night made glad with her melody again, but the manager gave
her a chance to play a distinctively different type of role--a woman
of the world who is getting on in years, what might be called a bud-
ding dowager, but who still has a serpent's eye for beguiling men,
and a serpent's tongue for puncturing their ego.

Abbott has also brought back Jack Durant, of the once-noted
vaudeville team of Mitchell and Durant, who seemed likely to run out
his days in the segregated world of the night clubs. Durant plays
a Broadway agent with the glib bluster of the Ritz Brothers, Alexander Carr of Potash and Perlmutter, and Smith and Dale of the
Avon Comedy Four, and then, just when you least expect it, he re-
lieves his rush of words to the head by turning flip-flops. Come to
think of it, those flip-flops shouldn't be so surprising, for a Broadway agent has been known to reverse himself suddenly before this.
Incidentally, Durant wouldn't be a bad choice for the title role of
The Show Off in case Abbott, the great resurrecter, decided to revive this as a musical. His fluent clowning robs his blackmailing
scenes of the nastiness you usually have to admit is inherent in black-
mailers, whether any of them are your personal friends or not.

The same applies to his accomplice in extortion, June Havoc,
who has been delved out of vaudeville and pictures and who has just
the cockeyed demureness that the part requires, enhanced by a chaste
Danielle Darrieux hair-do above a cockatoo face. Leila Ernst, playing
the cute blonde trick whom Pal Joey might love if he could stop loving himself for a moment, is another of the performers whom this en-
trepreneur--his name slips us for the moment--has dredged out of
summer stock. And Abbott--ah, yes, that's the bird we're talking
about--seems to have recalled his early success with Lee Tracy in
Broadway, for he has chosen as a bit player and chorus leader a
young bozo named Van Johnson who seems slated for stardom, since
he looks like a combination of Lee Tracy and Gene Raymond, with
Jack Whiting's smile and legs thrown in.

The remarkable thing is that these and other members of the
cast repeatedly play for Abbott, since in spite of a lack of billing--
which is supposed to be manna and mince pie to actors--they keep
coming back for more, year after year. Jean Casto, who lends a
Boston accent amusingly to the role of a hard-boiled newspaperwoman,
and who gives a very deft burlesque of a burlesque strip-tease, has
acted almost exclusively for Abbott. Maybe this attitude by his actors
is traceable to a feeling of compassion for Abbott. In spite of his
numerous successes he still looks like a simple country lad just landed
on Broadway from the West and quite bewildered by the bright lights.

A good deal of the success of Pal Joey is undeniably due to the
music and lyrics of Richard Rodgers and Lorenz Hart, who despite
their twenty-one years in the business can still squeeze out their an-

nual song hit in "Bewitched, Bothered and Bewildered." We take
great personal pride that these boys still drip persuasive scores, for
we can claim to be the first to give them critical recognition, having
covered their first effort, the Columbia varsity show, two decades
ago, when we predicted a great future for them. We meant it, instead of handing out the usual polite drool for amateur efforts. And
the boys responded nobly by making good.

There's a lot to be said for John O'Hara's book from his New
Yorker sketches, which has a totally different type of musical hero--
a suave cad who uses love as a stepping-stone for his dancing steps.
The characterization here is exceptional for musical comedies, and
Pal Joey remains true to type to the final curtain, using women only
to further his dream of having a night club of his own, and not being
diverted even by a blonde. There is some curious shuffling of the
plot, when the cute trick who loves him surrenders him without much
fight to the seasoned charmer, then takes him back for a meal, and
finally surrenders him with a casual smile. But somehow Abbott has
knit it all together into a triumph of sophistication, a jaunty but
frank picture of callous Broadway night life which has something of
the fascination of the snake house at the zoo.

And the chorus girls have plenty of snake hips. That undoubtedly accounts for the predominantly masculine gender of audiences at Pal Joey. In fact, to judge by the scarcity of femininity,
you might think you were in a burlesque house. But these audiences
are quicker to respond than burleycue patrons, catching innuendoes
on the fly even before the cast bat them out. We've often wondered
whether burlesque performers are so lackadaisical because the audiences are so comatose, or vice versa. Certainly no such complaint
can be leveled against players or spectators in this show, and both
sides of the footlights are quite unflagging in digging for dirt.

--Frank Vreeland in Rob Wagner's
Script, Vol. 25, No. 598 (May 3,
1941), pages 26-27.

PANAMA HATTIE (Book by Herbert Fields and B.G. De Sylva, Mu-
    sic and Lyrics by Cole Porter; Forty-Sixth Street Theatre,
    October 30, 1940)

STORY--Trying to grasp the vague misfortunes that actuate
a musical comedy plot and put them on paper is somewhat like trying
to hang on to a wet dog in a swamp at midnight. You know it's
there but it keeps slipping away from you.

However, Panama Hattie, a gal from down town in Panama,
loves Nick Bullett, who has something to do with the locks. Nick
has a daughter, age eight, and the daughter no like Hattie's clothes.

Leila Tree, from up town, loves Nick also, and she tries to blow up
the lock.

ACTING--Ethel Merman, in full throat and gusto, plays Hattie.
The lady has an easy, carefree way on a stage and this part was cut
right to her measure, and a good fit it makes.

Joan Carroll, a roundly engaging young thing, plays the little
daughter with rare savoir faire, aplomb, and ease. Child actresses
are apt to make you sit up and take notice of the nearest exit, but
not this one. You'll like her.

For comedy, the Messrs. Pat Harrington, Frank Hyers, and
Rags Ragland, as three sailors, do their bit effectively. Mr. Ragland, late of burlesque, rates a special nod. Arthur Treacher makes
his butler part funny. Betty Hutton throws herself around.

PRODUCTION--Smooth, sumptuous, and tasty covers the production. For dancing take note of Nadine Gae, a very agile and lith-
some miss. Also dancing you will find Miss Carmen D'Antonio, and
if there is any movement that can be worked into a dance Miss D'Antonio has not thought of, I am sure you will not be able to think of
it either.

Cole Porter's score comes up to scratch, with the usual quota
of tricky rhythms.

CUE SAYS--Mr. De Sylva has certainly developed a talent for
the musical comedy form. First Du Barry Was a Lady, then Louisiana
Purchase, and now, by gum, he has hit it again with Panama Hattie.
You will have a good time at it.

> --Oliver Claxton in Cue, Vol. 9,
> No. 46 (November 9, 1940), page
> 38.

THE PETRIFIED FOREST (Robert Emmett Sherwood; Broadhurst Theatre, January 7, 1935)

Let it be recorded at once that Robert E. Sherwood's melodrama,
The Petrified Forest, seems to be exactly the kind of show that the
public and the reviewers are crazy about, and then let it be recorded
in a small and doubtless wholly unimportant voice that it still isn't
the kind that this particular critical picklepuss has much taste for.
It is shrewdly manufactured; it is not without a modicum of theatrical
interest even so far as the aforesaid picklepuss is concerned; and it
achieves at least part of its author's purpose. But I trust that its
author will not refuse to take off his hat to me and bow low when we
pass on the boulevards if I write that, once you have nominated it a

very smart box-office show, you have said the best about it that you
honestly and critically can.

I may be doing the agreeable Mr. Sher.vood a gross and rightly
resented injustice when I hazard the opinion that he aimed much higher in his own mind than the mere creation of such a good box-office
show and that he imagined he was writing something pretty tony in
the way of a symbolical-philosophical exhibit, even though it did contain four gangsters, three machine guns and two bottles of whiskey.
I hope for his reputation's sake that he didn't, although there is evidence in the manuscript that leads us doubtfully to scratch our heads.
This evidence refractorily suggests that Mr. Sherwood pleasured himself with the idea that he had some profound cosmic philosophies to
unload, along with some pretty fine symbolism, and that his melodrama, down in his secret heart, took second place to them. But
despite the fact that the evidence in question has been accepted at
its face value by almost all the reviewers, who have enthusiastically
elected Mr. Sherwood to a metaphysical niche only a couple of inches
below that occupied jointly by Plato and Socrates, I like to believe
that Mr. Sherwood was kidding himself very little and the critical
boys a lot, and that much of the stuff they have fallen for he wrote
with his tongue in his cheek. If he didn't, may God and the head-
master of the Oswego School For Young Boys have mercy on his future.

Mr. Sherwood, whatever his deficiencies as a thinker and a
dramatist of any bulk, is certainly not a cheapjack. There is a
measure of pride in him, and a seeming resolve to try to do something
better than the common run of Broadway mishmash. But he is no
philosopher, and he himself, let us trust, will be the first to know
and to admit it. What he is is a hardworking playwright who thus
far has succeeded in producing nothing of any real quality, but who
is clearly so eager to and so sincere about his job that it is conceivable that someday, when he grows older and a little more impatient
with himself, he may. As of today, he still betrays the youthful
wish to intellectualize plays that would be twice as good if he allowed
them to pursue their simple emotional and dramatic courses, and he
still has not achieved the artist's contempt of mob reaction to his
characters. He still relishes the sure-fire, if dramatically corrupting,
laugh and he still surrenders to the quick and facile, if internally
dubious, effectiveness of situation and character. Thus, in this
latest play of his, though he knows as well as you and I do that his
young heroine, her fancy thrillingly wrapped round his artist hero,
would no more suddenly decide to go out and roll in the grass with
a hick lunchroom employee than you and I would suddenly decide to
go out and guzzle a magnum of strawberry pop, he permits her to do
that very thing merely to prick his audience. Thus, though he is
too experienced to believe for a moment that his rich Middle-Western
married woman would propose to a gunman whom she had just laid eyes
on that he take her for a roll in the hay, he also permits her to do
it in order to get an easy audience laugh. And there are a suffi-

ciently illuminating number of other such thuses. That's not honest
dramatic writing, Mr. Sherwood, as you, being an honest fellow personally and something of a good critic too, will agree, even if it does
make a wad of money at the ticket-till.

Leslie Howard, Humphrey Bogart, Charles Dow Clark and Miss
Peggy Conklin head the presenting company and turn in first-rate
performances.

--George Jean Nathan in Life,
March 1935, page 30.

* * *

There are about thirty plays on Broadway at the moment, and
though I may be shot for saying so, most of them are worthwhile.
They must be to survive more than a week run. To me, a season
is an artistic success if ten good plays have been presented. Certainly we have had that many already, and this is written before the
Lunts and Elizabeth Bergner arrive.

Leslie Howard, our first-English-gentleman-of-the-American-
stage, has added further luminosity to our theatrical horizon--as was
to be expected--by his charming performance in Robert Sherwood's
delightful melodrama, The Petrified Forest. We're all wondering just
what Mr. Howard thinks of the invariable use of the word "charming"
when used to describe any performance of his, or his personality on
or off stage. Some objectors say the term should be used only in
reference to women, and that it implies limitations when used about a
man, particularly such a competent actor as Leslie Howard. But to
this statement I strenuously object, for as many men as women possess the quality of charm--though there are altogether too few of
either--so why shouldn't we use the term to convey the added pleasure given us by this rare characteristic? Recently I heard Wm.
Lyons Phelps say, "One hesitates to call a man charming for fear
sissiness may be implied, but certainly that is not true when describing Leslie Howard. He is one of our finest actors and though thoroughly he-mannish, has tremendous charm."

Also, I heard John Mason Brown (N.Y. Post's brilliant dramatic
critic) discuss Mr. Howard's charm and ability at length without
apologizing for the use of the term. He stressed his belief, however,
that the time has definitely arrived for Mr. Howard to take a decided
step forward to more powerful acting parts. Out of the charm groove,
possibly, into some of the great Shakespearian characters. He mentioned Richard III particularly.

Although The Petrified Forest is vigorous melodrama full of
gangsters in an Arizona gas station and lunch room, it also is full-
up with what is known as serious thinking. The idea of Leslie Howard in any character fitting into an Arizona scene was somewhat
quaint to me, but really no other actor could possibly have played

the part. He is the intellectual element on the loose in an unintel-
lectual environment, giving voice to Mr. Sherwood's profound philosophy of these troubled times. Being one of the rare actors of our
time, he plays with a delicate pathos which wrenches the emotions
and makes women feel protective about him, and also with a smooth
suavity which is so agreeably stimulating to one's brain action. Had
Mr. Sherwood chosen, he might have made his Petrified Forest a
very important tragedy, but he keeps it par-excellent melodrama for
you to enjoy with or without your mind. But bring it along; there's
much more than appears on the surface.

> --Essey Oppey in Rob Wagner's
> Script, Vol. 12, No. 303 (January
> 26, 1935), page 30.

* * *

If Robert Sherwood's The Petrified Forest, squarely set up at
the Broadhurst Theatre under the well measured direction of Arthur
Hopkins, was boiled down to a mathematical equation, the result
would be aliquant.

Here surely there is more than meets the eye and more than
the normal ear heeds. Mr. Sherwood has set aside both a quality
and a quantity for his own inner satisfaction and for the deeper
penetration of the suspicious and suspecting cynical.

As Alan Squier, an undistinguished writer who has taken to
tramping the long road in a realized futile search for the end of disillusionment, Leslie Howard, in contrast to Mr. Sherwood, does his
work in full scope measure. Does it with the assistance of fewer lines
than are given to the average star, radiates his personality, during
many moments in which he is wordlessly involved, and completely
overwhelms even the most immune. It would seem that the infectious
Mr. Howard needs only his pipe, his well modulated voice and its ear-
pleasing inflections and two gracious hands, to captivate the most
meticulate followers of high histrionic standards.

Nevertheless, none of this accoladian evaluation of Mr. Howard's playing in The Petrified Forest is meant as a negative reflection on the play itself. I'd call Mr. Sherwood's latest a literary out-
burst against decadency, set in a melodramatic frame.... But I
wouldn't be too sure of my description. Mr. Sherwood's motivation
may, at the beginning, be of the slow walking variety. But later
on it breaks into a satisfactory, swift, running mood.

Alan Squier arrives at a filling station and lunchroom not far
from Arizona's petrified forest. There he meets Gaby Maple. Gaby's
father is an ambitious member of the American Legion. Her mother
deserted them during Gaby's childhood, to return to her native
France. We learn that the father and mother had first met during
the World War. Brought to America, Gaby's mother had rebelled

against the desert.   Divorce from it and her husband was the ultimate solution.

Gaby hates the desert just as her mother did.   The poetry of
François Villon and the romantic thoughts it has inspired in her, plus
a questionable artistic talent, make her yearn for a trip to Europe.

Alan, as he gets to know her, feels that the girl should have
her opportunity.   The gas station is temporarily taken over by a gang
of Dillinger-type outlaws.   Duke Mantee, its head, satisfies Alan's
whim to frustrate the futility of life by substituting death, and makes
it possible for Gaby to try to avoid earthly petrification and secure
freedom from the desert, by means of Alan's sole material possession
--an insurance policy.

High minded discussions, ranging from politics to eudemonics,
highlighted by deft comedy touches, are Mr. Sherwood's tools in the
unfolding of a broader plot than is herein indicated.

Peggy Conklin's Gaby is as much at home with sodden vernacular as with adolescent romantic desire and expression ... Humphrey
Bogart's Duke Mantee is all the more convincing because of his underplaying ... Charles Dow Clark brings a thoroughly human touch to
the role of Gaby's grandfather, who has somewhat of an admiration
for American desperadoes.

Frank Milan, Blanche Sweet, Robert Hudson, Robert Porter-
field, Ross Hertz, Walter Vonnegut, Slim Thompson and others--from
top to bottom--are all seen to fine advantage.   Raymond Sovey's
lunch room is an excellently atmospheric job.

The Petrified Forest is one of the season's most alive offerings.
                                    --D. Frank Marcus in Cue, Vol. 3,
                                    No. 12 (January 19, 1935), pages
                                    10-11.

THE PHILADELPHIA STORY (Philip Barry; Shubert Theatre, March
      28, 1939)

STORY--Tracy Lord, of the Philadelphia Main Line Lords, is
about to embark on matrimony for the second time.   Destiny Magazine threatens to run a piece about Seth Lord, her father, that
tells all about his mistress.   In return for killing the story, the
Lords allow the magazine to send a girl photographer and a bright
young man reporter to the wedding, and they arrive as house guests
the night before the nuptials take place.   The general idea is to see
that the pictures and the reporter's story are also never used.   Such
publicity would not be in keeping with the dignity and position of the
Lords.

Also present, the night before the wedding, is the groom,
George Kittredge, coal miner who has worked his way up in the world,
and Dexter Haven, first husband of Tracy and a pleasant young man.
Tracy gets all tangled up between these two and the reporter.

ACTING--Katharine Hepburn plays the pleasant, but somewhat
lightheaded, Tracy, and does a grand job of it. She has a good part
and makes the most of it. Van Heflin plays the reporter and is excellent, as is Joseph Cotten in the part of the ex-husband. Lenore
Lonergan, aged eleven, is swell as Tracy's meddling little sister.
Vera Allen, Forrest Orr, Frank Fenton, Nicholas Joy, and the others
in the supporting cast, contribute to a smooth and finished performance.

PRODUCTION--The Theater Guild with, at last, a good play to
work with, has given The Philadelphia Story a smooth production,
well set and lighted by Robert Edmond Jones.

CUE SAYS--Philip Barry, discarding metaphysics, has written
a fine, light-hearted comedy that is a delight to have in town. It
is recommended heartily and happily.

--Oliver Claxton in Cue, Vol. 7,
No. 24 (April 8, 1939), page 43.

* * *

Philip Barry has this season provided theatergoers with dramatic expressions from each side of his much-discussed dual nature.
After probing the vagaries of the human soul in Here Come the
Clowns, he is now back in his Holiday mood, writing a superficial,
smart comedy of the fashionable rich. The Philadelphia Story is
light, pleasant playfare, important because it returns Katharine Hepburn to the legitimate stage and because it gives the Theater Guild
the only box-office success it has enjoyed this year.

For The Philadelphia Story is a real smash-hit. It is the only
Broadway show to have withstood constantly business competition
from the World's Fair. It is also the only woman's starring vehicle
to have scored this season. The play is a tailor-made vehicle for
Hepburn, and she plays her role of a Philadelphian prig with lively,
charming confidence. Previous failure has taught Hepburn a lot.
She has substituted poise for uncontrolled nervous energy, and she
has learned how to sustain a long acting part. Even the harshest
critics of The Lake have conceded that much, and when she returns
to Hollywood, she's going to make those movie theater-owners once
listing her as "box-office poison" eat their own words. It is the
name of Hepburn that is packing them in at the Shubert Theater
every night, and it is Hepburn herself who lights up this innocuous
trifle with the flare of a theatrical personality.

The Philadelphia Story is about an heiress-divorcee who, about to marry a second time, discovers that one marital blunder hasn't taught her much about marriage. A writer for the Dime, Spy, and Destiny magazines (obviously the Time, Life, and Fortune publications) sets her on the right track, and she, in turn, does as much for him. It is polite comedy, styled with Barry witticisms, easy to take as a peppermint lozenge and as readily solvent. Shirley Booth, Vera Allen, and Joseph Cotten give particularly handsome support to the star, but it's Hepburn's evening.

> --DeWitt Bodeen in Rob Wagner's
> Script, Vol. 21, No. 510 (May
> 27, 1939), page 25.

PINS AND NEEDLES (Book by Arthur Arent, Marc Blitzstein, Emanuel Eisenberg, Charles Friedman, David Gregory, Music and Lyrics by Harold J. Rome; Labor Stage Theatre, November 27, 1937)

With no fanfare but with a great deal of purpose the first undertaking of Labor Stage, Inc., was launched Sunday evening, June 14th, in the studios of the Princess Theatre in New York with the Contemporary Theatre Company. It was a satirical musical revue, Pins and Needles, which succeeded in being genuinely entertaining, if occasionally over-ambitious.

This revue was the initial tangible product of the decision of the American Federation of Labor at its last convention, when, for the first time in the history of the American labor movement, the concept of theatre as a means of education for workers was officially endorsed in the formation of Labor Stage. This first effort was watched critically by labor leaders and theatre people alike. Neither group had cause to be disappointed.

Presented in a tiny studio (because the Princess Theatre proper in which Labor Stage will ultimately place its productions will not be completely renovated for several weeks yet) and presented on a still tinier stage, Pins and Needles managed to project a charm and vitality that one often finds missing in Broadway revues whose production costs run several hundred times that of Pins and Needles.

An unusually good looking and gifted cast of girls, among them particularly Peggy Craven and Elizabeth Timberman, a supporting cast of men with Lee Hillery and Louis Latzer deserving special mention, with Harold Rome and Earl Robinson supplying the music with two pianos, all contributed to the general success of the program.

Harold Rome, who supplied the major portion of the lyrics and music, displayed a fresh and engaging talent in his work. S. Syrjala, who was responsible for the production design, created some extraordinarily simple but effective settings for the various revue numbers.

Of the eighteen numbers in the show, several were outstanding, including "Pass At Me," "Not Cricket," "You Gotta Dance," and "Magic at Sea," the first three of which were contributed by Rome. The production, which now runs well over two hours, might be cut and tightened up to some advantage, although the timing, an important part of any revue, was splendidly handled, considering the limited playing area.

Emanuel Eisenberg's "Mother! Let Freedom Wrong," a good humored, if caustic bit of fun poking at the social theatre, got the least rise of any of the production material out of this reviewer, although the audience seemed to enjoy it. It was a particularly sophisticated piece of burlesque which apparently attempted to establish the fact that the labor theatre was healthy enough to laugh at itself.

In general, however, Labor Stage has made a valuable excursion into the field of the social revue, and brought forth some really worthwhile material. The new theatres throughout this country, which are working closely with the Central Labor bodies in their communities, will do well to follow the example of Labor Stage and make further experiments with the vaudeville form, a native and important theatre technique.

The Contemporary Theatre Company, which intends to stay together as the permanent company of Labor Stage, has indeed made an auspicious beginning.

--Ben Irwin in New Theatre, Vol. 3, No. 7 (July 1936), page 24.

* * *

It is the theory of the Labor Stage that working-class drama need not be humorless. To substantiate that opinion, they are now offering players from the International Ladies Garment Workers Union in a bright revue entitled Pins and Needles, a musical show which, by reason of its freshness and unique staging, has taken New York by storm.

The opening number, "Sing Me a Song with Social Significance," sets the pace of the entertainment, but it is an odd comment on the revue itself that when the numbers deliberately strive to be socially significant, they become only flatly obvious. On the other hand, when such sprightly numbers as "Dear Beatrice Fairfax," "Vassar Girl Finds a Job," and "Slumming Party" (with its now famous "Doing the Reactionary") are in the limelight, Pins and Needles becomes not only excellent fun but offers a subtle commentary on its social theme.

The revue is happily staged within the intimate Labor Stage,

thus acquiring the divertissement quality of a théâtre intime. It is
also fortunate in having most of its songs composed by Harold J.
Rome, who in his lyrics displays a delightful sense for natural
rhythms and rhymes. Marc Blitzstein has taken time out from his
Mercury activities to contribute to a really funny satire on Federal
Theater methods called "F.T.P. Plowed Under."

     The actors are all former workers in union shops, billing them-
selves, along with their union labels, as "plain, simple, common,
ordinary, everyday men and women who work hard for a living."
Now, although they've taken out Equity memberships and are professional actors, I'll bet they find that they work twice as hard and
sometimes think back fondly to the halcyon order of their one-time
thirty-five-hour week. Three of the girls--Ruth Rubinstein, Anne
Brown, and Millie Weitz--would be comely additions to any revue,
and demonstrate capably here that they know how to put across a
song.

--DeWitt Bodeen in Rob Wagner's
Script, Vol. 19, No. 452 (March
5, 1938), page 12.

THE PIRATE (Book and Lyrics by S.N. Behrman, suggested by a
     play by Ludwig Fulda, Music by Herbert Kingsley; Martin Beck
     Theatre, November 25, 1942)

     It is a little hard to understand just why S.N. Behrman was so
enchanted by an old Spanish play called The Pirate that he felt
obliged to revise it for the Broadway theatre. At its best, the exhibit at the Martin Beck is a handsomely staged and acted comedy,
distinguished by Mr. Behrman's usual precise and intricate wit; at
its worst, it is an old-fashioned piece of rascality dressed up to
look like art.

     Ludwig Fulda, the playwright who was originally responsible
for The Pirate, thought it would be pretty funny if a group of
strolling players turned up in a West Indian village, circa 1800, and
the leader of them impressed the local belle by pretending to be a
celebrated buccaneer for whom she had formed a literary attachment,
much as I myself have for Lizzie Borden. The point of the joke is
that he alone knows that the real bandit is the lady's husband, now
grown fat and respectable. I have little or no confidence in the
clarity of this synopsis, but I doubt if it matters. If you go to the
Martin Beck, it will be to see the Lunts in a characteristically stylized
performance and to listen to Mr. Behrman's graceful manipulation of
the English language. The plot, as Miss Gertrude Stein might easily
have described it, is a plot is a plot.

     Presuming that you ask no more from the theatre than light

and color and the spectacle of two talented people operating brilliantly in a vacuum, you ought to enjoy The Pirate. You will see Mr.
Lunt pretending to walk a tightrope in one of the most ingeniously
contrived scenes I can remember, Miss Fontanne giving about the
same sort of sardonic and cryptic performance she once gave in a
somewhat similar work called The Guardsman, and a great many
costumes and settings of unusual charm. Mr. Behrman's dialogue is
full of those balanced, exquisite lines for which he is celebrated, and
there are some pseudo-Shakespearean grace notes which I imagine
would be admired by Max Beerbohm. It may be that sometimes the
characters are called on for epigrams too involved and ornamental
for successful delivery on the stage, but, generally speaking, the
author has done well enough by his cast. I only wish that I could
overcome a suspicion that the whole thing is too cute for its own good,
and possibly just a little bit of a bore.

Operating under the majestic shadow of the Lunts are Estelle
Winwood, Alan Reed, Clarence Derwent, and Lea Penman. What I
could see of them I liked very much, as I did a large company of
colored actors, who appeared to be enjoying The Pirate a good deal
more than most of my neighbors in the audience.
                              --Wolcott Gibbs in The New Yorker
                                 (December 5, 1942), page 37.

                         *   *   *

If you don't regard a dull play as too much of a hindrance,
you may have a rather pleasant time at The Pirate. The Lunts are
in it up to their necks, for one thing; and it would take more than
just a dull play to dampen the spirits, or wreck the success, of the
Lunts. What with its gorgeous trimmings, its glints of wit, and its
bouts of vaudeville, The Pirate should do nicely for them.

It's possibly inaccurate to call The Pirate a play in the first
place. Call it an extravaganza, an opera bouffe, a vehicle, a period
piece, a costume job, a high-styled bore, a polished impromptu--any-
thing, indeed, except a play. It enables Mr. Lunt to act a strolling
player and impersonate a pirate, to walk (or almost walk) a tightrope,
perform magician's tricks, make fantastic love in high bravura fashion
and mesmerize his loved one. All this he does in the style to which
we are accustomed--with plenty of prancing verve and swashbuckling
dash and comic extravagance. The Pirate also enables Miss Fontanne,
with her training, mocking voice and her deftly stylized manner, to
react mischievously to Mr. Lunt's boisterous advances, and to look
incredibly young.

There are, to continue, Lemuel Ayers' gay and charming and
witty sets, and Miles White's glowing and brilliant costumes. The
eye has looked on nothing so fine this season. There are Herbert
Kingsley's happy bursts of music--half evocative, half derisory.
There are also Mr. Behrman's own flashes of wit, admirable but far

from abundant, and his success at times with extravagantly elegant,
deliberately artificial dialogue. But to sustain that kind of thing is
the hardest thing in the world, and Mr. Behrman can't begin to do
it. He gets his best effects when he suddenly swoops down from
high-sounding utterance to present-day slang; but that, too, is a
trick that's soon played out. On the whole, Mr. Behrman does not
quicken his play with words; he merely smothers it.

The play itself is the least—and the worst—of the matter, but
you might want to know that it tells of an early 19th-century West
Indian lady who enlivens her marriage to a fat, middle-aged dullard
by reading tales of romance, particularly one about a pirate called
Estramudo. Comes a strolling player who falls in love with the lady
and, to win her favor, boasts of being Estramudo himself. As a result of his boast, he is in a fair way to hang; and as though that
didn't complicate matters enough, it turns out that the actual Estramudo is the lady's fat husband—he having reformed some years back.
To get by with such folderol, you must obviously have one of two
things: a first-rate musical-comedy score, or a lady and gentleman
from Genesee Depot, Wis.

> —Louis Kronenberger in PM (No-
> vember 26, 1942).

PORGY AND BESS (Adaptation by DuBose Heyward and Ira Gershwin
    from the play by DuBose and Dorothy Heyward, Music by George
    Gershwin; Alvin Theatre, October 10, 1935)

That there are several merits to George Gershwin's so-called
American folk opera, Porgy and Bess, is readily to be allowed, but
it seems to me that the chief of them is ambition. As to Mr. Gershwin's ambition there can be no doubt. It is a fine and adventurous
thing. But it, like certain other fine and adventurous ambitions in
the American theatre, still lacks the sufficiency of soaring wings.
(Mr. Anderson's ambition in the direction of poetic drama and Paul
Green's and Lynn Riggs' in the direction of folk drama are illustra-
tive cases in point.)

Among Mr. Gershwin's other merits is the ability to confect
better than usual popular Puccini-flavored music-show tunes, several
samples of which are present in Porgy and Bess, e.g., "Bess, You
Is My Woman Now" and "I Loves You, Porgy." He is also talented
in humorous revue melodies and, with his clever lyric-writing brother
Ira, offers a good specimen here in "It Ain't Necessarily So," with
such Cole Porter rhyming trickery as "Jonah was at home in, the
great big whale's ab-do-min," or something like that. And he indicates on this occasion that in the loftier matter of chorals and in ingenious contrapuntal devices, albeit sometimes paraphrasings which
are not unrecognizable, he has a praiseworthy skill. But these quali-

ties, meritorious in their several ways though they are, are not sufficient unto the composition of a folk opera and, as a consequence,
Porgy and Bess (based upon the Heywards' familiar play) is considerably less a folk opera in any true sense of the term than an inde-
terminate, wobbly and frequently dull mixture of operetta, musical
comedy, and drama-with-music.

The recitative passages are completely nude and interruptive
of the exhibit's flow. Certain numbers, for example, "I Got Plenty
o' Nuttin'," "Summer Time," and most certainly the clogging Mr.
Bubbles' (of the Buck and Bubbles vaudeville hoofing team) "There's
a Boat That's Leavin' Soon for New York," seem much more in key
with something like Show Boat than with something that purposes
being a real folk opera. There are, it must be emphasized, passages
in the score that flutter toward musical dignity and even some mild
musical standing, but in the aggregate the enterprise is without the
coherence, the compositional drive, the orchestral background and,
above all, the exaltation that are the prerequisites of any kind of
opera, folk or otherwise.

The stage direction of Rouben Mamoulian, the settings of Ser-
gei Soudeikine and the singing troupe headed by Todd Duncan and
Anne Brown get the tributes of this critical department, which also
applauds the Theatre Guild's generosity in producing a valuable, if
not successful, experiment.

> --George Jean Nathan in Life, De-
> cember 1935, pages 21 and 46.

* * *

*When the Theatre Guild launched the George Gershwin musical
version of Du Bose and Dorothy Heyward's play Porgy recently, and
rechristened it Porgy and Bess, the cult of critical Negrophiles went
into journalistic rhapsodies, hailed it as a "native American opera,"
avowed it "typical" of a "child-like, quaint" Negro people and declared it "caught the spirit" of a "primitive" group. The huzzas
filled the columns, were quoted by second-hand intelligentsia, and
echoed in the banalities of the subscribers. No one, however,
thought to ask Negro musicians, composers and singers their opinions of the Gershwin masterpiece.

Accordingly, I sought out Edward Kennedy ("Duke") Ellington,
Negro orchestra leader and composer. He has neither axes to grind
nor pretensions to support, but busies himself reproducing and creating the most genuine Negro jazz music in the world. Objective
critics have likened his work to Sibelius; his band is distinctive. Un-
fettered by hot-cha exploitation, his energies might be released to
the serious efforts his genius warrants.

---

*Although not a professional review, this piece, titled "Duke Elling-
ton on Gershwin's 'Porgy,'" seems too important not to include.

"Well, Duke," I began, "now that you have seen Porgy and Bess, what do you think of it?"

"Grand music and a swell play, I guess, but the two don't go together--I mean that the music did not hitch with the mood and spirit of the story." Then he added: "Maybe I'm wrong, or perhaps there is something wrong with me, but I have noted this in other things lately too. So I am not singling out Porgy and Bess."

"But sticking to Porgy and Bess, Duke, just what ails it?"

"The first thing that gives it away is that it does not use the Negro musical idiom," replied Ellington. "It was not the music of Catfish Row or any other kind of Negroes."

"Then I don't suppose it could be very true to the spirit, scene or setting of impoverished Charleston Negroes if the musical expression failed to consider the underlying emotions and social forces of the Gullah Negroes," I suggested.

"That might be it at that," agreed Ellington, "but I can say it better in my own way. For instance, how could you possibly express in decent English the same thing I express when I tell my band, 'Now you cats swing the verse, then go to town on the gutbucket chorus'!"

"You would intend for the boys to play the verse in rhythm, and finish the final chorus with improvisations, accented beats and a crescendo," I laughed.

"Sure, but for all your fifteen-dollar words you didn't gave the same impression, did you?" he argued. "If you hadn't been around the band and if you did not know the backgrounds of the musicians you couldn't interpret them or use their idioms, could you?"

"I think I get your viewpoint," I answered, "but why did you say the music was 'grand'?"

"Why shouldn't it be?" he smiled amiably, "It was taken from some of the best and a few of the worst. Gershwin surely didn't discriminate: he borrowed from everyone from Liszt to Dickie Wells' kazoo band."

Ellington turned to the piano, and playing said: "Hear this? These are passages from Rhapsody in Blue. Well, here is where they came from--the Negro song "Where Has My Easy Rider Gone?" Now listen to this--this is what I call a 'gutbucket waltz.' See, it's a waltz, but it still has the Negro idiom. I have taken the method but I have not stolen or borrowed." He played on, evidently pleased with his innovation.

"Will you ever write an opera or a symphony?" I asked.

"No," Ellington declared positively. "I have to make a living
and so I have to have an audience. I do not believe people honestly
like, much less understand, things like Porgy and Bess. The critics
and some of the people who are supposed to know have told them
they should like the stuff. So they say it's wonderful. I prefer to
go right on putting down my ideas, moods and themes and letting
the critics call them what they will. Furthermore, an opera would
not express the kind of things I have in mind."

"Where would you consider Porgy and Bess offered opportunities that you should have used that Gershwin missed?" I asked.

"Several places," Ellington said, "he missed beautiful chances
to really do something. There was one place, though, where he
made the most of his music: the hurricane passages, when no one
was on the stage. But when he tried to build up the characterizations he failed. What happened when the girl selling strawberries
came on the stage? Did he get the rhythm, the speech, and the
'swing' of the street-vender? No, sir, he did not; he went dramatic! Gershwin had the girl stop cold, take her stance, and sing
an aria in the Italian, would-be Negro manner."

Ellington warmed up to his subject. "Bubbles, who is a great
dancer, built up the character of Sportin' Life with his dance. The
music did not do that. And other actors had to make their own characterizations too. There was a crap game such as no one has ever
seen or heard. It might have been opera, but it wasn't a crap game.
The music went one way and the action another. If a singer had
lost his place, he never would have found it in that score. Still,
the audience gasped: 'Don't the people get right into their parts?'
and 'Aren't they emotional'!"

"Would you say that an honest Negro musical play would have
to contain social criticism?" I asked.

"Absolutely," declared Ellington. "That is, if it is expected
to hold up. In one of my forthcoming movie 'shorts' I have an episode which concerns the death of a baby. That is the high spot and
should have come last, but that would not have been 'commercial,'
as the managers say. However, I put into the dirge all the misery,
sorrow and undertones of the conditions that went with the baby's
death. It was true to and of the life of the people it depicted. The
same thing can not be said for Porgy and Bess."

It was very evident that here was one colored composer who
realized the cramping forces of exploitation which handicap not only
him and his colleagues, but the Negro masses as well. That is why
their expression is filled with protest. He is also fully conscious
that there are imitators and chiselers, always ready to capitalize on

specious products purporting to "represent" the Negro. They are
totally lacking in social vision, and their art is phony.

No Negro could possibly be fooled by Porgy and Bess. Mamoulian's direction has added nothing to his old superficial tricks of ani-
mating inanimate objects, such as rocking chairs, with rhythmical motion to fit a song. (This business was used in Porgy which he directed in 1927.) His Negroes still wave their arms in shadowed
frenzy during the wake. The production is cooked up, flavored
and seasoned to be palmed off as "authentic" of the Charleston Gullah
Negroes--who are, one supposes, "odd beasts."

But the times are here to debunk such tripe as Gershwin's
lamp-black Negroisms, and the melodramatic trash of the script of
Porgy. The Negro artists are becoming socially-conscious and class-
conscious, and more courageous. Broadway will find it harder to
keep them on the chain-gang of the hot-cha merchants. The Elling-
tons and the Hughes' will take their themes from their blood. There
will be fewer generalized gin-guzzling, homicidal maniacs, and more
understanding of rotten socio-economic conditions which give rise to
neurotic escapists, compensating for overwrought nerves. There
will be fewer wicked, hip-swinging "yellow-gal hustler" stereotypes,
but more economically isolated girls, forced into prostitution. These
themes are universal. They will be particularized and vivified in
ringing language, and charged with the truth of realities. The music
will express terror and defiance in colorful Negro musical idioms which
have remained melodious despite a life of injustices. They will com-
pose and write these things because they feel the consequences of
an existence which is a weird combination of brutality and beauty.
                                          --Edward Morrow in New Theatre,
                                             Vol. 2, No. 12 (December 1935),
                                             pages 5-6.

PRESENT LAUGHTER (Noel Coward; Plymouth Theatre, October 29,
    1946)

    One of the characters in Present Laughter says that she feels
as if she were in a French farce, and that just about sums up Noel
Coward's latest play (title taken from the clown's song in Twelfth
Night), now on view under John C. Wilson's auspices. If Coward's
name hadn't appeared as author, it's doubtful if the piece would have
found a theater, for it's so shabby that it frequently plays as if some
unpracticed dramatist were imitating the Noel Coward manner.

    Clifton Webb, as star, acts a vain, petulant matinee idol, who
can't keep a flock of women admirers from losing their latch keys and
spending the night in his spare room--one at a time, of course. He
has an estranged wife, tolerantly amused at his philanderings, and a

female secretary who rules him as if he were her spoiled brat. The play concentrates on gilded discussion of sexual infidelity with occasional bounces of the more brittle Noel Coward wit.

Reversing an old wheeze, the leading player, in protecting one of the occupants of his spare room, says, "That was no prostitute. That was the wife of one of my dearest friends!"

The piece is directed at such a deadly pace (doubtless to avoid the slamming-door, quick entrance method) that the cast is handicapped. Nevertheless, I found Mr. Webb by no means as satisfactory as he was in Blithe Spirit, or in the movie, Laura. As the secretary, Evelyn Varden is wryly amusing whenever the proper line turns up. Doris Dalton, as the wife, lacks the style for Coward fripperies and Martha Linden makes a middle-aged siren suitably seductive.

The single setting of a duplex studio apartment has been elegantly contrived by Donald Oenslager.

--Russell Rhodes in Rob Wagner's Script, Vol. 32, No. 744 (December 7, 1946), page 26.

* * *

Present Laughter is Noel Coward's weary version of an Al Woods boudoir frolic. Clifton Webb keeps things moving cheerfully, and Doris Dalton and Evelyn Varden also lend energetic and artful efforts in this direction. Funniest and most outré moment in the current theater is when Miss Varden peers into the library, off-stage, and says lethargically, "Good heavens, young man, what are you doing to yourself?"

--Herb Sterne in Rob Wagner's Script, Vol. 33, No. 749 (February 15, 1947), page 12.

PRIVATE LIVES (Noel Coward; Times Square Theatre, January 27, 1931)

There is little to be said here about Noel Coward's Private Lives except that it has caught the public fancy beyond the most sanguine expectations of its author and producer and now ranks as what the academicians call a smash hit. Mr. Coward and Miss Gertrude Lawrence, two of the theatre's most charming people, make it so. If done by anybody else, I doubt if its success would be so great, but these performers are expert in the delivery of the sophisticated--I hate that word, but sometimes there is no synonym for it--dialogue which Mr. Coward knows so well how to write. The opening

situation finds each of them, after a five years' divorce, married to
somebody else, and embarking on the first night of second honeymoons
in adjacent balcony rooms of a hotel on the French Riviera. They
light a great many cigarettes, but they are by no means nonchalant
about it, for the curtain finds them in flight to Amanda's apartment
in Paris, leaving their respective spouses to figure things out as
best they can. Their former marital bickerings resume themselves in
the second act, with a good deal of scratching and clawing, and the
end finds the flat a complete wreck as the abandoned pair walk in
upon the combat. The denouément features an amusing breakfast
scene, with Mr. Coward and Miss Lawrence again sneaking off, leaving Jill Esmond and Laurence Olivier, who also do well by the piece,
similarly embattled.

> --Baird Leonard in Life (February
> 20, 1931), page 18.

REUNION IN VIENNA (Robert Emmett Sherwood; Martin Beck The-
    atre, November 16, 1931)

    Hot, savory, and satisfying. The pungent Fontanne-Lunt re-
cipe for spontaneity is infallible. No one cares whether they reune
in Austria or Asia, just so they do it often.

> --Don Herold in Life (May 1932),
> page 42.

                              * * *

    Hurray, there's something more to spend your money on!
While Reunion in Vienna, by Robert E. Sherwood, is no great shakes
as a play, it is such gay and exciting entertainment as presented by
the Theatre Guild that you must go, budget or no budget. The
Guild has accomplished this by invoking the services of that Mr. and
Mrs. Midas: Alfred Lunt and Lynn Fontanne.

    My suspicions about the value of the comedy qua play are based
largely on the first act, in which Mr. Lunt does not appear and to
which the chief contribution of Miss Fontanne is a beauty which is
downright sensational after her last season's hagdom.

    Miss Fontanne plays Elena, the wife of a great Viennese psycho-
analyst. A party in celebration of the centennial of the birth of the
late Emperor is being planned by such relics of the old régime as
have remained in or been able to return to Vienna, and as Elena,
ten years before, was the mistress of the Archduke Rudolph Maximil-
ian von Hapsburg, she is urged to attend it. There is a possibility
that the exiled Rudolph, now driving a taxicab in Nice, may slip back
for the festivity. Shall she go, or shall she not? Her husband,
being a stage psychoanalyst, decrees that she must.

May I make a note here that jokes about psychoanalysis are dangerous things? They belong to the overfacile, or mother-in-law, category of jokes. Unless they're terribly good, a kindly silence is preferable. Psychoanalytical jokes wham-bang all over Act I.

Act II, however, places in the hands of Mr. and Mrs. Midas an excellent situation. Both Rudolph and Elena come to the party. (You knew they would, didn't you? And I imagine that you've guessed, or perhaps read, that it is Alfred Lunt who plays the mad, charming, erotic Hapsburg.)

Rudolph takes for granted the resumption of their former relationship. Elena, who loves her husband, intends that nothing of the sort shall happen. There follows an electric series of seductive attacks and evasions; cruel, tender, with and without music. The lady, after almost losing, scores a complete moral victory; then, at the last moment, sees in Rudolph not the arrogant Hapsburg of her youth but a taxi-driver wearing his tattered archduke's coat very gallantly. Therefore, taking a shortcut to everyone's satisfaction which was once known as "The Road to Rome," Elena cuckolds her psychoanalyst. He doesn't know it, and is none the worse, while the Archduke, and the audience, can go home vastly pleased.

Miss Fontanne plays Elena with the brilliant distinction she lavished on the heroine of Caprice. Mr. Lunt surcharges Rudolph with incredible vitality. Whenever they are visible, one has an exhilarating sense of being regaled with the very best that the modern stage can offer.

In addition to their surpassing excellence, Minor Watson contributes a sterling and thankless performance as the husband, and Helen Westley snaps and snorts most engagingly as a bad, miserly, cigar-smoking old woman.

> --Charles Brackett* in The New
> Yorker (November 28, 1931),
> pages 28 and 30.

ROBERTA (Book and Lyrics by Otto Harbach, based on the novel by Alice Duer Miller, Music by Jerome Kern; New Ambassador Theatre, November 18, 1933)

Max Gordon has sunk a pretty penny in the gowns in Roberta, and the gals will go wild about it. Don't take your wife, because she is apt to get ideas. Roberta is going to set New York husbands and daddies back a lot of dough before the winter is over.

---

*This review is unsigned, but The New Yorker's records indicate that its author is Charles Brackett.

I even liked this show myself, considerably, in spite of the
fact that I think it is going to incite a lot of reckless shopping just
when we men were about to get our feet on the ground again. And
in spite of the fact that it gets off to a rather yawny start, and that
I think love troubles of musical comedy sweethearts are zero in indoor
excitement. And, furthermore, while many people adore Lyda Ro-
berti, I happen to be a fellow who is never vamped by explosive
broken-English baby talk accompanied by shaking shoulders, a wry
face, and a hot-cha-cha. Maybe I need a blood transfusion. The
plot concerns a Haverhill halfback who inherits a half interest in a
Parisian gown business. But the Jerome Kern music, Bob Hope's
handling of some rather hopeless wisecracks, and the gowns by
Kiviette are better than the story.

> --Don Herold in Life, January 1934,
> pages 38-39.

THE SKIN OF OUR TEETH (Thornton Wilder; Plymouth Theatre, November 18, 1942)

Man having risen from primordial ooze to the high estate of
a two-legged vertebrate, and having managed to escape extinction
from ice, flood, pestilence and wars "by the skin of his teeth," today looks the Future in the eye and says, "Come on, I'll lick you
too." That, in one breathless sentence, is the essence of Thornton
Wilder's three-act cosmic comedy. Consider it a dramaturgical kick
in the pants for contemporary Down-in-the-Mouthers, and three
cheers and a tiger for the Thumbs Up crowd. Man keeps on getting
better, says Mr. Wilder, and you might just as well acknowledge it.

Now, not all of Mr. Wilder's cockeyed, anachronistic comedy
makes sense--but enough of it does to assume you a solid evening of
fun. And whether or not you succeed in figuring out what all the
allegorical shootin's for, by eleven o'clock you know you weren't
bored. In fact, you feel rather well treated, amused, and entertain-
ingly instructed in 500,000 years of history nut-shelled into three
acts and a happy ending.

Speaking critically, Skin of Our Teeth is a triumph of performance over script--a play which, but by the grace of a handful
of grand troupers, might well have been a dead pre-Thanksgiving
turkey. For Mr. Wilder has gone Saroyanesque. His dizzy fantasy
is acted on a skeleton stage with symbolic characters skipping in and
out of character as they alternately act their roles, chide each other
and chaff the audience. It is they who fill in the hazy ideas with
solid, humorous characterizations, and give the play life and meaning.

Act 1 is the home of Mr. Antrobus, primeval man at the thresh-
old of the Ice Age. That Mr. A's cave is a bungalow in Excelsior,

N.J., is disconcerting only for a little while. Shivering Mr. Antrobus, his family, and Sabina--perennial handmaiden and "other woman"
--sorrowfully send their antediluvian pets out into the cold, as they
call upon the audience to tear up the orchestra seats and add fuel
to the flickering home fires, thus outwitting the marching mountains
of ice. Act 2, some thousands of years later, is set in Atlantic City
as Mr. and Mrs. Antrobus address a convention of mammals. Mr. A.
dallies briefly along the primrose path with Miss Atlantic City 1942,
but leaps back to his family when the Flood sweeps up out of the
ocean. Act 3 is set in the near future, as Mr. A. returns home
from the War, despondent, disillusioned and wearied of man's bar-
barism and stupidity. However, he picks up courage again, decides
there is still hope, and determines to keep on fighting to make the
world a better, happier and safer place for posterity's bipeds.

Mr. Wilder is to be congratulated upon the superb cast that
producer Michael Myerberg has assembled; Tallulah Bankhead, as the
maid-of-all-work and temptress, gives a richly humorous and delightfully versatile performance; Fredric March and Florence Eldridge are
at the height of their form as Mr. and Mrs. Antrobus; and Frances
Heflin and Montgomery Clift are excellent as their children. Elia
Kazan's imaginative, space-leaping direction and Albert Johnson's
brief but effective sets are completely in the mood of this provocative, vastly amusing, and delightfully acted fantastic comedy.

                              --Jesse Zunser in Cue, Vol. 11,
                                No. 48 (November 28, 1942),
                                page 22.

                    *   *   *

The Skin of Our Teeth has created more advance talk than any
other play coming to Broadway this season, and it is safe to say that
it will continue to be the most talked about now that it is here. That,
I think, is what is really best about it--that, like Our Town, it
brings something different, surprising, untrammeled to the stage,
overturning the dramatic conventions with an insouciance and audacity
that in themselves--more, indeed, in themselves, than in what they
accomplish--are refreshing. If Mr. Wilder's imagination lacks wings,
at least it often has long sharp fingernails. If his sense of drama
flounders, his sense of humor frequently triumphs. The brightest
moments of the play are the best proof that, as a whole, The Skin
of Our Teeth is much less than it might have been. It seesaws too
often and struggles too palpably but in the face of Broadway's usual
fare, it is certainly an interesting evening in the theater.

It is not hard to see in The Skin of Our Teeth--and for more
reason than its reckless stagecraft--the same mind that created Our
Town. It, too, tries to throw a lasso round the universe. But
where, in Our Town, Mr. Wilder brought all humanity within the con-
fines of a small New England community, in The Skin of Our Teeth
he has sent it whirling through time and space. There is nothing

mystifying about what he has done, and nothing in the least profound; there is only something spectacular. For his Mr. and Mrs.
Antrobus, living in Excelsior, N.J., are also heirs of all the genera-
tions of man, shuttling between the Ice Age and Atlantic City, in-
venting the alphabet and talking over the radio. They and their
maid Sabina, who is also Lilith and the Other Woman and a floozy on
the boardwalk and their son Henry, who is Cain and all his descendants, are humanity's abiding types. They go through fire and flood,
war and pestilence, hanging on from age to age by the skin of their
teeth; and by that tiny margin, life itself goes on. If Mr. Wilder
winds up with a kind of worried optimism, it is an optimism based
not so much on faith as on experience, not so much on the promise
of the future as on the records of the past.

Dramatically Mr. Wilder cannot sustain what he set out to do.
Only his first act has a real freshness and lift, partly because everything is still new and sudden and amusingly incongruous, but partly
because it is full of impudent monkeyshines that, besides being hilarious in themselves, act as a kind of fourth-dimensional commentary
on the illogic of man's experiences. The play, after that, starts
bumping up and down. There are still hilarious moments, but the
humor on the whole is less frequent and more forced. Since there
is no narrative worth mentioning, it is only by fresh spurts of the
imagination that the play can sail ahead, and the spurts are not
many. By the third act, the play bogs down in talk, and Mr. Wilder
even succumbs to the temptation of orchestrating his theme with some
pretty set speeches.

It is not in Mr. and Mrs. Antrobus, but in their wildly inter-
ruptious and confidential maid Sabina that Mr. Wilder has come off
with a first-rate theater character; and Tallulah Bankhead has played
the creature with brilliant verve and vivacity. So much so, that one
does not so much follow the play, at times, as wait for Sabina to come
back on the stage. As the less colorful Antrobuses, however, Fredric March and Florence Eldridge perform with suitable vigor; while
Florence Reed, Frances Heflin, Montgomery Clift, E.G. Marshall and
others are also effective. Mr. Kazan's direction, no easy job, is for
the most part spirited and inventive.

> --Louis Kronenberger in PM (No-
> vember 19, 1942).

SONG OF NORWAY (Book by Milton Lazarus, based on a play by
Homer Curran, Lyrics and Music by Robert Wright and George
Forrest, adapted from Edvard Grieg; Imperial Theatre, August
21, 1944)

For sheer golden voiced song and beauty of production, take
Song of Norway, an operetta on the life and music of Edvard Grieg,

presented by Edward Lester at the Imperial. To get it over with
fast, the book is no great shakes and there's nothing to make you
die laughing, but who cares about that, as one of the Two Black
Crows used to ask. When you get good singing of rare music, ballet, and colorful costumes, you've gone a long way toward a box-
office hit.

You Californians probably know more about Song of Norway
than I can tell you, as it had its beginnings out there. The Los
Angeles and San Francisco Light Opera Companies form the vocal
chorus.

Anyway, here we have Grieg, Nina Hagerup and Rikard Nor-
draak in midsummer of the 1860's on the Hill of Trolls outside Bergen.
Rikard loves Nina; Nina loves Edvard; Edvard loves Edvard; Edvard
has a yen for Louisa Giovanni, girl friend of Count Peppi le Loup,
which, in the vulgate, might be translated as Pete the Wolf. The
A-Minor Concerto and "Hill of Dreams" take up considerable part of
the Rikard-Nina-Edvard triangle, which gets the three nowhere fast,
but does get Edvard louping off with the count's baby as his ac-
companist.

Then the mad--but mad--whirl of Continental sophistication for
composer and singer. Bergen, Copenhagen, Rome and back to Bergen, where Edvard composes the title piece and all is forgiven.

Everybody who is anybody knows something about Grieg music
and loves it and so the score rates ace high in Song of Norway.
Here you have the "Peer Gynt Suite" and "Norwegian Dance" and a
number of other originals renamed for purposes of the operetta as
"Strange Music," "Hymn of Betrothal," "Three Loves," "Waltz Eternal"
and "At Christmastime" which will make you want to go back to the
Majestic for a refill.

Singing superbly and acting to the hilt are Lawrence Brooks
as Grieg, Helena Bliss as Nina, Irra Petina as Louisa, Ivy Scott as
Mother Grieg and Robert Shafer as Rikard. Also such veteran
troupers as Walter Kingsford as Father Grieg, Sig Arno as Count
Peppi and Dudley Clements as Henrik Ibsen.

Alexandra Danilova, Frederick Franklin and Nathalie Krassovka
from the Ballet Russe de Monte Carlo with the corps de ballet bring
a fresh quality to the production in keeping with the high standards
of their act.

--Russell Rhodes in Rob Wagner's
Script, Vol. 30, No. 688 (September 23, 1944), page 31.

SOUTH PACIFIC (Music by Richard Rodgers, Lyrics by Oscar Hammer-

stein II, Book by Oscar Hammerstein II and Joshua Logan,
adapted from book by James A. Michener; Majestic Theatre,
April 7, 1949)

   The latest white magic to spring from that magic collaboration
called "music by Richard Rodgers, lyrics by Oscar Hammerstein II"
is based on a portion of James A. Michener's Pulitzer Prize-winning
book, Tales of the South Pacific. The Messrs. Rodgers and Hammerstein are distinguished for the winning way the one has with music,
the other with lyrics. But, I suspect, they are possessed of some
other facets of genius which, if less spectacular, are more rare.
They love to break rules and they break them delightfully.

   South Pacific is inspired by a book of loosely interrelated episodes which took place somewhere between the actual scenes of the
war in the Islands and the wondrously romantic imagination of its
author, James Michener. The first reaction to the news that a musical was to be made from this book about men and women, (sailors,
Seabees, Marines and natives) thrown together in the backwash of
war was, "It can't be done!" But a similar reaction was equally
valid in the cases of Green Grow the Lilacs and Lilliom which, as
Oklahoma! and Carousel proved that "impossible" themes merely
bring out the best in Rodgers and Hammerstein. If South Pacific
hasn't quite the spontaneity of its illustrious predecessors, it is perhaps because we've learned to take this kind of miracle for granted.
It certainly sets Mr. Michener's tenuous, romantic mood to music
much more successfully than anyone would have dared expect. And
it condenses the leisurely Michener stories into a unified plot, without destroying either the humanity of the characters or the fugitive,
dreamlike quality of the setting.

   But the most spectacular and successful break with tradition in
South Pacific is perhaps the choice of opera's number one basso,
Ezio Pinza, as the romantic lead. The big league Pinza voice quickly puts the average "operetta" star in his place. One of the small
flaws of South Pacific seemed to me to be the fact that Signor Pinza
wasn't heard more often, but he was seen quite a lot and in the
seeing proved that opera stars can be personable, professional actors when occasion demands it.

   Miss Mary Martin plays the Navy nurse who wins his heart.
She puts over songs, particularly the comic kind, with her accustomed
expertness and, in her spoken lines, becomes more and more reminiscent of Tallulah Bankhead, which is a mite disconcerting in view of
the visual dissimilarity of the two ladies.

   William Tabbert is the flesh and blood counterpart of Mr.
Michener's Lieutenant Cable whose conflict between the flesh and the
Main Line was his undoing, Betta St. John is unforgettable as Liat,
the unforgettable Tonkinese who is the cause of his destruction.

Her even more memorable mother, Bloody Mary, remains a four-dimensional figure in the hands of Juanita Hall, despite the fact that her English has been somewhat dry-cleaned for the occasion. The meatiest characterization, however, is Myron McCormick's inspired portrait of Luther Billis, the eternal "operator" without whom no unit of our armed forces was complete. But it's still the music that matters most. Suffice it to say that the master tunesmiths haven't lost their touch. I imagine the haunting love song, "Some Enchanted Evening," is the one you'll be hearing most often. But there are plenty of others, and all plenty good. I particularly liked "I'm in Love with a Wonderful Guy" and a laugh-happy tune called "Honey Bun" which was Miss Martin's own party.

Jo Mielziner's sets are a nice compromise between realism and romance. He recreates the Pacific Islands in a sort of blue-and-brown duotone, which is a pleasant touch of poetic license. The Messrs. Rodgers and Hammerstein were associated with Leland Heyward and Joshua Logan (of Mr. Roberts) in the production of South Pacific, and while we're distributing green laurels, we'd better point out that the latter also staged the book and musical numbers. Ballet, which got its musical comedy start in Oklahoma!, doesn't live here anymore. And nobody seemed terribly distressed about its absence.

> --Thomas Brailsford Felder in Cue,
> Vol. 18, No. 16 (April 16, 1949),
> page 26.

* * *

Having more than justified some of the most terrifyingly enthusiastic advance reports ever circulated, South Pacific soared exquisitely over the Majestic stage last night and made it quite clear that the theater is going to be blessedly enchanted for many months to come.

This is the ultimate modern blending of music and popular theater to date, with the finest kind of balance between story and song, and hilarity and heartbreak.

Mary Martin, whose star has been riding high for a number of shows, achieves a new heaven for herself here with an authoritative versatility nobody in the theater can equal. And Ezio Pinza, one of grand opera's greatest, proves that new surroundings like these only make one more natural home for a fine singing actor.

> --William Hawkins in New York
> World Telegram (April 8, 1949).

* * *

Few shows have been so handicapped by advance reports of
their wonders as <u>South Pacific</u>, which had its lavish opening at the
Majestic Theatre last night. And few have lived up so handsomely
to the out-of-town superlatives. For Richard Rodgers, Oscar Hammerstein 2nd and Joshua Logan have taken two stories and a number
of characters from James A. Michener's memorable <u>Tales of the South</u>
<u>Pacific</u> and weaved them into an utterly captivating work of theatrical
art. I do not think it is first-night excess which causes me to hail
it as one of the finest musical plays in the history of the American
theatre.

                                   --Richard Watts, Jr. in <u>New York</u>
                                      <u>Post</u> (April 8, 1949).

                              *   *   *

In considering the merits of this new <u>South Pacific</u>, which was
triumphant in its first performance, there are such vital factors as
the scope and range of an unhindered Joshua Logan as the director;
the frolicsome ways of an inspired Mary Martin as a wartime nurse;
the heroic singing of a star from the Met, Ezio Pinza, and the capacity of Jo Mielziner for stage design and lighting. Put all this with
the contributions of Rodgers and Hammerstein and you have a show
that is pretty wonderful.

                                   --Ward Morehouse in <u>The (New</u>
                                      <u>York) Sun</u> (April 8, 1949).

STAGE DOOR (George S. Kaufman and Edna Ferber; Music Box The-
      atre, October 22, 1936)

George Kaufman and Edna Ferber, ever embattled defenders
of the theater against the gilded encroachments of Hollywood, take
as their theme in <u>Stage Door</u> the plight of the anxious ingenues.
The opeful young ladies of the theater are shown in their scurryings
about the halls and bedrooms of an upper West Side glorified boarding
house, called the Foot-Lights Club. In this hive the young women
are displayed in all the motley moods peculiar to aspirants for stage
glory.

Mr. Kaufman and Miss Ferber are sympathetic to their puppets,

and depict the girls' various plights, as, entangled in the webs of
ambition, love, hate and sundry complicating emotions, they struggle
for whatever it is young women struggle for. Some--the congealed,
glossy, sentimentality of the tale reveals--find fulfillment on the
boards, one treads the primrose and sable path, another commits
suicide and a number find the stage-heroine's usual end in the toils
of true love. There is one ingenue, the leading lady, who prefers
Macy's basement to the freely tendered snares of Hollywood, and
slaves over a counter rather than do what Mr. Kaufman describes
as "piece work" for the camera.

These touching scenes are presented with the slick superfi-
ciality for which Mr. Kaufman has become notorious. The sentimentality is supplied by Miss Ferber, most of it happily bearing a
varnish of Kaufman wit which prevents the cast sinking too deeply
into its molasses consistency.

"What is Hollywood," says Mr. Kaufman, or words to that effect, "in two years you're a star, in four forgotten and in six, back
in Sweden"--or--"John Barrymore, what's he got--a yacht!" Stay
with the elder art, the legitimate, counsel Mr. Kaufman and Miss
Ferber, it is the only true reward. They end their amusing morality
tale with the heroine reading a part in a fine play which is to make
her a great actress.

The men in this play are, as might be suspected, only supplementary to the plot. Nevertheless, Mr. Kaufman never wastes an
actor and gets his fun out of each. The youth with a sweetheart
wanders diffidently in and out, the two cloak and suit gentlemen who
take out the girls on a catch-as-catch-can basis, the motion picture
talent scout, the radical playwright, each is used to the full; every
gag possible is distilled; even their actions are carefully worked out.
It is all a thoughtfully staged piece of work, expertly done, marvel-
ously developed and occasionally as rewarding as Mr. Kaufman apparently thought it might be.

It is about time to mention Margaret Sullavan and the other
participants. The returned cinema star lends an enormous conviction
to the part of the cinema-contemptuous girl. A good actress when
she left Broadway two seasons ago, she returns a fine actress, proving, perhaps, that Hollywood can teach acting in spite of Mr. Kaufman's crack about "piece work." The radical playwright, whose actual identity is no hurdle to the feeblest imagination, is a butt for
some of the most resentful remarks in the whole play. He is played
by Richard Kendrick, a good performer. Lee Patrick gets bitterness
and wit into every line, giving an expert performance of what is really only a good part. Frances Fuller, condemned by the script to
suicide, is more able than is required and others to whom we owe
gratitude for good playing in an artificial success, are Robert Thom-
sen, Onslow Stevens, Sylvia Lupas and Leona Roberts.

--Herbert Drake in <u>Cue</u>, Vol. 5, No.
1 (October 31, 1936), pages 12-13.

STATE OF THE UNION (Howard Lindsay and Russel Crouse; Hudson
    Theatre, November 14, 1945)

You might have known that when Howard Lindsay and Russel
Crouse got around to taking up politics in a play, they would do a
good job of it.   That is precisely the result in State of the Union,
produced by Leland Hayward at the Hudson Theater--which is owned
by Lindsay and Crouse.   This is no Of Thee I Sing, with burlesques
of a vice-president and Wintergreen (with an imitation of Jimmy Walker, a once-fabulous New Yorker) for President.   This may have in
mind a certain fighting Republican who lost the battle to Roosevelt in
the dimly remembered days before Governor Dewey ran against
F.D.R.

Whatever the real or imagined goings-on, Lindsay and Crouse
have turned out a smash hit that doesn't make dopes out of the Republicans, but still knows the funny side to rub, while keeping their
play from deteriorating into farce.

Ralph Bellamy, who seems to be enjoying his return to Broadway from Hollywood, does an excellent job as the Republican candidate who happens to be an airplane manufacturer and a forthright,
honest man who doesn't see why he shouldn't speak his mind instead
of being a cautious trader for votes.   Naturally, he risks the nomina-
tion because he stands up to labor and industry, but the playwrights
suggest that the election may not be lost.   The contemporary setting is accented in a sprinkling of such names as Stassen and Tru-
man, and the authors frequently discard the joking manner for a serious query as to why a candidate should be expected to "trade" in
politics and why he shouldn't be consistent in his discussions in all
parts of the country.

Ruth Hussey, as the candidate's wife who doubts his affection,
is splendid.   Minor Watson is excellent as the political boss, while
Myron McCormick, as an ex-newspaperman turned campaign manager,
gives a cynical portrait.   The staging is by Bretaigne Windust and
the settings by Raymond Sovey.
                                                    --Russell Rhodes in Rob Wagner's
                                                    Script, Vol. 32, No. 720 (Janu-
                                                    ary 5, 1946), page 28.

                                        *   *   *

To this reviewer, afflicted by long weeks of grim playgoing with
the theatrical shakes Mr. Howard Lindsay and Mr. Russel Crouse
seem, this morning, like a dogsled that has finally brought the serum
to Nome.   To be less metaphorical, the two of them have presented
us, in State of the Union, with an altogether enjoyable evening in
the theater that, between laughs and even through laughs, gets
something said that greatly needs to be said.   They have rung the

bell in terms of entertainment, and perhaps people will hear it in terms of something more important. For State of the Union is asking this country to work for an unselfish national unity and not revert, as it is already reverting--now that the war is over--to factionalism and strife. State of the Union is asking us also to work for world understanding and peace, and not to make a farce of the United Nations by stirring up international hatreds. And Mr. Lindsay and Mr. Crouse have dramatized their plea in a timely, plausible, concrete story about a man whom the Republican big boys try to groom for the Presidency in 1948, but who throws them over when he discovers the terms on which he would have to run.

State of the Union is not in the least a profound play; it is not really a play at all. It is a show. It bristles with wisecracks, it flashes with tag lines; much of it is slick, much of it breezy, some of it corn. But its very limitations are a virtue; by not trying to say too much, it says what it does with simple vigor; by not trying to cut too deep, it has its own kind of quick, sharp sting; by not becoming too involved about problems, it remains interesting about people. In spite of all its little tricks, its smartly tailored laughs, it is a really human play. Its characters, as far as they go, are lifelike and life-sized, believable and understandable. It is popular writing in a very good sense and a very useful sense; everybody will enjoy it and everybody will understand it.

The Grant Matthews whom Lindsay and Crouse are writing about is an enormously successful airplane manufacturer who, now in November, 1945, sees the unity his country achieved through war already lost. Industry, labor, farmers are sitting in their own corners, with strife brewing; and he wants to get them all together again before something tragic happens. His mistress, who owns a big chain of newspapers, has got the Republican bosses interested in him for the Presidency, and Grant himself has the bug to be President. The Republicans think him good timber if he can be kept in line; but, first of all, of course, his liaison with the lady must be tucked out of sight, and he must be reunited with the wife from whom he is estranged. His wife agrees; his wife believes in all that he does; his wife, moreover, knows him through and through--his bigshot side, his vanity, his vacillations. And as the Party chiefs preach compromise to Grant, Mary Matthews preaches courage. It is she who finally wins out; Grant breaks with the big boys, to campaign on his own for what he believes.

In the plot sense, State of the Union is a comedy as well as a drama; is, indeed, a 1945 version of What Every Woman Knows, of the wife who makes the decisions for her husband and cleverly lets him think he is making them for himself. It is Mary and not Grant who emerges as the most important and interesting character in State of the Union; who brings to the evening at once the most force and the most fun. This being a show rather than a play, she is entitled, moreover, to her somewhat cornier triumphs, whether of farce-comedy at a crucial dinner-party, or of romance, in winning back her husband from the Other Woman.

A virtually flawless production has everywhere enhanced the script of State of the Union. A cast that plays its human situations to the hilt, that gives a maximum of edge to its bright, breezy lines, makes you almost forget that State of the Union is over-long and in places under-nourished. Ralph Bellamy is a very good Grant, likeable and believable. Ruth Hussey, who seems at times like a defrosted Katharine Hepburn, is extremely effective and extremely attractive as Mary; she has something of a manner, but she gives it the value of a personality. Minor Watson is corking as a Republican big-shot; Myron McCormick just right as a newspaperman; Kay Johnson right, also, as the mistress; and almost every smaller part is very well played. Mr. Windust's direction is admirable.

State of the Union, a plea that never becomes a preachment, and a lot of fun to boot, deserves to be what it certainly will be-- a smash hit.

> --Louis Kronenberger in PM (November 15, 1945).

A STREETCAR NAMED DESIRE (Tennessee Williams; Barrymore Theatre, December 3, 1947)

A Streetcar Named Desire is by all odds the most creative new play of the season--the one that reveals the most talent, the one that attempts the most truth. It carries us into the only part of the theater that really counts--not the most obviously successful part, but the part where, though people frequently blunder they seldom compromise; where imagination is seated higher than photography; and where the playwright seems to have a certain genuine interest in pleasing himself.

That is the most important thing about A Streetcar Named Desire; a more important thing, it seems to me, than that A Streetcar is by no means always a good play. It falls down in places; it goes wrong in places. But what is right about it is also, in today's theater, rare. There is something really investigative, something often impassioned, about Mr. Williams' feeling for his material. There is something--in the play's best scenes--that reveals deeper intimations, as well as sharper talent, than most of Mr. Williams' fellow-playwrights can boast. And there is a willingness to be adventurous in the pursuit of truth.

The problem of truth isn't made any simpler because Mr. Williams' heroine happens to be the most demoniacally driven kind of liar--the one who lies to the world because she must lie to herself.

His Blanche Du Bois, whose gradual disintegration is the subject of
his drama, is Southern-genteel and empty of purse; highly sexed and
husbandless; full of fine-lady airs, and the town's most notorious
tramp. When she comes to New Orleans to visit her sister and brother-
in-law in their shabby quarters, she drags her whole paste-diamond
dream world--her airs and pretenses, her nymphomania posing as
straitlacedness--with her. But her brother-in-law, a warmhearted
but violent and no-nonsense roughneck, sees through her at once
and proves her nemesis. When he finds her trying to turn his
wife against him, and then trying to nab his best friend in marriage,
the brother-in-law gets the goods on Blanche and brutally shows
her up. She loses her guy; while her sister is in the hospital, her
brother-in-law takes her to bed; and when she blabs, her brother-
in-law argues that she is crazy, and has her committed to an asylum
where she would all too soon be due in any case.

In Blanche, Mr. Williams hasn't quite contrived a real, pro-
gressive study in disintegration; except toward the end, his method
is too static, with Blanche often a kind of fascinating exhibit--but
an exhibit none the less. What both she and the play need is less
repetition and more variety; there were times, toward the middle of
the play, when I found myself fairly bored. In the last and best
third, however, there is a genuine release of emotional excitement;
and the conflict between Blanche and her brother-in-law--which may
not be Mr. Williams' theme, but is certainly his story--is always good
theater, and quite often good drama. And just because it doesn't
much induce us to take sides, it comes to move us, in the end, as
part of the malignity and messiness of life itself. It brings a certain
dry pity, along with a certain new power, into Mr. Williams' work;
A Streetcar is an enormous advance over that minor-key and too
wet-eyed work, The Glass Menagerie.

It has had, moreover, a very good production. Mr. Kazan has
capitalized on all its vividness and innate sense of theater without
ever letting it topple over into mere theatricalism. As Blanche,
Jessica Tandy begins by seeming miscast--she doesn't, for one thing,
look the way you think Blanche should--but ends up little short of
triumphantly; hers is a performance that should not be underrated.
No one is likely to underrate Marlon Brando's brilliant performance of
the brother-in-law, the more astonishing for being like nothing else
he has ever played. There are good jobs, too, by Karl Malden and
Kim Hunter; and the whole thing looks right, thanks to Jo Mielziner's
set and Lucinda Ballard's costumes.

> --Louis Kronenberger in PM (De-
> cember 5, 1947).

* * *

It is gratifying to be able to report that a really great play
from the pen of a young American playwright has come to Broadway--
to stay for quite a while, if we are to judge by audience reaction to

the first performance of Tennessee Williams' new drama, A Streetcar
Named Desire.

In his latest effort Mr. Williams has added to his ability to create and maintain a mood, as evinced by The Glass Menagerie, a talent
for tense, elemental emotion and a feeling for suspenseful, provocative action. Although there is some superficial similarity between the
two plays, Streetcar is more arresting, more mature, more adroitly
constructed and it is painted in rawer pigments on a wider canvas.

The audience is invited to witness, at almost frighteningly close
range, the disintegration of a human mind. Neurosis turns inevitably
to psychosis in a series of scenes that mount with almost classic majesty to a tragic climax.

Mr. Williams has employed a no-holds-barred technique to tell
the tale of a fading Southern belle destroyed by a combination of
narcissism, alcoholism, and nymphomania. Raw passion, violence,
lust stalk naked across the stage. His characters are horribly believable, uncomfortably reminiscent of people you may have known.

You are drawn into the squalid life of the New Orleans Quarter
in the opening scene and kept there, spellbound, until the final curtain falls on a human document plucked whole from life and set upon
the stage.

Jessica Tandy is perfectly cast in the rich principal role. She
develops with seemingly effortless skill the enormously complex character of a gently bred girl whose mind is a fugitive from the sordid-
ness of her life. Outwardly an elegant aristocrat, she is inwardly
a monster of immorality, a Messalina of the magnolia blossoms, whose
amours are a sort of compensation for a marriage to a homosexual
which ended in his suicide.

Dismissed from her school-teaching job as the result of her se-
duction of a seventeen-year-old student, she seeks sanctuary in the
home of her younger sister who has married a man from the other
side of the tracks, a Polish-American laborer who is rough, even
brutal, but is occasionally tender and always erotically expert. This
role is played with perception and humanity by Marlon Brando who is
physically and psychologically right for it.

The guest in the house clutches at a last chance for security
in the person of a pleasant but unexciting friend of her brother-in-
law. But her past catches up with her and the marriage she had
counted on fails to materialize. Her violation by the brother-in-law
puts the final strain on her sick mind and leads to the pathetic
denouement.

Kim Hunter is sympathetically real as the sister torn between
family and connubial loyalties. Karl Malden portrays to the life the

callow, mother-dominated friend and all the supporting bits are exceptionally deft. The vibrant, vital production is by Elia Kazan, the brilliantly imaginative set by Jo Mielziner. Lucinda Ballard did the authentic costumes.

This is no light, easily digested dramatic dish, it is strong red meat for strong stomachs--and a nourishing contribution to the health of the American theatre.

> --Thomas Brailsford Felder in Cue,
> Vol. 16, No. 50 (December 13,
> 1947), page 18.

SUMMER AND SMOKE (Tennessee Williams; Music Box Theatre, October 6, 1948)

If I ever cherished an illusion it was that Mr. Tennessee Williams was invariably deft, original and poetic. His knack for creating credible characters and piloting them through incredibly pathetic but entirely plausible situations has not been equalled in the contemporary theatre. It was therefore a bitter experience to find myself watching a spectable that bears the same resemblance to The Glass Menagerie and A Streetcar Named Desire that the parody of Allegro in Make Mine Manhattan bore to the original. With one difference. Allegro deserved to be kidded. Tennessee Williams does not. Particularly by himself.

All of the elements that made his previous works outstanding contributions to the literature of the theatre are present. But in such senseless profusion that the total effect is parody. There is just one more neurosis and several more hysterical giggles than the traffic will bear and the plot, instead of having the inevitable reality one has learned to expect from Tennessee, is a mechanical device designed to prove an obscure point.

The beauty of language and the theatrical imagination that are Williams hallmarks are plentifully in evidence but the play as a whole has an ersatz quality that suggests an adolescent imitator rather than the real thing.

Its heroine is a young lady named Alma Winemiller who has nurtured a lifelong flame for the son of the doctor across the street. The fact that she is the daughter of the Episcopal minister in a small Mississippi town and that the action of the play takes place between 1900 and 1916 must, I think, excuse her position that wedding rings should precede other things. But Mr. Williams is quite content to see her destroyed by an attitude which, in such a place and at such a time, must not have been extraordinary.

The object of her affections finds plenty of what Dr. Kinsey would call "other outlets" including an uncomfortably incendiary dancer who was always leaving "a little nick or a cut" on him somewhere to remember her by. But the young man whom grandma would certainly have called carnal in the first half of the play turns out, rather surprisingly, to be an Eagle scout-style pillar of society in the second. He marries a young protegée of Alma's from the other side of the tracks (presumably because she knows when to say "yes") and poor Alma who reverses herself too late, turns to one night stands with traveling salesmen.

Summer and Smoke's symbolic sacred and profane lovers are played splendidly by Margaret Phillips and Tod Andrews. Anne Jackson who plays the girl he marries is an ingratiating new ingenue. Jo Mielziner has done a stimulating job with a set that re-creates the mystic world of Tennessee Williams.

> --Thomas Brailsford Felder in Cue,
> Vol. 17, No. 42 (October 16,
> 1948), page 22.

SUSAN AND GOD (Rachel Crothers; Plymouth Theatre, October 7, 1937)

This is both a good and a bad play by the lady with the magic playwriting pen, Miss Rachel Crothers. She calls it Susan and God because it deals with a woman who flies from her own troubles (dipsomaniac husband) into the arms of the fashionable Oxford Movement. The play is both good and bad because it starts out to present either of two things: a satire on the Oxford brethren and their blue book confessional parties, or a story of a woman who almost ruins her own happiness by butting into the affairs of others. One or the other makes a good theme, but somehow they do not combine to make a play. The two concerns of the playwright make her rush alternately in two directions.

Miss Crothers' observation of the contemporary American woman seems to us to be extraordinarily clear and incisive. She is, moreover, very witty, making of her really profound observations the materials of good laughter and good playwriting. If she only could have met herself coming and going somewhere in Susan and God she would have written a really fine play.

Gertrude Lawrence plays very hard at being the central character, but overdoes her arch mannerisms. Paul McGrath is excellent as the husband who never stops his reforming or drinking.

The heroine, incidentally, abandons the Oxford Movement for

her husband in time for the third act curtain, after suffering from
jealousy for a whole scene.

--Herbert Drake in <u>Cue</u>, Vol. 5,
No. 51 (October 16, 1937), page
17.

TEN LITTLE INDIANS (Agatha Christie; Broadhurst Theatre, June
27, 1944)

The squeals of terror and shrieks of fright that provide the
violent tremolo obbligato to the homicidal goings-on at the Broadhurst
these nights loudly attest to the accepted fact that few things are
so pleasant for an audience to contemplate as a nice bloody bit of
murder done upon actors onstage. When that murder becomes massacre in delightful variations, as in Agatha Christie's chilling little
piece, audience pleasure is increased in reasonable proportion to the
number of corpses that are discovered by fewer and fewer actors,
a) on stage, and b), laid out neatly in the butler's pantry, upstage
left.

The devices by which inventive playwright Christie manages to
do in her selected victims are quite entertaining, and guaranteed to
be without a yawn in a carload. The victims come each to his or
her end in the pattern of the nursery rhyme, which you may remember as "Ten Little Indians ..." who passed along by devious means
to the happy hunting grounds, until "... and then there were none."

The plot, a modification of Miss Christie's novel which was
serialized in a magazine under the title of And Then There Were
None, sees ten guests gathered together for a hectic weekend in a
lonely house on an island off Devon, England. Their host is unknown, but on their first evening together they are informed by a
sepulchral voice that seems to come from nowhere that each one has
in his time committed a murder, for which justice is now about to be
done. And in a number of uncomfortable cases, it is done. As each
victim dies--by poison, knife and axe--another little plaster Indian
on the mantlepiece topples to the floor.

Gleeful gluttons who take special delight in watching corpses
drop like daisy petals in a lover's count were heard between acts
opening night to quibble about the number of death rattles they got
for their $3.60. For those who count homicide on a cash register
basis, it might be remarked that--let's see--one, two, three, four
corpses become such in full view of the audience, and two meet their
screaming end just as they leave the stage. That ought to be a
full money's worth for anyone.

Some of the play sags. Some of it is tightly written, tense and

thrilling, but there are occasional moments when the limitations of
stagecraft are a little more obvious. These, in the general interest
of an evening's fun, may be forgiven. The performances are in the
good tradition of chill melodrama. Among the guests whose host is
death are: high court judge Halliwell Hobbes, private detective J.
Pat O'Malley, governess-secretary Claudia Morgan, army captain
Michael Whalen, retired army general Nicholas Joy, religious fanatic
Estelle Winwood, neurologist Harry Worth, butler Neil Fitzgerald,
housekeeper Georgia Harvey, and just plain victim Anthony Kemble
Cooper. Albert de Courville directed against an appropriately gloomy
Howard Bay set.

> --Jesse Zunser in <u>Cue</u>, Vol. 13,
> No. 28 (July 8, <u>1944</u>), page 12.

* * *

Even though eight people are murdered in <u>Ten Little Indians</u>--
and no two at a time, either--Agatha Christie's mystery play travels
all too lightly up the spine. For two acts the play merely holds your
interest in the mildest sort of way; and though in the third act
there are some tense and almost terrifying moments, the effect as a
whole is far too tame. There isn't enough of either physical or psychological excitement; there isn't drama enough in the situations or
continuity enough in the suspense. And these deficiencies are all
the more serious in that <u>Ten Little Indians</u> has nothing to fall back
on in the way of striking characterizations, vivid atmosphere or lively dialogue. It is as lacking in distinction as in drama.

The whole thing is, indeed, too elaborate ever to become intense. Eight people are invited to visit a stranger on an island;
when they arrive, their host fails to appear, but they--along with
the butler and his wife--are regaled with a gramophone record accus-
ing all 10 of them of having committed some kind of murder. By the
time each has offered his defense, Act I is well-nigh over without
anything having happened.

Thereafter, folks die like flies; but not till the party gets
painfully small, and the few survivors are violently suspicious of one
another, does the play begin to get tense. There is plenty of action
in the last 10 minutes, but it comes too late--and it also helps to
slur over a pretty foolish explanation.

The first act is almost entirely wasted; but beyond that, <u>Ten
Little Indians</u> suffers from being too much like a straight detective
story and too little like a play. A mystery novel aims at challenging
the reader's ingenuity; he studies the characters at close range, waits
for slips, watches for clues. But that is not easy to do, nor particularly worth doing in the theater; there must be drama and situation,
and <u>Ten Little Indians</u> has too little of either.

The entire cast plays competently, with no one distinguishing

himself--if only because no one is in a position to do so. The characterizations, like the play, are quite routine.

> --Louis Kronenberger in PM (June
> 28, 1944).

THIS IS THE ARMY (Music and Lyrics by Irving Berlin, Book by
   James McColl; Broadway Theatre, July 4, 1942)

Three hundred enthusiastic soldiers of the U.S.A.--buck pri-
vates, corporals and sergeants (no officers)--put on a rip-roaring
musical show last week that has its audiences cheering and rocking
the rafters of the Broadway theatre. First nighters paid $45,000
for first-night privileges. Nearly $100,000 in advance ticket sales
have already rolled through the cash boxes. Warner Brothers have
paid a first installment of $250,000 to film the show. It looks as
though the Army Emergency Relief Fund, beneficiary, will be at least
$1,000,000 richer before This Is the Army calls it a day.

Which is all to the good. For this is certainly one of the
grandest musicals to hit Broadway in years. There is such an abundance of entertainment riches that one hardly knows where to begin.
Irving Berlin's lyrics and music are delightful--he has sprinkled
dozens of song hits through the show, among them, the plaintive
"I'm Getting Tired So I Can Sleep," the hauntingly lovely "I Left
My Heart at the Stage Door Canteen," the hilarious "The Army's
Made a Man Out of Me," the air corps' "My Head's in the Clouds,"
and the rousing marching song, "This Is the Army."

The curtain raiser, a military minstrel show, sets a fast pace
and the 21 song and production numbers that follow keep step.
You'll like particularly the Russian Winter item, the Stage Door Canteen number, the hilarious dance ensembles, the vaudeville acts, the
Aryans Under the Skin satire, and the Negro soldier contingent's
offering, "What the Well-dressed Man in Harlem Will Wear."

Sgt. Irving Berlin, who was mainly involved in that other army
show, Yip, Yip, Yaphank (1918), wrote this one, with Sgt. Ezra
Stone directing, and Cpl. Milton Rosenstock conducting the orchestra. It's a grand show. You'll want to tell your grandchildren about
it--but first you'll have to see it. The Broadway theatre is at 53rd
St. Better get there early--but get there!

> --Jesse Zunser in Cue, Vol. 11,
> No. 28 (July 11, 1942), page 11.

* * *

A horde of people who not so long ago wouldn't have been
caught dead in New York on the Fourth of July streamed into the

Broadway Theater Saturday night, paying anywhere up to $27.50 for the privilege. They showed remarkably good sense. It was a special occasion, and it wound up an exciting one. Uncle Sam had turned producer, packing the stage with his soldiers for the benefit of Army Relief. And, everything considered, he put on a whale of a show.

The genius of the affair was Irving Berlin, who repeated the job he had done with Yip, Yip, Yaphank during World War I. Yip, Yip, Yaphank has acquired the glamour of distance, but This Is the Army has what is every whit as good, the vitality of the moment. It's a good marching show without being too military a one. It's a professional show without being too Broadway a one. It speaks for the Army with a touch of price that breaks through its lightheartedness, but it doesn't wrap itself up in the flag or assume that where entertainment is concerned, bugles have the edge on saxophones.

Some of the humor in This Is the Army is perhaps a little frail; a voice, here and there, can't really do justice to a song; and at moments the show has a certain kinship with the heartier type of college theatricals. But in general the underpinning is remarkably sturdy. The huge cast, a good part of which has had no Broadway experience, is very well trained. What it lacks in talent it more than makes up for in teamwork. And on that solid base, the show wheels and revolves in a youthful and individual style of its own. It has spring and verve and genuine gaiety. The people in it manage to shoot the works without rough-housing or falling all over the place. This Is the Army is a lesson in how much can be achieved not only without stars, or even without girls, but largely without actors.

The first act goes along casually for a while, offering a minstrel and then a vaudeville show to let the cast sing and juggle and tumble and crack jokes. Then This Is the Army catches the wind and fills its sails: there is a brilliantly costumed Russian number full of fast dancing, a Harlem number full of more fast dancing, and a lusty finale that turns the Navy loose on Army soil. The second act bounces to life with a sketch about the Stage Door Canteen, so good natured that it doesn't have to be brilliant, and studded with take-offs of Jane Cowl and Joe Cook, the Lunts and Zorina, Noel Coward and Gypsy Rose Lee. There is a fairly rousing tribute to the Air Corps called "Head in the Clouds"; and a fast, gay extravaganza called "A Soldier's Dream," which is probably the best thing in the show.

They instantly top it off, however--by bringing back the best thing in Yip, Yip, Yaphank. Indeed, the whole evening veers toward the nostalgic and climactic moment when Irving Berlin and a bunch of oldsters, in their doughboy uniforms, break into "Oh, How I Hate To Get Up in the Morning."

Nothing that Mr. Berlin has written this time is apt to catch

on as fast or wear as well, but his tunes are all serviceable and some
of the choruses ring out resoundingly. For all he has done, in composing and organizing alike, he deserves enormous credit. But
everybody deserves credit: the entire cast; Sergeant Ezra Stone
for his brisk direction; Private Robert Sidney and Corporal Nelson
Barclift for their vigorous dance routines; Private John Koenig for
his attractive sets; and the band which, under Corporal Milton Rosenstock, plays everything with zip--including "The Star Spangled Ban-
ner."

> --Louis Kronenberger in PM (July
> 6, 1942).

THE TIME OF YOUR LIFE (William Saroyan; Booth Theatre, October
25, 1939)

Story--The review above* deals with a play that gives a splendid production to practically no plot at all and works out as a heavy
bore. This review is concerned with a play that has even less plot,
an equally good production, and produces as delightful an evening
as the theater has seen for many a moon. In the two you find ample
demonstration that there can be no didactic answer to the question--
what is a play?

The Time of Your Life has an air, a flavor, an engaging overall quality that cannot be caught and transferred by a recital of its
doings. The characters sitting around Nick's Pacific Street saloon
in San Francisco consist in the main of a nebulous gent named Joe,
his errand boy, a prostitute, Nick, a hoofer, a man trying to hit
the jackpot of a pin ball game, etc. Kit Carson, a seedy soul, indicates the mood of the affair when he steps in and asks Joe, "I
don't suppose you were ever in love with a midget weighting 39
pounds?" Joe never was.

The only approach to rational behavior is during a love scene
between the errand boy and the prostitute and that does not come
off. Fortunately it only lasts a few short minutes.

For the rest of the time the characters sit around and air
themselves of opinions, ambitions, and prejudices. Not that there is
anything static in this. It all moves along briskly.

Acting--The whole cast does a superlative job. Eddie Dowling
carries off grandly the nebulous Joe, a man with plenty of money,
from no one knows where, and strange decisions and desires.

In perfect support are Charles De Sheim, Edward Andrews,

---

*Of The Possessed by George Shdanoff.

Julie Haydon, Reginald Beane, Celeste Holm, William Bendix, and
Len Doyle. Not to speak of a whole flock of others.

Production--This can be labeled a producing triumph by Eddie
Dowling and Mr. Saroyan, who both directed it.

Cue Says--If, like a movie, they had started the whole thing
right over again after the final curtain I would have gladly stayed
for another round. Cue says darn well go.

> --Oliver Claxton in Cue, Vol. 8,
> No. 19 (November 4, 1939), page
> 29.

TOBACCO ROAD (Jack Kirkland, based on the novel by Erskine
   Caldwell; Masque Theatre, December 4, 1933)

I am never in the first row of the crowd that gathers around
a sick horse. If somebody seems to have the situation well in hand,
I pass on and sell my papers. In fact, I never go in heavily for
any sort of misery for fun. I'm just not spartan, I'm afraid. So,
having heard something of Tobacco Road in advance, I went with the
expectation of staying through one act and then slipping out to get
some Marx Bros.' Duck Soup to take the taste out of my mouth.

But I remained the evening through, enthralled by ruthlessly
honest and vivid playwriting, and by movingly honest and vivid acting
by Henry Hull and his associates as poor white trash of the Georgia
back country. You can't run out on a show that good, even if it is
spoiling your evening. So conscientious seems the work of Mr. Hull
and his company that I doubt that they will take a bath as long as
this play runs, which (on account of the general unpleasantness of
the thing) may not be such a wait, after all. The picture is of the
lowest, laziest, dirtiest, most ignorant, most animally-sexual people
I have ever seen. And the actors get dirtier with each performance,
because the stage is covered with real soil which you can smell over
the footlights. Or was that, too, real acting? Each of the main characters has just the slightest glimmer of soul: the old man has a
strain of earthy humor; the old woman has a remnant of love in her
heart for at least one of her seventeen children (the fathers of some
of whom had evidently passed through in Packards); the worthless
son responds to the sound and shine of a motor car. I predict that
if the show has any run at all, most of the cast will soon come down
with colitis from eating those stolen raw turnips in the first act.

> --Don Herold in Life, January
> 1934, page 39.

* * *

Of all the plays I saw, the performance of James Barton in the part of Jeeter Lester in Tobacco Road was a job of outright genius. You can protest to the editor of this magazine if you think I'm careless with my adjectives--but in my mind, genius it was. I sat in the third row when I saw the play and I actually ached with mingled emotions of laughter and tears when the show ended. I was close enough to Barton to perceive every little futile gesture, to hear every muttered soil-grown obscenity, to observe each gleam of hope that died aborning in the eyes of that human wreckage that he characterized. He was superb! With the exception of the actor who played the part of Lester's half-wit vicious son, the rest of the cast were mere stooges to fill in the necessary parts of the play. The content of the play itself leaves the observer in a conflicting state of mind. He has witnessed a most damning indictment of the present social system, and at the same time no solution to the problem is presented other than stark defeat. Be that as it may, I'd walk ten miles backward any time to see Barton perform in a Theatre Union production.

--John Mullen in New Theatre,
Vol. 3, No. 5 (May 1936), page
26.

TOMORROW AND TOMORROW (Philip Barry; Henry Miller Theatre,
January 13, 1931)

Philip Barry's Tomorrow and Tomorrow was well received on the opening night by those who could see and hear it. My seat was so far back under the balcony that it was only by leaning forward and doing considerable ear-cupping that I could get any idea of what was going on behind the footlights. I am sorry to state that my impression, gleaned at such an uncomfortable disadvantage, was not particularly favorable, and if Osgood Perkins, my favorite actor, had not been in the cast, I could have quitted the playhouse earlier than the final curtain with few regrets. But Mr. Perkins spellbinds me. I should rather hear him say "Mrs. William A. Plant" or "Why not?" than listen to Hamlet's soliloquy done by the leading player of any given country. In this piece Mr. Perkins has the ignominious part of a private secretary, weaving back and forth with his employer's bags in that fine spirit of unspoken contempt for things in general which he has apparently cornered and which makes even his brief, infrequent utterances almost historical. He is, for me, the whole show.

The action begins several years ago in a small Indiana college town and is based on the thwarted maternal instinct of Eve Redman (played by Zita Johann), married to a numbskull who owns some kind of "works," talks horse, and tells her in detail about his class reunion. She is very nice about it, however. In fact, the whole play

is a subtle conspiracy to keep Gail Redman from finding out what
an ass he is. They are about to minimize their disappointment in
having no children by adopting an orphan when a distinguished lecturer comes to town, puts up at their house, falls in love with the
restless, groping Eve, and supplies the paternity which is necessary
to make her existence complete. When he comes back some years
later, she is sorely beset to decide whether to fly with him or remain at home with her wifely duties, and the Watch and Ward Society
will be glad to hear that her final decision is noble, and stupid. As
the curtain falls we see her standing in the sunlight with a far-flung
gesture of farewell which betokens the bravery of her resignation,
and although it is exactly what she should have done, a cynical observer might easily wonder why on earth, if things were as bad as
all that, she couldn't sneak an occasional trip to Chicago and thereby
eventually cure herself of an emotional malady which threatened her
peace for the remainder of her days and gave the play, crediting
Shakespeare with an assist, its title. I was somehow unconvinced by
the magnitude of her sacrifice, possibly because a woman who smiles
constantly when she talks and makes up things about the laurel along
the river does not strike me as a hot menace to boredom either as a
dinner companion or a life partner. But Mr. Barry has set down her
story with a great sincerity, and if his celebrated dialogue does not
crackle as much in Tomorrow and Tomorrow as I had been led to believe it would, it is at least sufficient for the business at hand, and
at one point touches the humanities so closely that a simple declarative sentence from a maid, "I hate trays," draws an instantaneous
sigh of appreciation from the entire audience.

                                    --Baird Leonard in Life (January
                                         30, 1931), page 18.

                              *   *   *

    Most people will tell you that this new play is Philip Barry's
best, but most people prefer Paris Bound to White Wings, and Holiday to Hotel Universe, and that being the case I think most people
are wrong. Nevertheless, Tomorrow and Tomorrow is among Barry's
best, if for no other reason than that he has conceived a simple and
beautiful story and here and there touched the edge of a vision he
had seen, and communicated to us a part of its beauty.

    A childless woman falls in love with a man who gives her the
sympathy and understanding she had unconsciously sought for and
missed in her husband. They have a child and upon him Eve concentrates all the accumulated affection of her being. Dr. Hay, father
of the child, is only a passerby, and immediately after their short
union he goes back into his world of scientific investigation. Some
years later he is summoned to the bedside of the child, who lies
dangerously ill as a result of a fear-complex, unconsciously given him
by his supposed father. The true father saves the child's life by
exorcizing the complex, and asks Eve to take the child and go away
with him; but Eve refuses. Like Candida, she must remain with the

weaker of the two men who have claims upon her; besides, she has at last all that life can give her.

The direction of the play, Gilbert Miller's (with doubtless more than a hint by the author) was generally carried out with understanding, and the acting, particularly that of Herbert Marshall, Zita Johann and Osgood Perkins, was of that restrained order that is emphatic by reason of its lack of emphasis. But somewhere, somehow, something went wrong, and the supreme point was missed. I believe it was Mr. Barry's fault, and because of it the acted play failed to ring entirely true. Let me see if I can put my finger on what was wrong.

To do this I must go back a little into the earlier history of the script, and incidentally reply to a falsehood which Mr. Barry himself would probably never bother to contradict. This is to the effect that in its original form Tomorrow and Tomorrow was a poor thing, vastly overwritten, and so ill-adapted to presentation on the stage that someone had to take it in hand and make it actable!

When I read the manuscript several weeks before it was contracted for, and presumably before the nameless investigator who occasioned the stupid gossip could have seen or even heard of it, I can assure you that in practically every respect--except for a certain fulness in the dialogue that nearly all playwrights cut before making their final revisions--it was the same play now to be seen at the Henry Miller Theatre.

If it weren't that this silly story had appeared in print and was believed by certain people who don't care for the play, I would never have mentioned the matter.

But in reading the script I remember making a mental note that when the play was produced it might be difficult to make credible the cure of the child, because this had to take place off-stage, and because it would be necessary to inform the audience of the precise terms of Dr. Hay's delicate problem. In order to save the child's life it was imperative that his real father should gain his confidence, carry him back to the time before he had learned fear from his supposed father, and somehow drag his mind back to the present, minus the old fear. Hay has been "working" on the child--just how we don't know--and in the nick of time the child sings a verse that is intended to prove that he has, mentally, reverted to the age of two.

All this I got from the typed words, and I get it now from the printed copy of the play, but I could not have got it from the acted play. From that I got little more than a confused sense that in some way the child had taken a turn for the better. As I see it, this very important scene, on which the meaning of the end of the play largely depends, fails of its effect because it is neither clear nor convincing. It could only be adequately treated in narrative form.

This is a rather long explanation, and I would not have made
it if it weren't that the weakness in the scene I refer to was purely
incidental. The same criticism, though to a lesser extent, applies
to that earlier scene where Eve and Hay are so restrained in dis-
cussing their feelings for each other that the audience doesn't know
just what is happening. Here again a novelist could make everything
clear in a paragraph.

I believe Mr. Barry could have simplified his motives and yet
preserved the broad outlines of his story and that he ought either
to have omitted all reference to the child's complex as a mental malady
and simply allow Hay's presence to work its effect, or by some device other than the one used, have made the cure more credible.

Why he fell into such errors I think I understand: he was
trying to explain, not merely to show, as many motives in the minds
of his two chief characters as would show us why they felt and be-
haved as they did, but owing to the limitations of the play form he
had to resort to a more or less arbitrary kind of psychological fore-
shortening. As in Holiday and Paris Bound his theme got the better
of him, and he allowed it to cast a shadow over his people. This is
the principal reason why ideas, theses, and problems are the natural
enemies of good playwrights.

Still, Tomorrow and Tomorrow ranks high among the Barry
plays. Though the surface of its simplicity is occasionally troubled
by a kind of writing that strives for serenity rather than achieves
it, and though it is unnecessarily overburdened with episodes that
lead nowhere, it marks an advance in Mr. Barry's development as an
artist. Its very defects are the result of that ambition to see beauty
in life and to write passionately about it, which places Mr. Barry
among the few of our best playwrights.

> --Barrett H. Clark in The Drama
> Magazine, Vol. 21, No. 6 (March
> 1931), pages 10-11.

TONIGHT AT EIGHT-THIRTY (Noel Coward; National Theatre, November 24, 1936)

Did the wit I heard declaiming "Coward's in His Heaven--all's
right with world" have his tongue in his cheek, or was he speaking
for the gentlefolk in the orchestra? I shall never know, because the
Rolls-Royce that whisked him away from the theatre was too fast for
me. But it is a damning commentary on the season and its patronage
that all its well attended new plays should belong to the featherweight
class, and that one of its most heralded events should have been a
triplicate Tonight at Eight-thirty that is little more than vaudeville
in full dress.

What New York has folded to its abundant bosom is a series
of one-act pieces; three sets of them, to be precise, each of which
consists of one miniature satire, one tragedy of passion and one song-
and-dance number. The two sets seen by this commentator, from
which the unseen items are not reputed to differ greatly, well performed divertissements at best, are two-thirds shoddy and one-third
slight comedy. If they can evoke an enthusiastic response from
large audiences which are rallied to infinitely better, let alone more
important, plays only on the rarest occasions what inducement have
playwrights and producers to lend their talents to so stony a field?
If every allowance is made for slickness by a press that is merciless
to imperfections in truly important work, what hope is there for a
non-subscription theatre? The briefest glance at the content of Tonight at Eight-Thirty should be conclusive--and rather disheartening.
The sole extenuating factor must be Mr. Coward's own expert acting,
and Miss Gertrude Lawrence's captivating performance.

Another reason for regret is that Mr. Coward can do better.
There is no place here to review this fertile playwright's work, but
the fact that he is the careless possessor of a talent is no longer
news. That it does not wear the sable garments of woe is also not
news; Point Valaine and such tragic duds among his current offerings
as Still Life and The Astonished Heart belong in the evidence. To
puff up a bit of erotica until it looks like a whale of an emotion is
to be tedious, as well as pretentious. A little bird might also whis-
per into the author-composer's ear that, for all their commodity
value, such numbers as Red Peppers and Family Album are at best
a thimble-full of humor in a bucket of mediocre tunefulness. Mr.
Coward is not descended from Orpheus. But several of his current
sketches again attest his equipment for crackling satire. Hands
Across the Sea is too slight and flip to really matter, but it is a
masterly reductio ad absurdum of upper-class ineptitude, snobbish-
ness included; the skit would be a gem in any ordered comedy of
manners. The first two scenes of Ways and Means, before it turns
mildly puerile, reveal the same talent, which consists in sharp observation and lean, nervous wit incalculably effective when it dangles
sophisticates from its line. The age could use a major satirist. But
Mr. Coward, who is too sparing with his red pepper while much that
passes for pepper with him is little better than old snuff, would have
to give himself full sway. It will doubtless surprise this eminently
successful playwright to hear that he is frustrating himself....

--John W. Gassner in New Theatre
& Film, Vol. 4, No. 1 (March
1937), page 32.

TWENTIETH CENTURY (Ben Hecht and Charles MacArthur; December 29, 1932)

A madhouse on wheels is Twentieth Century. The action takes

place on a trip of this w.k. choo-choo from Chi. to N.Y. (I ought
to pan the show; what little r.r. stock I own is Pennsylvanian; if
somebody will put on a play called Pennsylvania, I'll puff it to the
skies.) Eugenie (1000%) Leontovitch, Moffat Johnson and others
give recognizably 70 m. per hr. portraits of screen and stage celebs,
including the great Gabno and a blend of a certain erstwhile high-
priest of hokum and an extant producer of the "great-honor-to-be-
present" school. It's all wild fun, from the chalk of Ben Hecht and
Charles MacArthur.

If I had a whistle as good as that, I'd stay home and blow it
and never go anywhere and save some money.

> --Don Herold in Life (February
> 1933), page 32.

VICTORIA REGINA (Laurence Housman; Broadhurst Theatre, December 26, 1935)

Helen Hayes removes the satiric stigma from the words "charm"
and "sentimental" in her evocative portrayal of England's Queen Victoria in Victoria Regina, which is being splendidly set forth at the
Broadhurst by Gilbert Miller. The title carries an air of triumph with
it, a fitting enough introduction to one of the most compelling plays
of the year.

But it is not so much a play as a portrait. The author,
Laurence Housman, has not bothered to set it in the mold of mounting drama. He does not have to. The steady, victoriously bourgeois
career of the woman who made such an impress on the world in her
long span that the period was given her name, creates heights of emotional import rarely achieved in conventional forms of the drama.
Through the completely magnificent acting of Helen Hayes the play
has become transcendent theatre.

In ten scenes it traverses sixty years, from 1837 when the naive
but already determined young girl appears in nightgown and long hair
to hear of her ascendancy to the throne, to the Jubilee in 1897 when
the plump epitome of successful respectability, complaisantly happy,
reviews a life well spent in the cultivation and propagation of a conservative attitude of mind and emotions.

The conventional picture of Victoria is one of smug virtue and
stodgy living. In Helen Hayes' hands the Queen has come to life
with a rewarding richness of characterization. Her interpretation is
generous in human qualities, making of England's favorite monument
of the last century a vital figure, secure in her attitudes, eminently
just, a kindly creature, loving wife and a careful statesman. Her
noted prejudices here become only a part of the picture.

In the opening scene the new queen reveals her independence
immediately by taking charge of her German mother and serenely
moving into the position of mistress not only of her life but of the
Empire's. Her middle-class virtue of stubborness shows most clearly
when she chooses Albert for her Prince Consort over the wishes of
her advisers. With him she learns statecraft and tolerance, experiences pangs of jealousy which drive her to some of the few hasty
actions of her balanced life and through it all gives the play a quality of humor and compassionate understanding.

For there are very funny as well as many charming scenes.
Playing royalty has not removed the gay spirit of the Helen Hayes
of comedy. Her discovery of Albert shaving is a delightful moment.
The prim upbringing of the girl had made the masculine custom of
removing the beard a matter of hearsay. All of her scenes with Al-
bert--who is perfectly played by Vincent Price--are triumphs of sentiment in the best sense of the word.

While the play is practically the sole possession of Miss Hayes
and Vincent Price, there are a number of important, finely conceived
and superbly acted bits. The Disraeli of George Zucco is a masterpiece of studied eloquence. John Brown, played by James Woodburn,
is a delightfully humorous character and Helen Trenholme gives love-
liness and authority to Lady Jane, who had the temerity to look long-
ingly at Prince Albert.

Gilbert Miller has done extremely well by the supporting cast,
enlisting the evident talents of superior English players. But the
play is all Miss Hayes: She has blended the splendid qualities of
sentiment, whimsy, humour and a little of tragedy into a truly great
characterization.

> --Herbert Drake in Cue, Vol. 4,
> No. 10 (January 4, 1936), pages
> 6-7.

*   *   *

The strange thing about the present theatrical season is that,
while it has been the most generally interesting and certainly the most
financially successful one in half a dozen years, it has disclosed very
little in the way of authentic dramatic quality. What it has disclosed
is a greatly increased skill in the casting and direction of plays and
a beauty in stage production that surpasses anything that we have
had before. As an instance, there is the Gilbert Miller offering of
Laurence Housman's Victoria Regina.

One thing may be said for this man Miller. When it comes to
putting on plays, he isn't afraid to spend money, whether it is his
own or somebody's else. And even in the latter case, as when, with
Libel!, he gets a Hollywood movie company to back him, he exercises
the same excellent care and taste as when, with the Housman exhibit,

he digs down into the Miller sock. As reputable drama, Libel!, by
an Englishman who signs himself Edward Wooll, need not occupy our
meditations. Admirably cast, impressively set, and directed to the
last inch by the Viennese Preminger, it is, though better written than
most such box-office gymkhanas, the old courtroom mystery whiffle,
in this case doubling up on hokum by pulling out the venerable mis-
taken-identity stop. It is, in short, in the recherché Miller production, simply Al Woods in modern dress. The author belongs in the
company of those English dramatists who liberally employ good manners to conceal bad plays. For Libel!, from its heavily routine introduction of the inevitable comic witness of courtroom drama to its wife
out of Temple Thurston literature who cannot tell definitely whether
the defendant is her husband or not and from the affable sarcasms
of its opposing counsel to the author's studied failure to recall that
the defendant's family dentist, for one, could readily have identified
him and thus spared us the play, the whole affair is--as no less an
authority and engagingly honest a fellow than Mr. Miller himself has
confided to me--little more than a good movie.

The company is a first-rate one, the best performance being
that of Wilfrid Lawson as counsel for the defendants. The only flaw
in the casting is Joan Marion, in the rôle of the wife. Why Mr.
Miller had to import Miss Marion all the way from England to play a
rôle poorly that any dozen American actresses might easily have
played with both hands tied behind them, I, the customarily omniscient one, wouldn't know.

Victoria Regina is Mr. Miller's most triumphant production.
Everything physically concerned with it, from Rex Whistler's superb
settings to the capital casting of the various rôles and from the
shrewd selection of the incidental music to the Miller stage direction,
is just about as fortunate as the theatre has a right to expect. Nothing in its own alley has so gratified this patriarchal eye since first it
began to squint professionally at the stage. As to the exhibition within these matchless surroundings, there seems to be some dubiety on
the part of a number of my critical messmates. Consisting of ten
episodes in the life of the Queen--extracted from the sum total of
Housman's original thirty--it is their expressed conviction, very em-
phatically delivered, that it isn't a play. Just what it is, they do
not make any too clear, but that it isn't a play they are certain.
Without taking sides for the moment, maybe if it isn't a play that's
just what the audiences who are packing the Broadhurst Theatre like
about it. Perhaps the show business has been hurt by too many
plays and what the public wants when it goes to the theatre is something that isn't a play, or at least something that the critics decide
isn't a play. This isn't the only time that plays-declared-by-the-
critics-not-to-be-plays have drawn a deeply relieved and enchanted
trade. From the day of Shakespeare's Much Ado to Schnitzler's
Anatol and from the day of Kaiser's Gas to Shaw's Getting Married
and Toller's Hoopla, We're Alive!, the critics have been telling the
public that what it is seeing and enjoying are not plays, and the public has been eating it up nonetheless.

It may be quite true that Victoria Regina is not a play in the
sense that Satellite or Truly Valiant is a play, but that, surely, is
not much against Victoria Regina. It may also be quite true that
Victoria Regina, while it has a beginning, a middle, an end and several other such elements so dear and vitally necessary to the critic-
pundit heart (even though that heart has apparently here overlooked
the fact), is technically a mere series of episodes, but so, technically, are two of Shakespeare's historical-chronicle plays, so is Schitz-
ler's Reigen, so is Drinkwater's Lincoln. Many so-claimed not-plays--
without being in the least alecky or paradoxical about it--are a heap
better on all counts than many professorially endorsed are-plays.
It would take a pretty balmy person to contend that Shaw's Misal-
liance, for instance, which the critics insist isn't a play at all, isn't
surely a whopping lot better than any six gross of Moons Over Mul-
berry Street which, even as the critics denounce it as claptrap, they
yet freely allow is a play. But you simply can't please some of those
boys. When something like Victoria Regina isn't, to their way of
looking at it, a play, they complain and demand a play. Then when
you give them something like The Silver Tassie, they complain that
it isn't only a play, it's two plays. And when you give them something like Odets' Paradise Lost, they complain that the trouble with
it is that it's four or five plays!

The troupe selected by Mr. Miller to act Victoria Regina is a
marvel of accurate selection. Miss Hayes gives her best performance to date in the name rôle, for all the fact that one of my
esteemed colleagues profoundly observes that "she isn't Victoria."
(I suppose George Arliss was Disraeli, Philip Merivale, George Washington, and that Joseph Schildkraut is a matinée idol.) The very
considerable acting talent which she lends to the rôle has, of course,
been here and there partly disregarded in favor of the impressive
make-up trickery which she employs in the play's last episodes. The
craft of the dressing-room has been eulogized at the expense of the
acting craft, just as it has been from the day of Mansfield's Baron
Chevrial to that of Mildred Natwick's recent May Beringer. Vincent
Price, as Prince Albert, could hardly be bettered.
                                        --George Jean Nathan in Life,
                                        March 1936, pages 18-19.

THE VOICE OF THE TURTLE (John Van Druten; Morosco Theatre,
    December 8, 1943)

    John Van Druten's latest play is a theatregoer's delight--a gay,
witty, chuckling romantic comedy that is pure entertainment from beginning to end. It accomplishes, incidentally, what Broadway wise-
acres have long contended was impossible: a one-set, three-character
piece to hold your attention and never slacken pace through three
acts of fast, racy, hilarious fun. It's a writer's--but also a director's

and actors'--feat; and audiences headed for the Morosco may be
properly grateful therefor.

   The three players so happily chosen by producer Alfred de
Liagre Jr. to project Mr. van Druten's theatrical bonbon are Margaret
Sullavan, recently of Hollywood; Elliott Nugent, who from time to
time writes, plays, directs and produces movies as well as plays; and
Audrey Christie, last seen hereabouts with Mr. Nugent in last season's and la Hepburn's Without Love. Together, this expert trio
bring to Voice of the Turtle a deftness in playing that perfectly
points up the bright good humor of the lines and adds weight and
reality to what is essentially pretty light stuff.

   The plot is simple enough. A soldier on furlough has a weekend date in New York with a young actress, patriotically generous
with her favors. She stands him up; whereupon her girl friend, in
a spirit of simple friendliness and because rooms are hard to get,
offers the soldier a place to sleep in her apartment. He stays the
weekend, and by Sunday afternoon these two have found unexpected
resources in each other. They also discover in a tender moment
that they are in love--for it is Spring, and once more "the voice of
the turtle (dove) is heard in our land."

   The base is slender, but the conversational superstructure (of
which there is a great deal) is colorful, inventive, fancy, funny and,
in a word, always entertaining. There are tender, as well as racy
moments and a sympathetic understanding of the problems of young
people lonely in the midst of a crowded city. The play's moralities
are frank and unconventional, but they are recognizable and the
dramatic values involved sound and believable.

   Write Voice down as a play you'll enjoy--and allot fair credit to
all concerned, including designer Stewart Chaney for an extremely
pleasant three-room apartment setting.
                                   --Jesse Zunser in Cue, Vol. 12,
                                     No. 51 (December 18, 1943),
                                     page 14.

WATCH ON THE RHINE (Lillian Hellman; Martin Beck Theatre, April
   1, 1941)

   Lillian Hellman has written a profoundly moving play of today,
of Nazism, and done it in honest theatrical terms. Her play is made
of the stuff of the theatre--plot and character and grand writing.
The fulminations and terror of the modern world are background atmosphere, and doubly strong for being so. What I am fumbling to
say is that Watch on the Rhine avoids the errors of its predecessors
in that it does not rely solely on audience antipathy for the brutality
of the last decade, but gives that antipathy an immediate reason.

Sara Mueller, an American married twenty years to the German, Kurt Mueller, comes back home with her husband and their three children. Kurt has fought the Nazis by espionage and on the battle-fields of Spain and is in constant flight from the Gestapo.

In Sara's home are her mother, Fanny Farrelly, aged and hard bitten and of the old, set, well regulated world; her brother and two refugees, the De Brancovis. The husband, Teck De Brancovis, is scheming in this country, as he schemed abroad to straddle the fence, turn a penny, and in general keep alive. What comes of this conglomoration of people makes the play.

It makes the play with hard writing and tender writing and, in the case of the children, charming writing.

An excellent cast presents this. Paul Lukas plays the German and plays him with depth and great feeling. Mady Christians, as his wife, ably abets him with the best performance of her career. The three children are splendid, particularly Eric Roberts, as the youngest. As De Brancovis, George Coulouris does extremely well and Helen Trenholme is moderate in the unneeded part of his wife. Lucile Watson plays Mrs. Farrelly to perfection.

Jo Mielziner's set is good and the direction by Herman Shum-lin, who also produced the play, fine.

> --Oliver Claxton in Cue, Vol. 10,
> No. 14 (April 5, 1941), page 30.

* * *

Adolf Hitler has said that the place for women is in the home. Lillian Hellman in her latest play, Watch on the Rhine, says in effect that the place for Nazis, male or female, is least of all in the home. That is the main thought underlying Herman Shumlin's top-ranking new production, which an unsurpassable cast turns into the sort of drama that leaves you as breathless as the world has been while the Nazis clumped through the Balkans.

We may think, the dramatist says in effect, that the Nazis can-not reach out and challenge us in our homes--but "tut, tut," says Miss Hellman, with a very potent "tut." As an example she locates her play in a good, representative American home, very orderly and comfortable, in sardonic contrast to the title of the piece. It is a well-to-do residence in a suburb of Washington, D.C., and to listen to the dowager ruling this pleasant Jo Mielziner roost, you'd never think there was a war on--a war to the death, with whole struc-tures of civilization toppling like houses of cards.

Then this dowager's daughter comes home, a daughter who has been away for twenty years in Europe, married to a German whom she brings back, an exile, along with a brood of offspring who are

piquantly odd in their chirpy, European way. The Teutonic husband,
it develops, fought the Fascists in Spain and has continued to combat the Nazi regime underground, though his fingers have been
broken and his spirit mangled as a reward. In spite of the totali-
tarian fire and brimstone that awaits him in Germany, he is determined, now that he has settled his wife and children in America, to
return and try to free other anti-Fascist leaders who have been captured for ferocious enlightenment by the Hitlerites.

One of the house guests, another refugee from Europe, stands
in his way, threatening to betray his identity and his mission to the
German Embassy staff whom this refugee finds choice card-playing
comrades. At once, due to this insidious opposition, the removed
American household is swept by invisible but powerful currents into
the very vortex of the conflict that seemingly is so far away. And
the drama moves toward a tension so great that the audience feels
it has become the General Headquarters directing the far-flung battle
against the powers of darkness.

The play is a remarkable work because, so to speak, Miss Hellman does a right-about-face in so many directions. It has an amazing, regenerative spirit of compassion--hardly the spirit one would
expect of the authoress of The Children's Hour and The Little Foxes,
those sharp etchings done with corrosive acid. Maybe prosperity
breeds mellowness, and even Hitler might have been kinder if he'd
made money in his early days.

This drama has much more humanity and depth than Miss Hellman's previous pieces foreshadowed, a humanity that does not state
itself in idealistic terms or missionary twaddle. It has compunction
even for the Germans, pointing out that there are good folk among
the Teutons also--a fact that we are prone to forget amid the scream
of headlines. It can unfold the philosophy of harassed Europe with
understanding, putting it in the mouth of the driven and calloused
refugee, the obnoxious one who is very much on his aristocratic up-
pers. Though he is the man who demands blackmail by opposing the
German that enlists your sympathy, Miss Hellman says equitably,
"Stand back and give the louse a fair chance to speak!"

This individual, who is thus allowed to bolster his views in the
true spirit of democracy, is labelled a Roumanian, perhaps as an allegorical sidelight on the defection of that Balkan country from op-
portunistic motives. But it is the only whiff of allegory or community club pageantry in the play. Miss Hellman wants to deal with human beings in all their frailties, not with symbolical figures in modern
dress. Hence her anti-Fascist fights because he loves his comrades,
not for a remote glittering dream. Most of all he loves little children,
and says so in a poignant good-bye to his own youngsters that would
wring any heart not imbedded in Goering fat. The play in this way
becomes, with the indirectness of living art, an eloquent appeal for
the next generation likely to be suffocated in Nazi serfdom, and be-

comes so without squaring off in an attitude and proclaiming, "I believe in Youth!"

It is by far the greatest play of the war series, the best that
Miss Hellman has written, and possibly the finest that this reviewer
has seen in many seasons of marching to the Broadway theater in a
spirit of wary hopefulness. After years of showgoing during which
one inevitably acquires a deepening sense of looking at a stage, this
reviewer found himself hunched on the edge of his seat, unaware
that it was a play and intensely concerned over the fate of this nice
family--feeling like the men who occasionally grab an airplane's tail
and are afraid to let go but fearful of what may happen at the landing.

To say that the beginning is desultory and somewhat trivial
is to overlook captiously the fact that this leisurely and amusing start
only serves by contrast to speed up the throbbing, serious situations
later, and to keep the play from being excruciatingly taut. It is a
play that would be effective even after the war, and for once a commentator is almost paralyzed at trying to say the right thing in favor
of it--a strange state for a critic.

But instead of chewing our nails in a state of Slavonic per-
plexity, let us pitch on the acting of Paul Lukas as the anti-Nazi
German. There's a performance for the ages! We have never seen
a finer piece of histrionism on the stage, though of course we don't
date as far back as Edwin Booth. Without any obvious artifice Lukas
makes this shabby but unquenchable crusader so imperishably real
and touching that one wants afterward to go around to the stage door
and slip the poor guy a couple of bucks for the cause. Lukas keeps
well in the background until the real pressure comes in the last act,
yet he is always noticeable, even though he has shaved off the
moustache which has been part of his stock-in-trade as a screen villain.

He was in the Hungarian army during the last war, and you
gather from the gleam in his eye that he knows Prussianism down to
its hobnailed boots. We have never seen more intense, livid fervor
and sincerity in any actor, and when he makes a crumpled gesture
beckoning to his children with his broken hand, we could almost feel
the pain in his Nazi-tortured bones. But his performance is actually broader than this current crisis, for when he cries out passionately against the mess that man has made of this troubled world in a
thousand years, he gives an unforgettable slap at the complacent history textbooks.

People always knew that Lukas was a master of restraint on
the screen, but they will be truly amazed to see his consummate
artistry on the stage. Once he was known as the Hungarian Barrymore, and it is just such a performance as John Profile gave in
Justice and Resurrection. Infinitely affecting as his farewell to his

children becomes, it is never slobbery, and all the demonstrative emo-
tionalism comes from the audience, blowing its noses. His portrait
of the sensitive man who admits he is frightened of Nazi terrorism
but still has the moral courage to risk it, is worthy to rank with
Alfred Lunt's portrait of the scientist in There Shall Be No Night.
When he departs to almost certain death in Germany, one nevertheless has an exalted sense comparable to a happy ending, for one has
seen the triumph of the human spirit in downing the powers of evil.

The Roumanian whom he puts out of the way, much as it sick-
ens him, is splendidly played by George Coulouris, as one of the
rounded, genuinely incarnate figures whom the dramatist has con-
jured from her bag. Lucile Watson is another true individual as the
independent dowager, crackling with tart wit, living in the past era
of her late beloved husband, yet eventually rising to the emergency
of the present with quiet nobility. Mady Christians depicts her daughter with perhaps more Continental resonance than one might expect
in an American-grown woman, till one realizes that she has been
abroad long enough to catch the European plangency of style. Helen
Trenholme has trenchant moments as the wife of the Roumanian who
finally repels him, and the whole cast seems imbued with Lukas'
spirit, even to Eric Roberts as an amusingly knowledgeable small
boy, Peter Fernandez as his serious elder brother, and Anne Blyth
as his charming sister--three youngsters who have their children's
hour in this war-torn scene.

Herman Shumlin, who has staged Watch on the Rhine impressively by stressing the human rather than the theatrical elements,
again shows the wisdom in casting players against the grain--con-
trary to accepted practice. Perhaps recalling that Wallace Beery was
elevated to lasting screen stardom by the simple principal of changing
him from a frowning heavy to a personable character actor, Shumlin
took Lukas out of menace roles which he held on the screen even in
The Lady Vanishes and put him in a sympathetic part, to the lasting
adornment of the stage. Now Lukas, who had been rather shuffled
around in such characterizations of late in films, is being eagerly
sought by studio officials for new roles, and we may yet see him
playing Abe Lincoln--and we bet he could do it!

As a result of following this method, Lukas has been given a
re-vitalized personality, and Shumlin, who adopted the plan in casting
Ethel Barrymore away from type in The Corn Is Green, now offers
the two most satisfying shows on Broadway. If this idea catches hold,
Boris Karloff, at present scaring old ladies on both sides of the footlights in Arsenic and Old Lace, may yet be presented as a domestic
pet in a new version of Harold Lloyd's Grandma's Boy.

                              --Frank Vreeland in Rob Wagner's
                              Script, Vol. 25, No. 596 (April
                              19, 1941), pages 26-27.

WHERE'S CHARLEY? (Book by George Abbott, Music and Lyrics by
    Frank Loesser; St. James Theatre, October 11, 1948)

    The musical comedy that script-writer George Abbott and song-
writer Frank Loesser have made out of Brandon Thomas' classic
vintage-of-1892 farce, Charley's Aunt, is mostly Ray Bolger. Which
is all for the best. Whenever Mr. Bolger is onstage the proceedings
are full of verve and wit. Since he's hardly ever off, Where's Charley? is pretty steady fun. When he is, things slow down a bit while
the typically nineteenth century plot writhes toward its complex
multi-romantic conclusion.

    But Mr. Bolger deserves a little rest now and again. His per-
formance, if it were nothing more, would at least be written down in
the score book as a feat in physical endurance. But it is much more
than that. Even the traditionally billowy bombazine which intermit-
tently turns an Oxford student into a South American millionairess
fails to muffle Mr. Bolger's elfin agility. And his best dance routines are performed when his light is not hidden under a bushel of
yard goods.

    Mr. Bolger dances and capers and clowns his way through the
vicissitudes that lie between Charley and the object of his affections
with a limber grace that makes the ancient farce seem new and sprightly much of the time. The translation of Charley's Aunt to the musical
medium has made it possible to inject a Brazilian scene that is witty
and worldly as well as colorful and spectacular. And the ballroom
scene finale is an exquisite period piece which is equally striking.

    Allyn McLerie, as the lady Charley loves, is a deft foil for Bol-
ger's antics and, on occasion, a dancing partner who measures up to
the company she keeps. Which is no faint praise. Even to be no-
ticed in such close juxtaposition to America's best comic-dancer (or
dancing-comedian, if you like) takes some doing. The Bolger-McLerie
combination is at its effective best in a number called "Make a Miracle" and in the aforementioned Brazilian extravaganza. Mr. Bolger's best solo triumph is "Once in Love With Amy" in which he combines song, dance and comedy with extraordinary success.

    Byron Palmer and Doretta Morrow enact the secondary sweet-
hearts and give tongue to Mr. Loesser's most melodious ballad "My
Darling, My Darling." They are satisfactorily decorative and pleasantly vocal. The third romance, which involves Charley's real aunt
and his roommate's father, is handled by Paul England and Jane Lawrence who have a mite of warbling to do themselves--notably a musical salute to middle-aged romance called "Lovelier Than Ever."

    Horace Cooper, as uncle and guardian of the two girls has the
principal comic role in Where's Charley? and there is a populous supporting cast. But none of these people really matters terribly. Bolger's the thing in Where's Charley?

The Abbott book is simply a translation of the play into a play-with-music and the Loesser score is a nice but rather inconspicuous accompaniment to the proceedings. George Balanchine did the choreography. Secondary honors, if secondary honors they are, belong to the sets and costumes by David Ffolkes. He has recreated the fin de siècle scene more or less literally. There's only a hint of theatrical license in his Oxford backgrounds and the costumes have the authentic air of museum documents.

These vital elements superimposed on the Bolger wizardry add up to an entertainment that is pretty as well as good, clean fun.
                              --Thomas Brailsford Felder in Cue,
                                 Vol. 17, No. 43 (October 23,
                                 1948), page 22.

WHITE HORSE INN (Book by Hans Mueller, suggested by Oskar
     Blumenthal and G. Kandelburg, adaptation by David Freedman,
     Lyrics by Irving Caesar, Music by Ralph Benatsky; Center
     Theatre, October 1, 1936)

Everything from a prop cow to a singing waiter. A double decker as a spectacle; a gardenia for the rested business man.
                              --John W. Gassner in New Theatre,
                                 Vol. 3, No. 11 (November 1936),
                                 page 31.

WINGED VICTORY (Moss Hart, Music by David Rose; 44th Street
     Theatre, November 20, 1943)

Moss Hart's Winged Victory is fundamentally recruiting-poster art, and as such it is stunning. There are the usual clean, primary colors, the highly conventionalized but heroic design, the bold and professional execution, and the inescapable moral--it is dangerous but necessary and romantic to kill the enemy--written in block capitals at the bottom. Taken on this level--taking Mr. Hart, that is, as the theatrical counterpart of Flagg and Christy--Winged Victory looks very much like a masterpiece, or at least looks like the damnedest service show ever put on. Taken even remotely as something else, as an attempt to report the emotions and behavior of young men at war, I'm afraid it has something of the high-minded but vacant quality of a moving picture. If Mr. Hart's play had been written frankly only as a morale builder and a tribute to a group of very brave men, it would be silly to review it as if it were intended to be a permanent contribution to the theatre. However, unlike those responsible for This Is the Army, the author has chosen to employ the play form and an editorial attitude, and I don't see how he can escape

altogether some critical investigation of what he has to say and his
manner of saying it. Dissecting a patriotic and non-commercial enterprise at this particular moment is thankless work, but I can't help
feeling that the customers have a right to know just precisely what is
on exhibition at the Forty-fourth Street Theatre.

In the first place, it seems to me that Mr. Hart's thinking suffers seriously from what might be called the Light Brigade Fallacy.
There are tentative references in his play to freedom and tolerance
and other abstractions, but the strong, general implication is that not
one of the very attractive boys on the stage has the slightest idea
of what the war is actually about. They want to fly because they
have the "bug," they join the Army in order to be allowed to fly,
they are ready to get killed, not as a matter of moral principle, but
because it is all, obscurely, part of the game. Such total political
innocence is touching, I guess, but it is a little disturbing, too.
When Mr. Hart divorces heroism from any trace of adult perception,
when he puts it on a theirs-but-to-do-or-die basis, he not only
diminishes the heroism but even, it may be, gives it a remotely
Fascist quality. The adolescent, or posterish, effect of the play
might have been avoided to some extent if Mr. Hart had chosen to
include at least one character of a skeptical or even faintly disrepu-
table nature, but he hasn't. There are two hundred and twenty-
eight people in the cast, and there isn't an ignoble thought in the
lot of them.

My second major objection to Winged Victory as a serious dramatic offering is that Mr. Hart's plotting often seems to have come
directly out of a Hollywood story conference. It is the tough, nerve-
less cadet, the boy who never gave the outcome of his tests a second
thought, who is the first to fail; it is the cadet whose wife has just
discovered she is going to have a baby who gets killed on a training
flight; and it is just when the hero of the play is most obsessed with
the thought of death that he learns of the birth of his son. I could
multiply these examples of machine-made art almost indefinitely, but
I doubt that it's necessary. You can take my word for it that surprise is not part of Mr. Hart's strategy.

To conclude this dirge, I would like to say that the quality of
the prose at the Forty-fourth Street Theatre is simple, precisely as
advertised in the press, but I'm afraid it is the dubious simplicity
you sometimes get when a complicated man tries to represent common speech, rather than the actual, eloquent sound of the young men
talking. It occurred to me, in reading the reviews of Winged Victory,
that some of my colleagues might perhaps have been overpowered and
slightly deafened by the scenery. Certainly they overlooked what
seems to me one of the most peculiar lines I can remember. One of
the cadets has just come back from his first night flight. "Well, god-
damit," he says in response to some heckling, "it is romantic! And
you don't hate yourself in the morning, either!" The idea of sex as
inseparable from disgust, especially in a healthy young man who hap-

pens to be married, made me wonder just a little about the nature of
Mr. Hart's researches into Army life.

There are, of course, a great many fine things to balance all
this. The revolving sets are clean and massive, sometimes beautiful;
the acting has a youthful charm and sincerity, almost a dedicated
quality, that you don't often see on Broadway; there is an extremely effective employment of background and incidental music, though
the "Air Corps Song" may turn up just once or twice too often; the
technical details, such as the devices used in testing the cadets' re-
flexes, are fascinating and introduced to just the right degree; the
purely ritualistic portions of the dialogue--the recited oath of alle-
giance, the prayers, and the more or less set official speeches to
the candidates--have a grave, if calculated, effect; the play itself
has a sort of military construction--the action, you might say, takes
its point, consolidates it, and then moves on--that is a delight to
watch. All these are certainly things to admire without reservation.
I only wish that Mr. Hart hadn't felt obliged to dilute them with such
a very elementary play. Perhaps, however, I'd better end by saying
that the current odds are about five to one that Winged Victory
wins both the Drama Critics' Award and the Pulitzer Prize, two
trophies at the moment practically synonymous.

> --Wolcott Gibbs in The New Yorker
> (December 4, 1943), pages 53-
> 54.

* * *

In Winged Victory Moss Hart has written a great piece of popular theater. Its theme is the role of the Air Forces in the war, and
it treats it in simple, understandable, emotional terms. It is largely
a show, and Mr. Hart has made it much more of one with his brilliant directing. It is partly a spectacle, and Sgt. Harry Horner has
greatly enhanced the spectacle with his splendid sets. It is essentially a salute, and a big Army band under Sgt. David Rose makes
the salute more resounding. Winged Victory belongs utterly to the
moment--not merely the moment in history, but also the moment when
you sit before it. Its force starts evaporating as you exit. But it
is so wholly divorced from art that I suppose it is partly exempted
from criticism.

To a remarkable extent, Winged Victory is much less about war
than youth. The whole tone of the play is boyish, even Rover-
Boyish, for which there is the excuse that the Air Force, unlike the
rest of the Army, is made up of kids. That is why the first half
of Winged Victory, which follows cadets from their induction to their
graduation, is infinitely the better half. For Mr. Hart is writing of
kids at school--a very serious school, but a school for all that. The
school, like any other, has its ritual, its traditions, its ideal of com-
radeship; and Mr. Hart's youngsters are fired by the romance and
imbued with the gallantry in them. The stakes are far higher, but

his kids' worries about passing their tests or their excitement over getting their wings differs only in degree, not kind, from making the football team or winning your letter.

I think this was the real story Moss Hart had to tell, not only because it has its own inherent form and unity, but because it is what he had himself observed and directly responded to. When he pictures a teeming, lively scene of general camp life, or a scene where kids are told they have been washed out of the Force, or the full-stage spectacle of a graduation, one is touched or exhilarated. Mr. Hart's kids may be far too uniformly decent and starry-eyed. But they are youth, even if they are not very convincing as young people; and youth has its own kind of poignancy.

The second half of Winged Victory, which takes its fliers to the South Pacific, is a different kind of story, and a much more fumbling and fictional one. Here reality can't be so blithely ignored, and Mr. Hart never achieves it. Here, too, an emotional pattern is repeated with sharply diminishing returns. Such situations as boys about to take off for the Pacific and young wives left behind in shabby hotel rooms emerge as the merest stereotypes. In his South Pacific scenes Mr. Hart scrupulously avoids the rank melodrama of The Eve of St. Mark, but by the same token he sidesteps all the grimness of war. His warriors remain nice schoolboys to the end.

What is best about Winged Victory is that it is always simple: if at bottom much of it is corny, none of it is fancy or pretentious. What is worst about it is that it has nothing whatever to say. It is simply emotional entertainment.

In staging the show, with its immense cast and many scenes, Mr. Hart faced a stupendous job which he mastered completely. As a production, Winged Victory could hardly be bettered. If there are no standout performances, the general level of acting is good. In the larger roles Cpl. Mark Daniels, Pfc. Edmond O'Brien, Pvt. Dick Hogan, Pvt. Don Taylor, Pvt. Philip Bourneuf, Pvt. Lee Cobb, and Phyllis Avery and Olive Deering all come through with honor. And the band plays with martial Schmalz, never more so than in rendering the old Yale, "Whiffenpoof" song or the rousing anthem of the Air Force.

> --Louis Kronenberger in PM (November 22, 1943).

THE WINSLOW BOY (Terence Rattigan; Empire Theatre, October 29, 1947)

The author of this British drama is Terence Rattigan, who provided the fabulous Lunts with O Mistress Mine, the salacious comedy

in which they are presently titillating the Chicago chapter of their
vast following. It would be hard to believe, if comparing the play-
bills were not convincing, that both plays were knocked off on the
same typewriter or conceived in the same mind. O Mistress Mine is
frivolous and essentially immoral. Mr. Rattigan's present offering is
serious and reflects the admirable traits of English character.

Young Winslow is a naval cadet who is accused of forging a
money order and is expelled from his school. His father, believing
his son innocent, attempts to persuade the Admiralty to review the
evidence. When he is first ignored and then given a brush-off, he
takes his case to the courts and the public, and it finally bobs up
as a political issue in the House of Commons. Reviewers who are
better informed than I am say the story is based on an actual contest
between an English citizen and an agency of the Crown. Mr. Rattigan has squeezed out the bathos and maudlin sentiment which usually
envelop such case histories, compressing its significance into four
scenes of poignant drama.

The Winslow Boy is presented in The Empire by Atlantis Productions, a front for a triumvirate of British and American producers;
namely, The Theatre Guild, H.M. Tennent Ltd. and John C. Wilson.
Glen Byam Shaw directed, and the decor, apparently a nasty French
word, was contributed by Michael Weight. If decor means settings,
he has no reason to be ashamed of his job. On the interpretive side,
Alan Webb, the embattled father, and Frank Allenby, a barrister who
fights the case to a successful finish, are the kind of Englishmen it
is easy to like. Michael Newell, the persecuted youngster, is apparently a future star. Valerie White is good as the Winslow daughter,
and Madge Compton is a proper English wife. Supporting roles are
well done.

While silently applauding an English father's determined fight
for the honor of his son I was thinking backward, trying to remember if I have always been as loyal to my children. Retrospection is
one of the needs that frequently accompany the contemplation of virile drama, and introspection is another, but nowadays there are few
plays that induce either mood. The Winslow Boy is rather unique in
that it rises above the level of dramatic competence to the plane of
moral significance. It gives the audience something to take home and
think about.

While the flaws in Mr. Rattigan's writing are numerous and obvious, most of them tend more toward perfectionism than ineptitude.
There are times when he seems to be saying, "Just watch me build
up the suspense in this scene. Boy, am I good!" At other times he
is apparently thinking: "Better speed it up here, can't let the audience wait too long for their suburban trains." But most of his de-
linquencies appear toward the end of the play and none of them im-
pair its essential sincerity.

                              --Theophilus Lewis in America (No-
                                 vember 22, 1948), page 219-220.

* * *

There is certainly one thing to be said for meretricious writing: it imposes no obligations on us. We can enjoy it with a sort of
tolerant contempt; we needn't for a moment take it seriously. Perhaps
we should even be grateful to writers who let us first have fun and
then get acidulous. If so, I am grateful to Mr. Terence Rattigan for
The Winslow Boy. On the whole, I had a good enough time at it.
As a theater-piece, I found much of it interesting; as a theater production, I found more. But as anything beyond that, it struck me--
as has everything I have ever seen of Mr. Rattigan's--as evidence
of an incorrigibly trashy mind.

The Winslow Boy is, by classification certainly, a "serious"
play. I further imagine that in its author's mind it represents a
truly serious effort. Mr. Rattigan has dramatized that great cause
celebre of Edwardian England, the Archer-Shee case; and it is a very
good (if not entirely easy) case to dramatize. For surrounding it
are elements of melodrama and mystery, of human interest, of family
feeling, of rocklike personal character; while imbedded in it is a
real principle of individual human rights.

It is a story, as you possibly know, of a 13-year-old boy--a
naval cadet--who is dismissed from the British naval academy at Osborne for stealing and cashing a five-shilling money order. Young
Winslow insists to his stern but highminded father that he is innocent; and his father thereupon starts a long battle to clear his son's
name. It is a very tough battle indeed, even with the greatest trial
lawyer in England as the boy's counsel; for Mr. Winslow is up against
entrenched power with all its arrogance, and bureaucracy with all
its red tape. Moreover, his son must compete--on the agenda of the
Admiralty and the House of Commons--with matters of international
importance. But, though it undermines his health, ruins his finances
and threatens his family's happiness. Mr. Winslow persists; and
eventually Mr. Winslow wins out. His son's name is cleared.

It is a story that might easily be impressive, concerned as it
is not just with family honor but with the sacredness of individual
rights. It is not impressive; but the first half is very effective as
theater. In the second half--with the battle being fought in high but
offstage places, and half the cast running in and out in Greek-
messenger roles--the momentum and the excitement considerably abate.
Still, though things here are decidedly leisurely, they are not unduly boring; among other things, one can watch the fine teamwork of
a well-matched all-British cast. But Mr. Rattigan, finding the going
pretty tenuous and hence pretty tough, begins to maneuver and em-
broider, and falls back more and more on hokum and muted heroics.

Muted heroics are, of course, one of the greatest banes of
British drama--and one of the greatest swindles. The assumption
seems to be that because the English underplay their big scenes,

they can get away with an unlimited quantity of them. The further
assumption seems to be that anything underplayed is also honestly
played. But from the standpoint of truth and taste alike, Mr. Rattigan makes all such scenes very hard to take indeed. I have no
doubt that he wrote The Winslow Boy as seriously as he knew how;
but, like Noel Coward, Mr. Rattigan often thinks he is being serious
when he is only being sentimental; and his keenly-developed sense
of theater makes him unable to resist anything--relevant or irrelevant,
high-pitched or low-pitched--that he suspects may get across. As
a result, one takes what he has to offer for what it is worth in theatrical entertainment alone. It will require somebody else to make me
really care about the Archer-Shee case (or the principle underlying
it) on the stage.

The play has been ably staged by Glen Byam Shaw, and the
cast--as aforesaid--work together unusually well. Alan Webb's performance as Mr. Winslow is probably the best of the evening; Valerie
White's, as his daughter, is the most touching; and Frank Allenby's
--as the icy lawyer with the heart of an oven--the showiest and most
entertaining.

                                   --Louis Kronenberger in PM (Octo-
                                     ber 31, 1947).

                              *   *   *

In The Winslow Boy, which comes to us fresh from a two-season
run in London, Terence Rattigan, heretofore noted as a concocter of
deft comedy in the classic drawing room tradition (vide: O Mistress
Mine etc.) adds a measure of meaty content to his undeniable gift
for facile plot structure and polished dialogue. The result, though
not the greatest play ever to hit Broadway, is certainly a satisfactory evening in the theatre and definitely the best Rattigan product
that has yet been displayed hereabouts.

It tells, in robust dramatic terms, the story of a small struggle that involves big issues. The Winslow Boy, aged fourteen or
thereabouts, is the apple of a middle-class English family's eye. As
a cadet at the Naval Academy at Osborne he is wrongly convicted of
a five shilling theft and the play is built around the Winslow family's
gallant and costly fight to clear the boy's name.

The most embattled warrior in what often seems a disheartening and futile battle is the boy's father, a beautifully drawn distilla-
tion of democratic principles, beautifully interpreted by Alan Webb.
Father Winslow is a sort of English counterpart of our own crusty
and petty-despotic Father Day. But he seemed to us to be both more
sympathetic and more significant. Outwardly an autocrat of the breakfast table cast in the familiar mold of the pre World War I pater
familias, he is inwardly the eternal champion of the rights of man,
a bourgeois Voltaire, making up in courage and integrity what he
lacks in wit and dazzle.

His principal adherent and ally is his daughter, an advanced female (the action takes place on the eve of World War I) who believes in the "hopeless cause" of Woman's Suffrage and actually smokes cigarettes in public. In the course of the Winslow case, this indomitable twain is often urged to give up the struggle by other, more typically human members of the family who do not consider that five shilling's worth of honor justifies the expense and the notoriety.

In what becomes a cause celebre, the Winslow fortunes take such a drubbing that the rather doltish older son is forced to come down from Oxford, the aforesaid crusading daughter's callow fiancé steps out of the picture and even the boy's doting mother becomes convinced that the game is not worth the candle.

Thanks, however, to the eloquence and sense of theatre of a brilliant attorney, right is done in the end and the mighty Lords of the Admiralty have to bow down before the Winslow Boy. The role of the barrister perceptively portrayed by Frank Allenby, is almost Shavian in its blending of cynicism and honesty. A cross-examination of the boy by the attorney which brings down the first act curtain is a masterly piece of theatre and the high spot of the play. The second act never quite measures up to the promise of the first, but Mr. Rattigan cleverly avoids the obvious ending and leaves his characters more or less as he found them, a group of frequently muddled, occasionally noble, but always human people.

Michael Newell enacts the adolescent storm center of all these goings-on, Valerie White, Madge Compton, Owen Holder, Betty Sinclair are splendid as assorted members of the Winslow household. The set is by Michael Weight.

> --Thomas Brailsford Felder in Cue,
> Vol. 16, No. 45 (November 8,
> 1947), page 17.

WINTERSET (Maxwell Anderson; Martin Beck Theatre, September 25, 1935)

Maxwell Anderson's Winterset belongs to the living theatre and is similarly defeated by its inconclusiveness. This gifted playwright has been riding two differently colored horses for a long time. He has alternated between the full-blooded romanticism of historical tragedies like Elizabeth the Queen and Mary of Scotland and the sober realism of Saturday's Children and Both Your Houses. It was in the cards that he should try to fuse the separate facets of his playwriting, to amalgamate the poet and the prose writer, the romanticist and the realist. The effort was made in last season's Valley Forge, but the romanticist and the realist did not mix well. In Winterset they do not mix at all.

In the winter of his discontent Maxwell Anderson has returned
to an old wound, the Sacco and Vanzetti case which outraged his
sense of justice and drew from him that spirited, if confusing, collaboration Gods of the Lightning. In his new play he is still indignant. He brings his most competent dramaturgy and his most ringing
poetry to bear upon the judge whose guilty conscience has unsettled
his mind and the embittered son of the electrocuted man who would
clear his father's name. But Maxwell Anderson is not content to
treat a contemporary theme; it is his ambition to move on to the
eternal verities and he falls back upon one of the staples of the
poetic trade, "pure love," with the customary sprinkling of noble
sentiments. Rightly enough, Winterset sees the futility and hollow-
ness of personal revenge. The corroding single-tracked bitterness
of "Vanzetti's" son is an impasse that must be broken through.
Therefore, the play provides him with a vapid and melodramatic love
affair for the good of his soul, at the conclusion of which he dies
grandiosely and self-sacrificingly--and vainly, in a Romeo and Juliet
aura! The result is a play that labors like a volcano and brings
forth--a mouse. The conclusion is irrelevant; it is more than that--
it is an evasion of the logic of the play, which demands that "Vanzetti's" son should substitute social vision for private hatred. His
newly-found love might help him to find this solution, but must be
subsidiary to it. We may speculate on the mote in the playwright's
eye which prevents him from seeing this clearly. Is it not an aversion to the social struggle and a desire to rise above it even at the
expense of logic?

The author and his apologists evade the issue when they de-
fend the use of verse in Winterset. The theatre can most certainly
use exalted and colorful speech for the expression of significant experiences. The trouble with Winterset is not its manner of saying
things but what it says. Content naturally affects expression, and
Anderson's dialogue is weakest when its dramatic direction is weakest, just as the characters become wooden whenever they are steeped
in a miasma of poetic sentiments in which the direction of the play is
forced and needlessly complicated. Incidentally, Mr. Anderson shows
a surprising ignorance of working-class people, and the communist
in the first act is an inexcusable caricature in a play that purports
to be a fair-minded idealistic drama. Winterset is half masterpiece,
half pretentious melodrama and romance. Like last season's Within
the Gates, the play is significant as a landmark in a very talented
playwright's search for meaning in the world. There should be room
in the theatre for this search, especially when it is so ably supported
by Richard Bennett, Burgess Meredith, Jo Mielziner, who has designed excellent sets, and Guthrie McClintic, who has directed the
production as well as it was possible without altering the text.

--John W. Gassner in New Theatre,
Vol. 2, No. 11 (November 1935),
pages 9-10.

* * *

When it comes to staging, Guthrie McClintic, who has performed with Maxwell Anderson's Winterset, is no slouch either. Taking a script that reaches up bravely and imaginatively for the edelweiss of poetic dramatic beauty, if forsooth it succeeds most often merely in clutching various lowland dandelions, he has exercised upon it his uncommon directorial and production talents and has contrived to deceive the injudicious into seeing it in virtues that are not always present. What Anderson, ever commendable spirit, doubtless set out to accomplish was a tale of Sacco-Vanzetti revenge seen synchronously through the eyes of the Gorki of Night Refuge and the Gluck of Iphigenia, with minor variations by Schubert, but what we finally get from him is little more in essence than Maeterlinck and Samuel Leibowitz after a brief holiday in Russia with Jehudi Menuhin. In some of his lines there is authentic song; in some of his scenes there is the slumbering flame of drama; and in all of his intention there is dignity, and high aim, and courage. But the guts of true poetic drama and of true poetic drama's unified force are not there. The performances of Burgess Meredith and of the Hecht-MacArthur discovery, Margo, a young Mexican actress, are especially creditable.

--George Jean Nathan in Life, December 1935, pages 20-21.

WITHIN THE GATES (Sean O'Casey; Incidental Music by Milton Lusk and A. Lehman Engel; National Theatre, August 22, 1934)

Sean O'Casey, in Within the Gates, has a very simple tale to tell that is neither very original nor very dramatic. It is about a young woman who has become a Whore because she could not get a decent job, and about the Bishop who will not help her until he learns that she is his illegitimate daughter. Then there is the poetic pleasure of life with him. There are also a host of minor characters, well-drawn, earthy, vivid.

The trouble is that O'Casey has seen fit to fluff up this simple tale with a host of pretentious irrelevancies. In an advance article, O'Casey proclaimed his play an all-embracing allegory. The characters, though they stand quite well on their own feet in the play itself, are declared (in explanatory notes inserted in the program by a considerate management) to be "symbols" of all manner of weighty things. The playwright has woven in dancing and song, some of it artistically justified, and some of it--to put it mildly--out of place. In the dialogue, speeches of rich and substantial poetic imagery alternate with speeches of jagged poeticism, where the sensitive listener grits his teeth in unpleasant anticipation of forced and sustained alliteration.

O'Casey is here concerned with widespread "poverty of spirit." All his characters except the Young Whore and the Dreamer are af-

flicted with it. And here is one weakness of the play. The author
seeks to maintain this "poverty of spirit" as an abstraction, arising
wilfully in each person. So we witness the shameful spectacle of an
O'Casey who was once an Irish workingman, labeling two Chair At-
tendants who are fired for being "too old" as "symbols of life's wreckage who are wasting life by living it." And we see this O'Casey ad-
dressing a song to the poor suffering little bankers and industrial-
ists, who of course never taken time off to enjoy life on their country
estates, villas, and yachts, a song inviting them to come out and enjoy the beauties of nature. Then there is that ominous group of
Down and Outs, all afflicted with that same "poverty of spirit," be
they wealthy or poor, whom "life has passed by."

His "strong" characters are likewise significant. It is their
weakness that is the chief source of the play's weakness. There is
no adequate force to give battle to those afflicted with poverty of
spirit. The Young Whore who has not succumbed is none the less
life's wreckage. Only a new and decent social system (but of this
there is no hint in O'Casey) could give her a chance to live and
grow and make her contribution to society. As for that other strong
one, the Dreamer, "symbol of a noble restlessness and discontent;
of the stir in life that brings new things and greater things than
were before ..." the Dreamer, a purposeless young man with minor
creative gifts, who in the play is actually a rather ordinary, not altogether real fellow (despite the praiseworthy efforts of Bramwell
Fletcher)--we can show Mr. O'Casey half a dozen such young men
in as many minutes, any summer day on the steps of the New York
Public Library. If this were the hope of the world, the outlook
would be dark indeed.

In its technical aspects, Within the Gates abounds in weaknesses which O'Casey seeks to rationalize theoretically. In the aforementioned article, he comes forth with the "new" idea that poetry
and music and dancing belong in drama. Who denies it, that it must
now be reasserted so vehemently? Realism as a style of artistic expression arises in different social systems at definite stages of social
development. To consider briefly this very play: O'Casey, as an
artist of high talent, is sensitive to his social environment. He per-
ceives the decaying imperialism that is the British Empire today.
("The golden life of England is tarnished," says one of his characters.) Everywhere is poverty of spirit. So much O'Casey understands, but not how this has come about. To understand the full
social implications of this phenomenon requires a sharp break with
one's past viewpoint on many matters. It is a difficult process to accept the revolutionary conception that capitalism must be destroyed
and labor emancipated from wage-slavery if humanity is to survive
and progress. The first and natural reaction of many sensitive
artists to the unpleasantness of life ("poverty of spirit") is flight--
escape from reality. "The world is a sad place; in my works of art
I shall scorn reality. I will bring in poetry and music and dancing
and high thoughts, though the world be barren of them." Yet, this

flight from the field of battle, results in abandoning the world to
the ruthless overlords of profit, means influencing others to abandon
the field with you, means doing very much what O'Casey denounces
the Down and Outs for doing.

This is the trend of O'Casey's present theorizing. His plays,
however, do not wholly succumb. Within the Gates, with all the
artificiality so inartistically puffed into it, retains a high degree of
realistic vigor, a flavor of the solid earth, an alive-and-kicking quality deriving from the robustness of the common characters. O'Casey's
roots in proletarian soil stand him in good stead. His workingclass
background is his strength.

Within the Gates is excellently acted by a large cast, featuring
Lillian Gish as the Young Whore and Moffat Johnson as the Bishop.
The play is a difficult one to stage, but Melvyn Douglas has done it
admirably. James Reynolds' simple part setting is a thing of beauty
and power, dominated by the unforgettable statue of the unknown
soldier with massive body and small head, wearing a trench helmet.
The music, written by Milton Lusk and A. Lehman Engel, reflects the
minor pastoral tone of the dances excellently. Special mention should
be made of the music for the Song of the Down and Outs, a weird,
powerful, ominous chord of the damned. Probably it is the beauty
of all these elements of the production (together with the poetic
virility of much of O'Casey's dialogue) that hypnotized a drab-sated
Brooks Atkinson to acclaim a play that contributes no fresh understanding or insight into life, but only confusion, as a "great" play.

--Ben Blake in New Theatre, Vol.
1, No. 11 (December 1934), page
19.

* * *

Just as anyone with an intelligence quota a few degrees higher
than that of a Nazi trombone player had about given up hope that
the local stage would ever again divulge anything that anyone with
an intelligence quota a few degrees higher than that of a New Masses
editorial writer against Nazi trombone players could sit through without suffering an attack of cephalomeningitis, Mr. Sean O'Casey came
along and threw the theatre a life-line in the shape of Within the
Gates. With this splendid and gleaming play the business of dramatic
criticism, after two long, dreary months of enforced snoring, was
again privileged to roll out of bed and earn for itself the right to
make a living. That some of its practitioners unfortunately did not
do themselves especially proud and revealed themselves as more magnificently equipped to pass upon the art works of Mr. Tom Powers,
Mr. Owen Davis, Mr. J.C. Nugent and other such local dramaturgic
magnificoes is beside the point. For the point is that here was--
and is--a drama in the true tradition of genius and, unless I am
hopelessly cuckoo, one of the finest things that, since the same author's The Plough and the Stars, has come to give a renewed breath

of life to a stage that has seemed disconcertingly to be edging toward the morgue.

That I have been, for many months, prejudiced in favor of the play, everyone around town who has had the misfortune to encounter me sufficiently knows. The moment I laid it down in the manuscript that O'Casey, whom I had then never laid eyes on, had sent to me, I began to buttonhole the drunk and the sober on streets and in alleyways and to harangue them on its virtues. I have long noted, I wish to confess at this point, that whenever I am seized with a great personal enthusiasm about a play it seems to be the custom of almost everyone to whom I seek to impart some of it to eye me skeptically, as if I were a cocaine sniffer, and arbitrarily not only to disagree with me but to insist upon an elaborate and even rambunctious contrary view, particularly if they have not read the play.

This was true again in the present case. Those who hadn't read it airily nosed me and attributed my unwonted ebullition, it seemed, (1) to the probable circumstance that I must have had some personal quarrel with Eugene O'Neill and was merely trying to put over another favorite by way of putting O'Neill in his place; (2) that I was simply up to my old business of retailing another dubious European genius at the expense of such American geniuses as hang out at Tony's; or (3) that I must have a new girl. Those who read it, when I had it sent to them via the more diplomatic Mr. Richard Madden, either reported that they could see absolutely no merit in it or alibi'd themselves out of committing themselves the one way or the other. The Theatre Guild, wrought up to a high twitter over the magnificence of the zero called A Sleeping Clergyman, politely allowed that its board of directors considered it pretty lousy. Mr. Rowland Stebbins, stewing in the glories of Tight Britches and Lost Horizons, averred he couldn't make head or tail of it, and, anyway, what the hell about all that symbolical stuff? Mr. Max Gordon, agog over the wonders of Spring Song; Mr. Guthrie McClintic, hardly able to contain himself over the dazzles of Divided By Three; the Messrs. Shubert, lost in admiration for the manuscripts of College Sinners and Spring Freshet; Mr. Brock Pemberton, a-swoon over the esthetic excellences of Personal Appearance; and almost all the other saviours of the American stage followed--in more or less paraphrased phraseology--suit.

It remained for a couple of odd boys named Tuerk and Bushar, who are seldom invited to these other notable producers' lunch parties and who probably wouldn't go if they were, to see anything at all in the play, to risk their reputations and the esteem of their profound colleagues by admitting it, and to dig down into their pants for the money to give it a hearing. That hearing you may now enjoy at the National Theatre, unless the play turns out by this time to have been as unwelcome to the tastes of the audiences that are just crazy about Small Miracle and Merrily We Roll Along as it was to those of the producers of such rare gems as The Bride of Torozko and the like. But

whether it runs for three nights or three months or three years,
this Within the Gates--and take it out on me in the future if I will
be found to be wrong--remains one of the truly sizeable and living
plays, as its author remains one of the few real dramatic artists, of
the modern theatre.

--George Jean Nathan in Life, December 1934, page 26.

THE WOMEN (Clare Boothe; Ethel Barrymore Theatre, December 26,
1936)

A deservedly savage satire on the useless women of the fast
set. Excellent portraits by an all-female cast, with Ilka Chase shining like a naughty deed.

--New Theatre and Film, Vol. 4,
No. 1 (March 1937), page 47.

* * *

Unless you desire your young and impressionable son to develop into a Harvard man, it is suggested that you deny him the right
to see The Women during his tender and formative years. It might
well have a subversive and devastating effect upon his sex life.

Boasting a cast of forty females, there isn't a "lady" in the entire ensemble. If Clare Boothe, who penned the excrutiating exposé,
is to be trusted, 1937 has done little to develop the gentler facets
of the fair and un-fair sex.

The flaying, done in terms of broad yet searching comedy,
scalpels the darlings right down to their emotional underthings and
doesn't stop there; a layer or so of not-too-soft epidermis is lifted,
and the sight is one to lower the matrimonial--and, very possibly,
the birth-rate, of the year. "L'amour! L'amour!!" grimaces the playwright. And then sets forth to show that Park Avenue cuties have
claws that make those of jungle beasties seem, by comparison, like
Dennison's crepe paper.

Uncannily discerning direction by Robert Sinclair keeps the
vicious plottings taut and exciting diversion. The writing is smooth
and malicious. There is the unusual stance of a completely feminine
world of which the generating pivot, the male, is felt but unseen for
an entire evening. "There is only one tragedy for a woman: to
lose her man." To protect what they feebly believe to be at once
their anchors and heritage, the Eves connive and plan and seduce
with utmost guile. Even the ordinarily sympathetic figure of the
long-suffering wife, so often played with great advantage to the Hand-
kerchief Manufacturers of America by the Mesdames Kay Francis, Ann

Harding, and Ruth Chatterton, is an unprepossessing wench. Possibly this fault lies in part with Margalo Gilmore who weeps and stag-
gers through the part with a dreary genuflection towards the routine.
It isn't that I quarrel with Miss Gilmore for recalling most of the
technique endorsed by the less worthy schools of the drama. But it
is a bit thick (or thin; depending on the individual viewpoint of
such matters) to have her project the entire gamut of cliches in lieu
of a performance.

Queen of the cats is Ilka Chase, who denudes a gossip monger
with no uncertain skill. Her timing is a delight, and she makes the
lackadaisical gym workout alone worth the price of admission. Then
there is Jane Seymour as an acrid novelist; she has been furnished
with a fine set of quips and sells them expertly. Enid Markey (Bill
Hart's favorite Western heroine) does a neat job as manicurist. Phyllis Povah is accurate as a perpetually pregnant frau. Scores of no
mean proportions are also made by Audrey Christie and Edith Gres-
ham.

Though a number of the 40-Girls-40 are beauties, a strong
baritone voice and a pair of tweed trousers would have been welcome
to ear and eye before the third-act curtain. Which only goes to
show that even our favorite vices can be overdone.

Male laughter predominated in the audience, but the ladies enjoyed themselves, too, though in a more repressed manner. To men
who would know women, and to women who would know themselves,
I heartily suggest the mirror Clare Boothe holds up to the Sex in
play form.

> --Herb Sterne in Rob Wagner's
> Script, Vol. 18, No. 430 (Sep-
> tember 25, 1937), pages 10-11.

THE WOULD-BE GENTLEMAN (Bobby Clark, adapted from Molière,
        Music by Jerome Morass, adapted from Lully; Booth Theatre,
        January 9, 1946)

Comics come and comics go, but Bobby Clark goes on forever.
If I may speak quite personally, he is my bid for tops in the laugh
routine, with the possible exception of Bert Lahr, who's coming up
in a show later.

Most of the boys who write about plays for the New York
papers were a bit stuffy when it came to reporting The Would-Be
Gentleman, in which Bobby stars for Michael Todd at the Booth The-
ater. They thought it mostly Bobby Clark and precious little Molière.
And so what of it? Bobby has made Molière seem a better playwright.
What may have made the Sun King laugh in Seventeenth Century

France is pretty dull, except for students who love to study period drama.

On stage most of the time, Bobby as Monsieur Jourdain, a wealthy tradesman who wants to be a snob, takes singing lessons, fencing lessons, and lessons on how to speak prose properly. Growling and baying like a love-lorn wolf, getting tangled up with his sword and leering like mad all over the place, Bobby, in a variety of outlandish costumes, panics the customers.

He doesn't wear spectacles painted around his eyes, nor does he smoke interminable cigars. He doesn't need these props, for he's a great clown in the tradition (and with undoubtedly more ingenuity) of Grimaldi. A snuff box serves him just as well.

Quite subordinate to the star are gifted June Knight, as the Marquise Dorimène; Edith King, as Madame Jourdain; Ann Thomas, as a comic maid; Ruth Harrison and Alex Fisher, dancers; Gene Barry as the Count Dorante; Frederic Persson as the philosopher, and Le Roi Operti as the tailor.

John Kennedy is mentioned as responsible for the staging and he must have had his hands full. Scenery by Howard Bay and costumes by Irene Sharaff are rich and colorful.

> --Russell Rhodes in Rob Wagner's
> Script, Vol. 32, No. 724 (March
> 2, 1946), page 30.

YEARS AGO (Ruth Gordon; Mansfield Theatre, December 3, 1946)

A celebrated actress has dramatized an episode from the early years of her life, and the resulting play about a family living near Boston has been given a sensitive interpretation by Fredric March, Florence Eldridge, Patricia Kirkland and company at the Mansfield. Ruth Gordon's Years Ago glimpses the actress when she was just sixteen, called Ruth Gordon Jones and aspiring desperately to a stage career over the objections of a rather gruff but good-hearted father. Writing of herself and her family in about 1912, Miss Gordon remembers even their faults with a good deal of fondness, which is accurately communicated until one cannot help liking the Jones family of Wollaston, Mass. Years Ago is a sort of combination of Life With Father and I Remember Mama, without the former's great high comedy or the latter's deeply touching characterizations; but as handled in this Max Gordon production, it still has considerable charm and good humor.

Dominating the stage at the Mansfield is Fredric March as Clinton Jones, Miss Gordon's father and a crusty down-easter, who

says damn all the time because he acquired the habit at sea, wants
his daughter to be a physical culture instructor, pinches pennies,
hates the telephone and just generally stands for no nonsense. The
role is for the most part an amusing caricature, coming into three
dimensions only briefly, when the father recalls his pitiable and even
tragic childhood in order to explain himself to his wife and daughter.
Clinton Jones presents a great temptation to overact, and indeed
there are times when March's imitation of New England accent and
gestures becomes a bit too broad. Elsewhere, however, the March
performance is projected most vividly, as he runs through the mannerisms of an excitable and opinionated father who is thrifty out of
caution rather than avarice and supports his daughter to the hilt
when the real emergency arises.

Miss Gordon remembers her mother as a woman who catered to
her husband in little things but could stand up to him on the big
ones, was capable of being cajoled by a strong-minded daughter into
such daring actions as installing a telephone, was a sympathetic wife
and mother and liked a little glass of Moxie now and again. As
played by Florence Eldridge in this show, Mrs. Jones is both recognizable and appealing. Miss Gordon's memory of herself at sixteen is
a personality motivated by two strongly dominant qualities: naivete
and an obsession for all things theatrical. The self-portrait is a
rather conventional one, and there is the feeling that in this case
the author is holding herself back. Nevertheless, Patricia Kirkland
has brought a good deal of acting talent to this role, and she makes
Ruth Gordon Jones a fairly likeable young woman.

Since the play revolves entirely around the Jones family, the
outsiders are all small parts, all of which have been suitably cast.
Garson Kanin's direction creates just the right sort of small town parlor atmosphere for his wife's script, and the Donald Oenslager setting
and the John Boyt costumes enhance this polished production. As
an extra added attraction there is a cat named Punk who seems to
respond to direction as well as anyone. Years Ago is a light and
undemanding autobiographical tintype of a family; and with March,
Miss Eldridge and Miss Kirkland in the picture, it is pleasant to look
at and worth the effort of Miss Gordon's memory.
                                        --Cue, Vol. 15, No. 50 (December
                                        14, 1946), page 22.

YOU CAN'T TAKE IT WITH YOU (Moss Hart and George S. Kaufman;
    Booth Theatre, December 14, 1936)

For the sake of a gag the Messrs. Kaufman and Hart have gone
Utopian on us in You Can't Take It With You. They present a Washington Heights family who have achieved the ideal state, an Elysian
existence where work is rarely known and all are not only free to in-

dulge themselves in any pursuit or hobby but wherein they do so
with gusto. The result is a household containing a fire-cracker maker,
a home-made candy manufacturer, a middle aged gent who amuses
himself with mechanical toys, an amateur operator of a printing press
who copies things out of Trotsky's works and wraps the candies in
them, a ballet dancer, a playwright and a Russian Grand Duchess
who works in Child's and is a good cooker of blintzes.

The result is hilarious vaudeville with four laughs a minute
and a screaming good time. The physical strain of controlling the
stomach muscles is considerable so when you attend this mad play,
as you will eventually, go prepared to see the funniest uproar in
several seasons, to hear many, many memorable cracks and to carry
away with you a set of risibilities so tickled as to last you for several weeks.

This strange, self-indulgent family believes in taking things
easy, in tolerating strangers to the extent of permitting a visiting
ice man to move in and live with them for eight years. They think
it quite the thing to raise snakes in the living room, to run a printing press there, to make fire crackers in the cellar and to test them
in the living room. They entertain the mother and father of the boy
their daughter wants to marry by having a shirtless Russian ballet
instructor teach their other daughter to dance to the music of a xylo-
phone, also in the living room. In fact everything takes place in
that one abused room, including the visit of the income tax collector
who fails to get his money because several years ago a visiting milk-
man (in residence four years) died without ever telling them his
name. So they buried him under the rightful title of the grandfather.
Ergo, grandpa, on whose small income they all live, is legally dead.
What an idea!

It must be obvious from the above that this is no play in the
proper meaning of that term, but it is a superb vaudeville act, the
best this variety fan has ever seen. It almost makes it seem that
vaudeville died because Kaufman and Hart were too busy with the
legitimate theater. You might go so far as to call it a play of character, to dignify it a little, for the actors participating have some of
the most delicious things to do and say that have been awarded
Equity members in a long, long time.

Josephine Hull, that portly, fluttery matron, is the mother, a
woman who took to writing plays because of a typewriter delivered
to the house by mistake. When not getting her characters into in-
extricable situations she is a portrait painter, but with a difference.
She keeps the pictures up to date, adding bald spots, for instance.
It is a triumphant piece of work in a tailor-made part.

Henry Travers is the grandfather whose tolerant amusement
holds the crowd together. He has a succulent part to nourish the
audience with and he administers the Kaufman-Hart lines with the

unction they deserve. Also playing mad people with excellent re-
source and the suspicion that they are having as good a time as the
spectators are George Tobias, with a beard, Frank Conlan, the over-
due ice man, Frank Wilcox, the father who plays with a Mecanno set,
Paula Trueman, the ballet dancer, and Margot Stevenson, Hugh Ren-
nie, Jess Barker, Anna Lubowe and George Heller, all grand performers in a wow of a show.

--Herbert Drake in Cue, Vol. 5,
No. 8 (December 19, 1936), pages
13-14.

INDEX BY CRITIC

Edward, My Son
The Heiress
High Button Shoes
An Inspector Calls
Kiss Me, Kate
The Madwoman of Chaillot
Me and Molly
Miss Liberty
Mister Roberts
South Pacific
A Streetcar Named Desire
Summer and Smoke
Where's Charley?
The Winslow Boy

GILBERT W. GABRIEL
Bell, Book and Candle
Call Me Madam
The Cocktail Party
Come Back, Little Sheba
The Country Girl
Gentlemen Prefer Blondes
Guys and Dolls
Hilda Crane
The Innocents
The Lady's Not for Burning
Lost in the Stars
The Member of the Wedding

JOHN W. GASSNER
Dead End
Jumbo
On Your Toes
Tonight at Eight-Thirty
White Horse Inn
Winterset

WOLCOTT GIBBS
Arsenic and Old Lace
The Corn Is Green
Death of a Salesman
Lady in the Dark
The Pirate
Winged Victory

WILLIAM HAWKINS
South Pacific

DON HEROLD
Ah, Wilderness!
Alice in Wonderland
As Thousands Cheer

Biography
Dinner at Eight
Dodsworth
The Gay Divorce
Mary of Scotland
Mourning Becomes Electra
Of Thee I Sing
Reunion in Vienna
Roberta
Tobacco Road
Twentieth Century

BEN IRWIN
Pins and Needles

ELIZABETH JORDAN
Blithe Spirit

IRENE KITTLE KAMP   see
IRENE KITTLE

WALTER KERR
Bell, Book and Candle
Call Me Madam
The Country Girl
Guys and Dolls
Hilda Crane
The Lady's Not for Burning

IRENE KITTLE (KAMP)
Anna Lucasta
Annie Get Your Gun
Born Yesterday
Carousel
The Glass Menagerie
The Late George Apley
On The Town

LOUIS KRONENBERGER
All My Sons
Annie Get Your Gun
Another Part of the Forest
Born Yesterday
Brigadoon
The Glass Menagerie
Harvey
The Hasty Heart
High Button Shoes
The Iceman Cometh
An Inspector Calls
John Loves Mary
The Late George Apley

Cabin in the Sky
Claudia
The Corn Is Green
Lady in the Dark
My Sister Eileen
Native Son
Pal Joey
Watch on the Rhine

RICHARD WATTS, JR.
South Pacific

JESSE ZUNSER
Blithe Spirit
Oklahoma!
One Touch of Venus
Othello
Over 21
The Skin of Our Teeth
Ten Little Indians
This Is the Army
The Voice of the Turtle

INDEX

TITLE INDEX TO SERIES

The number following each title indicates the number of the volume in which reviews for that production appear. Volume 1 covers 1900–1919, Volume 2 covers 1920–1930, and Volume 3 covers 1931–1950. Productions are listed alphabetically in each volume.